TWO MINUTES TO MIDNIGHT

1953 – THE YEAR OF LIVING DANGEROUSLY

ROGER HERMISTON

Biteback Publishing

ISBN 978-1-78590-737-1

10 9 8 7 6 5 4 3 2 1

A CIP catalogue record for this book is available from the British Library.

Set in Minion Pro

Printed and bound in Great Britain by
CPI Group (UK) Ltd, Croydon CR0 4YY

To Eileen

GORGEOUS
Just a pleasant Thursday with a high between 78 and 85.

The Detroit Free Press

THURSDAY, AUGUST 20, 1953   On Guard for Over a Century   38 Pages   Vol. 123—No. 107   Seven Cents

METRO FINAL
EXTRA

REDS FIRE H-BOMB

U.S. Confirms Soviet Blast

Jealous Wife Kills Husband

Test Revealed By Moscow

But AEC Official Hints We've Set Off Weapon Twice

WASHINGTON — (U.P.) — The United States Atomic Energy Commission confirmed Thursday that Russia has exploded a hydrogen superbomb.

In a formal announcement by the Atomic Energy Commission, it said that information received by the United States "indicates that this test involved both fission and thermonuclear reaction."

The thermonuclear reaction is the reaction of the hydrogen superbomb. The fission reaction is the reaction of the atomic bomb as a base trigger for the H-bomb.

Atomic Energy Commission Chairman Lewis L. Strauss issued the confirmation a short while after Moscow announced Russia had exploded an H-bomb recently in an experiment.

HERE IS the text of Strauss' announcement:

"The Soviet Union conducted an atomic test on the morning of Aug. 12.

"Certain information in this effect came into our hands that night. Subsequent information on the subject indicates that this test involved both fission and thermonuclear reaction.

"It will be recalled that more than three years ago the United States decided to accelerate work on all forms of atomic weapons. Both the 1951 and 1952 Eniwetok test series included tests involving atomic reaction.

"When Moscow did not elaborate on its information in 'our hands,' he presently meant that radioactive particles soared into the atmosphere by the explosion were picked up by the United States detection instruments stationed at many points around the world for that purpose.

IN MOSCOW, the Government said the explosion in Russia "a few days ago" set off a "thermonuclear reaction of great force" that showed the H-bomb is "many times stronger" than the atom bomb.

The announcement, published in the official newspapers Pravda and Izvestia, said "one of the types of the hydrogen bomb was exploded for experimental purposes."

It said there was "no foundation whatsoever" for any alarm the Soviets would use the weapon to stop up an aggressive race.

On Aug. 8, Premier Georgi Malenkov announced to the Supreme Soviet that Russia possesses the secret of the H-bomb.

The announcement underscored the determination to put Russia ahead of the West in building the weapon.

Soviet power, it said, to "strengthening the peace," and thrives on a test to convey weapons safeguard their national control.

The announcement concluded a sensation in Moscow as the newspapers hit the streets.

A FEW days ago in the Soviet union one of the types of

Other H-Bomb Stories on Page 38

10,000 Families To Go Homeless

That's Yearly Toll of Tragic Evictions of Detroit's Needy

Eviction Story Ires Council

Family of 9 Losing Even Its 'Rat-Hole'

Loads Gun As He Sits Watching

Northville Tragedy Follows Many Rows

BY RAY POOCE
Free Press Staff Writer

---

2 Detroiters Rescued From Alaskan Peak

AF Helicopter Picks Up Hunters Marooned After Crash of Plane

Beasts At Bay

New Envoy

You'll Find:

'A Man Called Peter'—Page 17

Fund for Taft

The Soviet H-bomb – front page of the *Detroit Free Press*, Thursday 20 August 1953.

© *Detroit Free Press*

CONTENTS

INTRODUCTION

1953 is usually described as being one of the 'monochrome' years in the early Cold War. In Britain, this meant an ostensibly comfortable, conservative, moral world where family came first, authority was respected and class barriers remained in place. The governing elite (the term 'establishment' was not coined until two years later) could sometimes face the occasional democratic wrath of public and press, but still retained its grip on power and influence.

But even if the tide of life appeared to be flowing sedately in 1953, strong currents were developing, bringing with them major societal change in the fields of science, music, sex and sport. In the first of those, on the afternoon of Saturday 28 February in Cambridge, England, Francis Crick, a brilliant, brash 36-year-old scientist from the university's Cavendish Laboratory, burst into The Eagle public house across the road from his lab to make a startling declaration.

'Gentlemen, we have discovered the secret of life!' he exclaimed to the assembled patrons, most of whom were fellow researchers, lecturers and students. By 'we' he was referring to himself and his 24-year-old Chicago-born colleague James Watson, who was among the audience of drinkers that day in the dim surrounds of the classic, dark woodpanelled English hostelry.

Crick and Watson were already recognised as an impressive research double act; the American's intense nature was balanced by the natural ebullience of the Englishman, which earned them the title of the 'scientific clowns' around the university. Now, as Crick excitably indicated, they had made arguably the single most important scientific discovery of the twentieth century.

By dint of their own chemical reasoning, patient model-building and undoubted genius – and by drawing on crucial X-ray crystallography evidence from another outstanding young scientist at King's College London, Rosalind Franklin – Crick and Watson had unravelled the 'double helix' molecular structure of the chemical deoxyribonucleic acid, better known as DNA.

It was already known that DNA was at the heart of every cell of almost every living thing, including those of man. This fundamental substance carried within it all the information for an organism to build, maintain and repair itself. By working out its structure, Crick and Watson had unlocked many of the mysteries of exactly how living things actually make and replicate themselves – 'the secret of life' indeed.

After the dramatic pronouncement in The Eagle, Crick and Watson went about publicising their discovery, first with a paper in the scientific magazine *Nature* on 25 April. 'Clue to the Chain of Life', the *New York Times* science correspondent would later write, hailing the discovery 'as important to biologists as uranium is to nuclear physicists'.[1]

On Saturday 18 July the arrival of a flamboyantly dressed, sultry-looking eighteen-year-old assembly worker with long greased-back hair at the home of Sun Studio on 706 Union Avenue in Memphis, Tennessee, would change the world's popular music scene, and with it youth culture, for ever.

Despite his rebellious appearance, the teenager who walked into the studio that day was a shy, polite character who wanted to record a disc to present to his mother for her birthday. His name was Elvis Aaron Presley.

Young Elvis proceeded to sing the classic ballad 'My Happiness', made popular at the time by the Ink Spots, the well-known American vocal jazz group, and recorded a second number, 'That's When Your Heartaches Begin', for the flip side of his demo. Marion Keisker the studio secretary, who kept notes on artists for future opportunities, was impressed by the purity of Elvis's voice. 'Good ballad singer – Hold', she wrote, as she made an additional recording of his songs.[2]

Presley would return to the studio in 1954 to meet its famed proprietor and record producer Sam Phillips, ultimately winning him over with a startling 'rockabilly' version of a piece by the famed bluesman Arthur 'Big Boy' Crudup, entitled 'That's All Right Mama'. This would be his first single, and within two years the hits would start to flow – 'Heartbreak Hotel', 'Don't Be Cruel', 'Love Me Tender' and 'All Shook Up'.

The future 'King of Rock and Roll' performed his unique blend of African-American blues, Christian gospel and country music with a free and passionate dance style, reeking raw sexuality with his unique gyrating hips. In 1953, sexuality – or the public discussion of it – remained more or less taboo. But all of that changed when the work of Alfred Kinsey, whose second publication, *Sexual Behavior in the Human Female*, hit the nation's bookstalls in late summer.

Fifty-nine-year-old Dr Kinsey had started his professional life as a zoologist, writing a bestselling textbook on biology (which had sold 400,000 copies) and establishing himself as the world's number one authority on the gall wasp.[3]

Then in 1938 he switched tack to make a study of sexual behaviour and eventually founded the Institute for Sex Research at Indiana University in 1947. The following year he published his first report, *Sexual Behavior in the Human Male*, which had sold 250,000 copies by 1953 and was translated into thirteen languages.[4]

His follow-up was no racy publication. *Human Female* was 842 pages of often ponderous scientific prose, complemented by scores of tables and charts. Kinsey and his team had gleaned their information from interviews with 6,000 women, reporting findings that seemed quite startling at the time, such as the fact that nearly half of the women said that they had engaged in premarital sex, and two-thirds reported they had experienced overtly sexual dreams. Female 'frigidity', Kinsey concluded, was man-made, not a product of innate physiological incapacity.

The book was attacked in many quarters as an affront to the dignity of womanhood. In Britain, *The Times* chose to ignore it completely, the *Daily Express* devoted an editorial to explain why it refused to print 'a word of the stuff', while the *Sunday People* – which did publish its main conclusions – warned its readers that 'those in this country should appreciate that British women are notoriously more reserved and less promiscuous than their US sisters'. The *Daily Mail*, however, reached perhaps the wisest conclusion: 'Sex', it stated, 'is undoubtedly here to stay.'

A revolution on the football field also took place on the afternoon of Wednesday 25 November at the Empire Stadium, Wembley, before an awed 105,000 spectators. This was the 'Match of the Century' between home side England, the inventors of the game, and Hungary, the mystery men from behind the Iron Curtain who were the finest team in the world at that time.

Before the kick-off, England captain Billy Wright looked down at the opposition's footwear. He noticed that the Hungarians had on these 'strange, lightweight boots, cut away like slippers under the ankle bone'. Turning to his colleague Stan Mortensen he commented: 'We should be all right here, Stan, they haven't got the right kit.'[5]

Instead the hosts chased forlornly on that fogbound afternoon as the Hungarians passed and dribbled their way around them. Wright himself, normally such an unflappable defender, was left sprawling, foxed by the footwork of the brilliant Hungarian captain Ferenc Puskás as he fired in his side's third goal. This was the first instance of 'Total Football', and the leaden-footed and confused Englishmen would succumb to an even heavier defeat at the hands of these football revolutionaries, 7–1 in Budapest, six months later.

Eight years on from the end of the Second World War and Britain was debt-ridden, her cities still remained scarred by German bombing, some raw materials were in short supply and rationing was still largely in place – although sugar and sweets were finally freed from controls early in the year. Looking enviously across the Atlantic at their war-time ally, Britons saw an America that was young, dynamic, rich and exciting.

Films and magazines informed them that for most young American couples an affordable, attractive home was within reach, equipped with a gleaming white refrigerator, dishwasher and of course a television, while a long, sleek car with white-walled tyres was invariably parked on the drive next to the front garden.

A new American urban middle class was developing, living in the suburbs, eating at McDonald's, watching drive-in movies and staying in new motels as they travelled for new experiences around the country. The supermarket, with its huge display and variety of hygienically packaged goods, was the ultimate symbol of American abundance.

But the rising tide of affluence did not extend to everyone, and life remained particularly grim for black people in the south who were still wholly segregated in housing, education, health and transport by law and custom.

America's new President Dwight D. Eisenhower grew up in rural Kansas with no black friends or teachers, and spent his career in the segregated US Army. In his new administration he employed just one black man, former CBS publicist Frederic Morrow, who impressed the President--elect's election campaign team when travelling around the country with them, helping to provide a bridge to African-American voters.

Racial tensions were on the rise in America, even if the civil rights movement was yet to swing into top gear. In Britain things were very different; by April 1953 Commonwealth immigration had created a permanent Asian and black population of just 36,000 people – 15,000 West Africans, 9,300 Indians and Pakistanis and 8,600 from the Caribbean.[6]

The latter had first come over on the *Empire Windrush* in June 1948 to fill jobs in the new NHS and other public services. But those numbers were soon to rise after the Truman administration, through its punitive 1952 McCarran–Walter Act, ended the practice of allowing West Indians to enter their favoured destination of the United States under the category of British citizens. Instead America set a new quota of just 800 individuals per year – shifting Caribbean emigration to the United Kingdom.

In 1953 Britain's immigrant population was concentrated mainly in the big cities of London, Manchester and Liverpool. Racial tensions were few and far between, but early in the year *The Observer*'s correspondent J. Halcro Ferguson went to visit the district of Liverpool 8, whose 8,000 'coloured inhabitants' made up perhaps the biggest black community in Britain.[7] He discovered some evidence of an unofficial colour bar in housing and employment, and foresaw the 'great danger that the coloured population, more closely integrated within itself, will tend to become ever more isolated from the life of the general population, and to regard the "Johnny Bulls" with even more suspicion and hostility'.

On both sides of the Atlantic the prospects for the advancement of women in the professions had gained little ground. Millions of women had entered the workforce in the war, holding down jobs in heavy industry and the armed forces, as well as excelling in more 'glamorous' roles as special agents and codebreakers. But in peacetime the traditional male-dominated tilt of society largely resumed, and women invariably left their wartime work to become homemakers.

In politics, there were just nineteen women MPs in the House of Commons. Churchill and Eisenhower found room for just one woman in their respective Cabinets – and Florence Horsbrugh and Oveta Culp Hobby were both given the 'soft' post of education (although Hobby had health and welfare thrown in for good measure).

Homosexuality was a crime in 1953, and it was the case in America that many assumptions about gay people mirrored common beliefs about the principal foe of the time, communists. Both were seen as morally weak, godless, undermining the traditional family and shadowy figures with a secret sub-culture. The FBI targeted the State Department in particular and unpleasant congressional hearings about supposed homosexual activity within the office took place.

Pressure from the American intelligence agencies led to Britain following suit. Encouraged by Home Secretary Sir David Maxwell Fyfe, the new Commissioner of the Metropolitan Police, Sir John Nott-Bower, instituted a new purge against homosexuals in London and nationwide – especially against those in the public sphere, to whom a blind eye might have been turned in the past.

After four years' deliberation Britain's Royal Commission on Capital Punishment reported in 1953, not on whether to consider abolishing the death penalty, but whether to limit or modify it. It recommended raising the minimum age for sentence of death from eighteen to twenty-one, and removing the mandatory death penalty to give juries the power to convict of murder 'with extenuating circumstances', which would not carry the ultimate punishment. This was a radical departure from the normal British legal practice of the jury pronouncing the verdict, but never the sentence. Additionally, the committee – led by Sir Ernest Gowers – floated the possibility of lethal injection replacing hanging as the means of execution.

Sir Ernest – author of the acclaimed *The Complete Plain Words*, a guide to writing straightforward English for the civil service, which became a surprise bestseller – was generally applauded for his committee's work. *The Times* reckoned that 'the report should reassure the country that, assuming our conscience is at peace about retaining the gallows at all, we have little to reproach ourselves with about the way in which the community uses it.'[8]

Stagnation in some areas, quiet revolutions underway in others; this was the fascinating paradox of 1953. But there was a dark side to the year too, and this is the – often untold – story of this book. In 1953 many observers believed that the ongoing Korean War was the harbinger of an even greater geopolitical and military crisis – the invasion of western Europe by an emboldened Soviet army, backed by swarms of tanks, artillery and jet aircraft.

For those in government and their advisers, a Soviet invasion of Europe was not only possible, but quite likely, and something that North Atlantic Treaty Organization's (NATO's) outnumbered conventional forces appeared all but powerless to prevent. But this was also the new nuclear age, with the United States and the Soviet Union – both equipped with atom bombs, but now bent on building bigger thermonuclear devices that could eclipse the terrifying destruction of Hiroshima and Nagasaki – squaring up in political and military battles all over the globe.

This was capitalism versus communism, supposed freedom versus assumed tyranny. The Berlin Blockade between 1948 and 1949 – when the Soviets cut off all supply links to the western sectors of the city – had been the first precarious confrontation between the erstwhile wartime allies in this new Cold War. Four years later mistrust had deepened, political uncertainties abounded and nuclear arsenals had mushroomed. 1953 would be the year of living dangerously – but it would be shaped first and foremost by an event way out in the Pacific Ocean, in November 1952.

PROLOGUE

The largest explosion in the history of the planet took place at 7.15 a.m. local time in the Marshall Islands, out in the vast expanse of the Central Pacific Ocean. On the east coast of America it was 2.15 p.m. on 31 October; perhaps appropriately the afternoon of Halloween.

A radio signal from the USS *Estes*, the command ship of Joint Task Force 132 situated 30 miles away, simultaneously triggered ninety-two detonators on the world's first ever thermonuclear device, the so-called 'super' bomb codenamed 'Mike'. 'Holy Cow! That sure makes the A-bomb a runt,' exclaimed one of the sailors on *Estes*, gasping in astonishment at the enormous forces released before him. Scientists on board who had helped fashion this monster cheered like fans celebrating a touchdown at an American football game.

Back in Berkeley, California, physicist Edward Teller, the 'father' of this new weapon, soberly monitored events while sitting in front of a seismograph in a darkened room in the basement of the university's geology building. When the dot on his screen did a little dance, he knew the blast had been a success. Wishing to inform colleagues at the Los Alamos Laboratory – but aware of the stringent security surrounding the bomb – he dispatched a telegram to them which simply said: 'It's a boy.'[1]

But this was an event that was going to be difficult to conceal. Word that something extraordinary had happened out in the Pacific quickly circulated that afternoon among the better-connected Washington DC press corps, and the phone lines were humming in the White House and Capitol Hill. Enno Hobbing of *Time* magazine was quickest off the mark and utilised his superior contacts among his old employers the CIA to get through to Shelby Thompson, information chief at the Atomic Energy Commission (AEC).

'Is this the big day?' Hobbing asked Thompson. 'Why don't you tell me? What are you talking about?' was the startled reply. 'We understand the H-bomb has just been set off,' probed Hobbing. 'We have a standard policy of no comment about weapons tests. We haven't anything to say in that field,' retorted Thompson. 'Don't you have any releases coming out there this afternoon?' persisted Hobbing. 'I don't know offhand. I'll have to check,' stalled Thompson. 'I mean about the H-bomb,' continued Hobbing. 'No,' snapped Thompson before he promptly put down the phone.[2]

Other reporters with good sources within the Department of Defense – like Clay Blair Jr from *Life* magazine – also got wind of the explosion at the nuclear test site at the Eniwetok Atoll. But with no one in authority prepared to go on the record, the bomb would remain a secret to the American public – and the world – for the next week.

The government's defences were eventually breached on Saturday 8 November 1952 when readers of the *Los Angeles Examiner* woke up to the front-page headline 'US Explodes Test H-Bomb; Eyewitness Tells Blast Fury'. Now the story of the bomb could begin to be told.

In an arresting opening paragraph, Chris Clausen, the paper's science editor, wrote:

In a moment of fury, fire and violence that made the atomic bomb 'a runt' by comparison, the United States detonated a hydrogen bomb at the Pacific Proving Grounds, the *Examiner* learned yesterday from an eyewitness to the historic event. The long-rumoured test of the world's most horrendous weapon, a hundred times more powerful than the atomic bomb, took place on a small atoll in the Eniwetok group of islands.

Given that a huge contingent of 11,650 awestruck scientists, engineers, technicians and military personnel had observed the explosion of the device – the operation was codenamed Ivy Mike – it was inevitable that some would break cover to tell family and friends back home.

The *Examiner*'s anonymous correspondent vividly described the scene as he stood on the deck of a ship more than 30 miles away from the blast.

Everyone waited tensely as the loudspeaker announced the minutes, then seconds, four, three, two, one.

Then, right on the nose through glasses so dark absolutely nothing could be seen, appeared a huge orange ball, materializing out of nothing, which grew larger and brighter until it appeared as if no dark glasses were there at all. An intense heat struck us almost immediately and the ball of fire started to rise and slowly lose its intensity. We took off our glasses and saw water vapor suddenly form around the column.

Then it rushed into the base of the column and up, clearing the air so that you could see countless tons of water rushing skyward – drawn up the column by that tremendous, unseen force.

The column went up and up and finally mushroomed. About three minutes later, the report, like a nearby cannon shot, hit us and was followed by seconds of dull rumbling. Then the mushroom expanded into a free halo, growing with tornado-like speed and reaching nearly over our ship before it appeared to cease growing.

Mike was not a deliverable bomb capable of being dropped from an aircraft. Instead the giant weapon was an experimental device, a prototype of a hydrogen bomb. It was a piece of clunky apparatus that looked more like a small building: it was about 20ft in height, 7ft in diameter and weighing over 80 tons. The device's assembly was contained in a steel casing 80 inches wide and 244 inches long, with walls 12 inches thick. It used a Hiroshima-style fission bomb as the trigger to set off fusion reactions in a large dewar of super-cooled deuterium, or heavy hydrogen.

There had been uncertainty – and great apprehension – among sections of the scientific community involved in its creation. Their fear was that an overwhelming fireball might ignite the atmosphere and cloak the earth in a blazing Armageddon, similar to that which supposedly killed the dinosaurs thousands of centuries earlier.

Terminal disaster was averted, but the full wrath of Mike had been severely miscalculated. The device was estimated at about 6 megatons, but it clocked in at a staggering 10.4 megatons – over 700 times the size of the weapon dropped on Hiroshima seven years earlier. It produced a 150-million-degree fireball many times the strength of the sun that stretched 3 miles in diameter, with a heat wave measuring 180 degrees.

Just ten minutes after the wind and the deafening roar of the detonation, the giant mushroom cloud had climbed 25 miles into the stratosphere. It would eventually spread to an astonishing 100 miles across.

The placid Eniwetok coral atoll, with its ring of forty-two verdant islands of palm and coconut trees surrounding a deep sapphire lagoon, was transformed into a moonscape. At the heart of the destruction was the island of Elugelab where Mike was placed. For centuries the natives, now all forcibly relocated to other remote islands, had come to this northernmost spot on the atoll in their beautifully constructed canoes to gather coconuts and roots, fish its reefs for lobsters and turtles, and shelter from raging storms.

That morning Elugelab was blown to kingdom come. Ninety million tons of coral, sand, reef, palm and coconut trees were vaporised in a second, metamorphosing the tiny little island into a deep-sea canyon. Elugelab was now just a subterranean crater, a mile in diameter and

164ft deep – the equivalent of fourteen Pentagon buildings, placed end-to-end.

Fifteen more eyewitness accounts from sailors and soldiers found their way into America's local newspapers – and were promptly syndicated, so that within days the whole country had a fair idea of what happened. On 10 November in Ohio's *Lima News* the writer described Elugelab 'turning a brilliant red and burning for six hours, gradually becoming smaller with a huge chunk just seeming to melt away'.

Two days later in the Michigan City *News-Dispatch* a sailor claimed that the bomb had been on his ship for its Pacific voyage, guarded by FBI agents while kept in a compartment welded shut with huge chains across the door. He described the heat from the blast as being 'like someone putting a hot iron on your back for a split second'.

By 13 November correspondents were no longer hiding behind a cloak of anonymity. Richard Burns, storekeeper third class, was a crewman on the USS *Oak Hill*, cruising 30 miles from the site of the explosion. In his letter to his parents which they passed on to the *Daily Pantagraph* of Illinois he told how the booming sound wave hit the ship two minutes after the explosion, and likened the growing cloud of smoke and debris and vapourised water 'to the head of a cauliflower, white and fluffy ... with the middle section turning white and forming into shapes resembling pine tree branches'.

It would not be known for some time that Mike had, inadvertently, claimed a victim that day. Ninety minutes after the explosion, Captain Jimmy Priestly Robinson was up in the mushroom cloud in the cockpit of one of four F-84 Thunderjets on 'Red Flight', sent to collect high-quality samples for the physicists at the Los Alamos Laboratory.

Jimmy, just twenty-eight, was a war veteran, holder of a Purple Heart and Air Medal, who had flown a B-24 Liberator named 'Dazzlin' Duchess' before being shot down over Romania and taken prisoner. After the war he transferred to fighter jets, and had already made a practice run through a smaller atomic blast in Nevada.

Once he had entered Mike's radioactive smoke, Jimmy hit a pocket of severe turbulence and his plane began to spin out of control. He accidentally hit the jet's microphone, and his wingman could hear him struggling to stay conscious and right the plane.

Finally he regained control at about 20,000ft. His vision impaired by thick cloud and heavy rain, he could not spot a tanker on which to refuel. So Jimmy set course to return to the airstrip at Eniwetok. But the bomb's electromagnetic storm had affected his instrument panel and he could not lock onto the homing beacon at the airfield. A rescue helicopter was dispatched, and Jimmy's last transmission was: 'I have the helicopter in sight and am bailing out.'[3]

The helicopter pilot saw the plane drop its wing tanks – and 'possibly' eject the cockpit canopy. He then watched it fly into the water, bounce and flip over, before disappearing beneath the surface.

All the search discovered that day was an oil slick, a glove and some maps. A month later Brigadier-General Frederic E. Glantzberg, commander for Operation Ivy, wrote to Jimmy's widow to tell her that the quest for his body, and his plane, had been discontinued. In October 1953 Mrs Robinson accepted the award of a posthumous Distinguished Flying Cross, for those showing 'extraordinary devotion to duty combined with a personal disregard for one's own safety', on behalf of her late husband.

There would be one remarkable postscript to this tragedy. Working through the samples that the other planes on Jimmy's mission had gathered on their specially fitted wing filters, scientists at the Los Alamos, Berkeley and Argonne laboratories discovered two new chemical elements to add to the periodic table, which were allotted the atomic numbers 99 and 100.

In 1955 these two new elements would be named einsteinium and fermium, after the great physicists Albert Einstein and Enrico Fermi, who both died in the preceding months.

If the White House had been eager to let the world know in 1945 just how destructive the atom bomb had been – in order to hasten the end

of the war – its attitude towards publicity for the hydrogen bomb programme was markedly different. There was an arms and technology
race on with the principal Cold War foe the Soviet Union, and outgoing
President Truman had been scarred by the betrayal of nuclear secrets
to the enemy by the likes of Klaus Fuchs, the German-born physicist
who worked on the secret wartime Manhattan Project to develop the
first atom bomb, and Julius and Ethel Rosenberg, the New York couple
convicted of being key members of a separate spy ring.

Having publicly, if sketchily, launched the 'superbomb' programme
nearly three years earlier, Truman had promptly gagged his administration and the Atomic Energy Commission from openly discussing
the topic. So when the AEC was forced to make a statement about Ivy
Mike on 16 November, two weeks after the explosion, it contained only
the briefest acknowledgement that something extraordinary had happened in the Pacific.

The press release read simply:

In furtherance of the President's announcement of 31 January 1950,
the test program included experiments contributing to thermonuclear
weapons research … scientific executives for the tests have expressed
satisfaction with the results. The leaders and members of the military
and civilian components of the Task Force have accomplished a remarkable feat of precision in planning and operations.

By saying next to nothing the US administration was faithful to its
policy of 'strategic ambiguity'. While everyone now effectively 'knew'
America had the H-bomb, the advantage of not announcing its arrival
was that the US government could shield itself from any criticism from
allied countries who decried the project. The very vague details disclosed could also mask a number of acute weaknesses – the principal
one being that it was not yet a deliverable military weapon.

At this moment when the world moved from the kiloton to the

megaton era, the two men who, above all, would have to grapple with the consequences of Mike were very differently engaged.

Republican candidate Dwight Eisenhower was in the final days of an exhausting campaign to become the 34th President of the United States. When Mike exploded at 2.15 p.m. Eastern Standard Time on Friday 31 October, he was receiving the cheers of hundreds of thousands of onlookers as his motorcade progressed through downtown Chicago.

Eisenhower had been very broadly told about what was about to happen at Eniwetok. A week later, while basking in the afterglow of his election victory at his favourite place on earth – Augusta National Golf Club in Georgia – he was hand-delivered a top-secret memorandum by Gordon Dean, chairman of the AEC.

It related in detail the events of the morning of 1 November on the Marshall Islands. 'We have detonated the first full-scale thermonuclear device,' the President-elect read. 'The island of the Atoll which was used for the shot – Elugelab – is missing.'[4]

Roy Snapp, secretary of the AEC, who had brought Dean's letter, awaited Eisenhower's response. This revelation of the awesome power of the nuclear weapons soon to be at the disposal of the new President met with a sobering, somewhat enigmatic reply. 'Complete destruction', reflected Eisenhower, 'was the negation of peace.'[5]

When Mike exploded at 7.15 p.m. Greenwich Mean Time, Prime Minister Winston Churchill was sitting down to dinner at his country house, Chartwell, in the company of Derrick Cawston, his tropical fish adviser. Their discussion, among other things, about the possible addition of the brightly coloured Pompadour to Churchill's pond was a relaxing prelude for the PM ahead of a busy Saturday hosting a visit by the Queen Mother.

Only eight days earlier Churchill had stepped up to the dispatch box in the House of Commons to proclaim his country's own advancement in weapons of mass destruction. To the resounding cheers of MPs, he revealed that Britain had joined the nuclear club by successfully exploding her own atom bomb on board the frigate HMS *Plym* in the Monte Bello Islands off the coast of north-west Australia.

'We live in a very terrible age,' admitted the Prime Minister, 'but there is no reason why we should lose our spirits.'[6] Questioned by Labour MP Frank Beswick about the need for the 'closest possible cooperation' with the United States on military – and civil – nuclear affairs, Churchill was outwardly optimistic. 'There are a very large number of important people in the United States … who have been most anxious for a long time that Britain should be kept better informed,' he replied.[7] 'This event will greatly facilitate and support the task which these gentlemen have set themselves.'

But America's policy of 'strategic ambiguity' was not relaxed to let the Prime Minister in on the H-bomb secret. Indeed, the 'special relationship' Churchill had fostered so assiduously with Roosevelt in the war was beginning to fray at the edges.

The juxtaposition of Conservative and Republican administrations should have given Churchill heart. But instead, contemplating the new leadership of Eisenhower and his fiercely anti-communist Secretary of State John Foster Dulles, the Prime Minister confided to his private secretary Jock Colville: 'For your private ear, I am greatly disturbed. I think this makes war more probable.'[8]

As 1952 drew to a close, the Korean War had lost its intensity but there was little sign of the conflict ending. In the Soviet Union, Stalin – sitting on his own stockpile of fission weapons and not too far behind the United States in the development of a hydrogen bomb – had embarked on another mad persecution, this time of Jewish doctors. In Egypt, Iran and Kenya, British colonial power was wavering. And in Europe, a plan to bind France and Germany together in a new European army was stalling.

Now mankind had invented its most fearsome weapon yet. Churchill was right to be concerned. Statesmanship of the highest order would be required in the anxious months to come.

Dwight Eisenhower – soldier turned politician, the first Republican President in twenty years.
© Fabian Bachrach

John Foster Dulles – Eisenhower's powerful, unbending US Secretary of State.
© US Department of State, public domain, via Wikimedia Commons

CHAPTER 1

'TWO SCORPIONS IN A BOTTLE'

It fell to President Harry Truman, who had reluctantly sanctioned the dropping of the atom bomb on Hiroshima and Nagasaki eight years earlier, to warn the American public – and the world – about the dawn of this even more frightening nuclear age.

The news was delivered in familiar coded fashion, but this time accompanied by a disturbing assessment of the world order. In his final State of the Union speech on 7 January 1953, the outgoing President was two-thirds of the way through his 10,000-word address before he finally, obliquely, referred to what had happened in the Marshall Islands in November.

'Recently, in the thermonuclear tests at Eniwetok, we have entered another stage in the world-shaking development of atomic energy. From now on, man moves into a new era of destructive power, capable of creating explosions of a new order of magnitude, dwarfing the mushroom clouds of Hiroshima and Nagasaki.'[1]

Truman continued, chillingly:

We have no reason to think that the stage we have now reached ∴ will be the last. Indeed, the speed of our scientific and technical progress over the last seven years shows no sign of abating. We are being hurried forward, in our mastery of the atom, from one discovery to another, towards yet unforeseeable peaks of destructive power.

The President then delivered a clear ultimatum to the men in the Kremlin. Unless and until the Soviet Union could be persuaded to enter international agreements over atomic energy, America would continue to lead the race for ever-more powerful weapons. His vision was a bleak one.

> The war of the future would be one in which man could extinguish millions of lives at one blow, demolish the great cities of the world, wipe out the cultural achievements of the past – and destroy the very structure of a civilization that has been slowly and painfully built up through hundreds of generations.

'Truman Warns Stalin of Atom War Ruin to Russia,' proclaimed the *Los Angeles Times* the morning after. 'Truman Says Atomic War To Kill Millions', was a typical interpretation, from the *Kingsport Times News* in Tennessee. In Britain, *The Guardian* warned of the 'Perils of a Third World War'.

Of course the Cold War superpowers were already squaring up on the battlefield in Korea. It was now two and a half years since 75,000 soldiers from the Korean People's Army in the north – with a nod and a wink from Mao and Stalin – had poured across the 38th parallel of this divided country.

The Truman administration had responded vigorously, shouldering the main burden of a United Nations response to what it perceived as a clear threat from international communism, and dispatching troops, planes and ships to Korea.

America would do the bulk of the fighting, take the majority of the casualties, and pay nearly all the bills, but fifteen other nations joined the UN coalition – principal ally the United Kingdom, Turkey (the third largest contributor of combat forces), France, Belgium, the Netherlands, Luxembourg, Greece, South Africa, Australia, New Zealand, Canada, Philippines, Thailand, Colombia and Ethiopia.

After the coalition's successful fightback in the heady days of late summer 1950, when the brilliant, if unpredictable, General Douglas MacArthur pushed the North Korean troops far back – so far that he wanted to carry on and invade China herself – the tables were turned a few months later when Mao's 300,000 combat-hardened People's Volunteer Army (PVA) entered the fray and forced the coalition forces to retreat.

From mid-1951 onwards the battle lines were drawn roughly where it had all started, around the 38th parallel. Brief ceasefires had come and gone but peace talks had never materialised. The attritional war on the ground continued while the battle in the air intensified.

In the febrile moment following the H-bomb success in late 1952, some Republican members of the US Congress Joint Committee on Atomic Energy (JCAE) began openly suggesting that the incoming President should reserve the right to deploy atomic weapons on the battlefield in Korea if his generals recommended it.

'If the war can be shortened by a single day – or if any lives can be saved – then the atomic bomb should be used,' declared Congressman William Sterling Cole from New York, who was favourite to become the new committee chairman.[2]

But for all the power of the message, the messenger was about to become yesterday's man. Truman would leave office on 20 January 1953, and the nuclear arms race, and the fate of the West's relationship with the communist East, now rested primarily with his bitter political opponent, Republican Dwight Eisenhower, abetted by Winston Churchill, Britain's ageing Prime Minister.

These new custodians of the special relationship could not have had more different beginnings. The 'simple country boy' (as 'Ike' would disarmingly refer to himself) was the son of a railroad worker raised in a shack next to the tracks in rural Texas, while Churchill was an aristocrat with a famous military and political lineage who was born and brought up in a palace in pastoral Oxfordshire.

The pair had first met fleetingly in Washington in December 1941; Eisenhower had just joined the general staff of the US Army when Churchill visited Roosevelt, with America still shaken from the shock of Pearl Harbor. A more substantial encounter followed in the White House on 21 June 1942 when Britain experienced the very bleakest of war days.

That afternoon Churchill was in the President's study when Roosevelt's Army Chief of Staff General George Marshall walked in with a note informing the two leaders that Tobruk in present-day Libya had fallen to Erwin Rommel's army, with the surrender of 33,000 men.[3] This setback in the North African campaign was another hammer blow to Churchill following the demoralising loss of the 'impregnable fortress' of Singapore in February.

But Churchill's spirits slowly revived as, together with the President and their key generals, serious planning began for Operation Bolero, the build-up of US forces in Britain ahead of a possible cross-Channel invasion of Europe in 1943. Then later in the afternoon the Prime Minister was joined in his room by two more senior American officers – General Mark Clark and General Eisenhower.

'I was immediately impressed', Churchill recorded, 'by these remarkable but hitherto unknown men.'[4] Days later, Eisenhower was appointed commander of all US forces in the European theatre, and a close working relationship between the two was underway.

Despite their very diverse backgrounds there were fascinating parallel experiences that bound the two men together. Both were graduates of elite military academies – Churchill from Sandhurst, Eisenhower from West Point. Their ideas about military strategy were aligned – in the First World War both were advocates of the tank, and, observing the futility of static trench warfare, both embraced the new doctrine of more flexible, mobile combat.

They shared an enthusiasm for flying; Eisenhower was the first President to hold a private pilot's licence, while Churchill would have done too had his concerned wife Clementine not put a stop to his exploits. For relaxation, both painted – mostly landscapes – to a reasonable standard; Eisenhower (whose main passion was golf) had come to this pastime late and was very much pupil to Churchill's master.

There was even an unspoken emotional bond between the men. Both had lost young children in the same year, 1921, three-year-old Doud Dwight Eisenhower to scarlet fever, and two-year-old Marigold Churchill from a blood infection.

In the war years the Prime Minister and the general often fundamentally disagreed on strategy and tactics. Churchill wanted to hit the Germans hard on the 'soft underbelly' of their conquered empire – in Norway, North Africa and the Balkans. Eisenhower preferred to tackle the enemy head on and make straight for northern France and from there on to the Rhine and the Ruhr.

In the spring of 1945 the two men disagreed over the importance of capturing Berlin ahead of the Russians. Eisenhower contended that capturing the German army, not the German capital, was the proper objective, and wanted a quick surrender. Churchill, perceptively, watching as the Russian army were also poised to enter Vienna, wired Eisenhower: 'If we deliberately leave Berlin to them, even if it should be in our grasp, the double event may strengthen their conviction, already apparent, that they have done everything.'[5]

Churchill liked to hold his military commanders close, so throughout the war the pair spent a great deal of time in each other's company. Whenever Eisenhower was in London there was a regular Tuesday lunch date, and often dinner on Friday at Chequers, the Prime Minister's country home. The general, no socialite or night owl, stoically endured Churchill's 2 a.m. working sessions but also enjoyed the hours when the two men – with their military academy backgrounds – fell into lively historical discussions about the roots of wars and the campaigns of the great commanders.

Churchill certainly valued Eisenhower highly for what he considered was his broadmindedness and wisdom, and while they might argue long and hard in private, loyally backed him to the hilt in public. On D-Day, in those uncertain early hours, he told the House of Commons firmly: 'General Eisenhower's courage is equal to all the necessary decisions that have to be taken in these extremely difficult and uncontrollable matters.'[6]

In the years after the war the two largely lost touch. Churchill was in opposition and preoccupied with writing his history of the war, while Eisenhower was serving a stint as US Army Chief of Staff, then a term as president of Columbia University, before spending a year as the first ever Supreme Allied Commander of the newly formed NATO. But Churchill's return to Downing Street in November 1951 and Eisenhower's decision to enter the political arena six months later kindled the Prime Minister's hopes that the 'Big Men' of world politics could get together to halt the Cold War.

There were already glimmers of what would become Churchill's final 'mission'. 'He told me that if Eisenhower were elected President, he would have another shot at making peace by means of a meeting of the Big Three (USA, Britain and the Soviet Union),' wrote his private secretary Jock Colville on 15 June 1952. '[He said] for that alone it would perhaps be worth remaining in office.'[7]

Great comradeship in the heat of battle could only guarantee so much political cooperation in a vastly altered world. Churchill now needed to get the measure of his old wartime ally, to find out how far the military man – who had been offered the Democratic presidential nomination four years earlier, which he declined – had travelled on his political journey to the right.

The Prime Minister carefully manufactured a stopover in America on the way to a scheduled winter break in Jamaica, arranging for informal talks with Eisenhower at the New York home of their mutual friend Bernard Baruch, financier, philanthropist and adviser to several Presidents.

In three short sessions with the President-elect, there was much to chew over. From Britain's perspective, the Korean War showed no signs of ending, Stalin was continuing to prove an implacable and immoveable opponent, and in Iran Prime Minister Mohammad Mossadegh had cut off diplomatic relations and was refusing to return Britain's share of the oil industry he had nationalised.

Churchill looked to Eisenhower to help solve these problems, hoping that a revived Anglo-American relationship could create a common front 'from Korea to Kikuyu and from Kikuyu to Calais'. The reference to Kikuyu was to the region – and the tribe – that supplied most of the recruits for the increasingly bloody Mau rebellion against British rule in Kenya, where a state of emergency had been in place since October 1952.

The Prime Minister was hoping for at least moral support from the President for this and other problems of Empire. But Eisenhower was disinclined to aid Britain in her battles with her colonies. He had welcomed the Labour government's post-war retreat from India, Burma and Palestine, and wished – as did most of the American political class – for more of the same. He accepted that Churchill did not propose to 'disregard legitimate aspirations among weaker peoples', but at the same time worried about his rather 'old-fashioned, paternalistic approach' towards nations craving self-dependence.

Churchill's romantic notion of the special relationship, born out of his close rapport in the early years of the Second World War with Roosevelt, had not dimmed. But the most influential figures in the new administration, although broadly ideologically sympathetic in their views with the 78-year-old British premier, were a new generation of politicians who looked on the 'Old Man' as a figure – although revered – of the past, and not necessarily equipped to deal with the future.

Eisenhower, Churchill's junior by sixteen years, reached that conclusion after his final, hour-long, conversation in the study of Baruch's Manhattan apartment. He wrote in his diary that Churchill was 'as charming and interesting as ever, but he is quite definitely showing the effects of the passing years'.[8]

The President-elect was dismissive about the Prime Minister's desire to rekindle the special relationship.

> He has developed an almost childlike faith that all of the answers are to be found merely in British–American partnership. Winston is trying to relive the days of World War II. In those days he had the enjoyable feeling that he and our President [Roosevelt] were sitting on some rather Olympian platform with respect to the rest of the world and directing world affairs from that point of vantage … in the present international complexities, any hope of establishing such a relationship is completely fatuous.

In particular what Eisenhower wished for in these early exchanges was an indication that Churchill would exert British leadership in Europe, taking some of the moral, political and financial burden off the United States. He wanted Churchill to make the Schuman Plan – for a European Coal and Steel Community – work, and also make a success of the project for a European army, otherwise known as the European Defence Community (EDC).

However, in his diary he regretfully noted that 'Europe's feeling [is] that Britain is not greatly concerned and will not help them politically, economically and otherwise'.[9]

All this led Eisenhower to the conclusion that 'much as I hold Winston in my personal affection and much as I admire him for his past accomplishments and leadership, I wish that he would turn over leadership of the Conservative Party to younger men'. That would leave his old wartime colleague with a kind of Prime Minister emeritus role: 'He could perform a very great function by coming forward with his inspiring voice only when critical circumstances so demanded.'[10] But the new President knew Churchill would never acquiesce to this semi-active position in politics.

As for Churchill, he left New York with mixed impressions of the principal characters in the new administration, and their willingness to re-engage with Moscow.

Somewhat surprisingly, Eisenhower had asked Churchill if he would object if he met Stalin, one-to-one, on neutral territory, for instance Stockholm. The Prime Minister replied: 'I would have objected strongly during the war when our contributions in forces was about equal. Now I don't mind. But don't hurry. Get your reconnaissance in first.'[11]

But in a clue as to how Eisenhower would view the special relationship, the President-elect hinted strongly that the days of the Big Three summits were numbered. 'Evidently he did not want Britain. That would involve asking France and Italy,' a perturbed Churchill told his Foreign Secretary Anthony Eden and Chancellor of the Exchequer Rab Butler.[12]

As for the Republican leaders surrounding Eisenhower, Churchill was unimpressed with what he perceived as their brashness, impatience and naïvety. Of the members of the new President's Cabinet, he took particular exception to John Foster Dulles, the soon-to-be Secretary of State, who had already made it clear that Churchill's presence at economic talks in Washington at the beginning of the following month was unwelcome. As Colville wrote following a dinner hosted by Bernard Baruch and attended by both Dulles and Churchill:

> [Dulles] explained that the American public thought Winston could cast a spell on all American statesmen and that if he were directly associated with the economic talks, the fears of the people and of Congress would be aroused to such an extent that the success of the talks would be endangered.[13]

John Foster Dulles, it seemed, had always been destined to become America's foreign policy chief. Both his uncle and his grandfather served as Secretary of State. At thirty he was appointed by President

Woodrow Wilson as legal counsel to the US delegation at the Versailles Peace Conference at the end of the First World War. In the Second World War he first helped prepare the founding Charter of the United Nations, then afterwards, as Truman's negotiator, fashioned the peace treaty that Japan signed with forty-eight Allied countries.

Dulles was an imposing individual, a tall, gangly, muscular man, whose mouth habitually drooped at the corners, giving his face an expression of extreme gravity. His spectacles were a legacy from contracting malaria in British Guiana when a young man, which left his sight impaired and meant that he had a permanent tic in his left eye.

Yet there was more to Dulles than the stereotypical public portrait of the austere, humourless, puritanical lawyer (he had been a partner in the elite New York firm of Sullivan & Cromwell). This son of a Presbyterian minister loved a good joke and his powerful, contagious laugh could set off a Washington drawing room. He was able to relax easily – during breaks in meetings he could be seen slumped in his chair, doodling or sharpening pencils, seemingly without a care in the world. He valued his 'down time', buying his own tiny island – Duck Island in Lake Ontario – where he and his wife Janet would retreat to 'rough it' for a week, hauling water, chopping wood and cooking fish, swimming and sailing.

His rapid conversion from internationalist to implacable Cold War warrior came between 1946 and 1950. By then for him the world struggle had become a kind of spiritual determinism, a confrontation between universal faiths: Christianity versus communism. To understand his enemy better, Dulles memorised – and often carried around with him – Stalin's basic work *Problems of Leninism*, believing it to be a plan for world domination akin to Hitler's *Mein Kampf*.

The new Secretary of State would have made particular note of one chilling paragraph in Stalin's book: 'The coexistence of the Soviet republic side by side with imperialist states is unthinkable; one or the other must triumph in the end; and before that end, a series of frightful collisions between either side must occur.'[14]

Dulles did not mind ruffling feathers. His State Department staff, already harangued and belittled over recent years by communist witch-hunter Joe McCarthy, were unimpressed when their new boss gave them an introductory speech in the car park on a rainy day in January. There were few warm words, and Dulles spoke darkly of the necessity of 'positive loyalty' from all of them. Fisher Howe, deputy special assistant, recalled: '[He] just bombed. It was so awful in contrast to what [his predecessor] Acheson had done.'[15]

At the back of Churchill's mind might also have been Dulles's admiration for Hitler in the early 1930s, his support of the nativist, neutralist America First Committee, and a speech he made in December 1939 decrying Britain's declaration of war against Germany and asserting there was no reason for the United States to become a participant.

Dulles's early flirtations with Nazi Germany were no doubt partly driven by his distaste for fascism's ideological enemy, Bolshevism. But by 1953 Churchill and Eden feared that Dulles had moved to the extremes and become a blinkered, unbending, fanatical anti-communist. His brusque intervention at dinner had put the Prime Minister's nose out of joint, and subsequent other, quieter conversations did little to alter his general impression of the man.

'He said he would have no more to do with Dulles whose "great slab of a face" he disliked and distrusted,' recorded Colville.[16] Churchill would later subsequently refer disparagingly to the American as 'dull, duller, Dulles'.

So it had not been a promising start to the post-war Churchill–Eisenhower relationship. While the new US administration's strategy on dealing with the Soviet Union had clearly yet to emerge, there was early evidence that the President-to-be was unwilling to support Britain in her struggle to deal with the unruly parts of the Empire, such as Egypt and Sudan. Then, of course, there was Eisenhower's insistence that Britain should take a lead in Europe.

'I have had a dreadful flurry of business in New York and Washington both with Democrats and Republicans,' Churchill wrote to Lord Cher-well, his close friend and scientific guru, the day after he had left America. 'There are lots of difficulties ahead.'[17]

* * *

It could have been right out of the pages of a novel by the thriller writer Ian Fleming, who in 1953 was about to introduce James Bond to the world in *Casino Royale*. Extraordinarily, on the very day that President Truman revealed America's major advance in weapons of mass destruction, a frantic hunt was underway on a Pullman sleeper train at Washington's Union Station for a document that actually contained vital secrets of the H-bomb.

That this precious manuscript had gone missing was down to 41-year-old John Archibald Wheeler. Johnny Wheeler (as he was known to his friends) was on his way to becoming one of the great figures in American science, an original thinker in the fields of relativity and quantum theory, and the man who coined the term 'black hole'. He was a key figure in America's Manhattan Project, which created the first atom bomb, and was now head of Project Matterhorn B, the H-bomb project based at Princeton University, where he had been professor of physics since 1938.

Early on Tuesday 6 January, Wheeler received a call at work from friend and fellow nuclear physicist Dr Ernst Krause, inviting him to attend a conference at the US Naval Research Laboratory in Washington the following day. This laboratory had played a key part in the Ivy Mike operation: Dr Krause now wanted to bring together scientists from the two major H-bomb laboratories, Los Alamos and Project Matterhorn, to analyse the very latest weapon development.

Wheeler agreed to come, and said he would along bring his close colleague at Project Matterhorn, Dr Jay Manton Berger. At 4.50 p.m., in preparation for the next day's meeting, Wheeler unlocked his office safe and took out three documents. One was a report by Dr Krause to be discussed at the conference, the second was a short inconsequential paper relating to Project Matterhorn and the third was a document of six pages.

The latter document was an extract from a much bigger file entitled 'Policy and Progress in the H-Bomb Program', a top-secret 91-page paper detailing the entire history of the development of the H-bomb project, compiled by John Walker, a congressional staff member, for his boss William Borden, executive director of the Joint Committee on Atomic Energy. Wheeler himself had played a part in its creation, offering up editing suggestions to Walker when he was shown a draft a fortnight earlier.

'Policy and Progress' was no dry as dust record. Instead, it set out in compelling detail all the major policy reports and events from the wartime period to the present, chronicling all the scientific – as well as moral and ethical – debates between those champions of the H-bomb, Edward Teller and Enrico Fermi, and its staunchest critics, the likes of Robert Oppenheimer and Hans Bethe.

Crucially, it also included scientific reports and data 'showing the broad, technical outlook for H-bombs at the time each policy was made'. It chronicled Klaus Fuchs's betrayal of the atom bomb project to the Russians, reminding its readers that a secret 1950 report reckoned that 'with regard to thermonuclear weapons, Fuchs' information [to the enemy] was hardly less complete'.[18]

The report was right up to date, and in among its pages were nothing less than the crown jewels of the US thermonuclear project. As its authors proudly proclaimed in the introduction, 'so far as is known, no similar document is in existence'.

Wheeler's six-page extract included the most sensitive details from 'Policy and Progress'. Pages one and two, written on bonded paper and stapled together, covered the principles of atomic energy; pages three, four, five and six, written on onion-skin paper and also stapled together, summarised the current debate on atomic theory.

Having only received it the day before, Wheeler had not yet had time to examine the document in detail, so he sealed it in a brown manila envelope, along with the two other documents, and took it back to his house, where he carefully placed it in the small overnight suitcase that he was taking for his trip.

At 8.45 p.m. Wheeler left home by taxi on the first leg of his rail trip to Washington DC. It would take him on a succession of short shuttle runs before arriving in Philadelphia at 10.06 p.m.

There he wasted no time in boarding the last train of this trip, the Pennsylvania Railroad sleeper to Washington DC. He went immediately to his berth, lower no. 9, in the Pullman car 101, named 'Bettsville'. After undressing and closing the curtains, he drew out his top-secret document and began to go through it carefully, making a number of pencilled notes in the margins. Shortly after 11 p.m. he replaced the extract – and the Krause report, which he had also read – in the envelope, closed his suitcase, and went to sleep. In the meantime no one had taken the upper bunk in his berth, and the car was only about half full.

On Wednesday 7 January, at 2.43 a.m., the train left Philadelphia, arriving at Washington's Union Station at 5.15 a.m. Passengers were entitled to remain on the sleeper until 8 a.m., so Wheeler scheduled a wake-up call from the porter for 6.45 a.m.

Rising immediately after the call, Wheeler headed straight for the men's washroom at the far end of the train, taking his shaving gear and his suitcase with him. Having placed his equipment on a washstand, he withdrew the manila envelope from the suitcase – aware he should be keeping it close at all times – and took it with him while he visited one of the toilet stalls. Before using the toilet, he placed the envelope between the steam pipes and the wall under the window at floor level.

So far, so good, even if since the previous afternoon Wheeler had breached any number of security regulations in his stewardship of this ultra-sensitive document. But then it all started to go wrong. Wheeler left the cubicle but forgot to take the manila envelope with him.

And almost immediately, another man entered the very same stall and locked the door behind him.

Shock flooded through his system when Wheeler heard the click of the door and immediately registered that he had left the envelope behind. It prompted desperate measures: setting aside propriety, he climbed on a washstand so he could peer through a metal grating at his successor on the toilet. From his vantage point he was reassured to see that the man was not reading anything.

Immediately after the man had finished his business and left the toilet, Wheeler dashed in behind him and found the manila envelope where he had placed it. He put it back in his suitcase, finished his ablutions and returned to his berth.

As soon as he had finished dressing, the porter, Robert James Jones, directed Wheeler to vacate berth no. 9 and move to berth no. 6 on the Pullman, which had been made up into daytime seating mode. It was now 7.20 a.m. and Wheeler, once settled, opened up his suitcase again and drew out the manila envelope to double-check that all was well.

The feeling of enormous relief since he left the washroom now turned to one of sheer panic, as Wheeler discovered that the vital document containing the H-bomb secrets was no longer inside the envelope.

He rummaged frantically through his suitcase in case it had dropped out among his clothes – but to no avail. Just then his Princeton colleague Jay Berger appeared, and while the distraught Wheeler urged the porter to help him search his berth and the washroom, Berger was delegated to stay behind to guard the suitcase.

A ten-minute trawl of all the cushions and linens in the berth, and a dig through bins in the washroom, brought no reward for Wheeler and Jones. The despairing scientist now began ripping up copies of the general reading matter in his suitcase – *Science*, *The Economist* and *Physical Review* – and other harmless personal correspondence, scattering the pieces all over the train's floor.

At 7.55 a.m., as they were required to, Wheeler and Berger exited the train. Leaving Berger to order breakfast for two at the Gateway restaurant, Wheeler hurried through the two other restaurants at Union Station in a desperate attempt to locate two of the other three men whom he believed he could identify during his time in the washroom. But it was a futile exercise, and at 8.10 a.m. Wheeler and Berger reported the loss of the document (without of course disclosing its top-secret details) to the Pullman Company's lost and found department.

Dejectedly contemplating his future, Wheeler ate a cursory breakfast with his colleague. The two men then headed for the nearby congressional office building to report the loss to the Joint Committee on Atomic Energy. Francis Cotter, security officer for the JCAE, on receiving the grim news, immediately contacted officials of the Pennsylvania Railroad and the Pullman Company to get them to put an official hold on the car so it would not be sent out for business again.

Following a hasty interview by JCAE staff, Wheeler, accompanied by director William Borden, chief of special projects Kenneth Mansfield and staff member William Bergin, traipsed back to Union Station to search 'Bettsville' once more.

They went through all upper and lower berths, drawing room, washrooms, bins, cushions, closets, vents and all possible places where the document might have lodged. But two and a half hours later their exhaustive search had failed to turn it up. And so, soon after midday, Borden bowed to the inevitable and picked up the phone to the Federal Bureau of Investigation's Washington field office and recounted the sorry story to Howard Fletcher, the assistant special agent in charge.

* * *

The missing document may not have included a total description of the H-bomb complete with drawings and diagrams, nor did it contain production rates of critical materials, details of the US weapon stockpile or scheduled dates for when the military could effectively deploy them.

But with its notes about current atomic energy and atomic theory, there was plenty that would have excited Soviet nuclear scientists. As Wheeler told his FBI investigators, deductions 'could be drawn by a potential enemy who knows how to make a conventional atomic bomb, but who has not yet cracked the thermonuclear field'.[19] He outlined the key points in the document as follows:

1. The US is on the way to a successful thermonuclear weapon.
2. There are several varieties of the thermonuclear weapon considered to be practical.
3. Lithium-6 is useful.
4. Compression is useful.
5. Radiation heating provides a way to get compression.

In his statement to the FBI, Wheeler reckoned that of all these pieces of information, 'the qualitative idea of radiation implosion … is the most important revelation. It is difficult to assess the importance of this notion without knowing the present state of thinking of a Russian like Landau' (Lev Landau, world-renowned physicist and key figure in the Soviet's bomb programme). But he admitted, 'the revelation could conceivably be very important indeed'.[20]

But mention of lithium-6 as a vital ingredient, the fusion fuel for America's H-bomb, would also have aroused the interest of the Kremlin. This could have been entirely fresh information – or at the least very helpful confirmation if Russian scientists had already started making lithium-6 part of their plans.

An anxious Gordon Dean, chairman of the Atomic Energy Commission, had little doubt about the significance of the document. 'It contained the most recent developments in thermonuclear devices,' he told FBI chiefs, and possession of it by a foreign power 'would seriously affect our national security'.[21]

John Walker, the author of 'Policy and Progress', was also deeply concerned. In his FBI interview he acknowledged 'the information lost was very serious and could conceivably advance the enemy's H-bomb progress, assuming certain factors'.[22]

Wheeler himself signed off his own statement to the FBI with an equally sombre evaluation. 'It is the conservative thing to assume that the information is indeed in the hands of a potential enemy, regardless of the alternative possibility of simple loss. Additional incentive therefore exists for the US to increase its efforts in the weapons field.'[23]

The FBI's investigation, led by Special Agent Charles Lyons, would prove to be one of the most painstaking and wide-ranging in its 45-year history. Immediate scrutiny fell on the fifteen individuals who had travelled in the Pullman that night. But quickly the inquiry narrowed in on Wheeler and Berger, the porter Robert James Jones, and the five other men who took neighbouring berths on the 'Bettsville' car that night.

The five – Gulf Corp engineer Charles Kottcamp, chemical engineer David Rest, aeronautical engineer James Luckman, traffic manager Claude Getty and warehouseman Howard Shipp – were quickly eliminated from inquiries.

African-American porter Robert James Jones was rigorously interviewed, but FBI agents found no reason to doubt his account of his actions on the night, or his general honesty and integrity. The 57-year-old married man had worked for the Pullman Company for thirty-two years and told his investigators he had handed over thousands of mislaid items, many of great value.

Two other Pullman sleeping cars had coupled together with the 'Bettsville' in Washington in the early hours of 7 January – the 'General Ewell', which arrived from New Orleans at 1.25 a.m., and the 'McCaslin', which came in at 7 a.m. from Jersey City. Exhaustive checks were made of passengers and staff on these vehicles to eliminate them from inquiries.

At a time of dread of the communist threat and fear of the skill and cunning of the Russian secret service, one theory had to be at the fore-front of the minds of FBI agents. Had Wheeler spun a clever cover story to disguise the handover of the H-bomb secret to a Soviet spy? But there was precious little evidence to back up that notion. Wheeler's FBI file, held at the Washington field office, did show that in 1946 he was listed as a member of the American–Soviet Science Society (later renamed the National Council of American–Soviet Friendship) – a body which encouraged the interchange of scientists and scientific in-formation between the Soviet Union and the United States.

More interesting to FBI boss J. Edgar Hoover was Wheeler's pro-test, along with ten other scientists, at the charges of disloyalty levelled at fellow nuclear physicist Dr Edward Condon, then director of the National Bureau of Standards. Hoover had long believed Condon was part of a Soviet network, telling President Truman he was 'nothing more or less than an espionage agent in disguise'.[24]

As the trawl for his communist connections continued, the best the FBI's informant on Wheeler could come up with was that the professor had travelled to Poland in 1947 to attend the congress of the International Union of Pure and Applied Physics. Thin pickings in trying to make out a case of espionage and treason.

Nor did Hoover's agents get very far with Berger. It was of interest that his parents had come from behind the Iron Curtain – his father Louis born in Russia and his mother Rose in Poland. A search of his file showed that in 1950 a car registered to Berger was reported by an informant to have attended a Progressive Party gathering in Cleveland, Ohio, which was a branch 'reportedly dominated by the Communist Party'.

As the investigation proceeded, there were some worrying gaps in the FBI's knowledge about the other occupants of 'Bettsville' that night. Agents were unable to track down an 'ordinary, plainly dressed' couple, thirty to forty years old, and their small child, who had bought a last-minute ticket from the conductor and taken up the lower and upper bunks in berth no. 1.[25]

The couple carried a 'makeshift' bag and purchased a one-way ticket from Philadelphia to Washington. By the way they were asking questions, staff deduced that it was their first trip on a Pullman. But with no record of sale and no name, it proved impossible to find them.

But Special Agent Lyons and his colleagues were even more frustrated – and concerned – at being unable to identify the individual who occupied the lower bunk in berth no. 8, which was the one next to Wheeler.

They succeeded in identifying the ticket for this berth, no. 6447, as a last-minute over-the-counter sale at the Pennsylvania Railroad downtown office in Chestnut Street, Philadelphia. But the name written on the company's seating chart was not clear as it had seemingly been written over another name, which was presumably a cancellation.

It looked as if the last name could be 'Magenbright', 'Magenknight', 'Wagenbright' or 'Wagenknight'. The chart was sent off to the FBI laboratory in Chicago, but after examination the technicians were unable to crack the writing. If this mystery man – or woman – did indeed occupy their berth, they had done so extremely discreetly, because the porter, Robert James Jones, and his conductor were unable to give even the slightest detail about him or her.

The FBI worried far more about ticket no. 6447 than they did about the unidentified 'ordinary couple'. Nevertheless, because they had a description of the family in berth no. 1, they considered placing an advert offering a reward for their identification.

As he pursued the theory of theft by a Soviet spy or accomplices, Special Agent Lyons asked his men to account for the movements of all Soviet diplomatic personnel on the morning of 7 January.

Lyons also initiated a probe into what he described as a 'delegation of radicals' heading for the capital on Monday night, possibly on one of the trains on which Wheeler had travelled.

A group were certainly outside the White House on Tuesday morning, carrying placards urging President Truman to commute the death sentence for spies Julius and Ethel Rosenberg.

Agents from the FBI's Washington office took numerous still photographs and shot five 100ft reels of film of this protest and then made Wheeler study them to see if he recognised any of the individuals from his various journeys on 6 and 7 January. But he was unable to provide a positive identification and so the hunt for the missing document continued through February.

*   *   *

If it wasn't a challenging enough job to track down the H-bomb document, the FBI had to contend with some fallout from the 'political war' in the community of atomic scientists which – certainly in the early days of the inquiry – obscured the disturbing reality of the secret paper from the bureau's senior figures.

Back in January 1950, President Truman's exhortation to the Atomic Energy Commission to go ahead and build the hydrogen bomb had not been greeted with universal approval within the organisation. Strong characters on the AEC's general advisory committee, such as Robert Oppenheimer, head of the Los Alamos Laboratory in the war, Enrico Fermi, leading architect of the atom bomb, and James Conant, adviser to Truman on the bomb's use, questioned both the morality and the military necessity of building the 'Super'. Other critics who were less exercised by ethical concerns still doubted whether the concept of the fission–fusion bomb could be translated into the reality of an effective weapon.

Among those lined up on the other side as advocates of the programme were Edward Teller, leading theoretician of the new weapon (he disliked the sobriquet 'father of the H-bomb'), and Hans Bethe, another Los Alamos veteran who did have moral reservations but was irked by suggestions that a working H-bomb was not feasible, and was determined to prove the doubters wrong.

John Wheeler, too, was furious at those that he felt had tried to put the brakes on the project. 'The professional handwringers who kept us from getting it [the H-Bomb programme] … have much to answer for,' he would later tell Kenneth Cole, biophysicist and fellow Manhattan Project veteran.[26]

Teller and Bethe looked to Congress for support, and received it from the Joint Committee on Atomic Energy, the body charged with political oversight of the country's nuclear programme. And in William Borden, the committee's director, they found a more than willing ally.

Thirty-two-year-old Borden was something of an evangelist for nuclear weapons. Seven years earlier, when a law student at Yale University, he had written an eye-catching book entitled *There Will Be No Time: The Revolution in Strategy*, in which he argued that unless a system of world federalism was established to eliminate nuclear danger, atomic war was inevitable. He insisted that the United States must prepare for such an eventuality by constantly retaining nuclear superiority over her potential enemies. Optimistically, he concluded that a nuclear war could be won with only limited damage.

The book brought young Borden to the attention of movers and shakers in Washington, among them influential Democratic Senator Brien McMahon, himself a Yale alumnus, who had put forward a bill that placed atomic research in the hands of scientists. His Atomic Energy Act also created the Joint Committee on Atomic Energy, which provided political oversight – and McMahon, naturally, was its first chairman.

Borden saw it as his mission to further the cause of the H-bomb, and to campaign, overtly or covertly, against its critics. 'Policy and Progress' was his creation, designed to frame the case for the 'Super' through a very partial history of its development. The 91-page document was directly fired at the AEC's general advisory committee members who were lukewarm or plainly opposed to the H-bomb, casting them in a poor light, even hinting that they had, treasonably, tried to sabotage this vital project of national security.

Into this battle of the scientists stepped the FBI on 7 January 1953.

Special Agent Charles Lyons was straight away told by Borden that he personally had no intention of informing the Atomic Energy Commission of the loss of the document – although he added that he would not want to stop the FBI from doing so if it wanted.

Borden also attempted to play down the significance of the missing paper. Telling J. Edgar Hoover's assistant Louis Nicholls – correctly – that the document did not give 'specifics as to numbers and products on hand', he suggested that it was merely 'like some of the top-secret material that the Alsops had been publishing'.[27]

He was referring to the Alsop brothers, Joseph and Stewart, journalists of some influence and key Washington insiders (Joseph had CIA connections) whose columns in the *New York Herald Tribune* were syndicated to newspapers around the country and thus read by millions. But for Borden to suggest that the H-bomb document was merely akin to one of their exposés was, at best, disingenuous.

But Lyons did tell the Atomic Energy Commission, and its leading lights soon briefed him about the extreme danger of the document falling into enemy hands. Gordon Dean, AEC chairman, was the first to warn that it would 'seriously affect our national security'.[28]

Then on Thursday 12 February, Dean's fellow AEC commissioner Thomas E. Murray went to see J. Edgar Hoover at his office in the Department of Justice building on Pennsylvania Avenue. Murray, a commissioner since 1950, had previously talked publicly about 'dismantling the era of terror'. He was a 'dove', on the Oppenheimer side of the H-bomb argument, and believed that America should stop further tests and instead equip her armed forces with thousands of small atomic bombs as a means of protection in limited wars.

Hoover told Murray all he knew was that Wheeler's document was 'confidential and contained something about the work of the AEC'. When Murray told him exactly what was in the papers, the FBI chief was stunned. That afternoon he wrote to his senior aides Clyde Tolson, Milton Ladd and Louis Nicholls:

I was shocked to learn of the importance of this document and the fact that we had not been previously advised of its importance … I told [Murray] I would arrange to have the assignment made a special so we could give it top priority in an effort to locate the document or the person responsible for stealing it.[29]

From then on Hoover was hands-on in the investigation, demanding to be briefed on every significant twist and turn. He had already urged Alan Belmont, the head of the FBI's Domestic Intelligence Division, to contact the new administration with the bad news – specifically General Robert Cutler, Eisenhower's National Security Advisor.

On Monday 16 February, Hoover was summoned to the White House to learn of the new President's alarm about the missing document. The Attorney General, Herbert Brownell Jr, told Hoover that Eisenhower was stunned at the lack of security and perplexed 'how such a document could be forwarded by a committee of Congress to a professor employed by the Atomic Energy Commission.'[30]

Brownell told Hoover that the President had insisted on being briefed every day on the progress of the investigation, and that Eisenhower intended to personally handle the matter with the Joint Committee on Atomic Energy. The President had also demanded to be given a list of specific security regulations that had been broken – and by whom.

Next Eisenhower himself summoned Senator Bourke Hickenlooper from Iowa, a frontrunner for the job of new chairman of the JCAE, for a breakfast meeting the following morning. Hickenlooper was as startled as the President had been the previous day – because he too had been left in the dark in the last five weeks about the missing document. The senator found Eisenhower 'much agitated' over the incident, but, amazingly, also somewhat confused about what exactly had gone astray.

'He had the wrong pitch,' Hickenlooper told the FBI the next day.[31] The President seemed to think the entire 91-page document had gone missing; Hickenlooper had to reassure him 'that the document lost contained only the conclusions and the highlights and consisted of only four or five pages'.

Hickenlooper stayed for lunch at the White House, and bore the brunt of further presidential anxiety. In a brief aside before they sat down to eat, Eisenhower suggested that if he did become chairman of the JCAE, Hickenlooper should straight away hand over the security of the committee to the FBI.

Eisenhower vented his full fury the next day, summoning the five commissioners of the AEC to his office in the White House in advance of a scheduled meeting of the National Security Council (NSC). Gordon Dean, Thomas E. Murray, Henry DeWolf Smyth, Eugene Zuckert and general manager Marion Boyer were lined up like errant schoolchildren in front of the headmaster's desk.

Murray had 'never in his life seen anyone so agitated' as the normally calm President let rip.[32] 'He reverted to his military form', recalled DeWolf Smyth.[33] 'Dean tried to explain that this was a Joint Committee document, that we had nothing to do with it. But Eisenhower wasn't hearing. I guess he was never a top sergeant but he talked like one that day.'

Also pulled in for a dressing down were Hickenlooper and Sterling Cole, Republican congressman for New York – the two ranking Republicans on the Joint Committee. 'He gave us unshirted hell', said Cole.[34]

Gordon Dean had to work hard to convince Eisenhower that this was not necessarily an inside job with the document now resting in Russian hands. The President told Dean he was staggered that such sensitive documents seemed to be passing through so many hands in the AEC and the JCAE.

At the meeting of the National Security Council a few hours after his showdown with the commissioners, Eisenhower confessed that he was 'frightened and did not know how to proceed'.[35] He noted that there were only three people on the Joint Committee who could have released this document – and had they been in the armed forces 'they should have been shot'.[36]

Various members of the council were convinced that the loss of the papers was down to treason and espionage rather than carelessness. Vice-President Richard Nixon recommended that each member of the JCAE's staff should undergo thorough investigation by the FBI, and Eisenhower's earlier suggestion that the bureau should take charge of the committee's classified files was debated. In the end, no action was taken on that front.

A week later and the White House came back to the FBI again. Sherman Adams, Eisenhower's Chief of Staff, phoned Hoover to tell him Eisenhower was considering a suggestion that he should introduce an executive order banning the sending of highly sensitive documents by mail.

Executive orders are controversial as they allow the President to implement a policy initiative without seeking congressional approval. The FBI chief cautiously said that he would 'be very glad to try and handle it' for Adams, but foresaw problems ahead.[37] 'I thought we would probably want to talk to the security people in the Atomic Energy Commission, as there apparently was friction between the commission and the committee.' In other words, finding agreement between the warring sides in the H-bomb debate could be long and tedious for Hoover and his colleagues.

As the weeks rolled by, the White House had greater, more immediate concerns – first and foremost the war in Korea. The FBI's examination of every aspect of Wheeler's past and present life found very little that caused concern. His colleagues and associates routinely described him as 'a brilliant and excellent instructor', 'sober, reliable, responsible', 'personable', 'down-to-earth' – an 'excellent character with no reason to doubt his loyalty to the United States'.[38]

If Wheeler had a weakness, it was his carelessness with official documents – although how rash he had been in the grand scheme of things, given that he handled secret papers every day, was a moot point. Nevertheless, the FBI identified a number of familiar security violations in his past. Coincidentally, Wheeler had left a small black notebook and a collection of Atomic Energy Commission passes on a Pullman coach just six months earlier. Then in December he lost a book at Kansas City Airport – harmless enough, except that Wheeler had covered the brown paper envelope containing the book in mathematical formulae.

In the end, after FBI agents all over the eastern side of the United States had interviewed hundreds of people and supervised the search of miles and miles of railway track and dozens upon dozens of railway carriages, they were none the wiser. Neither the family from berth no. 1 nor the mystery man or woman from berth no. 8 could be tracked down.

Whether a spy had stolen the document and it had found its way to Moscow to aid the Soviet's H-bomb programme, no one could know. Maybe one day it would turn up in the archives in Moscow. Until then, it had to be assumed that it had been mislaid by Wheeler en route from Princeton to Washington, perhaps sliding away from his grasp as he dropped off to sleep on that Monday night, and somehow vanishing into the structure, equipment or bedding of the Pullman.

Wheeler's punishment was to receive a severe official reprimand from Eisenhower – delivered via AEC chairman Gordon Dean, who expressed the body's 'extreme displeasure and concern' with him and his careless action. But Dean told the JCAE that Wheeler was just too important to the H-bomb's future to be punished. 'We do not know anything we can do without cutting off our nose to spite our face.'[39]

So the scapegoat for the whole sorry episode was William Borden, who was fired from his post with the JCAE – really only because he had put the politicians in an embarrassing position with the President and his new administration. After all, he had created the document, not mislaid it.

Borden returned to private law practice nursing dark thoughts about the whole affair, even wondering whether his old foe the Atomic Energy Commission might have had something to do with the theft. An obsessive enmity towards Robert Oppenheimer in particular developed, and would resurface in dramatic fashion later in the year.

As for Wheeler, he later mused in his memoirs: 'It is interesting, even now, to wonder whether my document was purloined by a Soviet agent. It could hardly have vanished into thin air.'[40] He comforted himself by thinking that 'if Soviet scientists saw it, they would have learned only that their side and our side were thinking along very much the same lines'.

That luxury of thought was not available to those pursuing the case in January and February 1953. For them, this was a desperately worrying moment in the heart of the Cold War.

* * *

At the same National Security Council meeting on 18 February when he laid bare his fears about H-bomb secrets being stolen by the Soviets, President Eisenhower was confronted with a penetrating, but worrying, analysis of the state of the arms race.

On the council's agenda was a report entitled 'Armaments and American Policy', a hangover from the Truman presidency which had been commissioned the previous summer by the then Secretary of State Dean Acheson. Acheson had asked a five-man panel of 'consultants' to take a fresh look at America's approach to the ineffective disarmament discussions currently taking place at the United Nations. But once they had started their inquiry, the panel broadened it out into a much wider examination of the accelerating build-up of nuclear weapons by the two global superpowers.

Dr Julius Robert (always referred to as J. Robert, or simply Robert) Oppenheimer was the chairman of the inquiry and his colleagues were a mix of scientists and civil servants: Allen Dulles (deputy director of the CIA, and brother of John Foster); Vannevar Bush (inventor and science administrator); Joseph E. Johnson (State Department and United Nations official); and John Dickey (president of Dartmouth College, the renowned Ivy League university).

The 48-year-old Oppenheimer, son of a wealthy German Jewish immigrant father, and a mother from Baltimore who was a painter, was the country's most famous scientist, feted for his outstanding leadership as wartime head of the Los Alamos Laboratory, which successfully manufactured and tested the world's first atomic bomb. He was the Leonardo da Vinci of his age, comfortably straddling the worlds of science and the arts: a brilliant theoretical physicist, he spoke eight languages (including Sanskrit) and studied philosophy and Eastern religion.

A childhood prodigy, Oppenheimer started a rock collection at the age of five and was admitted to the Mineralogical Club of New York when just eleven. 'Ask me a question in Latin and I'll answer you in Greek,' he once urged a fellow student. Another oft-quoted story was that on a train journey from San Francisco to the east coast, he read all seven volumes of Edward Gibbon's *The History of the Decline and Fall of the Roman Empire*.

It was typical of this cultivated scholar that he codenamed the atom bomb 'Trinity' after the poetry of John Donne, and when he watched the first of its kind explode with a blinding flash in the New Mexico desert on 16 July 1945, at that moment he turned in his mind to the Hindu scripture, the Bhagavad Gita, for an appropriate response: 'I am become death, the destroyer of worlds.'

Six foot tall, thin and a little stooped, with sharp blue eyes and an alert, expressive face, 'Oppie' charmed students, fellow scientists and politicians alike with eloquence, quick humour and the incisiveness of his mind. With a cigarette constantly in hand and his trademark broad-brimmed brown porkpie hat on his head, he was a familiar figure on the Washington power circuit, not to mention the capitals of Europe.

But after the experience of Hiroshima and Nagasaki Oppenheimer constantly fretted about the morality of nuclear proliferation. The A-bomb, he told fellow physicists in 1947, had 'dramatised so mercilessly the inhumanity and evil of modern war'. Six years on, Oppenheimer had now become the best-known opponent of the hydrogen bomb.

But he still remained the man that Presidents and members of Congress turned to for the shrewdest analysis of the nuclear arms race. Oppenheimer did not personally attend the NSC meeting to present his report, but the findings of his committee, detailed in clear, powerful language with at times vivid imagery, were disturbing to the President and his colleagues. The report described the character of the atomic arms race as one in which 'unprecedented destructive power was accumulating, probably on both sides, at a quite phenomenal rate'.[41] The report calculated that the Russians would have the material to make 1,000 atomic bombs in just a few years' time, and while little was known about their enemy's H-bomb programme, the commission cautioned that it would be the 'height of folly' not to expect the Soviets to 'learn what we have learned'.

The panel argued that in this atomic age, the destruction of the large modern industrial society – beyond any hope of recovery – was inevitable in the wake of a sustained attack. Scoffing at some people's optimism that America, with careful preparation and planning, could survive a first strike attack of up to 2,500 A-bombs, Oppenheimer wrote caustically that 'the term survival must have a rather specialised meaning'.[42] Who would survive in a country of radioactive ash?

The consultants queried America's attitude and policy. 'There is now in our posture a rigidity and totality of commitment which seems very dangerous,' Oppenheimer and his team wrote, with the 'widespread feeling that the United States is clutching the atom to its bosom and may at any time get angry and hurl it in the general direction of the Kremlin'.[43]

The reality was that at the beginning of 1953 the United States had something in the region of 1,000 nuclear warheads, while the Soviet Union possessed just over 100. However, because American and British spies had failed to penetrate the Iron Curtain to any significant degree since the end of the Second World War, it was generally believed that the Russians had a far greater atomic capacity.

But as the Oppenheimer report pointed out, it was just a matter of time before 'the Soviet Union will have "enough" bombs – no matter how many more we ourselves may have'. This now was the essential truth – that no country, in any meaningful sense, could win a nuclear war.

The evening before this meeting Oppenheimer had spoken to a closed meeting of the Council on Foreign Relations, whose members were Washington's leading military and political policy-makers, lawyers, bankers and journalists. His speech was on the same lines as his report, but in characteristic fashion it contained a dramatic passage that lived long in the memory of those who were in that room:

> The atomic clock ticks faster and faster ... we may anticipate a state of affairs in which two great powers will each be in a position to put an end to the civilization and life of the other, though not without risking its own. We may be likened to two scorpions in a bottle, each capable of killing the other, but only at the risk of his own life.[44]

Oppenheimer and his panel offered various recommendations to step off this road towards mutual destruction. The disarmament discussions in the United Nations – their early remit – should be scrapped. Soviet intransigence had rendered them feeble in the extreme, and in any case the world was very different now than in 1946 when they had started.

Instead, US leaders should make determined efforts – barely considered to date – to communicate far more directly with the rulers in the Kremlin. Stalin would not be there for ever, and those jockeying for the succession might have different mindsets. 'The danger of the arms race must be much increased if Soviet leaders fail to understand its real character; we believe that careful communication may materially reduce the chance of a disastrous Soviet miscalculation.'[45] Of course, best efforts to start a conversation might be rebuffed, but Oppenheimer and co. felt it 'well worth a try'.

But the panel's principal message to Eisenhower and Dulles was that they must show openness and honesty – 'candour' was the word they employed – about the nature of the arms race and its likely terrifying consequences. Candour with the American people and government, and candour at the political and military level, with their Western allies.

Oppenheimer believed most Americans had little idea of the growing destructive power of atomic weapons. The truth of the arms race was currently 'buried in a few informed minds'.[46] He was convinced that this long period of concealment and deception should be ended, and a straightforward statement, backed up by facts and figures, was now necessary. 'This country does better when it knows the truth,' and people should learn about the rate and impact of America's atomic production, but also learn about the Soviet Union's growing capability. They should be warned that beyond a certain point 'we cannot ward off the Soviet threat merely by keeping ahead of the Russians'.

Summing up this new concept of 'candour', the panel concluded:

It is bad enough to be in a very dangerous world; it is still worse to be unaware of the danger … in the end it is the province of the nation to make its own foreign policy, and we are not among those who believe that we are necessarily wiser than the people and government of the United States, when they are truly informed.[47]

At that NSC meeting Eisenhower praised the report and urged all members of the council to read and digest it fully. At this stage he only demurred from the recommendation to quit the disarmament talks.

However, a week later the President's enthusiasm for 'candour' had seemingly cooled. He pointed the finger at Oppenheimer and Bush, the two scientists, and suggested that they had little grasp of the need for security and that their recommendation for openness clearly went beyond the law – the stringent Atomic (McMahon) Act of 1946, under which any information about nuclear weapons was classified as 'restricted data'. He made it clear that he was wholly opposed to letting the American people know the size of the country's stockpile of nuclear weapons.

Allen Dulles, the only member of the panel at the NSC meeting, explained that they had never been expected to approach the problem as a purely scientific one. He defended the concept of 'enoughness' – when the Soviet Union possessed a stockpile of sufficient size to deal the United States a damaging blow, enough even if the US possessed a stockpile many times bigger. He added that a policy of candour was not designed to scare the public, only to give them a realistic picture of the dilemma that they might face.

In the end the NSC decided to postpone any decisions on the Oppenheimer report. A new subcommittee, under the chairmanship of Vannevar Bush, was sent away to consider how best – if at all – to implement the recommendations.

Oppenheimer's stock with Eisenhower was still high. Although the President now appeared to have reservations about the report, it was he who had encouraged Oppenheimer to deliver his speech to Washington's movers and shakers to ensure they were aware of the thinking of the 'father of the A-bomb'.

The two men were certainly no strangers. Although Oppenheimer opposed the development of the H-bomb, he had lobbied hard for the production and improvement of lower-yield bombs – specifically battlefield tactical nuclear weapons. As a key figure in Project Vista, a joint study between the military and the scientific community on tactical warfare and the defence of Europe, he visited Paris in November 1951 for a series of meetings with Eisenhower, who was then Supreme Allied Commander of NATO.

But the charismatic, ambitious, artfully persuasive and at times arrogant Oppenheimer was collecting powerful and determined enemies who were jealous of his achievements and furious at the direction in which he wanted to take America's nuclear policy.

His speech to the Council on Foreign Relations infuriated the US Air Force (USAF) generals. Referring to America's growing stockpile of atomic weapons and the strategy for employing them, he declared: 'It is generally known that one ingredient of this plan is a rather rigid commitment to their use in a very massive, initial, unremitting strategic assault on the enemy.'[48]

He was, of course, criticising the Strategic Air Command's core war plan. In 1948, outlined in Operation Halfmoon, the command had called for the dropping of fifty atomic bombs on twenty Soviet cities. Two years later its planning became increasingly apocalyptic when General Curtis LeMay pushed for implementation of 'Emergency Plan 1-49', which would have involved the delivery of America's entire stockpile of atomic bombs in a single massive attack – 133 nuclear weapons dropped on seventy Soviet cities.

But there was one man in particular in the council audience that night who came away seething at Oppenheimer – and with a resolve to bring him down. Admiral Lewis Lichtenstein Strauss, naval officer, businessman and eminent public servant, had recently been appointed as Eisenhower's atomic energy adviser and was widely tipped as the next chairman of the Atomic Energy Commission.

Strauss's path to influence in Washington's defence and scientific establishment had been a very different one to the man he would now make his chief foe. Born in 1896 in Charleston, West Virginia, Strauss wanted to study physics, but his family did not have enough money to send him to college. Instead the young man spent the First World War serving under food administrator (later President) Herbert Hoover, helping channel 27 million tons of food to Europe after the armistice of 1918.

After the war Strauss worked at Kuhn Loeb, the investment bank, and eventually became a partner and self-made millionaire. In the Second World War he had a reserve commission in the US Navy, and joined its ordnance bureau to work on weapons production. Then in 1947 President Truman appointed him as one of the first five commissioners on the newly created Atomic Energy Commission.

The prickly Strauss was on the opposite side to Oppenheimer on the H-bomb argument. Now he violently disagreed with this notion that the public should be informed about America's nuclear stockpile – or indeed that any matters of nuclear strategy should be publicly debated.

Back in 1947 Strauss, as chairman of the trustees at Princeton, had actually offered Oppenheimer the job as director of the university's prestigious Institute of Advanced Study. But before he could be cleared to accept the post, Oppenheimer had been forced to declare some embarrassing details of his far-left past and connections.

The details had come via a twelve-page report from FBI boss J. Edgar Hoover, which highlighted Oppenheimer's association with communists. But he survived the scrutiny to take up his position, with Strauss voicing no opposition. Six years on, however, and Strauss now deeply distrusted the nation's most famous scientist – and with a vital place in the White House he was in a position to make life very uncomfortable for Oppenheimer. Reviewing the evidence and pondering it anew, Strauss even began to believe that the man responsible for the research and development of the atomic bomb might be a Soviet spy.

Robert Oppenheimer – 'father of the A-bomb', now keen to lift the veil on nuclear secrecy.
© Ed Westcott, public domain, via Wikimedia Commons

CHAPTER 2

'A GOOD TARGET'

In the closing days of the 1952 presidential campaign, before an enthusiastic crowd of 5,000 in Detroit's splendid neo-Gothic Masonic Temple, Eisenhower had made the pledge that surely clinched his election victory.

At the heart of a powerful foreign policy speech he vowed to cast aside the 'diversions of politics' and concentrate on ending the Korean War. 'That job requires a personal trip,' he told his audience. 'I shall make that trip. Only in that way could I learn best to serve the American people in the cause of peace.' Then came the simple, resonant phrase that made the headlines the next day: 'I shall go to Korea.' 'Eisenhower Scores With Korea Pledge' was a typical response on the front page of Michigan's *News-Palladium*.[1]

An America desperate for the stalemate to be broken and for the boys to come home now clearly believed that the general – who, after all, helped draw down the curtain in Europe at the end of the Second World War – was the man best equipped to end the two-year conflict.

The President-elect duly fulfilled his promise on 2 December when he touched down in Seoul for a three-day visit that was conducted in conditions of great secrecy. A cover story – that he was working on his final Cabinet selection at his New York home – had successfully put political reporters off the scent.

When details of his visit were eventually released, it was clear that he had kept as low a profile as was possible, eschewing major public appearances to concentrate on visiting the frontline with the generals. An appearance alongside the excitable and unpredictable South Korean leader Syngman Rhee before an appreciative crowd in Seoul had been declined.

In the film footage that followed the lifting of the press embargo, Eisenhower could be seen clad in regulation general infantry winter clothing, touring considerable stretches of the west and west-central fronts, talking to UN combat units, watching practice manoeuvres by South Korean troops and visiting a mobile surgical hospital. It was an accomplished public relations exercise and whetted the appetite for his move into the White House in late January.

Two months on from that visit and little had changed in Korea. One million communist troops faced 768,000 UN soldiers along static battle lines that had not significantly shifted in the past two years. The last important land contest, for 'Triangle Hill', had ended only days before Eisenhower arrived.

That battle had been a blow to UN morale after its troops failed to take the strategically important hill mass. Although the Chinese People's Volunteer Army suffered 11,500 casualties in the 42-day assault, they had slowly exhausted the US 8th Army and the PVA leaders had become emboldened by their attritional strategy. But as the sub-zero temperatures and deep snow of December and January turned to the winter rains of February, transforming the battlefield into a muddy quagmire, the pace of combat ground almost to a halt, with the minimum of daily shelling, sniping and raiding by both sides.

The air war, however, remained as frenetic as ever, and here the UN – primarily US Air Force – had notable successes in February 1953. While the B-29 bombers and F-84 Thunderjets struck successfully at munitions factories, steel mills and locomotives, the lively escorting F-86 Sabre fighters were harrying the experienced Soviet MiG-15s.

In one of the highlights of the air war, four F-86s took on a formation of forty-eight MiGs south of the Sui-ho Reservoir, shooting down two enemy aircraft and, through evasive manoeuvres, causing two others to crash. In this battle Captain Manuel Fernandez Jr, using the characteristic stealth and cunning that would later win him the Distinguished Service Cross, achieved ace status by downing his fifth and sixth MiGs.

Back in Washington, on Wednesday 11 February, Eisenhower chaired a meeting of his new-look National Security Council to search for ideas to plot a way out of the Korean impasse.

It was early days in his presidency, but Eisenhower was determined to establish the NSC as the top policy-making body on foreign and security affairs. President Truman had set it up in 1947, but then somewhat neglected it. Eisenhower wished to revive it by encouraging free-flowing, free-thinking debate among his Cabinet ministers, military chiefs, CIA officials and even civilian representatives.

The President had handed over the organisation of the NSC to Robert Cutler, his National Security Advisor. The intense, energetic 57-year-old Bostonian was quickly acquiring a reputation as one of the new administration's sharpest and toughest minds.

'Bobby' Cutler was a man cut from a different cloth to the usual government recruit, plucked as they usually were from narrow strata of the political, business and military classes. Class poet Cutler graduated *cum laude* from Harvard in 1916, then wavered between a career in literature and the law. He wrote two novels, *Louisburg Square* and *The Speckled Bird*, in between serving as an infantry officer during the First World War with the American Expeditionary Forces on the Western Front.

After the war he finally plumped for the legal profession, graduating from Harvard Law School. Cutler would become one of New England's most successful lawyers, eventually rising to the position of president of Boston's Old Colony Trust Company.

Cutler developed a taste for government towards the end of the Second World War when he was appointed special assistant to Henry Stimson, Secretary of War, while also working on assignments for the

US Army Chief of Staff George Marshall. He won the Legion of Merit for his wartime work for 'foresight and careful planning, consummate tact, unusual ability and vigour'.

Cutler moved in Republican circles, and Eisenhower recruited him for his 1952 election bid to write speeches and help advise on policy. At times fussy, terse and over-assertive, 'Bobby' did not endear himself to everyone on the campaign trail, but Eisenhower was impressed enough to entrust him to run the NSC.

What the President did not know was that Cutler was gay. Very few people did, outside of Washington's small circle of closet homosexuals. Aside from his running of the NSC, Cutler had also been asked to draft Eisenhower's Executive Order 10450, a piece of harsh legislation – complementing the McCarthyite crackdown on communism – designed to weed out those in federal government deemed to pose a security risk.

The definition of such untrustworthy individuals in Order 10450 was wide-ranging: 'Any criminal, infamous, dishonest, immoral, or notoriously disgraceful conduct, habitual use of intoxicants to excess, drug addiction, or sexual perversion.'[2] Given the mores of American society at the time, Cutler might well have found himself fitting the fourth and final categories on that list. But by helping frame such castigatory legislation with its slant against gays and lesbians – and several thousand of them would lose their jobs as a result – he found, perhaps, perfect cover for his own sexual proclivities.

All of this was incidental to Cutler's main preoccupation with the NSC, a body into which he breathed new and energetic life. All those attending the weekly meetings (which usually took place on Thursday mornings) in the White House Council Chamber were well briefed beforehand, and encouraged to contribute their views in a relaxed atmosphere.

'It is the single most important agency in the Executive Branch,' avowed Eisenhower. Cutler controlled the length and tempo of the meetings, introducing subjects and moderating the discussion. Eisenhower and John Foster Dulles were clearly the main players and the central focus, but through the President's urging, the NSC was a forum where others could provide him with innovative thinking, as much as being a body for decision-making.

'Eisenhower is quite creative in a conference. He feels very free … to throw up almost outlandish ideas just to see what will happen,' his young Vice-President Richard Nixon recalled.[3]

While other council members talked, Eisenhower would doodle on any paper he could find – agendas, memos and other official documents. Some of his sketches would be of heads of the participants round the table; many were 'of cups in saucers, carefully drawn in proper perspective'.[4]

Despite this compulsion, Eisenhower was a careful listener. 'Doodling had no effect on the President's retentive memory or attention to business,' Cutler noted.[5]

On this particular day in February the subject matter could hardly have been more serious. First Allen Dulles, who was shortly to take over the reins at the CIA, kicked off the meeting with the latest intelligence on the war in Korea. He told members that three new Chinese armies had recently appeared in or around the battlefield – although they were thought to be replacements, not reinforcements. Dulles also commented on the intensifying air battle, noting how there had been a high number of Soviet MiG flights the previous month.

But the main focus of the discussion was provided by General Omar Bradley, Eisenhower's indispensable lieutenant in the Second World War, who was now chairman of the Joint Chiefs of Staff. He brought to the table disturbing views from the commander of UN forces, General Mark Clark, another of the President's able subordinates in wartime.

Clark's first piece of intelligence was that the so-called 'Kaesong sanctuary' was now packed with troops and equipment, which had convinced him that a communist attack on UN troops was forthcoming. Kaesong was the location of the ancient capital of Korea, 35 miles north-west of Seoul. It became a 'sanctuary' – i.e., neutral territory, covering 28 square miles – at the time of armistice negotiations in 1951. In reality, though, it was firmly under communist control.

Clark was requesting an end to the immunity of the Kaesong sanctuary, and that when it was obvious that the communist offensive was imminent, he should be granted permission to attack. The commander's other plea to the NSC via Bradley was for authorisation to expand the war into China herself, to destroy enemy aircraft that he believed were massing in Manchuria to support that new troop contingent in Kaesong.

The previous month, scientists at Los Alamos had triumphantly reported the successful testing of a battlefield atomic weapon. Now, for the first time, members of this new National Security Council openly debated whether a variety of the weapon which had caused such catastrophic death and destruction in the cities of Hiroshima and Nagasaki should be deployed on the Korean battlefield.

It was back in the dark days of the winter of 1950, when UN forces were pushed all the way back to the 38th parallel after the Chinese intervention – the longest retreat in American military history – that the use of the atomic bomb in active warfare was first contemplated.

A powerful group in the military had pushed for use of the A-bomb as a tactical weapon, and one of its chief advocates was Major General James Gavin, former commander of the 82nd Airborne Division and then a member of the weapons evaluation group for the Secretary of Defense. He recommended using a Hiroshima-type device against massed enemy troops, which dropped from an altitude of only 2,000ft would be the equivalent of 8,000 medium artillery shells per square mile and could wipe out a whole division (up to 25,000) of troops.[6]

In public, military chiefs had been cautious, but sent out signals that nothing could be ruled out. Asked by a *US News & World Report* reporter whether the bomb would be effective on the Korean battleground, General MacArthur had replied inscrutably: 'My comment at this time would be inappropriate.'

On 30 November 1950, at a press conference, the President had stated that he was prepared to take 'whatever steps were necessary' to end the war in Korea and then was more explicit when asked by a reporter if the measures might include the atomic bomb. 'That includes every weapon we have,' Truman retorted. 'Mr President,' the reporter followed up, 'you said "every weapon that we have" – does that mean there is active consideration of the atomic bomb?' 'There has always been active consideration of its use,' Truman replied.

'President says A-bomb will be used if necessary' was a common headline the following day, and a convulsion of international proportions followed. A nervous Prime Minister Clement Attlee, with Britain as America's chief ally in the UN force in Korea, flew out to Washington immediately for urgent talks, which eventually resulted in public assurances that there was no trigger-happy mood and that the two leaders had agreed to close joint consideration of questions involving atomic weapons.

Yet the US military secretly continued to plan for the last resort of an atomic attack. In April 1951, when the Chinese launched their massive Fifth Phase Offensive against the 8th Army, Truman ordered nine Mark IV nuclear bombs to be transferred from the United States to forward Strategic Air Command bases in Guam and Okinawa. Examination of atomic use continued in the autumn of 1951 with Operation Hudson Harbor, an exercise which tested US ability to drop A-bombs on troop formations in difficult terrain.

The reality was that Truman, who had shouldered the awesome responsibility for the bombs dropped on Japan, was desperate to avoid another nuclear attack in Asia. But at the NSC meeting in February 1953, the new man in the White House made it clear that the current status quo in Korea was not acceptable. Eisenhower declared that the use of atomic weapons should be considered on the Kaesong area, 'which provided a good target for this type of weapon'.[7]

General Bradley thought that it was necessary to discuss the end of Kaesong's immunity with America's allies, but believed it would be 'unwise' to broach the subject of the possible deployment of atomic weapons.

But John Foster Dulles backed the President, squarely confronting the moral inhibitions of using this weapon of mass destruction. The Soviets, the Secretary of State said, had convinced much of the world that atomic weapons should be placed in a special category, aside from all other weapons. But it was his opinion that 'we should try to break down this false distinction.'[8]

With the bit between his teeth, Eisenhower added that if America's allies 'objected to the use of atomic weapons, we might well ask them to supply three or more divisions needed to drive the communists back, in lieu of the use of atomic weapons.'[9]

By the end of the meeting the subject of the A-bomb had been put to one side. For one thing, Eisenhower was not convinced about the accuracy of General Clark's intelligence about Kaesong. He also made it clear that, at this stage, he did not want any discussions with Britain and other allies about atomic weapons or any other military plans. He would leave it to Dulles to broach the subject of the ending of the Kaesong sanctuary.

But this meeting was a key turning point. The atomic genie had now been let out of its bottle, and the NSC would return to the subject multiple times in the coming days and months.

* * *

Back in December 1945, four months after the first atomic bombs were exploded at Hiroshima and Nagasaki, Robert Oppenheimer had been called to give evidence before a special congressional committee on the future of atomic energy.

The committee held in-depth interviews with a number of Manhattan Project luminaries and others on how atomic bombs were built, their effects, and what was needed from the scientific and military worlds to sustain the nuclear programme.

The testimonies ranged far and wide. There was a discussion on the latest experiments on atomic-powered ships, and a suggestion – from Rear Admiral William R. Purnell – that submarine-launched ballistic missiles might be the best way to deliver atomic weapons.

The general enthusiasm of the witnesses for atomic weapons was not shared by Oppenheimer, who made it clear that he was firmly against the idea of building up a stockpile of nuclear weapons: '[They] would give us an absolutely illusory security. An atomic bomb which you do not use is of no use to you,' he told the committee.[10]

But Republican Senator Eugene Millikin of Colorado pressed Oppenheimer on the future threat to the United States. He asked the scientist whether there was any way of detecting a nuclear bomb smuggled into the country in, say, a shipping crate.

'In normal warfare we … have mine-detecting devices which are rather effective if used thoroughly,' noted the senator. 'I was wondering if anything of that kind might be available to use as a defence against that particular use of atomic bomb?'[11]

Oppenheimer's typically colourful reply sent a chill down the spines of the committee men:

If you hired me to walk through the cellars of Washington to see whether there were atomic bombs, I think the most important tool would be a screwdriver to open the crates and look. I think that just walking by, swinging a little gadget, would not give me the information.[12]

Thus the spectre of nuclear terrorism was already in the minds of US politicians in 1945. In the wake of Oppenheimer's dispiriting analysis, the Atomic Energy Commission asked two of America's brightest young physicists, Robert Hofstadter and Wolfgang Panofsky, to investigate whether it would be remotely possible to detect 1 cubic inch of enriched uranium or plutonium – the key ingredient in an A-bomb – if it were smuggled into the country in a crate or a suitcase.

Their work, named the 'Screwdriver Report', was highly classified and has never been publicly released. To the unease of Congress, they backed up Oppenheimer's testimony, concluding that although it might be possible to detect passive radiation from plutonium and, less likely, from highly enriched uranium, 'you can't detect a nuclear device unless you are close to it'.[13] And the chances of detection would be even smaller if the bomb was surrounded by an effective shield.

Eight years on from Oppenheimer's evidence, and with the Soviet atomic bomb a reality since 1949, fears that a nuclear weapon could be smuggled onto American or British soil had only been heightened. So when Churchill, working late on a Thursday night in the Cabinet Room at 10 Downing Street, was brought the early editions of the newspapers he was alarmed to read this short piece in the *Daily Telegraph*.

'Atom bomb checks' ran the headline. The article revealed that Rear Admiral Alfred C. Richmond, assistant commandant of the US Coast Guard Service, had disclosed that his men were regularly searching vessels approaching New York and neighbouring ports 'for atomic bombs, other types of explosives and bacteriological weapons'.[14]

The admiral was quoted as saying that thirty to forty vessels were now being searched every month – most of them from countries behind the Iron Curtain. In total, 1,500 ships had been searched during the past two years. So far, however, nothing untoward had been discovered.

The Prime Minister, via a memorandum from his private secretary Anthony Montague Browne, demanded of the Home Office whether the British port authorities had anything similar planned – and how effective such searches were deemed to be. What Churchill had forgotten was that just under a year ago his Cabinet Secretary Norman Brook had sent him a note on this very subject – attaching to it a copy of a secret report he had compiled for the previous premier, Clement Attlee, back in July 1951.

Brook's report, in his customary succinct yet elegant prose, had set out the history of the Attlee government's plans to counter the potential threat of a clandestine atomic attack from the Soviet Union. The government's worries first surfaced in the autumn of 1950 when the Cold War was heating up, only a year after the Soviets exploded their first atom bomb, and just a few weeks into the Korean War.

The British Chiefs of Staff of the armed forces, after receiving concerned soundings from the Joint Intelligence Committee, urged that greater consideration be given to a surprise atomic attack by the Soviet Union. At first their best guess was the enemy would begin the next world war with an atomic attack on London on the model of the Japanese air strike on Pearl Harbor – without warning, and with no declaration of hostilities.

But there were other possibilities that the committee wished a top-level, secret committee, set up by the Ministry of Defence (MOD), to explore. So on 28 September 1950 the strangely named Imports Research Committee (IRC) held its first meeting. The committee was given a deliberately ambiguous title aimed at foxing the rest of Whitehall and beyond about its true remit – much as the equally dull-sounding wartime Tube Alloys programme had disguised its true purpose, to research and develop Britain's first atom bomb. Still, at least the Imports Research Committee had a title and subject matter, however vague the description of the latter. An even more secret committee, tasked with developing Britain's atomic weaponry, merely went by the acronym NNC, which stood for No Name Committee.

Chaired by a senior MOD civil servant, the IRC had an impressive cast list, including Martin Furnival Jones (later director general of MI5); Michael Perrin (deputy controller of atomic energy at the Ministry of Supply); George Turney (of the MOD's Directorate of Scientific Intelligence); and Captain Michael Laing (former director of the trade division at the Admiralty).

The committee concentrated on two scenarios. First, that a complete atomic bomb could be concealed in a merchant ship arriving in Britain from the Soviet Union or one of her satellite nations. Second, and more intriguingly, that the bomb might be broken down into numerous parts, placed in, say, fifty small packages of equal weight, then smuggled into Britain by different routes – perhaps some of them disguised as ordinary merchandise on ships, and others as diplomatic freight through the Soviet embassy in London.

The committee had studied the transcript of the Oppenheimer 'screwdriver' testimony and knew that it was nigh-on impossible to detect an atom bomb, or its key components, if it was hidden and shielded in a package or a suitcase. So tighter control of shipping or closer inspection of diplomatic baggage appeared to be the only options to eliminate this particular threat.

The IRC calculated that a complete plutonium bomb could be packed into a box about 4ft tall by 4ft wide and 10ft long, weighing 2 to 2.5 tons. The only components emitting any kind of 'characteristic' radiation would be the fissile material and the neutron source – and those would be barely detectable. So Oppenheimer's screwdriver would be the only way to uncover the bomb.[15]

As for an enemy agent assembling a bomb once the fifty packages had been smuggled into the country – that would be relatively straightforward:

> It could be carried out in any premises having the normal equipment of a small garage, including lifting tackle. It is a skilled assembly job, which could probably be completed in about twenty-four hours by half a dozen men of the skilled fitter type together with a supervisor – provided they had been carefully trained and in possession of precise and detailed instructions. No special precautions, beyond those normally required in handling high explosives, are necessary.[16]

Turning to the scenario of the complete bomb smuggled in on a ship, the IRC noted that if a war looked inevitable, the period just beforehand – which civil servants dubbed the 'precautionary stage' – would make it easier for rigorous searches to take place. But the enemy would probably make its move in a period of relative calm between nations when less attention was paid to security risks. February 1953, for instance, was such a period.

The IRC looked across the water and noted enviously that Congress had passed an emergency act in July 1950 giving its customs officers additional powers to search foreign ships. Within days of the passing of that legislation the Polish liner MS *Batory* – the ship in which the Communist Party leader Gerhard Eisler escaped from America the year before – had been stopped and searched for atomic weapons when docked in New York harbour. Nothing suspicious was found.

If the fifty parts of an atomic bomb were smuggled into Britain for the device to be assembled here, the Soviet embassy's diplomatic freight or 'diplomatic bag' – which had immunity – would be an obvious route. In theory, both could be examined for any abuse of customs duty. The horror of the Foreign Office at such drastic action could be imagined. In the furore that would inevitably follow, there would be tit-for-tat action aimed at the British embassy in Moscow, and, the IRC concluded, 'it could not fail to increase international tension'.

In concluding his report of the IRC's deliberations, Norman Brook acknowledged that 'it would be practicable for the Russians to introduce an atomic bomb into this country by clandestine methods'.[17] 'It is equally clear', he added, 'that there is no certain method of preventing them from doing so.'

However, Brook told Attlee that he was 'very doubtful' that the increased security involved in any of these measures could 'outweigh the very serious disadvantages, political and economic'. Would not a military aircraft 'do the job' more effectively than any of these elaborate clandestine methods? And when it really came down to it, why would the Soviets invite immediate atomic attack against themselves when the Americans had such an overwhelming advantage in their A-bomb arsenal?

Brook suggested Attlee should discuss the IRC's findings with a small group of ministers including his Foreign Secretary Herbert Morrison and Defence Secretary Manny Shinwell. But that briefing never happened as a few months later Attlee called an election and was then ousted from No. 10.

Churchill had clearly forgotten about the Import Research Committee before Brook's report was dusted off and landed on his desk in March 1952. Perhaps not surprisingly, as his attention would have been focused on the momentous development, and ultimately successful testing, of Britain's own A-bomb.

Now that the Prime Minister had set this hare running again, his civil servants and military advisers were keen to set the hounds on it. General Sir Nevil Brownjohn, chief staff officer at the Ministry of Defence, told George Mallaby, undersecretary for foreign affairs at the Cabinet Office, that 'it would be fruitless to resurrect this subject and a waste of time to undertake any further examinations'.

Nevertheless, the chairman of the dormant IRC, George Wheeler, was obliged to consult with the Americans – and the Belgians and the Dutch, who were believed to have stepped up their searches of Soviet vessels.

When he reported the results of his inquiries, his aim was to put Churchill's concerns to bed. 'The reply from America confirms our impression that the American examination [as reported in the *Daily Telegraph*] is largely window dressing.'

Wheeler told General Brownjohn, who was in charge of this new Whitehall inquiry, that he had also consulted his colleagues on the IRC. 'The general feeling is that no harm would be done [to look at the matter afresh] – but nobody expects to reach any different conclusions. In the circumstances I think a re-examination of the general problem would be a waste of time.'[18]

Brownjohn himself consulted Vice Admiral Charles Hughes-Hallett, head of the British Naval Mission in Washington, who advised him that the American searches were 'somewhat superficial … and, for economic and manpower reasons, restricted to the ten major US ports'.[19]

'You will see from all this that the US measures are not as effective as the press accounts would lead us to believe,' Brownjohn wrote to Norman Brook. The Prime Minister's hare had now been dispatched, although the Defence Committee would take another look at the subject later in the summer.

Thirty years later, the plot of a bestselling thriller was based on one of the scenarios discussed by the IRC.[20] In *The Fourth Protocol*, under the Kremlin's Plan Aurora, Soviet agent Valeri Petrofsky arrives under deep cover in the United Kingdom and establishes a base in a house in Ipswich. From there, he travels around the country collecting packages from various couriers from behind the Iron Curtain who have smuggled them into the country either hidden in or disguised as seemingly harmless artefacts.

After assembling the device in his Ipswich garage, Petrofsky plans to explode his atom bomb near RAF Bentwaters, making it look like an accidental detonation of a US weapon. The Kremlin's plan is for a wave of anti-Americanism to follow, support for unilateral nuclear disarmament to grow, and a sympathetic left-leaning Labour government to win power and begin to dismantle the Western alliance.

Happily, the plot is foiled by John Preston, ex-Parachute Regiment solider turned MI5 officer, Petrofsky is killed and the bomb made safe. In 1953 Britain fortunately never came close to such drama – even if the imagination to envisage it was in the minds of some in Whitehall.

* * *

The fear of the Russian threat manifested itself in a variety of ways. For instance, the renowned efficiency and the reach of the Soviet spying operation led the British security services to contact 10 Downing Street with concerns that the Prime Minister's hearing aid might be bugged.

Churchill's state-of-the-art apparatus was under the care of the electronics company Multitone, run by father and son Joseph and Alexander Poliakoff, Jewish émigrés who had fled Russia after the revolution of 1917.[21]

The Poliakoffs had been regular visitors to Downing Street over the past year since Churchill returned to Downing Street, and were even on occasions welcomed into the Prime Minister's bedroom – where he tended to work on papers in the morning – to brief him on the effectiveness of their equipment.

But MI5's suspicions about any Russian citizen – past or present – with links to the offices of power had hardened after the extraordinary discovery five months earlier of a bug that had been planted in the US embassy in Moscow.

A routine electronic sweep of the embassy had picked up the voice of the ambassador, George F. Kennan, but no one could discover from where it was being transmitted. Eventually, after a painstaking search, it was traced to a wooden replica of the Great Seal of the United States in the embassy study, which grateful Soviet schoolchildren had presented to the US government in 1945 to mark the end of the war.

When the seal was smashed open with a hammer, security experts found a pencil-shaped microphone within it, housed in a metal chamber approximately 10 inches long. It became clear that this bug had been relaying every word that Kennan uttered in his study very clearly to his Soviet eavesdroppers. Even more galling to the Americans was the thought that the Soviets had been listening in to conversations in that study for the previous seven years.

The sophistication of the bug astounded Western experts. It did not have its own power source and was not connected via wires. Instead it was illuminated by a strong radio signal from the outside which powered and activated it, and gave it a virtually unlimited life.

The revelation of 'The Thing' – as the Soviet bug was quickly dubbed

– clearly worried Roger Hollis, deputy director general of MI5, who was still reeling from the discovery of Soviet agents (Klaus Fuchs, Guy Burgess, Donald Maclean) at the heart of Britain's scientific and political establishment.

So when he wrote to Churchill's principal private secretary Jock Colville on 16 February, he set out in full his misgivings about the Poliakoffs. He detailed Joseph Poliakoff's past role as technical adviser from 1924 to 1927 to the All-Russian Cooperative Society (ARCOS), an organisation set up by the Soviets to encourage trade between the United Kingdom and the USSR – but whose employees the security services suspected of being spies.

Indeed, the police – working on information gathered by MI5 – had carried out a high-profile raid on the ARCOS headquarters in May 1927, taking away scores of documents that they would later claim proved the company was engaged in military espionage and other subversive work.

Not that there was remotely any evidence to implicate Joseph Poliakoff in any such activities. In his letter, Hollis next noted that during the war Multitone had employed two people with 'considerable Communist records' – although he could not say whether they were still employed by the firm.[22]

Finally, Hollis observed that the Russian Trade Delegation – another body that MI5 considered to be a front organisation for espionage – had been in touch with the Poliakoffs in 1948 in connection with some equipment that it had bought from Multitone two years previously.

It was hardly damning stuff – and Hollis admitted that an examination of Churchill's equipment had uncovered no evidence of bugging. He told Colville he had not made any further inquiries into Multitone but suggested the following: 'I imagine you will probably think this is unnecessary and that you can decide on the information before you that it would be safer not to employ the Poliakoffs ... on the maintenance of the equipment in the Cabinet Room.'[23]

After being shown Hollis's letter, Churchill had ringed '1948', suggesting that the link with the trade delegation concerned him. Eight days later Colville wrote back on his behalf to tell Hollis: 'Mr Churchill agrees that in the circumstances Mr Poliakoff must not be allowed here anymore.'[24] Hollis then went ahead and found an alternative company to deal with the Prime Minister's hearing aids – Bonochord Ltd – rigorously and satisfactorily vetting the three engineers who would work in 10 Downing Street. Meanwhile, MI5 continued to keep the utterly guiltless Poliakoffs under surveillance.

Even before MI5's concerns about the Poliakoffs, after the startling discovery at the US embassy in September 1952 Churchill had put one of Whitehall's 'big beasts' onto a vital investigation into bugging.

Sir Frederick Brundrett was vice-chairman of the Defence Research Policy Committee and deputy scientific adviser to the Minister of Defence. During service with the Royal Naval Volunteer Reserve after the First World War, he was involved in pioneering research work on underwater communications with submarines. Soon afterwards, at the Royal Naval Signal School, he played a leading role in the development of short-wave radio.

But Brundrett never claimed to be a great scientific innovator, once joking that he was the worst circuit engineer in the history of the Royal Naval Scientific Service (he became its chief in 1946). This short, wiry, energetic man was instead one of the great science administrators, and he perfectly understood the vital role that scientists could play in government and was able to win the trust of service chiefs and Cabinet ministers alike.

Along with the likes of Lord Cherwell (Churchill's favourite scientific adviser), Sir Henry Tizard and Sir John Cockcroft (both instrumental, among other things, in developing Britain's radar capability), he had galvanised Britain's technical and scientific contribution in fighting the Second World War. Now he was being asked to apply his personality and his methods to winning the Cold War.

In a report to the Chiefs of Staff, Brundrett advised that 'intensive work' needed to be done to enable Britain to match the Soviets' eavesdropping skills.[25] He ordered this work to take place under 'special arrangements' at two venues – the Marconi Research Laboratories at Great Baddow, Essex, and the Post Office Research Laboratories at Dollis Hill, west London.

Both sites would employ four extra scientists on the project – with Brundrett insisting, because of the 'peculiar nature' of the task, that they should be drawn from the defence sector, rather than from industry. He emphasised that close liaison with the Americans 'through the MI5/FBI' channel was essential.

Brundrett, whose brief as scientific adviser ranged far beyond improving eavesdropping techniques, had no illusions about Britain's woeful lack of intelligence about the intentions of the Soviet Union. 'This war is fought with spies, not soldiers, at least in the short term … [but] to be frank the situation is not good,' he concluded.[26]

With no agents being successfully run behind the Iron Curtain, technical and scientific proposals had to fill the gap. Much depended on Brundrett's famed creativity and leadership.

*   *   *

Brundrett knew the value of cooperation with the United States in sharing scientific knowledge for application in the military arena. Aside from eavesdropping, he would also work closely with Washington in the coming months on the development of chemical and biological weapons.

But Churchill's chief scientific adviser Lord Cherwell – known to friends and associates simply as 'the Prof' – on the other hand, was tired of the obfuscation of Congress and the White House over the sharing of atomic secrets, and had embarked on a mission to prise his master away from the grip of a relationship that he now considered far from 'special'.

It was a long, tortuous process, however, and Cherwell was becoming increasingly exasperated at what he saw as Churchill's erratic attitude and unrealistic expectations about American cooperation in the atomic field. All the same, he was doing his utmost to persuade him that Britain's future lay equally in a Commonwealth effort with Australia and South Africa, which held the biggest deposits of ores in the world.

Correspondence between Cherwell and Churchill on scientific matters was akin to that of master and pupil in the classroom. Cherwell, one of Churchill's oldest friends and advisers, was perhaps the only man in Whitehall who could lecture, and chastise, the Prime Minister in the way he did.

Cherwell – previously Sir Frederick Lindemann – had been at Churchill's side for over thirty years. German-born (but with a deep dislike of the country of his birth), with some far-right views, 'the Prof' was teetotal, a vegetarian and a non-smoker and was an outstanding tennis player who had won tournaments all over Europe and even played in singles and doubles matches at Wimbledon.

Professor of experimental philosophy (physics) at Oxford, Cherwell could be frosty, arrogant and boastful when confronted by academic rivals. But the Churchill family – Churchill's wife Clementine was his tennis partner – and circle were very fond of him, and over time he had become indispensable to the Prime Minister, who brought him into his wartime government to run his statistical branch, and had now lured him back again to be a key figure in his second administration.

Cherwell's enthusiasm for the atom was based as much on the promise of its civil application as it was for military use. But he had applauded the Labour government's secret £100 million investment in an atomic bomb – Parliament knew nothing about it – and had fought to stop Churchill's vacillating attitude on the subject.

Churchill's enthusiasm – all too evident in the war, with the establishment of the Tube Alloys bomb project – was now tempered by

economic worries (the Conservative government inherited a huge balance of payments deficit), and, more often than not, his desire to seek
American approval, cooperation and financial help before committing
to shared projects.

To the Prof's bafflement and fury, Churchill had, on occasions, even
suggested that he was not even an advocate of an independent British
project. 'I have never wished since our decision during the war that
Britain should start the manufacture of British bombs,' he wrote to
Cherwell in November 1951, soon after taking power.[27] 'Research however must be energetically pursued,' he continued. 'We should have the
art rather than the article.'

The Prof swiftly disabused Churchill of that notion. He persuaded
him that ownership of the atom bomb was a necessity for Britain's independence and prestige. The idea that Britain should merely 'rank
with other European nations who have to make do with conventional
weapons' appalled him.

So in December 1951 Churchill privately authorised the first atomic
test, and on 17 February 1952 came the public announcement from
10 Downing Street that the test would take place later in the year in Australia. On 3 October, Britain became the world's third nuclear-armed
power after successfully testing her own atomic bomb, exploding the
device on an anchored frigate, HMS *Pym*, in the uninhabited Monte
Bello Islands off the north-west coast of Australia.

America was of course now a giant step ahead following her thermonuclear test a month later (which Churchill was not informed about),
but Britain had at last triumphantly proved her independence in the
atomic field – and Cherwell, with a key Cabinet role (he had the nomi-
nal title of Paymaster-General), continued to make the case for quicker
and further nuclear advancement.

When writing to Churchill at the end of 1952, he deployed his characteristic crystal-clear language to make his case, allied with a grand
sweep of history that he knew the Prime Minister would appreciate.

In a memorandum entitled 'Atomic Energy – Future UK Programme' he reminded the Prime Minister that the enormous advances in the Victorian era were due to 'the men who had the imagination to put and keep England ahead for 60–80 years in the use of steam power for industrial purposes'.[28]

Now, as Britain's coal prices soared and reserves dwindled, prosperity in the coming century would 'depend on learning how to exploit the energy latent in uranium (1lb is equivalent to 1,000 tons of coal)'.

The Prof added: 'No one, of course, knows exactly how and when these developments will come; but nobody knew 150 years ago the part the steam engine would play'.[29]

Cherwell had presented a paper to the Defence Committee in early December 1952, advocating – on behalf of the Chiefs of Staff – the building of two new plutonium 'piles', which would not only go towards making new bombs but also potentially generate electric power. Churchill had baulked at the plan, primarily on cost grounds.

'I was shocked by the line you took,' the Prof wrote in response.[30] 'Even if Eisenhower were to give you fifty bombs … we should still need the dual-purpose piles which I proposed. We need these not only for the plutonium they would yield but also to learn how to design and use reactors for electricity.'

The Prof brushed aside the Prime Minister's worries about the expense – £6 million a year spread over four years – describing it as 'negligible' compared to the £1,500 million spent annually on defence or the £250 million on food subsidies.

Cherwell teased Churchill by stating that he wondered whether the Prime Minister wanted to give up making 'bombs of our own' and merely rank with other European nations who made do with conventional weapons.[31] With a final flourish he wrote: 'I cannot believe that you would contemplate adopting such a disastrous line which might in the long run spell national suicide.'

The reality was that Churchill hankered back to the days when he and President Roosevelt signed what he considered was a major lasting international treaty on nuclear power – the Quebec Agreement – and also put their names to a further aide-memoire, agreed at Roosevelt's Hyde Park home, on the same subject.

The secret Quebec Agreement, which was signed in August 1943, had required America and Britain to pool resources to develop nuclear weapons, stipulated that neither country would use them against the other and stated that none of this shared information should be passed to other countries. It effectively merged – or subsumed – the British Tube Alloys programme into the American Manhattan Project. Worryingly for the British scientific community, the document, in paragraph five, also gave America a veto over British post-war commercial or industrial use of nuclear energy.

The short 'Hyde Park Aide-Mémoire', which was signed in September 1944, defied calls to share nuclear secrets with the Allies, insisting all knowledge and development of the bomb should remain solely in US and UK hands. It also foreshadowed the terrible events of Hiroshima and Nagasaki, stating that when an atomic bomb was finally available 'it might perhaps, after mature consideration, be used against the Japanese, who should be warned that this bombardment will be repeated until they surrender.'[32]

In opposition Churchill had fulminated about the relevance and importance of the Quebec Agreement (the Hyde Park paper, known to so few anyway, had quickly slipped from memory), but the harsh reality was, as Attlee would patiently tell him in private, that the era of wartime cooperation with the United States was long gone. Instead, in the Cold War, it was the Atomic Energy Act of 1946 that essentially defined US–UK dealings on nuclear power.

Otherwise known as the McMahon Act (after the Democrat senator who introduced it), it was unfortunately framed – as far as the British were concerned – just at the moment when it became clear that Soviet spies had been stealing vital atomic secrets. One figure at the centre of this affair was the gifted British physicist Alan Nunn May, who, after helping to develop radar technology, first joined Tube Alloys before eventually moving to Canada and working on nuclear reactors on the fringes of the Manhattan Project – where he was recruited by Soviet military intelligence.

The principal objective of the McMahon Act was the transfer of control of nuclear research and development from the military to civilian authorities, by setting up the Atomic Energy Commission in the United States. But fears about the loss of nuclear secrets led to the introduction of the controversial Section 10 on 'restricted data', which barred any other country, including Britain, from receiving any information on American nuclear technology.

It fuelled great resentment from Britain's political and scientific community, and encouraged the Attlee government on its way to developing its own atomic bomb. 'We've got to have this thing over here whatever it costs … we've got to have the bloody Union Jack on top of it,' Foreign Secretary Ernest Bevin had famously told the secret Cabinet committee at the crucial meeting in October 1946.[33]

In 1951 the McMahon Act's tight security regulations were relaxed slightly, allowing the US to share certain atomic information outside the field of military weapons – such things as reactor development and production of fissionable matter.

By early 1953, with the British bomb in place and American permafrost no longer thawing despite Churchill's best endeavours, Cherwell was keen to press onwards to a bright nuclear future without Washington's help. A crucial milestone for the Prof was reached on Wednesday 14 January, when the Cabinet, after months of wrangling, agreed in principle that the responsibility for atomic research and production should be transferred from a government department – the Ministry of Supply – to a new independent authority.

Cherwell had waged a long and hard battle over the past eighteen months to, as he saw it, free this exciting new industrial enterprise from the 'dead hand' of government and civil service control. He wanted the brightest and the best scientists to be attracted to an organisation that combined 'efficiency, elasticity and rapidity of decision [making]' – and to be better rewarded for their expertise.[34] He looked to the leaders of the new authority to possess 'qualities of mind and outlook which we may hope to find in those who control large and growing industrial enterprises'.

His chief adversary in Cabinet had been an old foe, Duncan Sandys, the Prime Minister's son-in-law, who, as Minister of Supply, had the most to lose. The two men had clashed repeatedly in Churchill's war-time Cabinet, most notably over the threat from Hitler's long-range rockets. On this the Prof, who had been highly sceptical about the dangers, could by and large be adjudged to have lost the argument.

But on the matter of a new civil body to look after Britain's atomic affairs, Cherwell most emphatically won. Churchill, dithering on the issue, had set up a small Cabinet subcommittee to consider the arguments, comprising Harry Crookshank (Lord Privy Seal), Harold Macmillan (Minister of Housing and Local Government) and Walter Monckton (Minister of Labour).

The language of their report delivered at the Cabinet meeting on 14 January showed how well Cherwell had successfully lobbied them and stoked their enthusiasm in the subject. 'It is said that the harnessing of atomic energy will prove to be the most important scientific development since the discovery of fire,' they declared.[35] 'The industrial use of atomic energy … is coming, and its effects will be far-reaching. We cannot afford to be left behind in this race; for the whole of our industrial future may turn on its outcome.'

In the end, they calculated that if left to a government ministry, the 'full potentialities of this new source are not likely to be realised … the heads of which must inevitably be preoccupied with many other important problems'. Instead, atomic power 'will be more energetically and efficiently pursued if responsibility is transferred to an organisation … with a structure more akin to that of a large industrial organisation'.[36]

Cherwell might have written the report himself. He had finally won the day. Churchill was absent that day, and there was only one dissenter, Rab Butler, the Chancellor, who said to his colleagues: 'I don't think this is sound', suggesting that Lord Waverley, who would be asked to chair a committee to see it through to fruition, should first consider the principle of the decision.[37]

But Butler conceded, 'I can't press my view further', while even Duncan Sandys now halted his fire, grudgingly admitting: 'In the long-term there are probably advantages in making the change.'

The Prof now pressed on with his quest to wean the Prime Minister off his reliance on American cooperation. The new Congress had already shunned any suggestion that the US should lower her security bar and once again share some atomic information with Britain. In a survey conducted by the Associated Press news agency at the beginning of the year, Congress members lined up almost two to one against an open interchange of data with their Second World War ally.

Republicans were far more hostile than Democrats, although the latter too took a generally negative stand. 'British security system doubtful, too dangerous,' commented Chester Holifield (California), with a nod to Klaus Fuchs, the British scientist involved in Tube Alloys and the Manhattan Project, who had been unmasked as a Soviet spy.[38] Some of the observations on any exchange of information were scathing. 'We would be trading a horse for a rabbit,' remarked William Harrison (Wyoming).[39]

It was against this background that Cherwell wrote to Churchill some weeks after the Cabinet decision, informing him there was 'little doubt' that opinion in Washington circles about cooperation was 'less favourable' than ever.[40] Churchill, using his purple marker (as opposed to his red one that he used in the war), circled the phrase 'less favourable'.

The Prof went on: 'The congressional committee is less flexible and more nationalist than it was and Senator Hickenlooper and

Representative Cole, between who the chairmanship seems to lie, are far less well disposed to us than Senator McMahon was.'

Once more Cherwell urged Churchill on another course. Reminding him that he had written in January about the lack of benefit Britain derived in this sphere, he once more spelt it out. 'The time has probably come to free our hands from some of the restrictions it [the relationship with America] imposes in order to build up a great Commonwealth enterprise. The Foreign Office has apparently been thinking on similar lines.'[41]

When Churchill forwarded this memorandum to Anthony Eden for his comments, the Foreign Secretary backed up Cherwell, initialling the paper and stating: 'I agree with the Paymaster-General.'

Churchill, however, did not, and continued to harbour hopes of a close relationship with Eisenhower and his administration, on this matter and others. But in the coming months Cherwell would continue to make the case, patiently and firmly, for Britain striking out on her own.

* * *

In these early months of his administration, President Eisenhower showed little interest in the continent of Latin America, beyond insisting that its rulers – the majority of whom were dictators – should do all they could to tackle the menace of communism.

He certainly believed, as he would spell out to Churchill, that colonialism was 'on the way out as a relationship among peoples' and that the 'fierce and growing spirit of nationalism' should be accommodated.[42] But in February 1953 he made no move to intervene in his own 'backyard' when Churchill decided to send a warship to the region to protect a sliver of British Empire.

The territory in question was Deception Island, which to all intents and purposes, as one American commentator put it, was 'really just a grain of sand sticking in the international hour glass'. Set against the background of the Korean War and the atomic arms race, an international dispute over the provenance of this tiny corner of one of the earth's bleakest, coldest, remotest regions baffled most global observers.

But for the Prime Minister, natural defender of the Empire, the crown colony of the Falkland Islands in Antarctica – of which Deception was a part – was strategically, politically and symbolically important. So he had no hesitation in sending a frigate and a contingent of Royal Marines thousands of miles to deal with Argentinian and Chilean incursion on the island. This was for him no 'neo-Palmerstonian' act – simply a matter of defending Britain's sovereignty.

Just 7.5 miles long and 7.5 miles wide, Deception is one of the numerous South Shetlands islands, which lie more than 500 miles south of their big brother in the region, the Falklands. Of its kind Deception was unique, however, because its circular harbour was formed and then kept ice-free by a huge warm spring, heated by an underwater volcano which, when active, enveloped it in a cloud of steam.

British interest in this area of the planet may have dated as far back as 1592, when the explorer John Davis, one of Queen Elizabeth I's chief navigators, sighted the Falklands on his ship *Desire*. Two years later Sir Richard Hawkins is reputed to have followed in his footsteps and mapped the island. Then just under a century later Captain Sir John Strong actually stepped on the land – after his ship HMS *Welfare* was driven off course – and promptly named it after his sponsor, the Viscount of Falkland, MP and commissioner of the Admiralty.

As for little Deception, it seems that Captain Cook – who visited 'nearby' South Georgia – missed the island on his major voyage around the Antarctic in 1775. American sealer Nathaniel Palmer may have been the first recorded visitor in 1820, staying just two days, but nine years later British interest was firmly established when a naval expedition under Captain Henry Foster (who lent his name to the harbour) spent an extended period on the island, conducting valuable topographic and scientific experiments.

For much of the rest of Deception's history the chinstrap penguins, brown skuas and snowy sheathbills were disturbed only intermittently by hardy seal and whaling expeditions – often British, but also American and Norwegian.

Then in the Second World War, Churchill's coalition government authorised Operation Tabarin (named after a racy Paris nightclub) – ostensibly a secret mission to block the Germans and their allies from gaining a grip in the region, in particular denying U-boats safe passage and anchorages.

But in reality, Tabarin – whose first base was on Deception – was all about creating a permanent foothold and reinforcing Britain's territorial claims in the Falkland Islands and its dependencies, at a time when serious challenges loomed from those countries with the nearest land masses, Argentina, first and foremost, and Chile.

The British government claimed the Falklands by right of discovery and continuous occupation, while the Argentinians demanded the territory by dint of geographical proximity and the assumption that they 'inherited' Spanish claims in the region.

When the post-war leader of Argentina General Juan Perón and his charismatic wife Eva set themselves up as the leaders of a new aggressive South American nationalism, the cause of 'repatriating' Las Malvinas (Spanish for the Falkland Islands) was firmly on their agenda. Perón boasted that by the time he left his post, not an inch of soil, nor a breath of air, would be alien-owned in 'Argentina's Antarctic sector'.

Much political hot air was expended in Buenos Aires and Santiago. British government suggestions that the Falklands dispute should be decided in the International Court of Justice in The Hague were firmly rejected by the Argentinian dictator and his Chilean counterpart, General Carlos Ibáñez del Campo.

Under Perón, Argentina did establish her own small base of sorts in 1947 on Deception, although the British controlled the island. The dictator then sanctioned – or turned a blind eye to – numerous other minor incursions into the Falklands, including one in February 1952 when a landing party from a British survey ship was forced by armed Argentinians to withdraw from Hope Bay (although they eventually returned, along with an escort of Royal Marines).

Churchill fumed about that incident, and a subsequent report from his defence chiefs concluded that while they saw no likelihood of a full-scale invasion of the Falklands, they could not rule out a landing on an unoccupied outer island.

Their prediction was realised within the year. In early January 1953, a party of Argentinians and Chileans were landed on Deception Island. The ship bringing them transported 10 tons of soil from Argentina, supposedly for the garrison to grow vegetables – but in reality, the earth was a symbolic gesture to reinforce the view that Deception Island was an integral part of Argentina.

Even more provocatively, the Argentinian party erected a hut, tent and flagpole on the airfield, just a few hundred yards away from the six-man British base. The Chilean group, meanwhile, also built a hut and then in a further act of needling marked out a football pitch and painted 'Chile' in large white letters in the middle of it.

This was an affront too far for Churchill's administration. At a Cabinet meeting on Thursday 12 February, once the perennial subject of the forthcoming Coronation was out of the way, ministers settled down to hammer out the final details of Britain's response.

Lord Simonds, the Lord High Chancellor, wished to ensure that any response – with a military dimension – was legally watertight. Having assured colleagues of Britain's 'clear title' to Deception Island and the 'right to resist aggression', his advice was that the British landing party should tread carefully, treating this incursion as 'illegal entry' rather than an 'act of war'.[43]

The frigate HMS *Snipe*, with thirty-two Royal Marines on board equipped with Sten guns, rifles and tear gas, was dispatched from Portsmouth. The military operation, which was carried out on the afternoon of Sunday 15 February, went without a hitch. A whaler and motorboat were lowered from *Snipe* at around 2 p.m., containing Major Edwards and his thirty marines, along with the chief constable of the Falkland Islands Dennis Ikkint and his translator, police constable D. J. O'Sullivan.

They encountered no resistance from the two naval ratings stationed in the Argentinian hut, which was found to contain a rifle, two pistols and a flare gun. Alongside stood a tent, where the marines found some stores – and a cat, which had apparently wandered from the British base.

The Chilean hut was unoccupied, an even more fragile construction containing a single bunk bed and 70lb of tinned food. Commander of HMS *Snipe* Denis Hall-Wright then ordered the Argentinian flag to be pulled down and asked the dozen marines who were staying on to destroy the two huts. He then transported the compliant prisoners to South Georgia in the South Sandwich Islands, where the chief constable and keeper of prisons Kenelm Pierce-Butler supervised their transfer, along with their stores and equipment, onto the ship SS *Quilmes*, whose destination would be Buenos Aires.

The Secretary of State for the Colonies, Oliver Lyttelton, conveyed the success of the mission to Churchill with ironical flourishes that were typical of him. 'I have the honour to report that my war, or the first phase of my war, has now been successfully completed,' he wrote.[44] 'The strength of the hostile detachment turned out to be two, and we were therefore in overwhelming force.'

So as it turned out, this had hardly been a major encroachment on British territory. But by tweaking the lion's tail, Perón was satisfied that he had further stoked the fires of nationalism back home. The front page of independent evening paper *La Razón* was headlined: 'Brutal outrage in Antarctica against Argentine sovereignty.' It went on to claim 'over a million square kilometres of Antarctica lands belong to Argentina. Our country's rights, supported by the sacrifice of Argentine sailors, seventeen expeditions, and permanent action at the service of mankind, will prevail.'

Police stood guard outside the British embassy and other British buildings in Buenos Aires as indignation mounted, with parading youths chanting 'Down with Britain' and 'The Malvinas are Argentine'. Foreign Secretary Anthony Eden offered to take the dispute with Argentina and Chile to the International Court of Justice in The Hague – an offer which was, once again, turned down.

Three months later there was an intriguing footnote to the incident. Perón sent his special envoy, Rear Admiral Alberto Teisaire, to the Queen's Coronation celebrations, during which he asked Foreign Office officials to a private meeting at London's Park Lane Hotel.

There, Teisaire, the acting president of the Argentine senate, made an unexpected offer on his President's behalf – to buy the Falkland Islands. He told the British diplomats that 'he wished to see Anglo-Argentine economic relations put on a firm basis, and that their proposal was, as part of some long-term arrangement, Britain should surrender all ... rights and claims to the Falkland Islands'.[45]

Teisaire even attempted to point out that there was a precedent for the deal in America's lend-lease agreement with Britain in 1940, when fifty ageing destroyers were exchanged in return for vital bases in the West Indies and North America.

The Foreign Office officials at the meeting were not inclined to take the admiral seriously. Kenneth Pridham, head of the American department, witheringly observed: '[His] major mistake was coming to the Coronation not only without a uniform but without any decorations at all. The result was that at the major functions he looked unhappily like a rather inferior waiter.'[46]

It fell to Lord Reading, the junior Foreign Office minister, to flatly reject Teisaire's proposition, telling the admiral: 'The inhabitants of the Falkland Islands were British, and if a plebiscite was held, they would vote practically unanimously to remain under the British flag.'[47] Even Teisaire had to admit that 'this was probably true'.

Reading went on to inform Teisaire candidly: 'It was inconceivable that any British government should consider the sale of the islands. If they were to do so there would be at once a terrible outcry from the public, and the government would be overthrown.'

And that was that. Public bickering and the occasional minor confrontation would characterise the relationship between Argentina and Britain over the next thirty years, even after Perón and Churchill had departed from the scene. It would take a new military dictator, Leopoldo Galtieri, to attempt to take control of the Falkland territories again – and another Conservative Prime Minister to retaliate.

Joseph Stalin lies in state at the Hall of Columns, Moscow.
© Keystone/Getty Images

CHAPTER 3

'NO CROCODILE TEARS'

The Cold War received a massive jolt in early March 1953 when Joseph Stalin died in his dacha at Kuntsevo, just outside Moscow. He was seventy-four. It was, as his daughter Svetlana put it, a 'difficult and terrible death' – if not as terrible as many of the millions of deaths the dictator had himself ordered, or, as in the case of the Jewish doctors who were the latest victims of his growing paranoia, was still planning.[1]

Stalin had been discovered barely conscious on the floor of his bedroom four days earlier on 1 March, after a typical all-night drinking session with his cronies. But it was not until the following day, when he was paralysed and speechless, that the doctors were summoned. Almost too frightened to touch him, they eventually announced that he had suffered a massive stroke. His inner circle – Georgy Malenkov, Vyacheslav Molotov, Lavrentiy Beria, Nikita Khrushchev and Nikolai Bulganin – scurried in and out of the dacha each day, dithering one moment and plotting the next, unsure of what to do, while rumours spread that they or some of them had taken a hand in putting an end to the great leader.

Finally, at 9.50 p.m. on Thursday 5 March, Stalin's eyes opened and Svetlana watched him 'cast a glance over everyone in the room. It was a terrible glance, insane or perhaps angry, and full of the fear of death. He suddenly lifted his left hand as though he were pointing to something up above and bringing down a curse on all.'[2] After this parting gesture, the man who had brutally led the Russian revolution for three decades was finally gone.

The news of Stalin's death was released to the outside world by Moscow's foreign services. But Radio Moscow said nothing, although seasoned listeners understood a momentous event was in the making because for several hours solemn orchestral music spilt out of the loudspeakers of Moscow, 'filling the night with an eerie atmosphere of tragedy and sorrow'.

Then at 2.55 a.m. the music suddenly stopped. The sound of pealing bells replaced it, followed by a minute's silence and then the majestic strains of Alexander Alexandrov's Soviet national anthem. Finally, at 3.05 a.m., the voice of Yuri Levitan, the announcer who during the war had brought Russians powerful exhortations to defend their homeland, eventually succeeded by heartening news of victories, spoke to the nation.

His pathos-steeped announcement stated that 'at 9.50 Joseph Vissarionovich Stalin … died after a serious illness. The heart of the collaborator and follower of the genius of Lenin's work, the wise leader and teacher of the Communist Party and of the Soviet people, stopped beating.'[3] In the following hours there were repeated broadcasts of this communiqué to reassure the populace, and to proclaim Stalin's immortality.

The dictator's corpse was transported to the laboratory attached to Lenin's mausoleum in Red Square just two hours after the first announcement, where state embalmer Boris Zbarsky should have been responsible for preparing the body for the funeral. But Zbarsky, who had embalmed Lenin, was currently in a labour camp in Siberia, one of the casualties of Stalin's recent purge of Jewish doctors.

Instead it fell to Zbarsky's deputy Dr Sergei Mardashev and his assistant Dr Sergei Debrov to perform the work, with Stalin's bodyguards watching their every move intently. Debrov was struck by how different the despot's face, littered with pockmarks and liver spots, looked from the doctored image used for propaganda purposes.[4]

The death of Stalin plunged millions of Soviet men and women into a state of almost mental and emotional disorder. Schooled by years of political education, they had come to believe that their leader was a great and good man, and that his ideas – despite the scale of human suffering they brought to so many families – were just and right. Trained to believe that Stalin was taking care of them, they were lost and bewildered without him.

This was the leader who had mobilised their heroism in the Second World War, urging them to enormous sacrifices that made the defeat of the German invader possible. This was the man who, after the war, extracted every ounce of strength from them to rebuild their devastated land, and who then drove the nation to the forefront of the world's industrial powers.

In the hours after the announcement there was a muted atmosphere on the streets of Moscow. America's acting ambassador Jacob Beam had dispatched his staff across central Moscow to gauge early reaction, and he reported back to Washington that there was 'a surprising lack of response' – in contrast to the death of President Roosevelt and King George VI.[5]

Perhaps it was momentary shock. Soon tidal waves of mourners from across the country and torrents of poems and speeches lamenting the passing of 'the deathless leader' washed over the capital, while old and young publicly wailed in schools, factories, offices and the streets. As millions streamed to the Hall of Columns in the House of Trade Unions for a last glimpse of Stalin's body – by the third day the queue had stretched to 6 miles – scores perished, trampled to death in the stampede.

When Eisenhower first learned that Stalin was either dead or dying, he was persuaded to publish a moving message which barely referred to the dictator. At Robert Cutler's prompting, he wrote:

The thoughts of America go out to all the people of the USSR – the men and women, the boys and girls – in the villages, cities, farms and factories of the motherland. They are the children of the same God who is father of all everywhere. And like all peoples, Russia's millions share our longing for a friendly and peaceful world.[6]

Appealing over the heads of the Kremlin directly to Soviet citizens was a shrewd propaganda ploy. But Eisenhower was frustrated that no one in his administration had prepared any political plan in the event of Stalin's death.

At the Cabinet meeting on 6 March he fumed:

Ever since 1946 I know that all the so-called experts have been yapping about what would happen when Stalin dies and what we, as a nation, should do about it. Well, he's dead. And you can turn the files of our government inside out – in vain – looking for any plans laid. We have no plan. We are not even sure what difference his death makes.[7]

When he heard the news, Churchill sent a simple message of 'regret and sympathy' to Moscow. That was too much for the pro-Labour *Daily Mirror*, who responded with the front-page headline 'Crocodile Tears'.[8] 'Let no tears be shed,' was the equally condemnatory verdict of the *Daily Sketch*.[9] 'The world is well rid of him. No honest man or woman can fight villainy for years then regret the end of one of its authors.' Even the *Church of England Newspaper* was moved to say: 'About the dead say nothing but good – but suppose there is nothing good to say?'[10] It declined to be hypocritical of a man who inflicted 'intolerable cruelty' on millions.

Churchill was angry at the *Daily Mirror*'s tone and coverage about his old wartime colleague and adversary, telling his doctor Lord Moran that the paper was 'dancing on his tomb'.[11] The physician also noted in his diary that 'the PM feels that Stalin's death may lead to a relaxation in tension'.[12] 'It is an opportunity that will not recur, and with Anthony away [Eden was sick at the time] he is sure he can go straight ahead. He seems to think of little else.'

With the funeral out of the way, the race for the succession in the Kremlin began. First out of the blocks were the grey apparatchik Georgy Malenkov, appointed Premier, and the feared secret police chief Lavrentiy Beria, First Deputy Premier and head of the Ministry of State Security (MGB), which was soon to be renamed KGB. The latter was assumed to be the real power behind the throne in these early post-Stalin days, although Nikita Khrushchev was coming up in the ranks after securing the crucial role of First Secretary of the Communist Party on 14 March. Vyacheslav Molotov, Stalin's long-standing Minister of Foreign Affairs and the only contender whom Churchill and Eden knew from the wartime days, seemed to be slipping behind the leading pack.

Churchill, still believing in the diplomacy of 'big men', moved quickly to try to seek the blessing of Eisenhower for an easement of relations with these new leaders in the Kremlin – with the goal, as yet undeclared, of a future summit meeting. Two days after the funeral he telegraphed the President:

Now there is no more Stalin I wonder whether this makes any difference to your view about separate approaches to the new regime or whether there is a possibility of collective action … I have the feeling that we might both of us together or separately be called to account if no attempt was made to turn over a leaf.[13]

Eisenhower's immediate response was non-committal. Writing the same day, he 'by no means' rejected the possibility of an approach to the Kremlin by Western leaders. But he warned:

I tend to doubt the wisdom of a formal multilateral meeting since this would give our opponent the same kind of opportunity he has so often had to use a meeting simultaneously to balk every reasonable effort of ourselves and so make of the whole occurrence another propaganda mill for the Soviet.[14]

Strangely, in the two British Cabinet meetings since Stalin's death there had been no discussion about the fate of the vast Soviet empire now under new management. Churchill and his colleagues were instead focused on trying to win (primarily American) support to establish order in Egypt, where Britain's 80,000 troops stationed in the Suez Canal zone were being increasingly harried in the early months of the new military regime. Nor did the Joint Intelligence Committee have much to say about Stalin's passing, beyond the bald assessment that the three leading contenders for the succession – Malenkov, Molotov and Beria – were all judged likely to continue his policies.

By contrast, over in Washington on 11 March, the National Security Council held a wide-ranging, at times argumentative debate on what should be the approach to the despot's demise. Allen Dulles was first asked to take the floor with an assessment of how the country's spies thought Stalin's death would play out.

The CIA director was impressed with the smooth transfer of power, which now saw Malenkov as titular leader. But because he had risen to power on Stalin's coat-tails, it was not possible to 'estimate with confidence [his] capabilities' – and Dulles reckoned 'a struggle for power could develop within the Soviet hierarchy at any time'.[15]

Dulles told the committee that 'ruthless and determined' as he had been to spread Soviet power, Stalin had not allowed his ambitions to lead to reckless actions in foreign policy. However, now, the director warned, 'it would be unsafe to assume that the new regime will have Stalin's skill in avoiding general war'.

Dulles's brother John Foster counselled caution in the short term with a striking analogy. 'The Soviet was now involved in a family funeral, and it might be best to wait until the corpse was buried and the mourners gone off to their homes to read the will, before we begin our campaign to create discord in the family.'

By the 'family', John Foster Dulles was referring to the Kremlin's subservient eastern European satellite countries, and it was here that he wanted the administration's efforts concentrated. For the past eight years normal impulses of nationhood had been subordinated to the 'virtual worship of Stalin as a demi-god'.[16] Now was the time, said the Secretary of State, 'to play up this nationalism and discontent for all it was worth, to seize every opportunity by this device to break down the monolithic Soviet control over the satellite states'.

Eisenhower himself had begun the meeting with some unexpected observations about Stalin's hold on power. He told his colleagues that he had never believed Stalin had been the undisputed ruler of the Soviet Union – instead he always thought it had been 'something of a committee government'. Even more surprising – and this was from 'personal experience' – the President believed that Stalin, at the end of the war, wished for 'more peaceful and normal relations with the rest of the world ... [but] in some degree at least, he had had to come to terms with other members of the Kremlin ruling circle'.

A few days earlier Eisenhower's – and Churchill's – old friend, the power broker Bernard Baruch, had passed on a memorandum to the President written by Sam Lubell, the well-respected writer and political psephologist. Eisenhower was greatly impressed by Lubell's views, and now used them to press his case before the NSC.

Lubell had suggested a way out of the Cold War with a 'butter over guns' strategy, in which the two great powers would agree a treaty limiting military spending to a percentage of their total budgets much smaller than that they allocated for domestic economic and social expenditure. 'The strongest single internal political pressure in Russia today is the hunger of the people for better living conditions,' Lubell argued.[17]

Eisenhower observed that after the completion of each Soviet five-year plan, the people had been promised that their needs and aspirations would be considered. Each time they had been let down. 'What we should do now is propose that the standard of living throughout the world be raised at once,' an enthused President suggested to the NSC.[18] 'We do need something dramatic to rally the people of the world around some idea, some hope, of a better future.' John Foster Dulles agreed, pointing out how eager the eastern European countries had been to have a slice of the aid provided by the United States under the Marshall Plan, only to be thwarted by the men in the Kremlin.

So Eisenhower sent his special assistant (for Cold War operations) Charles Douglas (C. D.) Jackson away from the meeting to frame a speech, an initiative, the focus of which would be 'on the common man's yearning for food, shelter and a decent standard of living ... [which] was a universal desire'.[19]

* * *

On the morning of Monday 9 March, a Bedford coach carrying a small contingent of national servicemen from RAF North Weald turned off the Brentwood to Chipping Ongar road, lumbered half a mile down a long, winding farm track, then disappeared into a wooded copse studded with impressive silver birch, ash and rowan trees.

The vehicle pulled up in front of a chalet-style bungalow, which did its best to blend in with its surroundings, and to a passing walker – if any had been allowed – might just have seemed like a farm dwelling of the modern variety.

But the bungalow was no innocent rural building. It was a guardhouse. And the men who alighted from the vehicle were not a group of arborists, or botanists, or country ramblers. Instead they were an advance party of teleprinter operators and fighter plotters, about to start their first day in a top-secret underground bunker, which would have a critical role to play on that fateful day if Soviet Tu-4 bombers swooped over the Channel with their atomic payload on board.

That eventuality was not immediately anticipated by military and intelligence chiefs. But if it came to pass, Kelvedon Hatch, hidden away in the gentle Essex countryside, would be on the frontline of the nation's vital air defences as the RAF's Metropolitan Sector Operations Centre, coordinating the work of nearby radar stations, and directing fighter planes from the area's airfields towards the enemy.

Kelvedon Hatch – one of six command and control centres around the country – was the jewel in the crown of the government's top-secret Operation Rotor, a badly needed modernisation of the country's early warning and detection system, which had either been only very basically maintained since the end of the Second World War, or simply abandoned.

Rotor, approved by the Air Council in June 1950, was a massive military engineering project, revamping the whole of the radar system and placing a network of control and operation rooms like Kelvedon Hatch in large, protected – usually buried – bunkers in the British countryside.

Deemed critical to the nation's defence back in 1950, Rotor seemed even more relevant in the wake of the Korean War. It was then promoted to 'super priority' status in August 1952 – equal to that of the development of atomic weapons and guided missiles – after a sobering analysis of Britain's readiness for war in a major policy paper drawn up by the Chiefs of Staff, entitled 'Defence Policy and Global Strategy'.[20]

The 25-page document was signed off by Bill Slim, hero of Burma in the Second World War and now Chief of the Imperial General Staff, Military Cross holder John Slessor, Chief of the Air Staff, and Admiral Sir Rhoderick McGrigor, First Sea Lord, who helped sink the *Bismarck* and distinguished himself in the invasion of Sicily.

In 'Global Strategy', they declared unequivocally that 'the Free World is menaced everywhere by the implacable and unlimited aims of Soviet Russia. Using communism as a convenient and dynamic instrument, Imperialist Russia seeks world-domination exercised from the Kremlin.'[21]

When they began to formulate their strategy a year or so earlier, the chiefs believed Russia might be contemplating an early attack. Now they were not so convinced that Soviet leaders would embark on a war in which, although 'fearful punishment' would be meted out to the 'Free World', they themselves would be faced by 'catastrophic devastation in Russia'.

The Chiefs of Staff drew much comfort from the West's main line of defence, the effectiveness of American atomic air power. The United States had a 'formidable' stock of atom bombs, and there was also an increasing number of the smaller bombs which could be carried by light aircraft.

But at the back of their minds they worried that a nuclear confrontation might still be sparked off. There was the risk that the Allies – in particular the Americans – would 'underestimate Russian reaction to some particular move, or that they will be provoked into precipitating war as a result of some comparatively minor injury'.[22]

Worryingly, they could foresee a time – three or four years hence – when, with the American economy exhausted by the military demands placed on it, 'there may well arise a mental outlook tending to the view that war is preferable to the indefinite continuation of the Cold War and thus to a demand for a showdown'.[23]

If the crunch came, the opening phase would be of 'unparalleled intensity'. The Soviet Union would attack the United Kingdom with atom bombs, hoping to neutralise the most threatening bomber bases from which US atomic attacks on the USSR could be launched. The chiefs were also certain that A-bombs would be launched against the main British ports, supported by an intense mining and U-boat campaign to sever sea communications.

After the report came out, Air Ministry officials scouted around in the summer of 1952 for venues for their new underground control and reporting centres. Secluded Kelvedon Hatch, just 25 miles from London and 6 miles from RAF North Weald, was quickly identified as strategically and geographically suitable, so officials approached the farmer whose land they wished to compulsorily purchase.

Jim Parrish, farmer and market gardener, was obliged to hand over 13 acres of pasture land, 10 acres of Highash Wood, and half an acre for a private roadway that the military could construct in the corner of the wood. Parrish, who was paid £100 an acre, had no complaints. 'I've fought two world wars and I have no desire for a third,' he told the men from the ministry.[24]

Building work began in late summer, with RAF guards positioned on top of the hillside overlooking the copse to ward off the curious. The hillside was bulldozed to a depth of 125ft, at the bottom of which 20ft of gravel was placed to act as a shock absorber and to aid drainage.

Concrete walls 10ft thick were erected, reinforced with 1-inch thick tungsten enhanced rods. Over these walls a lining of brick and pitch waterproof membrane was laid, and on top of that was placed wire-mesh netting called a Faraday cage. When an atomic bomb goes off it creates an electromagnetic pulse which wipes out all things electric. The Faraday cage would provide an 'electric field-free' space inside the Kelvedon bunker, protecting the sensitive electronic and communications equipment inside. All internal doors on the ground floor were lined with metal plates.

Having built the bunker, the workmen pushed the tons of dirt back over the top of the structure to bury it. Once the grass had grown back the hill was, to all outward appearances, the natural part of the landscape it had always been. The 27,000 square foot bunker, 20ft below the surface, was completely hidden from prying eyes.

Inside the bunker was arranged over three floors. The operations room was located in a large central well stretching up through all three floors. On the bottom floor stood two large map tables. One, 24ft across, was the general situation map, displaying the big picture, covering a region stretching from the Humber to Southampton and across the sea to France and Denmark. The smaller, 10ft across, was the fighter table, showing more localised aircraft firmly under Kelvedon Hatch's control.

The maps were the domain of the fighter plotters, who moved aircraft around the map with rods – like croupiers on a roulette table. Those gazing down on the maps from glass-panelled cabins, built into three walls on the middle and top floors, took their places in order of importance.

On the middle level were the ground executive, who gave instructions to radar stations, and the air executive, who directed airborne planes. The most senior officers – chief fighter controller, guided weapons controller, battle commander and electronics officers – occupied the top floor.

Finally, stretching from floor to ceiling for all to view, was the all-important tote board, the central source of up-to-the-minute information with aircraft availability and weather reports from airfields in the sector such as North Weald, West Malling, Biggin Hill, Manston, Tangmere, Bentwaters, Waterbeach and Marham. If an unidentified aircraft entered their air space, the plotters could turn to the tote board and know exactly how many airfields had planes that could be scrambled immediately, or ready within fifteen minutes.

One day later that summer, when no air activity or training was taking place, the tote board was transformed into a cricket scoreboard. England were locked in a tense battle with Australia for the Ashes, and at a crucial moment in the Headingley test, a full display of batsmen, bowlers, scores and wickets was displayed.

Although 'the Hole' – as Kelvedon was quickly christened by its staff – was 'activated' on that day in March 1953, it would be May before it was fully up and running. The devastating North Sea flood had caused serious delays in men and equipment.

When it was totally operational, Kelvedon could not have wished for better senior officers in charge – both of whom were heroes of the Second World War. New Zealander Alan Deere, commanding officer of RAF North Weald, was one of the outstanding fighter pilots in the war, earning the Distinguished Flying Cross (DFC) for covering the retreat to Dunkirk, and then winning a bar just months later for 'conspicuous bravery in pressing home his attacks against superior numbers of enemy aircraft'. In all, he was credited with notching twenty-two 'victories' and ten 'probables' – as well as being shot down seven times.

The tall, angular acting Air Vice-Marshal Thomas Pike's record was hardly less impressive. He worked in the Air Ministry early in the war before taking command of 219 night fighter squadron as a wing commander in 1941. Flying Bristol Beaufighters from RAF Tangmere, he played a leading role in the air defence of the United Kingdom, shooting down enemy aircraft and – like Deere – winning the DFC and bar.

By May 1953 some 500 personnel – almost all men – were employed at Kelvedon Hatch, with 100 down in the bunker at any one time. Nearly all were based in a camp at RAF North Weald, where they lived in prefabricated huts.

For some, the exercises they took part in felt very real; for others they were just war games, 'fairly remote from the actual picture'.[25]

All personnel had signed the Official Secrets Act, but day-to-day security was not over-burdensome. There was no special pass needed to enter the bunker – or indeed certain rooms in it. A uniform and an RAF 1250 pass were enough to get you on the bus from North Weald and virtually guaranteed entrance to Kelvedon Hatch after that.

'On reflection I realised security was quite lax – surprisingly after the efforts to hide "the Hole" in the first place,' recalled one fighter plotter.[26]

I knew the majority of people on the bus or at the site, but there were always a few strange faces around – RAF personnel, new postings, auxiliaries, detachments. The acquisition of a uniform and a fake 1250 pass would not have been difficult. Having flourished the identification and gained entry, an agent could note any items of interest, leave 'sleeper' devices or carry out any number of undercover activities.

The imagination may have run a little wild – but these were nervous times. Raymond Parmenter was a driver, seconded to the coach unit, and worked at Kelvedon Hatch from the very start.

> Certainly I knew this whole project was something unusual – but then you must remember as a young man, what was usual? The second bloody world war had only finished eight years earlier: London, my working and social environment, was almost a ruin, and men women and children were terribly scarred – if not physically, then most certainly mentally, by six years of war. Eight years on, food, clothing and fuel were still rationed or scarce. Luxury goods were only just becoming available.[27]

Kelvedon Hatch cost £1.5 million to build, and the whole Rotor network of fifty-four radar stations and control centres cost a staggering £240 million. The stations used up 350,000 tons of concrete, 20,000 tons of steel and thousands of miles of telephone and telex connections.[28]

The employees of 'the Hole' might have had some degree of protection if the atom bombs got through and began to fall – but what of the prospects for the general population? In the same week that Kelvedon Hatch was activated, the government's Home Defence Committee decided to commission a report on the likely conditions in Britain during the initial 'survival' phase of a future war, when the nation would grimly hang on after nuclear attack.

A committee was set up under the chairmanship of Robert Hall, head of the Cabinet Office's economic section, called the 'National Economy in War Working Party'. Hall and his colleagues had to work on the basis that the Soviets possessed a supply of 200 atomic bombs to drop on Britain. They would report back in July with their findings.

While all this planning was taking place in the event of a Soviet nuclear strike, there were those in the British intelligence fraternity who feared that it would be America, not Russia, who would precipitate a third world war.

Vice Admiral Eric Longley-Cook was one of them. He had been among the most respected naval commanders of the Second World War, in charge of the cruiser HMS *Argonaut* as she took part in the perilous Arctic convoys, and then played a key role in protecting the British troops who went ashore on Gold Beach on D-Day. He had won a Distinguished Service Order and the French Legion of Honour and was mentioned in dispatches on three occasions.

After the war Longley-Cook became Director of Naval Intelligence and a member of the Joint Intelligence Committee. For his parting shot before stepping down as director in September 1951 he submitted a concerning paper to Prime Minister Clement Attlee, entitled 'Where Are We Going?'

Longley-Cook, who had made regular visits to Washington in his three-year tenure as director and felt he understood the US military and political mindset well, laid out his basic views very clearly right from the outset. 'The Kremlin does not intend to commit the USSR to total war,' he wrote.[29] 'There is a very real danger of the USA involving herself and her allies in a "preventive war" against Russia.'

The vice admiral had observed the 'kinetic energy of American war preparations', and felt that since the Second World War 'America was less than ever inclined to listen to advice … [becoming] richer and stronger, though perhaps little wiser.'

He viewed the American people as 'mercurial and volatile … [able to] be whipped up to a state of war hysteria.'[30] Urban dwellers visualised 'in their own concentrated home town the ruins of Hamburg and Berlin. These and other Americans say: "We have the bomb, let's use it now while the balance is in our favour. Since war with Russia is inevitable, let's get it over with now."'

He worried that there was a 'considerable and growing body of opinion in the US establishment which does not regard the prospect of a third world war with complete disfavour'.

In his most apocalyptic language, he asserted that he 'knew of no case in history of a nation which has armed at this rate without finally going to war. It is doubtful whether, in a year's time, the US will be able to control the Frankenstein monster which she is creating.'

Britain's 'wisdom and experience' could bring restraint to bear on the Americans, Longley-Cook declared.

> But the United States should be left in no doubt that if anything in the nature of a 'preventive war' was engineered by them against the Soviet Union, they would have to fight alone, for even if HM government followed suit, how many of our people would willingly do so?

Attlee was interested in Longley-Clark's analysis but could not act on it after losing power in October 1951. Churchill, shown the document in December that year on the eve of a visit to Washington, was initially sceptical. 'It is the usual Communist approach of British intellectuals,' he scoffed, adding that he wanted a 'sharp eye' kept on the writer.[31]

However, after gauging the mood in the White House and the Pentagon, and as he settled into Downing Street in the early months of 1952, Churchill refined his scepticism. In April he told his private secretary: 'I want to see the secret report prepared by the former Director of Naval Intelligence and sent to me by the First Lord when I went to America. Let me have it back again.'[32] Sir John Slessor, his Chief of Air Staff, warned him: '[There is] to my mind a lot in what Longley-Cook says.'

The vice admiral may have been wrong in his 'worst-case scenario' prediction of a war in 1952, but with an even more hawkish US administration in place in 1953, the fears he had outlined remained in the minds of quite a few British policy-makers.

* * *

If the United States and the Soviet Union were to be drawn into direct conflict, it was generally accepted that it would happen in central

Europe, the epicentre of the Cold War across which the Iron Curtain had been drawn. Both sides saw war on the continent as a potential Armageddon that could bring total victory or catastrophic defeat. Both shaped their political, economic and military strategies and arranged their forces in preparation of fighting that war.

Tension was at its most fraught over Germany, which was still an occupied country in 1953. Following the war, America, Britain, France and the Soviet Union had divided the country into four zones of occupation – the Allies taking the western two-thirds, while the Soviets retained the eastern part.

Berlin, the historic capital, was where the clash of ideology and culture was at its sharpest and where flashpoints were most likely. Like the rest of the country, the city was placed under joint four-power authority and divided into four sectors, the Allies in West Berlin, the Russians in East Berlin. Thus split, the city sat like an island of democracy in a communist sea, 100 miles east of the line that divided occupied Germany from the western zones – and menacingly encircled by half a million Red Army troops.

NATO had been formed in 1949 to provide the West's military shield (the Soviet Union had immediately responded in kind with her own defensive grouping, the Warsaw Pact). But America – and Britain – were keen to strengthen West Germany's political and economic systems so it could serve as a bulwark against communism. To enable the former, the Federal Republic of Germany was officially formed in 1949, a parliamentary democracy with a capitalist economy and free churches and labour unions.

The Marshall Plan had ploughed some $1.4 billion into the German economy, recognised as the vital cog in the European industrial machine. The response was immediate, with the country's gross national product (GNP) growing by 10.5 per cent in 1951 and 8.3 per cent in 1952. On 27 February 1953, under the London Debt Agreement, West Germany's creditor nations took the next step and elected to cancel half of her debt – 15 billion out of a total of 30 billion Deutschmarks.[33]

With Germany's 'economic miracle' now underway, ideas aplenty for a new Europe were pouring out from idealistic statesmen. These were plans not merely to counter the Soviet threat but to bind the continent's nations closer together economically – and even politically. But would Britain, qualified by her role in the war for the leadership of western Europe, be prepared to jump on board?

In the immediate aftermath of the war Winston Churchill had wished the European project well, and by his high-flown speeches had even appeared to indicate that he wanted to be intimately associated with it. In his widely acclaimed speech in Zurich on 19 September 1946 he talked fervently about the need to 'recreate the European fabric … and to provide it with a structure under which it can dwell in peace, safety and freedom. We must build a kind of United States of Europe.'[34]

Then at the first Congress of Europe at The Hague on 7 May 1948, without being precise about what kind of continent he envisaged, he stirred the emotions of European enthusiasts with some particularly powerful words:

> We shall save ourselves from the perils which draw near only by forgetting the hatreds of the past, by letting national rancours and revenges die, by progressively effacing frontiers and barriers which aggravate and congeal our divisions, and by rejoicing together in that glorious treasure of literature, of romance, of ethics, of thought and toleration belonging to all, which is the true inheritance of Europe.[35]

But Churchill was no supra-nationalist, let alone a federalist; despite the rolling oratory he was a pragmatist. His big idea for Europe, outlined first in that Zurich speech, was for it to be strengthened by a Franco-German partnership – quite startling just a year after the war's end, with French wounds from invasion and occupation still raw. 'In this way only can France recover the moral and cultural leadership of

Europe,' he said. 'There can be no revival of Europe without a spiritually great Germany.'

To that end it was he who put forward a proposal for a European army. The day after Robert Schuman had first unveiled his plan for a European Coal and Steel Community in May 1950, Churchill stood up at the Council of Europe in Strasbourg to ask his assembly colleagues to vote for 'the immediate creation of a European army under a united command in which we should all bear a worthy and honourable part'. This army, he envisaged, should be 'subject to proper European democratic control' and should act in concert with the United States and Canada.

That speech immediately created feverish expectations that Britain might not only merge her army with her European neighbours, but could even be prepared to lead this new military force. But as time went on, it was clear that Churchill's objectives were focused on utilising West German military capability for the defence of Europe – without recreating a new German army – which would in turn fulfil his wider objective of binding France and Germany together. He knew the thought of rearming the Germans in any shape or form aroused the deepest emotions in the French: Britain's part in this European army would not be to lead it, but to be there essentially to hold the hand of a nervous France.

In the new Churchill administration of October 1951 there were certainly those keen to advocate British leadership in Europe: Home Secretary David Maxwell Fyfe; Housing Minister Harold Macmillan; President of the Board of Trade Peter Thorneycroft; Minister of Works David Eccles; and Minister of Supply Duncan Sandys.

But the bigger beasts in the Cabinet were more sceptical, and it led to an extraordinary government split over a European army, which was displayed for all to see on just one day. On 28 November in Strasbourg, Maxwell Fyfe told the Council of Europe he might not be able to guarantee 'full and unconditional participation', but that there would be a thorough examination of the possibilities ... and no refusal on the part of Britain'.

'We had agreed to the principle of joining the European army, which was the single greatest hurdle to overcome,' he would later record.[36] But a couple of hours on and his superior, the Foreign Secretary Anthony Eden, speaking to reporters after a NATO council meeting in Rome, promptly ruled out any British troop participation, only promising the 'closest possible association' with it.

The day after the Maxwell Fyfe–Eden split had come to light, Churchill laid a paper before Cabinet which stood – eighteen months later in March 1953 – as the clearest elucidation of his views about moves towards the economic, military and political integration of Europe. It was headlined 'United Europe – Note by the Prime Minister and Minister of Defence'.

'I am not opposed to a European Federation including – eventually – the countries behind the Iron Curtain, provided that this comes about naturally and gradually,' he wrote.[37]

> But I never thought that Britain or the British Commonwealth should, either individually or collectively, become an integral part of a European Federation, and have never given the slightest support to the idea. We should not, however, obstruct but rather favour the movement to closer European unity and try to get the United States' support in this work.

On the military front, he was already wearying of his idea for a European army, blaming the French for obfuscation and delay. 'The French seem to be trying to get France defended by Europe. Their proposed contribution for 1952 of five, rising to ten, divisions is pitiful, even making allowances for the fact that they are still trying to hold their Oriental Empire.'

On the economic side, he welcomed the Schuman Coal and Steel Plan as a 'step in the reconciliation of France and Germany, and as probably rendering another Franco-German war physically impossible'. But, he added, 'I never contemplated Britain joining in this plan on the same terms as continental partners.'

Then he spelt out the nature of Britain's relationship with Europe – and the wider world.

Our attitude towards further economic developments on the Schuman lines resembles that which we adopt about the European Army. We help, we dedicate, we play a part, but we are not merged and do not forfeit our insular or Commonwealth-wide character. I should resist any American pressure to treat Britain as on the same footing as the European States, none of whom have the advantages of the Channel and who were consequently conquered.

The final paragraph came to the crux of the matter. 'Our first object is the unity and consolidation of the British Commonwealth and what is left of the former British Empire. Our second, the "fraternal association" of the English-speaking world; and third, United Europe, to which we are a separate closely and specially related ally and friend.'

So Britain was merely an observer when on Monday 9 March 1953 Strasbourg was the setting for the most ambitious step yet, not merely on the road to reconciliation, but towards the desire of many for Europe to rise powerfully from the ashes of war and unite both economically and politically. In the council chamber of the temporary headquarters of the Council of Europe, the concrete, utilitarian-looking *La Maison de L'Europe*, it fell to the former Belgian Prime Minister Paul-Henri Spaak to stand up and paint the bright colours of a European dream.

With his fellow European idealists, Frenchman Jean Monnet and Luxembourg-born Robert Schuman, Spaak had been one of the central figures in the quest to build new European institutions to transform a fragmented, impoverished continent into an economic, military and political entity.

These days Spaak – who had played tennis for Belgium in his youth – was a bald, heavyset man with a round face and prominent dimpled chin, his eyes owlish behind horn-rimmed glasses, projecting an appearance of both benevolence and pugnacity.

He bore a resemblance to Winston Churchill, the likeness enhanced by his equally inspiring oratory and love of cigars. 'I am told that I look like Churchill and speak English like Charles Boyer,' Spaak once acknowledged, adding with typical wit, 'Of course I would rather speak English like Churchill and look like Charles Boyer.'[38]

Spaak himself had already had three spells as his country's premier, and was now president of the European Coal and Steel Community, the continent's first stab at economic integration.

The Belgian was widely acknowledged as ruthless, daring, tactful, amusing, receptive and intellectually brilliant. 'He has the cunning of Machiavelli and the obstinate idealism of St Francis,' one Italian commentator averred.[39]

On that day in March Spaak came to the chamber in *La Maison de L'Europe* to present the very first constitution for Europe and put the western part of the continent on the road towards political unification. It was an exciting moment for the ardent federalists in the so-called 'little Europe', the grouping of six nations that would make up the proposed European Political Community (EPC) – France, Italy, West Germany, Belgium, the Netherlands and Luxembourg.

The industrial arm of the new Europe, the European Coal and Steel Community, had already been established in April 1951 by the Treaty of Paris. The military arm, the European Defence Community, had been agreed, again in a treaty signed in Paris, in May 1952; the EDC was still some way off, however, requiring ratification by all national parliaments before any kind of European army could be formed.

A political 'roof' was now needed to complete the structure of this proposed new supra-national western Europe, and it was this that Spaak outlined to an audience of 1,000 in his speech that day. The draft constitution he presented, setting up a 'European Community of a supra-national character', contained 116 articles and two protocols. A proposed bicameral parliament would have a Chamber of the Peoples (with 268 members) elected by direct universal suffrage, and an upper house, the Senate (ninety-one members), appointed by the national parliaments. Parliament would not only have control over an Executive Council – the governing body of the EPC – but would also be a genuine legislative body.

The Executive Council would consist of twelve members, two from each country, led by a president who would be appointed by the Senate. Moreover, the constitution included provision for the establishment of a European Court of Justice and an Economic and Social Council.

Article 82 set out the EPC's principal task, 'to establish progressively a common market among the Member States, based on the free movement of goods, capital and persons'. In Article 67 on its international relations, the constitution asserted that the EPC could 'conclude treaties or agreements of association with third states'.

All this appeared to many like full-blooded federalism – or a quick route towards it. But Spaak declared that what was proposed was 'neither federal nor confederal'. The constitution steered a path between two 'extremes' – on the one side a purely inter-governmental system, merely linking countries which retain their entire sovereignty, and on the other a constitution which would immediately pool most of the activities of the states. 'This is a political community of a supra-national character … it respects the powers and competence which the governments of our countries have hitherto kept under their own control … and does not entail any fresh transfers of sovereignty.'[40]

Spaak said all members of the Council of Europe, the very first pan-European body, were welcome to join the EPC. The constitution encouraged the closest links with those other western European countries – 'in particular the United Kingdom'.

Britain's delegate in the chamber that day was forty-year-old Lord (John) Hope, Conservative MP for Edinburgh Pentlands. An Old

Etonian, Hope had had a 'good war', mentioned in dispatches for his service at Salerno and Anzio, and had settled down to be a caring MP, immersing himself in the problems of the woollen and paper industries in his constituency.

However, the presence of a mere MP, rather than a Foreign Office minister, indicated the low level of interest that Churchill's government had in this proposed European institution. Nor was there much commitment from the Labour and Liberal Party delegates – Alfred Robens and Lord Layton – who had left to catch an early train by the time Hope got up to speak.

Nevertheless, Hope gave a generous and witty response to Spaak's speech. 'This is an historic day for Europe,' he declared.[41] Great Britain, he promised, would 'work as closely as we possibly can with the new community'. But Hope was careful not to exceed his brief, saying that there could be no guarantee of peace in Europe 'which is not backed to the limit by the power and participation of the United States of America'.

And Hope warned:

> For any of us to feel that united Europe could or should become a 'third force', a neutral in the struggle for life upon which civilisation is now engaged, would be as tragic as it would be for our American friends to believe that united Europe could be strong enough to allow them to cut adrift from it. Either course would certainly enjoy the enthusiastic support of the Kremlin, and I pray that neither will ever be followed.[42]

Nonetheless, he concluded, 'Great Britain will never turn her back upon Europe. That is our determination, fixed and irrevocable … Gentlemen, it is not a question of whether we shall be with you if danger strikes. We are with you now.'

The draft constitution for a new EPC was voted through by 50:0 with five abstentions – an unexpectedly clear endorsement of the proposals. As the year wore on, its planned structure would become more elaborate, with the addition of a Council of National Ministers to 'harmonise the action of the Executive Council with that of the governments of member states'. Disagreements would start to surface about this, and the perceived dominance of parliamentary power.

Britain, working on her fraying relationship with the United States and bogged down in end of Empire problems, would continue to be on the outside looking in. But not all in the intelligentsia felt that this was the right approach.

A. E. Holdsworth, *Financial Times* journalist and London editor of the *Yorkshire Post*, and now a barrister on the south-eastern circuit, wrote an especially insightful – and provocative – letter to *The Observer* at the time when the treaty for the EPC was unveiled.

He observed that the logical conclusion of the project for such a community would be, in time, what Britain had always fought to prevent – 'the creation of a super state across the Narrow Seas'.[43] But were we right to want to stop it? It was all very well Britain priding herself on being the link between western Europe, the Commonwealth and the United States. But the importance of such a role, Holdsworth wrote, would be eroded as soon as 100 million west Europeans started to speak with one voice. 'The conception of the United Kingdom as a sort of trunk telephone exchange of the Western world might have for some an attractive gleam. But it confuses scope for diplomatic activity with the reality of power; the chance to talk with the ability to decide.'

Such arguments were just starting to be fought more keenly in 1953 in Whitehall and Westminster. It was the beginning of Britain's long agony over the nature of its relationship with Europe.

* * *

Idealistic plans for the future of Europe were all well and good. But the principal focus of the continent's leaders, just a week after the death of Stalin, was still firmly on Moscow. The world waited apprehensively for the new Malenkov regime to reveal its true colours, for any sign that a thaw in the Cold War might be possible.

Then, as predicted, right at the heart of Europe, on the dividing line between East and West, came a potentially precipitous moment that fell into the British Chief of Staffs' category of 'comparatively minor injury'; but a spark, nonetheless, that could light the fire of war.

Air combat between the Cold War's chief protagonists, the United States and the Soviet Union, had been raging above the battlefield in Korea for nearly two years. This 'war' was not one whose existence either side wished to draw attention to – Stalin because he wished to keep up the pretence of his non-involvement, and the UN because it was reluctant to ratchet up tensions any further. Nonetheless, this had been a key sector of conflict, even more so in the early months of 1953 as the war on the ground stagnated.

Now attention turned to a worrying new development – skirmishes in the skies above central Europe. The air forces of the West, primarily the RAF and the USAF, were regularly conducting training exercises close to the Iron Curtain, but also engaging in clandestine spy flights over Soviet territory, photographing sensitive military installations, testing response times of scrambled Soviet fighters and gathering electronic intelligence (ELINT), such as recording Russian radar emissions.

The Soviet Air Force reacted forcefully to these intrusions. The previous summer a Swedish Air Force DC-3, thought to be on a secret ELINT mission, was intercepted and destroyed by a Soviet MiG-15 fighter over the Baltic with the loss of all eight crewmen. Then on 10 March, the day after Stalin's funeral, a USAF F-84 Thunderjet was also shot down, again by a MiG fighter, after apparently breaching Czech airspace; the pilot managed to parachute to safety.[44]

This was the backdrop to the critical events of Thursday 12 March. Just after 9 a.m. that day at the Central Gunnery School at RAF Leconfield in East Yorkshire, 29-year-old Flight Sergeant Peter John Dunnell climbed into the pilot's seat of a four-engine RF531 Avro Lincoln bomber and set off with his crew of six on one of NATO's routine flights across north-west Europe.

These fortnightly missions were designed to provide radar tracking and fighter affiliation training for the RAF, and were a realistic sim-ulation of a six-hour high-level operational sortie, especially useful for trainee gunners. Normally the planes would fly from Leconfield to northern France, then along the 'safe' side of the East/West German border before returning via Holland to base in Yorkshire.

This particular exercise was codenamed Barrage. Peter Dunnell and his team had been preceded by another Lincoln, RF503 captained by Flight Sergeant Frank Denham, which had conducted its own realistic sortie, being 'attacked' by friendly NATO fighters – Dutch Thunder-jets, Belgian Meteors and RAF Vampires.

However, towards the end of its exercise RF503 had received a nasty shock. As it neared Kassel, inside the British zone, two MiG-15s appeared out of nowhere, settling underneath the Lincoln on the port beam. The Russian fighters conducted a series of high quarter approaches, as if they were about to attack the British bomber, before suddenly peeling away.

Whether the crew of the second Lincoln were aware of this incident when they left base is unclear. Certainly at this time the airmen had a heightened sense of concern about getting too close to the border, and of the threat of the fast and flexible Soviet MiGs.

Joining Dunnell in the cockpit that day was the new commanding officer of 3 Squadron, Harold Fitz, who had elected to take on the co-pilot duties to acquaint himself with his men's work. With them in the plane were Flight Lieutenant Stephen Wyles and Sergeants Ronald Stevens, George Long, William Mason and Kenneth Jones.

Their flight followed its scheduled plan successfully enough – until it approached Saarbrücken. Then the plane overshot its turning point and sped into the Soviet zone, where it spent seventy-two minutes, penetrat-ing at least 60 miles and flying for some 90 miles over the territory.

At around 1.20 p.m. the Lincoln made it back into the 20-mile-wide air corridor from Hamburg to Berlin, and was just west of the river Elbe, inside the British zone. It was travelling at 10,000ft, over the village of Bleckede, when suddenly it was attacked without warning by two MiG-15 fighters, which opened fire with their cannons from point-blank range on the unsuspecting crew.

The Lincoln plummeted into a steep dive, followed by the MiGs, which continued to strafe the crippled aircraft. The main body of the RF531, with four of the crew in the wreckage, crashed into a wood near Bolzenberg, 3 miles inside the Russian zone. The remainder of the plane came down on Lüneberg Heath, a British military exercise area 15 miles south of Hamburg.

There was no hope for the four airmen trapped in the main fuselage, which burst into flames before crashing into the ground. The other three men managed to bail out, but one parachute failed to open. The remaining two appeared to open theirs successfully, but several shocked German witnesses testified that one of the MiGs swooped low and hit them with cannon fire.

The body of the crew member whose parachute failed to open landed in the Soviet zone, where it was picked up by a passing Russian jeep, and later returned to British authorities. Of the two other parachutists, one was very badly wounded, shot in the shoulder and neck, when picked up by a passing car and taken to the hospital in nearby Lauenburg. He was pronounced dead on arrival.

The remaining parachutist was the rear gunner, Flight Lieutenant Stephen Wyles. Pilot Officer J. P. Massey from the RAF base at Lüneburg found him lying in a field near Holzen, and when crouching by the side of the stricken airman to administer basic first aid, asked him, 'How are you old chap?'[45] 'How are the others, did they all get out?' Wyles replied.

An ambulance was quickly summoned and Wyles was transported to Lüneburg Hospital. There, still able to be gently questioned, his opening remarks were, 'Was that a Sabre?' suggesting that a US fighter might have shot down his plane. Even in his semi-conscious state, Wyles was adamant – and this would be a bone of contention in coming days – that there had been no ammunition on board the Lincoln. He would die from his injuries at 6 p.m. on 12 March.

The RAF Police interviewed Wilma Muller, a housewife from Hittbergen, who heard the firing overhead as she drove home from Bullendorf. She believed the second bout of firing 'could only have been aimed at the pilot', and when she reached her house she was told that 'a pilot with a perforated parachute, [who was] injured by firing on his shoulder was found near the village of Rosenthal'.[46]

Hermann Dehne, an engineer at the Bleckede port, saw the incident with workmates and watched the descent of the parachutists. 'My colleagues and I are of the opinion that both parachutists were being fired at by the jet plane,' he told German police.[47]

The war of words over the death of the seven airmen was begun in earnest by General Vasily Chuikov, hero of the Battle of Stalingrad, now Commander-in-Chief of the Group of Soviet Forces in Germany. In a telegram sent at 2 a.m. the following day to the British Frontier Service at Wahner Heide, he heaped total blame on the Lincoln. He claimed that the British bomber had penetrated 75 miles into the territory of the German Democratic Republic. The pilots of the MiGs had called upon the Lincoln to follow them and land at the nearest aerodrome – according to Soviet Air Force rules – but Chuikov asserted that the Lincoln ignored that request: '[Instead] it opened fire on the Soviet aircraft ... which were compelled to fire warning shots. However, the offending aircraft continued to fire on the Soviet fighters ... which were compelled to open fire in reply.'[48]

Then came Chuikov's most contentious claim. He said that an examination of the wrecked Lincoln had revealed a cache of weaponry – two aircraft cannons, a heavy machine gun, ammunition and cartridge cases.

The British government's initial reaction was predictable and understandable. In Berlin, the British high commissioner in Germany, Sir

Ivone Kirkpatrick, described the act as a 'deliberate and brutal act of aggression'.[49] The Foreign Office denied that the Lincoln had been trespassing in Soviet territory, and Foreign Secretary Anthony Eden, who was in New York addressing the United Nations, labelled the attack as 'barbaric'.

Before he addressed the House of Commons the following Tuesday, Churchill summoned the Leconfield station commander, Group Captain Herbert (familiarly known as 'Tubby') Mermagen, to Downing Street so that he could be briefed on the nature of the Lincoln's exercise and the validity of Chuikov's claims. What Mermagen told the Prime Minister was that the Lincoln had been unarmed. The bomber was equipped with machine guns and cannons. But before the flight, the turret armourer at RAF Leconfield had removed all the ammunition from the tail guns and the mid-upper turret. In addition the belt feed mechanism had been taken out from the mid-upper cannons, rendering them incapable of firing.

A hint of suspicion would have been aroused by empty shell cases from a previous sortie that were found by the Russians in canvas bags underneath the mid-gunner's seat. For some unexplained reason, the armourer had been instructed not to remove them before the plane took off from Leconfield.

So when Churchill got to his feet on 17 March, after condemning the MiG attack as 'cruel and wanton', he was able to relay to MPs the thrust of what Mermagen had told him.[50] 'The Lincoln was unarmed … the Russian assertion that the Lincoln opened fire on them is utterly untrue,' he declared. 'The flight was part of the usual exercising of Allied air defences. Such exercises have been carried out by Flying Training Command over the past eighteen months.'

But why had the Lincoln strayed so far into 'enemy' territory? Chuikov's claim that it had ventured 75 miles into the Soviet-held sector was very much on the mark. Churchill did acknowledge to the House that, although the pilot and navigator were both experienced officers, 'the aircraft may, through a navigational error, have accidentally crossed into the Eastern zone of Germany at some point'.

Here is the mystery of the Lincoln's flight. The Air Ministry investigation would later reveal 'no technical failure' in the navigational equipment carried in the aircraft – wireless direction finding, radar position fixing or the homing beacon.[51]

Both the Lincolns had been carefully briefed that day about the probability of a strong easterly wind. The ministry's conclusion was that the plane veered so far off course because of 'an error in navigation due to an over-allowance for the strength of the wind – which had not been checked … against ground aids'.

There is one other theory about the Lincoln. While it may not have been on an airborne intelligence flight, it may well have been closely tracked by a British signals unit on the ground at RAF Scharfoldendorf in the British zone. That unit is said to have captured quite clearly the conversation between the attacking MiGs and Soviet ground controllers, which is thought to explain Churchill's very clear condemnation – having been briefed – of this 'wanton attack'.

The reaction in America – remembering that her Thunderjet had been shot down only days earlier – was even stronger than in Britain. 'Red Jets Kill 6 RAF Fliers', reported the *Daily News* in New York, 'British Accuse Reds of Murder', stated the *Newark Advocate* and 'War Scare Spreads in Western Europe', led the *Kingston Daily Freeman*.

The Associated Press wrote that the 'two incidents chilled Europe with fear', and wondered whether 'new shoot-to-kill orders may have been issued to communist fighters patrolling the western air frontier of the Soviet bloc'. In Congress there were dark and ominous mutterings. 'We can't be expected to let them continue to raid our territory without doing something about it,' declared Republican Speaker Joseph Martin.[52] Dewey Short, the Republican chairman of the House Armed Services Committee, was more explicit: 'We should shoot the hell out of them.'[53]

General Hastings Ismay, Churchill's chief military adviser in the

Second World War and now Secretary General of NATO, reacted more cautiously. At this stage he did not regard the shooting down of the two planes as 'war-like moves', but stated that NATO should 'take the matter up' if such attacks continued.[54]

The Times in London also adopted a more measured response.

The Western powers, though they cannot be expected to tolerate murderous attack upon their flyers, must aim at keeping matters under control. At this stage they should probably act on the assumption that nerves, rather than deliberately aggressive intention in Moscow, have been responsible for these grievous acts.[55]

The problem was that no one, in these early days of the new Soviet administration, had any real idea of the intentions of Malenkov and his colleagues. Were these simply two isolated incidents, in which 'trigger-happy' Soviet pilots made the attacks on their own initiative? Or did the incidents represent a coldly calculated, carefully planned move directed by the Kremlin towards the West? Was it a move designed to whip up war fever in Russia and the satellite countries, and thus attempt to consolidate support of the new Kremlin regime at home?

At a Cabinet meeting on Friday 20 March, Lord De L'Isle and Dudley, Secretary of State for Air, confirmed that the bomber was unarmed and could not have returned fire. 'The shooting was unprovoked – and probably without warning,' he told colleagues.[56]

Nevertheless, Churchill said that the government 'should be prepared for criticism on why these unsuitable aircraft were so exposed to attack. It doesn't look very good.' Lord De L'Isle went further and admitted the two Lincolns were guilty of a 'breach of discipline. [They] should have gone back when out of radar contact.'

More positively, Eden told his colleagues that General Chuikov had invited the four powers administering Germany – Britain, France, the Soviet Union and the United States – to a conference about air safety in the Berlin corridors. 'In principle I'm ready to go,' replied De L'Isle. 'So am I – but I [would] want diplomatic representatives as well as RAF experts,' Eden added.[57]

For several weeks, all NATO aircraft flying near the East German border operated on a fully armed 'fire back' basis. But Soviet aggression in the airspace above Germany continued. On 17 March, a British European Airways Viking was attacked by MiGs while on a scheduled flight in the Berlin air corridor. Then five days later an American B-50 bomber was attacked by MiGs but managed to drive them off with cannon fire.

Away from the European theatre there was another incident in this undeclared war of the skies. On 15 March, a Soviet MiG attacked an American B-50 bomber being used as a photo reconnaissance and weather observation plane, 25 miles off the Siberian coast. The US plane returned fire, but there were no casualties.

Eventually, grudgingly but still surprisingly, the Soviets expressed regret over the deaths of the seven-man Lincoln crew, and returned the four bodies and the wreckage from their zone to RAF Celle in Lower Saxony.

Then, as the talks about the air corridors got underway, these kinds of airspace incidents began to dwindle away. Glimmers of light appeared with some minor Soviet concessions in other areas: first, the withdrawal of the notice to the United Kingdom to quit her embassy in Moscow; then the agreement by Russia to the appointment of the Swede Dag Hammarskjöld as Secretary General of the United Nations.

In April 1953, Eden's diplomatic pressure paid dividends and Moscow announced that it would act immediately to obtain the release of nine British civilians and an Irish missionary from communist prison camps in North Korea. The best-known was Captain Vyvyan Holt, the respected minister from the British embassy in Seoul.

Cool heads prevailed, and the danger passed. The new masters in the Kremlin appeared to be adopting a more conciliatory tone – but Western leaders were taking nothing for granted.

Joe McCarthy – conducting a relentless fight against 'the enemy within'.
© DonkeyHotey, public domain, via Wikimedia Commons

CHAPTER 4

MIND BLOWING

They called it 'Annie', a comforting, intimate soubriquet, appropriate for that of a sister, lover or Hollywood movie star ('Nancy', 'Ruth', 'Dixie' and 'Ray' would follow). In fact she was a 16-kiloton atomic device, similar in size and destructive power to the bombs that killed 225,000 residents of Hiroshima and Nagasaki.

At 5.20 a.m. Pacific Standard Time on Tuesday 17 March 1953, Annie was dropped from a 300ft steel tower in Area 3 on the Yucca Flat in the Nevada desert and exploded. The event was watched by millions of Americans sipping their coffee in front of televisions or listening while huddled in pyjamas around their radio sets. The stupendous flash was seen outdoors by people living as far as 500 miles away in San Francisco.

They came from far and wide to witness this atomic show. A crowd of 250 newspaper, newsreel and television reporters, together with 360 state governors and mayors and scores of county and civil defence officials, were gathered together at a vantage point at News Nob, a craggy knoll of rock 7 miles from the explosion. Everyone there was fitted with heavy dark glasses but warned that even with this precaution they must not look at the explosion.

A select group of twenty journalists were taken to join the 1,000 infantry troops from the 6th Army taking part in Exercise Desert Rock V in trenches much closer to the detonation – just 2 miles south-west of the tower. The briefing sergeant calmly assured them: 'These are nice, deep foxholes, built by the 412th engineers. Kneel down, lean forward against the front of the foxhole, look down – and pray if you want to.'[1]

Almost everybody put their hands together. For those crouching reporters, their first experience was to witness the murky dawn light suddenly disappear, to be replaced by the brilliant, other-worldly white glow of the atomic flash. The light was so bright that they could read with ease the notes they had previously written on their pads.

What then followed was an eerie silence and a sensation of suspended time. Seven seconds later came the almighty report of the detonation, like a dozen huge cannons firing all at once right beside their ears. The blast pressure generated by the explosion sent dirt and gravel whistling over the trench, some of it spilling down on top of them.

'We were shaken like dice in a cup for brief, fleeting moments of terror,' Gene Sherman of the *Los Angeles Times* told his readers.[2] As he and his fellow reporters tentatively stood up and began to peer towards the detonation site, the dust cloud was initially so choking and blinding that it obscured their sight completely. Then, as they watched on in awe, they witnessed the atomic cloud emerging from beyond the cover of dust, rising in an ever-expanding ring above their heads, gradually assuming the familiar, sinister purple-coloured mushroom shape. Ultimately the cloud would reach 41,000ft above the earth's surface.

Back at News Nob young CBS news anchorman Walter Cronkite searched for a vivid description with which to capture this astounding sight for his viewers. 'The sun rose this morning some fifteen minutes after the blast itself went off – and the sun must have been embarrassed by the brilliance of the atomic explosion.'

Once the smoke had cleared, the war 'games' began. Within half an hour radiological safety personnel, accompanied by troops from the

15th Chemical Service Platoon, jumped into jeeps and set off with their monitoring equipment in the direction of ground zero. Once they had taken their samples and issued an all-clear, the soldiers in the trenches headed out on manoeuvres to attack an 'objective' just half a mile from the blast site. Others were airlifted to a slightly more distant site by a handful of marines in three helicopters, who were measuring the bomb's radiological after-effects on both man and machine.

If this was a military operation to test the effectiveness of the latest nuclear weapons coming out of the Los Alamos Laboratory, together with a scientific assessment of the effects of their radiation fallout, it was also a massive civil defence exercise (with yet another codename – Operation Doorstep) designed to educate American householders of the consequences of an attack from their communist foe. So once the soldiers were underway with their war scenario, observers moved cautiously towards a place named 'Doom Town' to see if any of its inhabitants and their property had survived the 16-kiloton blast.

This make-believe neighbourhood with the macabre name had been constructed along the lines of a traditional American suburb, with two two-storey colonial-style wood-framed homes erected together with a smattering of outbuildings, while some fifty cars of various type, colour and operating condition were parked along its streets.

One of the houses was just 3,500ft away from ground zero, the other 7,500ft. Government-surplus furniture and common household items were installed in these well-fitted-out buildings, which were also equipped with blast shelters in the basement; they were essentially complete homes minus interior finish, plaster and utilities.

But the greatest curiosity surrounded the fifty occupiers of house no. 1 and house no. 2. The well-established merchandising display company L. A. Darling, of Bronson, Michigan, and the Las Vegas department store JCPenney had teamed up to provide and clothe the buildings' occupiers.

Men, women, children and even baby mannequins had been fashionably attired, cast as ordinary people frozen while engaged in typical activities as the bomb went off.

They were arranged in domestic tableaux eerily reminiscent of the sitcoms and interior magazines of the time. Dad lounged in his easy chair reading the newspaper, Mum bent over the kitchen table, a spoonful of pears in her hands, twins played on the living room carpet, and baby sat in his high chair. The table was set. Refrigerators and pantries were stocked with fresh food. Outside, the 'neighbours' were sitting in their car.

Unsurprisingly, when Annie's blast came there was next to nothing left of house no 1. It was sheared off at the floor and 'looked as if it was a layer cake that had been worked on by a mad baker'.[3]

The mannequins that had given the house such a realistic lived-in appearance now sprawled in awful grotesquery, like broken dolls. The earth outside was scorched; the desert greasewood turned to dust; the decorative Joshua trees scarred and misshapen.

House no. 2 and its occupants fared a little better. The windows and doors had been blown out, and the 'people' on the ground floor flung about or crushed beneath scattered furniture. But the mannequins in the bomb shelter underneath the building held their positions and remained relatively unscathed.

Cars around the further site were flattened on top, as if a giant fist had crushed them, but strangely those with windows open suffered little damage: the theory was that the latter had let the pressure pass through, while the closed windows offered resistance that built up destructive pressure.

As the hours unfolded, America's reaction to Annie moved from initial trepidation to reluctant acceptance. The image of house no. 1 being torn violently to shreds was indeed a horrific and gripping demonstration of nuclear fury. The images of the frame smouldering from the heat micro-seconds before the whole structure was ripped apart by the blast were the stuff of nightmares.

But it was accepted – implicitly or explicitly – that the test was an evil necessitated by the Cold War. 'It is tragic, it is insane, it is fantastically costly – but the play must go on,' wrote the leader writer of Utah's *Deseret News*.[4] In the post-bomb euphoria, no real worries were voiced in the neighbouring states about potential radiation contamination to beast and man.

There was a barely a mention of the fate of scores of animals – primarily dogs and mice – that were placed in nearby shelters to test the effectiveness of the structures from neutron irradiation. A hundred rabbits were offered no protection – left out in the open, anywhere from 2 to 12 miles from the blast, to test the effects of thermal radiation on the eyes.

Ninety miles away back across the desert in Las Vegas, a kind of Armageddon tourism was starting to develop. This much-trailed test had attracted people from all over the country to Sin City. Hotel-casinos hosted parties on their rooftops that would last until dawn when they could witness the detonation while guests sipped Atomic Cocktails (equal parts vodka, brandy and champagne, with a dash of sherry – then, bang!).

Already on the market, the 'Atomic Hairdo' – a coiffure featuring an upswept mass of ringlets and curls in the shape of the mushroom cloud – grew ever more popular, clubgoers danced to the 'Atomic Boogie' and the 'Atomic Bomb Bounce', and the Miss Atomic beauty contest continued apace.

The economy of Nevada may have received a boost from Annie, but what the Federal Civil Defense Administration wanted was to promote Cold War preparedness on the home front. The nuclear theatre of Doom Town was aimed at searing the horrors of the nuclear age into the human psyche, promoting a mindset of motivation through fear.

It had brought home to Americans that nuclear war was eminently real, but that survival (after a fashion) from the Soviet Union's bombs was possible if they were trained and prepared.

Meanwhile, reverberating in the minds of the new administration in Washington were the worrying results of a defence survey completed a few months back at the Massachusetts Institute of Technology by the most renowned of America's physicists and engineers. The survey reported to the President that the Soviet Union had now about 150 atomic bombs and 700 big bombers to deliver them. It concluded that within two years the Soviets could deliver a 'devastating' and possibly 'decisive' atomic attack on American cities, against which the country had only the feeblest defence – the calculation being that just one plane in ten of the enemy could be downed.

So on this day in March 1953, as the Chinese prepared a major new offensive in the Korean War to try to seize the strategically vital Hill 355 at the heart of the front line, President Eisenhower accepted that Annie's live appearance was necessary to dismiss from the minds of his people that the bomb was just a vague, mysterious instrument of infinite disaster. Instead he needed them to grasp that it was a real and present danger to the American way of life.

But it was also a message that he wanted to send out to the Chinese military and to the new masters in the Kremlin, just two weeks after the death of Stalin, that America was ready, able and willing to develop and deploy – if pushed – her ever-expanding arsenal of weapons of destruction.

* * *

The pressure on President Eisenhower to consider the nuclear option to end the Korean impasse was mounting from various quarters of the political, military and intelligence establishment. Over at the

Department of Defense, US Air Force director of plans Major General Robert Lee wrote a memorandum which recommended using atomic bombs to achieve victory 'in the shortest space of time'.[5]

Attached to Lee's paper was a top-secret CIA special estimate, which stated: 'The Communists would recognize the employment of these weapons as indicative of Western determination to carry the Korean War to a successful conclusion.'

Then it was the turn of the Joint Chiefs of Staff, who took the extraordinary step of recommending that 'the timely use of atomic weapons should be considered against military targets affecting operations in Korea', as part of any operation against 'Communist China and Manchuria'.[6]

The practical difficulties of employing tactical atomic weapons on the Korean battlefield were discussed further at a meeting of the Joint Chiefs of Staff and Department of State strategists on Friday 27 March. General Joseph Lawton Collins of the US Army seemed somewhat sceptical of their deployment: 'The Communists are dug into positions in depth over a front of 150 miles, and they are very thoroughly dug in. Our tests last week proved that men can be very close to the explosion and not be hurt if they are well dug in.'[7]

However, Paul Nitze, director of policy planning at the State Department, quoted from a report by a group of civilian consultants. Their attitude was 'that we had gone to great expense to develop these weapons, we have tested them only in such tests as we could conduct ourselves, and we could certainly test them better under combat conditions'.[8]

General Omar Bradley (Joint Chiefs of Staff chairman) and General Hoyt Vandenberg (US Air Force Chief of Staff) voiced only cautious approval. 'Because of the casualties that will be involved in any stepped-up action, we may find that we will be forced to use every type of weapon that we have,' declared Bradley.[9] 'I hope that if we do use them, we use them in Manchuria against the bases. They would be effective there,' was Vandenberg's view.

But General Collins warned that American forces should be concerned about the defence of their own naval bases in the area if the Soviets retaliated. 'Right now, we present ideal targets for atomic weapons in Pusan and Inchon. An atomic weapon in Pusan harbor could do serious damage to our military position in Korea.'

And if America decided on a major amphibious operation – like the successful one that had been launched by General MacArthur at Inchon in 1950 – Collins worried that US troops would be vulnerable. 'An amphibious landing fleet would be the perfect target for an atomic weapon at the time when it was putting the troops ashore,' he explained. 'On the other hand,' he repeated once more, 'the Commies, scattered over 150 miles of front and well dug in, don't present nearly as profitable a target to us as we do to them.'[10]

Four days later Eisenhower convened a special all-day meeting of his National Security Council. There were twenty-seven around the table, key Cabinet members, representatives from the Atomic Energy Commission, civil defence chiefs and those civilian consultants who were pressing for the use of the A-bomb.

It was the kind of free-wheeling, wide-ranging discussion that the President liked to encourage, covering defence spending, the latest intelligence – or lack of it – on the new Malenkov regime, public attitudes to the atomic threat in the wake of the Annie exercise, and the latest developments in the atomic energy programme.

Inevitably, though, all roads led back to the stalemate in the Korean War. Before lunch Eisenhower brought up the subject of the use of atomic weapons. 'Admittedly,' he said, 'there were not many good tactical targets', but he felt that 'it would be worth the cost if, through use of atomic weapons, we could (1) achieve a substantial victory over the Communist forces and (2) get to a line at the waist of Korea.'[11]

John Foster Dulles, perhaps surprised by the direction of the President's thinking, deflected the issue, and instead expressed the thought that 'it might now be possible to achieve an armistice in Korea on the basis that the previous administration had sought in vain'.[12]

After lunch the council discussed the Joint Chiefs of Staff estimate of the time it would take to develop all the weapons they needed for all vital defence purposes; 1959 would be the earliest date. Then one of the civilian consultants, Deane Waldo Malott, brought the discussion back to the use of the atom bomb. Malott was the president of Cornell University, in his own words 'a Republican' and 'very conservative'. 'The so-called liberals of today', he once said, were radicals 'not tinkering with our institutions but out to destroy them'.[13] With his extensive links in the corporate world, he was known at the Ivy League establishment as the 'business president'.

Malott told his fellow council members there appeared to be 'public hysteria with respect to atomic weapons and the danger of atomic attack'.[14] Eisenhower replied that he was less worried about hysteria, more about complacency in the American public. Malott responded, startlingly, that he 'nevertheless believed that we ought to use a couple of atomic weapons in Korea'.

Eisenhower replied 'perhaps we should', but pointed out the effects on America's allies who would 'feel that they will be the battleground in an atomic war between the United States and the Soviet Union'.[15]

Nevertheless, the President made it clear that he and Secretary of State Dulles 'were in complete agreement that somehow or other the taboo which surrounds the use of atomic weapons would have to be destroyed'.

Dulles himself accepted 'that in the present state of world opinion we could not use an A-bomb'. But, agreeing with Eisenhower, he said, 'We should make every effort now to dissipate this feeling, especially since we are spending such vast sums on the production of weapons we cannot use.'

After that, the discussion moved on to the mutual security budget and how much foreign aid America could still afford to distribute to Europe, primarily, and the rest of the world.

This was a meeting where no definitive decisions were taken on strategy and operation. But if the genie was already out of the bottle on the use of the A-bomb, it had now flown a little further away.

* * *

By 1953, the CIA was only six years old and still had much work to do to cement a favourable reputation among the American public. In its brief history it had been found wanting in its assessment of the Soviet atom bomb project, had failed to predict the Berlin Blockade, and – most culpably – had been caught completely unawares by the invasion of South Korea.

But in the three years after that Korean disaster the agency had started to recover under the sage leadership of General Walter Bedell 'Beetle' Smith, Eisenhower's right-hand man in the Second World War and the American who had the satisfaction of signing the German Instrument of Surrender. Smith had revamped the agency from top to bottom, ruthlessly weeding out inadequate staff and rewarding those who remained with clearly defined career paths. He cemented the CIA's Office of National Estimates (ONE) – which was set up in 1950 to produce analysis predicting the future moves of Cold War rivals – and in the first month of his regime, ONE turned out as many intelligence estimates as it had done in the previous three years. In addition, Smith initiated the system of providing daily intelligence briefs for the President.

Now, in 1953, he had moved over to the White House to serve as Eisenhower's Undersecretary of State, to be succeeded by his deputy, Allen Dulles. The younger Dulles brother had been immersed in the diplomatic and intelligence world on and off since he joined the diplomatic service in 1916, mixing it with work as a Wall Street lawyer when he needed to make some serious money to better support his family.

In the First World War Dulles was based in Switzerland, and had tried, but ultimately failed, to lead Austria-Hungary out of the German camp. By the age of thirty-three he was chief of the Near East division of the Department of State. In the Second World War he set up the Office of Strategic Services (OSS, which was the CIA's predecessor) headquarters in Bern, and this office became a centre of the European resistance and one of the biggest and most effective intelligence-gathering units in the Allied world.

Dulles shared his brother's worldview, but his personality was cut from a very different cloth. A tall, hearty man who wore rimless spectacles and was rarely without a pipe, Dulles had a booming laugh and bouncy enthusiasm, and the air of an affable New England prep-school headmaster.

His wartime activities had given him a taste for the more glamorous side of an intelligence officer's work, namely psychological warfare and covert operations. Eisenhower shared his proclivity for both; in the Second World War the President appreciated the contribution made by Britain's spies and cryptanalysts, and had been impressed by how the OSS and his own military's psychological warfare teams had combined with resistance groups in German-occupied territory to distract the defence and prepare the way for his invasion force.

The CIA's primary function had always been to gather intelligence and international security information from foreign countries. But now Dulles, in his early weeks as head, was about to give his agency the go-ahead to pursue a startling covert operation on American soil.

The full story would not be laid bare for a quarter of a century. When it came out, it would reveal a dark tale about the production of mind-controlling and mind-altering drugs in CIA laboratories and of those drugs being administered to human guinea pigs – many willing, but a fair number unwitting. It would be the story of the involvement of eighty of the nation's universities and institutes, hospitals and prisons, some reluctantly compliant, some unknowing, some prepared to turn a blind eye and take the 'research grants' for the dubious experiments taking place on their premises.

It would be scarcely believable to learn that the CIA had run the outrageous Operation Midnight Climax, where agency safe houses doubled as brothels in two of America's biggest cities, in which moonlighting prostitutes plied unsuspecting victims with hallucinogenic drugs to assess the impact on their behaviour and sexual performance.

All this began on 3 April when Richard Helms, the CIA's ambitious 39-year-old chief of operations – responsible for intelligence collection and covert action programmes – wrote to Dulles, requesting money for a highly sensitive research and development project to study the use of biological and chemical materials in altering human behaviour.

In previous years the CIA had started to dabble in this field with Project Bluebird (authorised on 20 April 1950) and Project Artichoke (started on 20 August 1951), which were essentially defensive programmes in which the agency sought ways to insulate its agents from brainwashing attempts.

Now the goals had shifted, the ambition was greater. 'This area involves [the] production of various physiological conditions which could support present or future clandestine operations,' Helms explained to the new CIA director.[16]

Aside from the offensive potential, the development of a comprehensive capability in this field of covert chemical and biological warfare gives us a thorough knowledge of the enemy's theoretical potential, thus enabling us to defend ourselves against a foe who might not be as restrained in the use of these techniques as we are.

Also in that memorandum of 3 April was a warning from Helms that the CIA's fingerprints should be kept off this controversial project:

> It is highly undesirable from a policy and security point of view that contracts should be signed indicating Agency or Government interest. In a great many instances the work in the field must be conducted by individuals who are not and should not be aware of our interest ... in no case should any manufacturer or supplier be aware of Government interest.[17]

Within the agency, the project had to be kept within as tight a circle as possible. 'Even internally in CIA, as few individuals as possible should be aware of our interest in these fields and of the identity of those who are working for us.'[18]

Helms was becoming a key figure in the agency. He was a product of the eastern establishment – his grandfather had been president of the Federal Reserve. As a former newspaper executive, his major claim to fame was securing an exclusive interview for the United Press with Adolf Hitler in 1936. As with many newspapermen, he made the transition from journalism to intelligence when he joined the OSS for the Second World War.

The techniques of the communist foe had been worrying Helms and his colleagues for a number of years. Already struggling to match the powerful MGB in the 'conventional' espionage war, the nascent CIA was short of weapons with which to fight its chief opponent, and the Chinese, on a new battleground – for the control of the enemy's mind.

Writers like Arthur Koestler (*Darkness at Noon*) and George Orwell (*1984*) had already explored, in novelistic form, the techniques of mind control practised by the monolithic state machine as a key part of its own self-maintenance and preservation.[19]

Now real evidence of the apparent proficiency of the communists in this field was starting to mount up. The world had seen the pathetic figure of Hungary's Cardinal József Mindszenty in the Budapest People's Court in 1949, weak, emaciated, his eyes fixed in a vacant stare as he confessed to treason. Helms and his CIA colleagues wondered whether Mindszenty might have been drugged, in addition to being subjected to usual torture methods such as the use of dazzling lights, scant food and sleep deprivation.

The CIA was also disturbed the following year when American Robert Vogeler, an International Telephone and Telegraph Corporation executive, appeared in the same court and confessed to spying against the communist state, supposedly gathering information on rockets and radar and planning to smuggle its atomic scientists out of the country. The colourless monotone of Vogeler's 'confession' suggested he might have been beaten or hypnotised – or drugged.

Helms was also puzzled about the odd behaviour of the US ambassador to Moscow, George F. Kennan, at Berlin's Tempelhof airport in September 1952. Kennan, author of the famous 'Long Telegram' advocating containment of an aggressively expansionist Soviet regime, surprised reporters by using the most undiplomatic language.

He compared the status of Americans living in Moscow with his experiences during five months' internment by the Nazis in 1941. The Kremlin declared him *persona non grata*, and Helms wondered whether Kennan had been administered a drug that caused him to 'act in such an aberrant fashion'.[20]

But a big influence on the CIA's thinking came from the journalist Edward Hunter – no stranger to the intelligence world and another figure who had worked for the OSS in the war, this time as a propagandist.

Hunter, a long-time correspondent in China and the Far East, was noted for his anti-communist writing. He was fascinated by the successful mind control that he believed totalitarian regimes exerted on their subjects. It was he who originally coined the phrase 'brainwashing', a literal term he plucked from Chairman Mao's lexicon, which described the forced programme of indoctrination of communist beliefs on Chinese citizens.[21]

In early 1953, Hunter's sway on government and public opinion was as strong as ever. He had recently published *Brainwashing in Red China*, which pulled together all the evidence he had gathered over previous years.[22] The book was already cited in the congressional record as one of twelve textbooks on communism recommended for schools and libraries by Vice-President Richard Nixon.

In recent months the American public had read or listened to the broadcasts of a small number of their soldiers and airmen who had apparently turned their back on their homeland while in captivity and were telling the 'truth' about the war.

On 23 February 1953, a Chinese broadcast had featured Colonel Frank Schwable, Chief of Staff of the First Marine Air Wing, shot down and taken prisoner in July 1952. Schwable claimed that the US was establishing a 'contamination' belt across North Korea to choke off the movement of supplies to the communist front. Corsair planes, he claimed, were to drop first cholera, then yellow fever and typhus bombs, using five planes nightly from the 513th Fighter Squadron.

Schwable's wife, starved of any news about her husband's plight over the past six months, was elated on hearing his voice. She was, however, unconvinced by the content of his broadcast, telling reporters: 'That's the same old Communist malarkey. Nobody believes it.'[23]

Nonetheless, Hunter warned that this brainwashing was being done on a significant scale. He warned Americans not to be surprised if a number of their 7,000 prisoners of war in Korea who were eventually released talked and acted like communists. Their resistance would have been broken down by constant mental pressure, but also by physical threats, hunger, sleeplessness, hypnotism – and drugs.

Helms believed that it was America's 'responsibility' not to lag behind the Chinese or the Soviets, and the only way was to test drugs that could be used to control human behaviour. 'We all felt that we would have been derelict not to investigate this area,' Helms later explained.[24]

The CIA had learned of the Soviet use of a drug called bulbocapnine, which induced therapeutic stupor. The agency was also aware of the growing reputation and use of lysergic acid diethylamide (LSD), whose hallucinogenic effects were discovered by the Swiss scientist Albert Hofmann in 1943.

Increasing evidence was coming in at this time of the attempts the Soviet Union was making to acquire quantities of LSD. One report even suggested that the Kremlin had attempted to buy virtually the entire world's supply of the chemical – 10kg, enough for about 100 million doses – from Sandoz, the giant Swiss pharmaceutical company, which had a monopoly on the West's production of the drug.

The CIA was prepared to spend $240,000 to buy up all of Sandoz's product and trump the Kremlin. But when officers arrived at the company's headquarters in Basel (where Hoffman worked) they discovered that their source for this information – the military attaché in Switzerland – had hopelessly misinterpreted the figures he had been given. The Sandoz executives told the CIA men that nowhere near 10kg of LSD had been produced in the past ten years – the figure was nearer 40 grams (about 1.5 ounces).[25]

Such errors were born of anxiety and panic at this stage of the Cold War. 'We were literally terrified,' one CIA officer later recalled.[26] 'This [LSD] was the one material that we had ever been able to locate that really had potential fantastic possibilities if used wrongly.'

Whatever the availability of LSD, CIA chiefs were convinced that North Korea was using it in their interrogations of American prisoners, hence the false statements and 'confessions'. This tasteless, odourless and colourless drug, which created a kind of schizophrenia, even when taken in small quantities, would now be the CIA's first choice in its new mind-altering programme.

While he contemplated Helms's proposal, Allen Dulles publicly voiced his fears over brainwashing. In a lecture to the National Alumni Conference at Princeton University on 10 April, entitled 'Brain Warfare', he told his audience: 'I wonder [...] whether we clearly perceive the full magnitude of the problem, whether we realize how sinister the battle for men's minds has become in Soviet hands.'²⁷ The 'Red Menace' had secretly developed 'brain perversion techniques ... so subtle and so abhorrent to our way of life that we have recoiled from facing up to them'.

Dulles vividly described the condition of those subjected to communist mind control. 'Parrot-like, the individuals so conditioned can merely repeat the thoughts which have been implanted in their minds by suggestion from outside. In effect the brain under these circumstances becomes a phonograph playing a disc put on its spindle by an outside genius over which it has no control.'

So Helms had been kicking at an open door. Three days after this lecture, Dulles responded swiftly to his proposal, formally approving a top-secret programme to be called Project MKUltra. He gave it a generous budget of $300,000 ($2.8 million today), declared it exempt from normal CIA financial controls and authorised the agency's technical services staff – led by a trained chemist named Sidney Gottlieb – to forge ahead with research projects of their choice 'without the signing of the usual contracts or other written agreements'.²⁸

The cryptonym 'Ultra' was probably a nod to Dulles's and Helms's service with OSS, when Ultra – the designation given to intelligence gained as a result of the breaking of the main German code – was one of the biggest secrets of the Second World War.

Dulles had the backing of his counter-intelligence chief, James Jesus Angleton, whose career-long obsession about a Soviet mole operating at the heart of the CIA was well underway. He was certain that LSD, or something similar, would help root out the spy.

The President was not told about the project, and there would be no attempt to seek approval from Congress. Dulles and his senior colleagues were well aware of the consequences of the secrets of MKUltra spilling out. 'Precautions must be taken not only to protect operations from exposure to enemy forces, but also to conceal these activities from the American public in general,' wrote a CIA auditor when the project was up and running.[29] 'The knowledge that the agency is engaging in unethical and illicit activities would have serious repercussions in political and diplomatic circles.'

The international standard for medical experimentation had been set at the Nuremberg trials for Nazi war criminals. The Nuremberg Code stated that medical experiments should be conducted for the good of mankind and that a person must give full and informed consent before being used as a subject.[30] The US Department of Defense had just signed up to the code and now the CIA was preparing to flout it.

Helms, long a champion of Sidney Gottlieb because of his ability to cut through jargon and make science understandable to the layman, made sure that he was appointed to run MKUltra.

Gottlieb presented a curious character to the 'preppy' contingent at the CIA. The son of Hungarian Jewish immigrants – although he never practised the faith – he was born with a club foot and developed a stutter in childhood. But he pushed himself with unrelenting intensity to shrug off these afflictions and eventually became an enthusiastic square dancer and exponent of the polka.

Academically, Gottlieb was outstanding. As a student he was particularly gifted at science, and would graduate *summa cum laude* in chemistry from the University of Wisconsin in 1940. In 1948 he was recruited to the National Research Council, where he worked on plant diseases and fungicides, and had his first exposure to hallucinogens. Then in 1951 his fervent patriotism was satisfied when he was invited to work at the CIA, swiftly rising to become the head of its technical services staff.

It was Gottlieb's Office of Scientific Intelligence, in coordination with the US Army biological warfare laboratories, that would drive the project. In addition to the production of LSD and other 'truth serums', MKUltra would oversee scores of sub-projects involving radiological implants, hypnosis and subliminal persuasion, electroshock therapy and isolation techniques. MKUltra even spawned a smaller sister project, named MKDelta, for experiments on individuals abroad.

An early MKUltra document referred to the need to study substances 'which will promote illogical thinking and impulsiveness to the point where the recipient would be discredited in public'; substances 'which will enhance the ability of individuals to withstand privation, torture and coercion during interrogation'; and investigation of a 'knockout pill which can be surreptitiously administered in drinks, food, cigarettes as an aerosol, which will be safe to use, provide a maximum of amnesia, and be suitable to use by agent types on an ad hoc basis'.[31]

MKUltra began to pay hundreds of thousands of dollars to subcontracting institutions, hospitals, doctors, toxicologists, psychiatrists, hypnotists and other experts to carry out the testing of LSD and other drugs.

Most of the subjects were outcasts from society, prostitutes and their clients, mental patients, convicted criminals – the people 'who could not fight back', in the words of one of Gottlieb's colleagues.[32]

In these early days, these CIA 'researchers' would carry out their experiments with 'willing' participants. Drug addicts were given shots of morphine as reward for their test roles. Students were paid, soldiers were promised extra furloughs. Cancer patients were promised painkillers. Sexual psychopaths and the mentally ill were simply not told, because they did not need to be paid.

One of the first set of tests was conducted by the National Institute of Mental Health at its Addiction Research Center in Lexington, Kentucky, which was effectively a prison for criminals serving sentences for drug violations.

Volunteers, after being examined physically and signing a consent form, were then given LSD. One mental patient was given the drug for 174 consecutive days. Then, as a reward for their participation, the prisoners were supplied with a drug of their addiction.

At the Boston Psychopathic Hospital, students from Harvard University and the Massachusetts Institute of Technology were paid $20 each to drink a tall glass of water spiked with LSD, and then asked to participate in a series of psychological tests for ten hours. These were done under the auspices of the 'Society for the Investigation of Human Ecology' – simply a front organisation for the CIA's research.

Eisenhower may not have known about MKUltra, but he had encouraged his CIA chief to use covert methods and be bold and imaginative in confronting the communist threat, in whatever shape or form it came. MKUltra was one of the first significant secret programmes that Dulles authorised – but it was certainly not the last. However, it was high risk, and six months later it would suffer a high-profile casualty that would lift the dark curtain that shielded it from the outside world just a little.

* * *

One Communist on the faculty of one university is one Communist too many. One Communist among the American advisors at Yalta was one Communist too many. And even if there were only one Communist in the State Department, that would still be one Communist too many![33]

Ten months on from that rousing peroration – on 9 July 1952 – at the Republican Party convention in Chicago, and Joseph Raymond Mc-Carthy was at the summit of his power and influence. The respected economic and political ideologies of the world – capitalism, liberalism, conservatism, socialism, communism – required decades to take root in the political lexicon. In the febrile environment of the Cold War, a new 'ism', 'McCarthyism', had needed just three years to become recognised and familiar at home and abroad.

'One sometimes wonders who is the most powerful, the President or Senator McCarthy', Labour leader Clement Attlee pondered in a speech to the House of Commons.[34] The demagogic senator from Wisconsin, with his roughly handsome looks, burly stature and thick baritone voice, had etched himself vividly onto the canvas of American life with his relentless hunt – which many described as a witch hunt – to root out communist conspirators in every shape and form.

Day after day Joe McCarthy dominated the front pages and evening radio news broadcasts. His technique of the unsubstantiated accusation, the vilification of those unable to answer back, the charge of guilt by association and the counter-accusation as a method of defence remained constantly on show in this age of anxiety.

McCarthy justified his frequently dirty tactics in typically earthy language with the analogy of the farmer's son that he was. 'You learn early in life that you don't go skunk hunting with striped trousers, a silk handkerchief and a top hat … we're engaged now in … digging out a much smellier breed of animal than I dug out back on the farm.'[35]

'McCarthyism' was defined by the man who gave it the name as 'the fight for America'. Many Americans condoned McCarthy's aggressive behaviour and brutal investigations in the honest belief that he was performing work that was essential to the preservation of the American way of life. Many others were appalled, seeing the bullying techniques, the congressional hearings akin to Soviet show trials and the flexibility with the facts as classic methods of totalitarianism.

But in the new Eisenhower era McCarthy, with his national profile and his hold on the important minority grouping in the Republican Party, the ultra-conservatives of the Midwest, was not going away. In the recently elected Congress, McCarthy, because of his seniority, might have been eligible for the chairmanship of the powerful Senate Committee on Appropriations, with its jurisdiction over state and federal spending. Instead, he opted to head what was commonly regarded as a backwater body: the Committee on Government Operations.

Republicans, euphoric at winning the presidency and control of both houses of Congress after twenty years out in the cold, were worried about the unpredictable Wisconsin senator. But when Indiana's William Jenner drew the chairmanship of the Senate Subcommittee on Internal Security, whose brief included any anti-communist investigations, it looked as if they had shot McCarthy's fox. 'We've got Joe where he can't do any harm,' commented majority leader Robert Taft.[36]

But the shrewd McCarthy had chosen the Committee on Government Operations, ostensibly a minor 'watchdog' body, for a purpose. Allied to it was a Permanent Subcommittee on Investigations, which he was also entitled to chair. This subcommittee had been a sedate body in recent years, but in the past it had studied 'export policy and loyalty' as well as probing the 'employment of homosexuals and other sex perverts in government'. It had wide discretionary authority and full-time staff to boot.

McCarthy saw that it offered him unlimited scope to investigate whatever and whoever he wished. This would be the perfect stage from which to root out spies, traitors or merely undesirables in American society – and once more his main enemy, the US Department of State, was in his crosshairs.

It was in February 1950 that McCarthy rose from relative obscurity into the national limelight with the stunning claim in his speech in Wheeling in West Virginia that 'I have here in my hand a list of 205 … a list of names made known to the Secretary of State as being members of the Communist Party and who are nevertheless still working and shaping policy in the State Department'.[37]

The following day the 205 had been reduced to fifty-seven. Ten days later, on the Senate floor, it went back up to eighty-one. But by the time Democratic Senator Millard Tydings had finished his investigation into McCarthy's claims in July 1950, despite all his bluster, McCarthy had not produced the name of even one communist in the State Department.

The detail of McCarthy's accusations did not seem to matter to many Americans, who were living in a heightened climate of apprehension. Effective demagogues find an area of emotion and exploit it. The backdrop to McCarthy's Wheeling speech was the fall of China to Chairman Mao's communists, the successful explosion of the Soviet atom bomb, and the case of the State Department official, Alger Hiss, who had been accused of passing secrets to the Soviets.

Since McCarthy had become a household name, the Korean War had plunged American soldiers into unhappy battles with the communist monolith, while evidence of the enemy within – most recently Julius and Ethel Rosenberg, convicted of passing secrets to the Soviet Union – kept on coming. In 1953 McCarthy was still riding the wave of the Red Scare, which showed no great sign of subsiding.

Riding this wave alongside McCarthy in his new subcommittee was the young counsel Roy Cohn. Aged twenty-six, Cohn had already earned a reputation as a relentless questioner with a sharp mind and retentive memory. Working in the US Attorney's Office, he had helped prosecute William Remington, a former Commerce Department employee convicted of perjury relating to his Communist Party membership, and had also participated in the prosecution of the Rosenbergs.

Brash and arrogant, Cohn alienated others on McCarthy's staff. He ran hearings like a prosecutor before a grand jury, collecting evidence to make his case in open session, rather than offering witnesses a full and fair hearing. But McCarthy appreciated his zeal and gave him free rein to conduct investigations.

The subcommittee hearings were generally held in room 357 of the Senate Office Building. But McCarthy would often switch them to room 318, the spacious Caucus Room, where better television and radio coverage could be accommodated. If he wanted the extra glare of publicity he would move to New York City, working out of the Waldorf-Astoria Hotel or the federal courthouse at Foley Square.

The principal targets in those early months of 1953 were two subsidiaries of McCarthy's hated State Department: the Voice of America (VOA) and the US Information Service libraries, at home and abroad.

The Voice of America, established in 1942 to counter Nazi propaganda, had become a window into America society through dramas, essays, poems, folk songs and news. It stood third in terms of audience in the world's communication networks, behind Radio Moscow and the BBC. With seventy-five transmitting stations spread over four continents, it reached an estimated 300 million people in forty-six languages and dialects.[38]

Many of the VOA executives and senior editors took as their 'mission' the historic BBC approach, which insisted on presenting British policy without slanting the news or flooding the airwaves with political propaganda. But the VOA's main east European desks were manned by younger exiles with intensely anti-fascist or anti-communist leanings that coloured their radio commentary.

There was a clash of attitudes, and impartial news reporting was losing out. 'Congress expected us to "make propaganda" and we made it,' said one VOA official.[39] 'Anything more subtle than a bludgeon was considered "soft on communism".'

The guardian of this new approach in the VOA was a group called the 'Loyal American Underground' led by a Romanian exile, Paul Deac. It started feeding information about 'subversive employees to McCarthy and his retinue of friendly journalists'.

McCarthy told VOA officials in private: 'Your agency is full of Communists, left wingers, New Dealers, radicals and pinkos.'[40] His subcommittee initially carried out closed session interviews with VOA employees, and the senator made sure the 'results' were emblazoned across the front pages of influential newspapers.

So on Friday 13 February, timed to coincide with the first day of his subcommittee's open hearings, the headline in the *Chicago Tribune* read: 'Uncover Plot in "Voice" to Sabotage US'.[41] Reporter Willard Edwards wrote: 'A senate investigation of Communist influences in the Voice of America here [in New York] has uncovered amazing evidence of a conspiracy to subvert American policy in this nation's radio propaganda broadcasts abroad.'

The report went on to say that 'scores of witnesses, questioned night and day' had provided proof of the 'deliberate sabotage of American objectives in foreign propaganda'. Committee subpoenas were 'fluttering on desks like pigeons in Union Square and more than 100 witnesses have been lined up for questioning'.

So in the course of the next month a large nationwide television audience was treated to an often bizarre spectacle, as a variety of witnesses were sometimes cajoled, more often than not harangued, by Cohn and McCarthy, on the basis of obscure 'evidence' of communist sabotage at the VOA.

Roger Lyons, the director of religious programming, faced an accusation that he did not believe in God. This claim was made after a disgruntled employee reported a conversation with Edwin Kretzmann, chief policy adviser at the VOA, who had dismissed a question about Lyons's specific religious adherence with the off-the-cuff response that it was not a pertinent question to ask and by saying, 'For all I know, he may be an atheist.'

Lyons insisted during testimony, 'I am not an atheist, I am not an agnostic. I believe in God.'[42] He had to confirm he had been to church within the past month, and felt obliged to volunteer that he had recently contributed $10 to a local Lutheran church.

Dr Nancy Lenkeith, a scriptwriter in the French section, and effectively a witness for the prosecution, denounced her superiors after she was sacked for broadcasting a favourable book review of *Witness* by Whittaker Chambers (who was a former Soviet spy).

She told the committee her head of section had asked her to join a Marxist commune. She also reported a producer who had traduced the good name of Abraham Lincoln. When asked about the idea of doing a Lincoln's Day broadcast, he had apparently said: 'That damn Lincoln! Why do we have to talk about him again? We talk about him all the time, and he bores the French.'[43]

Tragically the stress of the subcommittee's interrogations arguably cost one man his life. The VOA's decision to locate two powerful transmitters – named Baker East and Baker West – in North Carolina and Washington State was criticised at the open hearings by a former VOA radio engineer, Lewis McKesson, who implied that those locations had been chosen because signals broadcast from these positions could be more easily jammed by Soviet transmitters.

Raymond Kaplan, a 42-year-old VOA engineer, had worked on the Bakers project and been interviewed at the Waldorf-Astoria in an earlier closed session. On 6 March he jumped in front of a truck in Cambridge, Massachusetts. The coroner ruled his death as suicide, and released the note he had left for his wife and son. 'I have not done anything in my job which I did not think was in the best interests of the country,' Kaplan wrote.[44] But he stated that he feared that 'he would be a patsy for any mistakes' and that 'once the dogs are set on you everything you have done since the beginning of time is suspect'.

The campaign against the Voice of America began to fizzle out by the end of March as McCarthy moved on to new targets. His investigation had claimed the scalps of several top executives, and the Bakers transmitters project had been suspended. The VOA's reputation in Europe had been badly damaged.

Quite what the President thought about it, and the circus that accompanied it, no one was quite sure. He stonewalled at his weekly press conference when asked directly if he thought that Senator McCarthy's investigation against the VOA was helping the fight against communism. 'It was a question he would not answer without a bit more preparation on it, because he just hasn't thought about McCarthy's particular function, what he can do and what would happen if he didn't do it.'[45]

In fact the President himself had already launched two independent inquiries into the VOA and other media operations – his own Committee on International Information Activities and the Advisory Committee on Government Organization. As ever with McCarthy, and especially in the early weeks of his presidency, Eisenhower was resolved to play the long game.

The other focus of McCarthy's subcommittee was on the 'subversive' books that were held in the libraries of 200 State Department information centres in sixty-three countries around the world. Under the Truman administration their purpose had been to offer a 'balanced view of the United States' and 'a balance of the opinion and thinking of the United States'.[46] Virtually no effort had been made to exclude the writings of controversial authors, including communists. Diversity of opinion was encouraged and the intellectual credibility of the collections preserved.

McCarthy set out to change all of that. His staff examined the State

Department's International Information Agency catalogues and calculated that there were over 30,000 volumes (out of 2 million) in agency libraries that had been written by 'communist' writers. They reached this figure by listing all the individual copies of books by 418 writers.

The State Department, cowed by McCarthy's Voice of America inquiry, now issued a directive banning the books, music and paintings of 'communists, fellow travellers, etc' from the Voice of America and ordering all overseas libraries to remove all publications from controversial authors from their shelves.

With the imprint of both Dulles and McCarthy on this new policy, panicked librarians across the world rushed to clear their shelves. As a rough guide, they selected books by any author about whom derogatory information had been offered before a congressional committee – particularly the House Un-American Activities Committee (HUAC) and, of course, McCarthy's Permanent Subcommittee on Investigations.

These banned books were strange bedfellows. Jean-Paul Sartre, French philosopher and apologist for the Soviet regime (at that time), was not a surprise. Nor was *Ten Days That Shook the World* by the American journalist and activist John Reed (who had died in 1920), or anything by one of Stalin's favourite writers, Maxim Gorky.

However, there were also some odd choices: Foster Rhea Dulles, the cousin of the Secretary of State, who wrote scholarly tomes about the Far East, and Dashiell Hammett, the genius of hard-boiled detective fiction, who certainly had far-left associations but whose books were largely devoid of politics. The stories of children's writer Helen Goldfrank were also on the banned list – but then she had been previously active in the Communist Party and was the subject of FBI investigation.

Some of the writers were summoned to room 357 of the Senate Office Building for a grilling. Goldfrank batted away thirty minutes' worth of questions by relentlessly pleading protection under the Fifth Amendment – the right under the US Constitution to remain silent so as not to incriminate oneself. When the frustrated questioner Senator John

McClennan asked if there was anything in America she was proud of 'except that constitutional right you invoke so freely and insistently', she asked to consult her counsel.

The deadpan reply then came back: 'I am proud of the entire Constitution of the United States, and on the basis of the Constitution I seek special privilege under the Fifth Amendment.'[47]

Hammett, one of Eisenhower's favourite writers, was marginally more cooperative when he was interrogated. Hoping to lure him into the territory of 'proletarian fiction', Roy Cohn asked him if any of his books dealt with 'social problems'.[48]

Hammett conceded that a short story titled 'Night Shade' did indeed fit that description, because it concerned 'Negro–white relations'. 'Did that story in any way reflect the Communist line?' Cohn asked. 'I would say no, it didn't reflect it. It was against racism.'[49]

In a lull between witnesses in April 1953, Roy Cohn and his 25-year-old 'chief consultant' David Schine embarked on a seventeen-day tour of Europe to purportedly investigate 'waste, mismanagement and security violations' in the United States Information Service, including the Voice of America. Handsome, somewhat oleaginous, Harvard-educated Schine was the wealthy heir to a string of hotels and theatres, and the owner of reportedly one of the largest collections of cigars in the world. He was no lawyer, but he was a fervent anti-communist.

Cohn and Schine's trip was an expensive publicity exercise – to the American taxpayer, for use of military transport planes; and the European taxpayer, for hotel rooms and other expenses. To the already worried State Department officials in Rome, Paris, Berlin and elsewhere it was just more torment to their already harassed lives.

'Insolence abroad' was the verdict of one French diplomat. The two 'junior Mc-men', as some American papers derisively dubbed them, reportedly engaged in high jinks along the way, brawling in a hotel lobby in Bad Godesberg in West Germany, and chasing each other around their bedroom and overturning contents, ashtrays and furniture.

Interviews with the press exposed their immaturity. At one, Cohn introduced Schine as a 'management expert', claiming that his colleague had written a book about the 'definition of communism'. A quick bit of research by journalists revealed that the book was a six-page pamphlet, not written by Schine but merely published by his hotel company.

The duo stopped just six hours in England, time enough for a visit to the American embassy, where 'officials of the BBC' – according to Schine – were also there to meet them. In actual fact there was only one BBC executive who met them – Hugh Carleton Greene, assistant controller of overseas programmes, and the brother of Graham Greene.

'He should, perhaps, be used to cloak-and-dagger conduct,' wrote the *Manchester Guardian* correspondent witheringly.[50] 'He is always familiar with American ways, though possibly not the ways of Senator McCarthy and his assistants.'

The rest of the British press poured a barrel-load of ridicule on Cohn's and Schine's heads. Viscount Brendan Bracken, Churchill's great friend and key wartime adviser, dismissed them in his *Financial Times* column as 'scummy snoopers' and 'distempered jackals'.[51]

The left-leaning *News Chronicle* commented: 'Let McCarthy's two precocious youngsters … be made familiar with the British hatred of bullying honest officials to serve the ulterior purpose of a fanatic in authority.'[52] It continued: 'McCarthyism has done more to bedevil Anglo-American relations than any other single factor.'

From the other side of the political divide the *Daily Express*, owned by another of Churchill's friends, Lord Beaverbrook, echoed those sentiments. 'McCarthy', its editorial declared, 'is seeking to promote bitterness between Britain and America, thereby playing Malenkov's game.'[53]

The British public looked askance at the rise and rise of McCarthyism with its smear campaigns, its purge of government officials, its blacklisting of writers and entertainers. The political establishment, as Attlee implied with his comment about McCarthy's influence in the House of

Commons, was concerned that Britain's closest ally in the Cold War was under the sway of aggressive, isolationist tendencies.

These fears were reflected in some of the cultural offerings on view in March. A week before Cohn and Schine set off on their European jaunt, BBC television's *Sunday Night Theatre* had broadcast a dramatisation of Irwin Shaw's novel *The Troubled Air*, a portrayal of a McCarthyite witch hunt on a popular American radio show. At the end of the drama, an American radio announcer is heard saying that the McCarran Act (with its strict immigration vetting) compelled even Prime Minister Winston Churchill to be examined on his arrival in the United States. The play's final scene was pure irony – a view of the Statue of Liberty.

Five million viewers watched *The Troubled Air*, and a few weeks earlier nearly as many had tuned in for *The Troublemakers*, a play about hysteria over communism on an American campus.

The Labour left had constantly maintained its opposition to McCarthyism and its attack on civil liberties. Now, however, it appeared as if the Conservative Party was becoming just as concerned.

The Home Secretary, Sir David Maxwell Fyfe, was not an obvious civil libertarian. He still believed in the death penalty, and had ignored a cascade of parliamentary and public sympathy in January when allowing the hanging of nineteen-year-old Derek Bentley (who had an approximate mental age of eleven) for his part in the murder of a policeman.

He was also the scourge of homosexuals, declaring that he wanted 'a new drive against male vice … to rid England of this plague'.[54] To many this campaign was akin to McCarthyism, creating a climate of paranoia and prejudice in which undercover police officers were deployed as agents provocateurs, and blackmail was not uncommon.

But Maxwell Fyfe had his liberal instincts too. He had made his name as one of the chief prosecutors at the Nuremberg trials with a brilliant cross-examination of Hermann Göring, and then played a vital part in drafting the European Convention on Human Rights.

In an interview with American reporters he voiced the fears of the

Cabinet about the climate in America – without directly referring to the Wisconsin senator. In this 'apparently endless Cold War', he said, it was vital to retain all the liberties that 'form the warp and woof of a free way of life, and particularly to preserve that freedom of controversy which is so vital to democracy'.[55]

He averred that a Communist Party member was entitled to hold a government post provided that his work did not involve secrets relating to the nation's security. He also had no worries about continuing the Labour government's policy of allowing the entry to Britain of foreign communists coming to attend open communist meetings.

Viscount Bracken, from the vantage point of his column in the *Financial Times*, concluded: 'Things have now reached a pass in the United States when to have made a mild speech twenty years ago at a college debating society, saying that perhaps there was a grain of truth in the doctrines of Marx and Lenin, is quite enough to blot a man's career.'[56]

As Marx, Lenin, Sartre et al. tumbled from the shelves of US State libraries across the world, librarians in America, cowed by McCarthy, were pulling down old favourites. Henry David Thoreau's *Civil Disobedience* apparently encouraged men to protest at American law and order. John Steinbeck's *Grapes of Wrath*, with all its pain and tragedy for the oppressed worker, with the rich causing the Depression and doing little to help its victims, was labelled as nothing short of Leninist propaganda.

This was troubling, but it would all briefly become the theatre of the utterly absurd later in the year when Mrs Thomas J. White of the Indiana State Textbook Commission reportedly called for the removal of references to the book *Robin Hood* from textbooks used in the state's schools. 'He robbed from the rich and gave it to the poor. That's the Communist line,' she said. 'It's just a smearing of law and order.'[57]

Pravda, the Kremlin's prime propaganda paper, lapped it all up, cheekily publishing a poem about the famed outlaw entitled 'The New Ballad of Robin Hood'. One Soviet commentator pondered: 'Can Wall Street succeed where King John failed?'[58]

* * *

Later in the summer, the advisory company Gallup polled the nation's prominent professional and business leaders – as listed in *Who's Who* – to measure feeling about McCarthy's campaign to ban books.

The poll found that 77 per cent said books by communist writers should not be banned from American library shelves, with just 18 per cent saying that they should. But on the question of whether those books should be banned from US libraries abroad, the result was much closer: 47 per cent said they should not, but 42 per cent said that they should.

The latter grouping typically felt that America should 'not help the Communists in spreading among foreign peoples the doctrines for which they stand but which are inimicable to our way of life'. A poll of the general public would very likely have eked out greater support for McCarthy.

While the campaigns against Voice of America and the libraries seemed unwarranted and unnecessarily bullying to many, McCarthy did find an issue that really resonated with the public. This was the 'scandal' of trade by the Western nations with Red China – at the time when the latter was killing UN troops, principally American soldiers, in the Korean War.

McCarthy's committee, with a bright new assistant counsel, 27-year-old Robert Kennedy, doing all the legwork, revealed that Western nations had profited to the tune of $2 million by shipping goods to and from China since the beginning of the war.

Young Kennedy, along with Senate investigator LaVerne Duffy, had combed through the Lloyd's of London shipping index, studied British parliamentary hearings, read reports from the Maritime Commission and even looked at intelligence from the CIA to show that Western vessels had handled 75 per cent of this trade.

Many of these ships, Kennedy claimed, were paid for with loans subsidised by US taxpayers and simply intended to help its Second World War allies rebuild their merchant fleets. Top of Kennedy and McCarthy's 'guilty' list was America's closest ally; more than half of the vessels carrying out this trade sailed under the British flag.

To make it even worse, not only food and other staples were being traded by the British, but also strategic materials, including rubber, fertiliser and petroleum. 'Natural rubber is needed for the tyres of jet planes,' Kennedy told one reporter.[59] But the most damaging claim was that some of those British ships had carried communist troops.

Kennedy had discovered that there was also a large Greek role in the trade with China. On Saturday 28 March, McCarthy called the Washington press corps in from their weekend off to announce that he personally – not the State Department – had negotiated with the Greek shipowners of 242 merchant ships to agree to break off all trade with China and North Korea.

Those ships were owned by the Greeks but flew the flags of various nations: seventeen were British; thirty-four were Canadian; fifty-one were Greek; fifty-two were Liberian; and eighty-eight were Panamanian. In the coming days McCarthy would add to the list so that eventually 327 vessels promised to stop carrying goods to China.

The State Department was furious. It had been carrying out delicate negotiations to try to persuade allied carriers to abandon trade with China: now McCarthy had usurped their role, and cast himself as the great protector of the boys in Korea.

The dispute between the two developed in hearings held two days later by McCarthy's subcommittee. Harold Stassen, the State Department's director for mutual security, angrily told McCarthy that he was interfering with the nation's foreign policy – and in any case, the department had won agreement from the Greek government to stop shipments a few days earlier.

This clash between the Republican administration and their most charismatic senator was doing the party no good at all, so

Vice-President Nixon, who was close to the Wisconsin senator, brokered a lunchtime meeting between Dulles and McCarthy. Out of it emerged a peace of sorts, with a joint statement that foreign relations were 'in the exclusive jurisdiction of the chief executive' but that McCarthy's activity 'was in the national interest'.[60]

The row with the accused British was not so quickly resolved. For Churchill and his Cabinet, this was the United States at her most isolationist and naïve. A cut-off in trade with China would cause great harm to Hong Kong and Malaya, and merely push Mao's regime towards trading more with the Soviet bloc.

Trade and shipping were the lifeblood of an island nation. It was already impossible for a British ship of over 500 tons, registered in the United Kingdom or her colonies, to proceed from any port in the world to a port in China or North Korea. It was acknowledged there had been a ten-fold jump in exports to China at the beginning of the year, mainly of textile machinery and woollen goods, but that was not inconsistent with UN resolutions or the terms of the Battle Act of 1951, which was concerned only with restricting the export of strategic materials to communist countries.

As *The Times* wrote:

> The McCarthy policy, if one can dignify it by such a name, would logically lead to the stopping of all trade with the whole of that part of the world under Soviet influence, without regard to the strategic or non-strategic character of the goods carried. It would mean, on the trade front, a general state of war.[61]

Clement Attlee stirred the pot again in the speech in which he questioned whether McCarthy should be placed alongside Eisenhower in terms of power and influence. He also spoke about how the American Constitution was 'framed for an isolationist state', and suggested that 'elements in the United States' did not want a settlement in Korea and preferred an 'all-out war against China, and communism in general'.[62]

He believed that China was not a puppet in Soviet hands and would 'wear her communism with a difference'. He suggested she might resume her 'rightful place' on the Security Council of the United Nations – after a Korean armistice.

This was a very big red rag to a bull. McCarthy, taking time off from his committee hearings, unsurprisingly responded in trenchant fashion. This was 'one of the most insulting speeches ever made in the legislative body of a recipient nation against an ally which has been pouring out her economic life blood for practically every other nation on earth'.[63] 'Perhaps Mr Attlee forgets that the US has suffered 130,000 casualties in Korea, while the British figure is roughly 3,700.'

'Let us examine this man Attlee,' he went on. 'He said he would distribute to senators a copy of a picture of the Labour leader reviewing Communist troops at a military review during the Spanish Civil War in 1937 with two Communist leaders, all three of them giving the Communist clenched-fist salute.' On his inquiry on trade with China, McCarthy said: 'If the British are trying to blackmail us into accepting the Communist terms on the grounds that they will withdraw from Korea if we don't, then I say "Withdraw and be damned". Then let us sink every accursed ship carrying materials that result in the death of American boys.'

Attlee, in response, said that McCarthy had revived 'an old canard that I reviewed Communist troops. The Spanish Republican Government was not Communist. The troops I reviewed contained Liberals and people of all kinds of view who stood for liberty against fascism. The salute given was at the time the ordinary salute of all anti-Fascists.'[64]

TASS, the Russian news agency, relished the 'growing discontent' in Britain with 'various aspects of American policy'. This row, however, fizzled out after a couple of weeks.

Nevertheless, the Cabinet felt it necessary to release a very full statement to the House of Commons to counter what was coming out of the

McCarthy inquiry. 'We cannot live without trade and we consider that this trade in non-strategic goods is to the advantage of the free world,' it said.[65]

And on the accusation that two British ships, or ships flying the British flag, had been ferrying communist troops, 'all information available to Her Majesty's Government indicate that these allegations are completely unfounded'.

Whatever the rights and wrongs of the shipping controversy, it cannot be denied that McCarthy struck a chord. When Kennedy's report eventually came out, it was widely praised for its well-marshalled arguments and restrained tone. 'An example of congressional investigation at its highest level,' wrote Arthur Krock in the *New York Times*.[66] While Doris Fleeson, the first woman in the United States to have a nationally syndicated political column, reckoned that it was 'that *rara avis*' for McCarthy: 'A documented and sober story.'[67]

So McCarthy still strode purposefully across the American political stage. A few days after his spat with Attlee, Eisenhower gave his reflections on the Wisconsin senator to his friend Harry Bullis. 'It is a sorry mess,' he conceded.[68]

> This particular individual wants, above all else, publicity ... at times one feels almost like hanging his head in shame when he reads some of the unreasoned, vicious outburst of demagoguery that appear in our public prints. But whether a presidential 'crack down' would better, or would actually worsen, the situation, is a moot question.

So a showdown was not in sight. The President would continue to refuse to debate or denounce McCarthy publicly, much to the frustration of his Cabinet colleagues.

Ronald Maddison, RAF engineer and tragic Porton Down volunteer.
© PA/PA Archive/PA Images

CHAPTER 5

'LEAST SAID,
SOONEST MENDED'

Eisenhower spent the first two weeks of April 1953 absorbed with a major speech he had agreed to give to the American Society of Newspaper Editors. He knew a response was expected to Georgy Malenkov's first speech to the Supreme Soviet, the country's foremost law-making body, on 15 March, which had led the *Manchester Guardian*, for one, to hail the new Premier as the 'Peace Monger of Moscow'.[1]

Gone was the usual Kremlin rhetoric, castigating the 'warmongers' and 'imperialists' of the West. Instead Malenkov declared: 'There is no such troublesome or unsolved question with the United States or any other nation which cannot be solved by peaceful means.'

Pacing around the Oval Office, an enthused Eisenhower spelt out a possible new approach to his speechwriter Emmet Hughes.

> We are in an armaments race. Where will it lead us? At worst, to atomic warfare. At best, to robbing every people and nation on earth of the fruits of their own toil …
>
> There could be another road before us – the road of disarmament. What does this mean? It means for everybody in the world: bread, butter, clothes, homes, hospitals – all the good and necessary things for decent living.[2]

But of course there had to be a quid pro quo. For the Soviet Union, the price of disarmament (which would include international control of atomic energy and atomic weapons) would include an 'honourable' armistice in Korea, agreement to a free and united Germany, the signature on an Austrian treaty, and the 'full independence of the east European nations'. The President's shopping list was one the Kremlin was clearly not going to accept.

Eisenhower hoped that his rhetoric about how the arms race was stealing the lives of ordinary people around the world would have resonance. But Charles Douglas Jackson, the President's propaganda chief, was unconvinced, 'genial, bourgeois talk about schools for the ignorant and the sick' would do much to halt the Kremlin's global ambitions.[3]

Secretary of State Dulles remained implacably opposed to any softening of the administration's position towards Russia: 'It's obvious that their overtures are … because of outside pressures, and I don't know anything better we can do than to keep those pressures up right now.'[4]

As for an armistice in the war, the hard-line Dulles told Hughes bluntly: 'I don't think we can get much out of a Korean settlement until we have shown – before all Asia – our clear superiority by giving the Chinese one hell of a licking.'

Churchill was sent a copy of the speech beforehand, and much to the surprise of Eisenhower and his aides, he had reservations – albeit from a standpoint which was the reverse of that of Dulles. While applauding the President's 'grave and formidable declaration', he wondered if it was a little premature.[5] 'I believe myself that at this moment time is on our side. The apparent change of Soviet mood is so new and so indefinite and its causes so obscure that there could not be much risk in letting things develop.' He also worried that Eisenhower's demands on the Soviets 'might quench the hope of an armistice'.

In classic Churchillian style, he colourfully illustrated his point of the need to wait for the 'full character' of the regime to emerge: 'I always like the story of Napoleon going to sleep in his chair as the battle began, saying "Wake me when their infantry column gets beyond the closest wood."[6]

Nonetheless, Eisenhower was determined to be bold. However, his 'Chance for Peace' speech at the Statler Hotel in Washington nearly ended in disaster. He began to experience disturbing chills and dizziness once he got underway, and sweat started to pour down his face. To steady himself he had to grip the lectern firmly, and he skipped some less important passages as he soldiered on.

He had been treated by his doctor for stomach pains the night before, and the conclusion would be that he was suffering from an inflammation of the ileum, a portion of the small intestine.

Among the many memorable lines written for him by Hughes, one stood out. 'Under the cloud of threatening war,' Eisenhower said, 'it is humanity hanging from a cross of iron' – evoking a famous phrase from the great Democratic orator and politician William Jennings Bryan.[7]

The speech was received with great acclaim at home and abroad. For the *New York Times*, this effort to wrestle the peace initiative from the Soviets was 'magnificent and deeply moving'.[8] In London, *The Times* said it had 'fired the imagination. Its timing is excellent, and in manner and substance it could scarcely be better.'[9] The *Mirror*, often a critic of the President, applauded it as 'a most heartening, far-sighted declaration on peace ... It has the ring of a leader on a world scale.'[10]

Political leaders also queued up to applaud Eisenhower. 'It had clearly presented the real aims of peace,' said French premier René Mayer. 'Honest and strong' was the verdict of Italian Prime Minister Alcide De Gasperi, while NATO Secretary General Lord Ismay thought it 'most important, most noble and most moving'. U. Ohn, Burma's ambassador to Moscow, trumped them all by declaring that it was 'in the best tradition of the Founding Fathers of the United States'.

Eisenhower had to wait nine days before the new Soviet leadership responded to the speech. The good news was that the main government mouthpiece, *Pravda*, took it seriously enough to devote its entire front page to his proposals – and printed the complete text of the address.

Normally *Pravda* would consign speeches of this sort to two or three paragraphs on the back page. Kremlin watchers also felt the tone of the response, although sharp and argumentative, was not as vituperative or belligerent as it often could be.

'The words of President Eisenhower were met with a feeling of sympathy when he said "We are seeking a genuine and complete peace in all Asia and the entire world,"' *Pravda* declared.[11] 'And also his declaration that "not one of the troublesome questions, be it great or small, is insoluble in the presence of a desire to respect the right of other countries."'

But that was as good as it got. As well as rejecting Eisenhower's preconditions for peace talks, the editorial in the Moscow newspaper had a sharp rebuke for its bogeyman John Foster Dulles, who had made a follow-up speech to 'Chance for Peace' two days later.

Dulles had dismissed the mood music of Kremlin pronouncements since Stalin's death, which some had characterised as a 'peace offensive'. 'That's incorrect,' Dulles told the same audience of the American Society of Newspaper Editors. 'It is a peace defensive … it is prudent, for the present, to assume that we are witnessing a tactical move of the kind which Soviet communism has often practiced.'[12]

The *Pravda* editorial criticised Dulles for trying to convert Eisenhower's speech 'into an act of war'. It went on to say that Dulles's 'militant pose would hardly achieve its objective'.

Churchill, with his own agenda for reconciliation with Moscow, looked on with keen interest. Despite his initial reservations, he hailed Eisenhower's speech as 'massive and magnificent' when addressing a party rally in Glasgow the next day.[13] 'Is there a new breeze blowing on the tormented world?' he asked.

The Prime Minister, who had just been granted a knighthood by the Queen, was in high spirits – relishing, at this vital moment, taking full control of foreign affairs while Anthony Eden was absent for a second gall bladder operation.

'I'm really wonderfully well, Charles,' he told his doctor Lord Moran at the end of the month.[14] Warned that he might be taking on too much with the Foreign Office, he replied: 'Oh, I like it. It doesn't add as much work as you think. You see, I've got to keep an eye on foreign affairs at any time … I am making speeches out of my head at the moment. They seem to go all right.'

In a couple of weeks' time, he would make one of those speeches – and it would have a dramatic effect on his relationship with Eisenhower and the drive to détente.

* * *

When nineteen-year-old aircraftsman Barry Barnes arrived at the top-secret Chemical Defence Experimental Establishment facility at Porton Down in Wiltshire on the afternoon of Tuesday 25 April, he was surprised to see a monkey roaming freely in its cage in a compound near the officers' mess run by the Royal Veterinary Corps. The beast appeared to be in a lively mood, leaping about and happily chattering away for the benefit of the new visitors.

But when Barnes came down for breakfast the following morning the scene was very different:

> The gate of the cage was open, and there were two soldiers lifting the body of the monkey onto the back of the truck. He was as stiff as a board. I remember joking nervously to one of the soldiers, 'He hasn't

eaten one of your breakfasts, has he?' To which I received a fusillade of abuse.[15]

Up to then, Barnes, an operations clerk at RAF Hawarden on the border of England and Wales, had had few qualms about travelling to Porton Down to take part in trials 'into the effects of the common cold on the operational capabilities of servicemen' – so the paper read that was pinned to the noticeboard at his base.

Volunteers would receive an extra week's pay, which in his case was 28 shillings – seven of which he normally sent home to his mother. But it was not just the money that made him sign up.

> Here we were in a Cold War, involved with the Russians. One of my friends had been in the Gloucester Regiment in the Korean War. I had uncles who had fought at Dunkirk and Alamein – and another who was taken prisoner at El Alamein.
>
> All those people I regarded as heroes. Now I just thought I could do something – in a small way – for my country. We still had that national spirit.[16]

On that first afternoon Barnes and his eleven colleagues were given a briefing by two army officers and a man in a white coat: 'A doctor, or a scientist, it wasn't made clear – we were not given any of their names.'

The servicemen were told they would be given a variety of tests.

> They said, 'We are not going to tell you what they are, but some will be for the common cold. Some will test various substances, some of which will be on your skin. Some will be to do with nerve gas, and there will also be a placebo. You don't have to worry about any of these things, because everything is under strict control. There may be a little discomfort, you may feel a little unwell, but don't worry, we have antidotes if that happens.[17]

Barnes was not unduly concerned. 'Of course then we had great faith in authority – be it the bank manager, schoolmaster or doctor. And of course you believe what you are told in the forces. We hadn't got to the cynical stage.'

The following day the volunteers first underwent a series of fairly basic psychological and intelligence tests. Then they were asked to put on gas capes, and after a pad was put on their arm, a liquid mixture was dripped on it. Nothing untoward happened – 'it was an easy start', recalled the serviceman.[18]

But the next day it was a very different story. The participants were told that they were going to be tested with some nerve gas and were taken on a bus way out in the countryside, to a concrete building in the middle of Salisbury Plain. There they were told to put on gas capes, respirators and helmets, and led to a room in the centre of the building, which featured a big window running down the whole of one side. 'We could see people with white coats standing behind the window with clipboards and goodness knows what, and in front of them a big bench with tubes on,' Barnes explained.[19]

It now became clear that they were standing in a gas chamber.

We were told to walk round the room for two minutes. We were then told they were going to pump in a dose of nerve gas. 'You will not see it, you will not smell it, and you won't feel anything at all. This may give you a bit of a headache and make you subsequently feel a little unwell, but don't worry, we have an antidote for this and your discomfort won't last too long.'

During the walk around the chamber, the men were instructed to stop and take off their respirators. At the end of the two minutes, they were told to move out of the room and remove all their protective clothing and respirators, which were quickly hosed down by officials.

Almost immediately Barnes started to feel very ill. 'I had a terrible pain behind both eyes. It was as if someone had knocked a nail right through them. Within minutes I could hardly see – it was like being in a room filled with black smoke.'[20]

All the other men suffered similar effects and each one had to be helped back to the bus. Back at Porton Down they were sat down and made to take basic aptitude tests similar to the day before. 'But I couldn't see – I felt like death,' Barnes recalled. 'I was then taken back to bed, but there was no way I could sleep, the pain was absolutely awful, agony.'

The tests continued on and off for a couple of days.

> I can't recall how I performed in them – it was just sheer torment, and I was still basically blind. I was given no antidote, no aspirin during all this time. We were taken to a laboratory at some stage and I think we had some sort of medical, but it was so vague. I was in such a state.[21]

Eventually he was told that he was being given an antidote, which consisted of drops in the eyes, and after a few hours the pain lessened a little and his eyesight began to return. It was then that Barnes was able to see that the airman who had been in the bed next to him was not there anymore.

'A chap came to collect his belongings the next day. I said, "Where is he?" And he replied "Oh, he's not very well, he's in hospital." I never saw him again.'[22]

That man was volunteer 702, James Patrick Kelly, a 21-year-old airman from Glasgow. He had collapsed in the gas chamber, with foam oozing from his mouth. His body then went into spasms, he was unable to breathe and he finally lapsed into a coma.

In hospital Kelly's airways were cleared of mucus and saliva, and he was administered oxygen and given 2mg of atropine, a drug equipped to combat the effects of nerve gas. Over four hours later he returned to consciousness, only able to mutter 'I feel terrible' in his strong Scottish accent. It would take him a month to recover.

Slightly differently from Barnes, Kelly had been told his visit to Porton Down would be to participate in a gas warfare course. He would say later: 'The staff did not explain anything about the test that we took part in. No one explained the substances that they were using … we received no formal briefing about Porton Down, or the work they were doing there.'[23]

Kelly's brush with death, in conjunction with the severe effects Barnes and the other volunteers suffered, might have persuaded scientists to call an immediate halt to the tests. Such a move was not seriously contemplated, however, even though there were those in the Porton Down hierarchy who suggested reducing the amount of the nerve gas – sarin – to the lowest range, 15mg to 30mg. That advice was ignored, although those in charge of the experiments did bring down the amount from 300mg to 200mg for the next round of experiments.

These were conducted nine days later, on Wednesday 6 May, when a further six subjects entered the gas chamber on Salisbury Plain. One of them was volunteer 745, twenty-year-old Leading Aircraftsman Ronald George Maddison, a wireless mechanic from Consett, County Durham.

Maddison was based at RAF Ballykelly in Northern Ireland, so he had set off for Porton on Saturday 2 May. He had confided to colleagues that he was looking forward to a 'jolly', a chance perhaps to see his girlfriend Mary Pyle and his family, and of course earn a bit of extra money. The money he would earn, 15 shillings, might buy an engagement ring for Mary.

Maddison was a short – 5ft 7in – slim, fit man who loved skating and playing hockey. Like Barry Barnes and James Kelly, his first couple of days at Porton Down had been uneventful, and involved taking the aptitude tests and undergoing a medical. He and his colleagues were given time to read and relax, but they also helped in the preparation of rabbits for tests, feeding and then shaving the skins of the animals.

Like Barnes and his group, Maddison was never told he was going to be given a hefty dose of a lethal nerve agent. When signing up for the tests, again like Barnes, it was indicated that the scientists would be looking for clues for a cure for the common cold. Once on site, Maddison and the others learned only that they were going to 'test various cloths with chemicals'.

Just after 10 a.m. on 6 May, while wearing a respirator, Maddison entered the gas chamber where he was exposed to a 200mg dose of sarin, dripped through a cloth onto his arm. A few minutes in, when asked how he felt, he replied, 'Perfectly well.' But half an hour later scientists noticed that he was sweating profusely, and Maddison told them he felt 'pretty queer'.

He was led from the chamber, his respirator and contaminated clothes removed, and walked over to a bench in the open air. But almost immediately afterwards he collapsed, his body violently shaking. An ambulance was summoned, and in the meantime he was given atropine intravenously.

Young ambulanceman Alfred Thornhill arrived on the scene to witness a terrible sight.

It was like he was being electrocuted, his whole body was convulsing. I have seen somebody suffer an epileptic fit, but you have never seen anything like what happened to that lad … The skin was vibrating and he was making a very strange bubbling noise that sounded to be coming from his throat. There was all this terrible stuff coming out of his mouth … it looked like frogspawn or tapioca.[24]

Thornhill asked the scientists standing around Maddison's body what had happened. 'He's taken his mask off too soon,' one of them replied. The ambulanceman could 'see the panic in their eyes'.[25]

Thornhill and his colleagues raced Maddison back to the medical centre at Porton Down. There, doctors fought for over two hours to save his life, injecting anacardone – a drug used to stimulate breathing in acute respiratory cases – yet more atropine, and then liquid adrenaline directly into the heart.

But it was no use, and at 1.30 p.m. Ronald Maddison was pronounced dead. Half an hour later Alfred Leigh Silver, Porton Down's medical officer, who had led the desperate efforts to save his life, put a call through to the Wiltshire coroner Harold Dale, only to discover that he was out of his office.

Leigh Silver wanted to brief Dale face to face, in private, so he drove over to his office in Wootton Bassett, accompanied by Harry Cullumbine, head of physiology (and in charge of human experiments), and medical officer Major Richard Adrian, the first to attend to Maddison on Salisbury Plain.

The telephone lines were soon humming between Wiltshire and Whitehall. This was a shocking, unprecedented event – but there was never any real thought of exposing it to public scrutiny. The government's weapons of mass destruction programme, chemical and biological – of which these tests were a part – was highly classified for reasons of national security.

As the internal investigation into young Maddison's tragic and unnecessary death got underway, politicians, civil servants, lawyers and scientists seemed to be guided by the words of the secretary of the Coroners' Society of England and Wales, Sir William Bentley Purchase.

Purchase was a vastly experienced coroner with the investigation of 2,000 deaths to his name. He told coroner Harold Dale that he should make up his own mind about whether to hold Maddison's inquest in secret. But he advised: 'At the present moment, the motto seems to be least said, soonest mended.'[26]

* * *

By a strange coincidence, at the very moment that Ronald Maddison was dying in Porton Down's medical centre, 90 miles away in White-hall Winston Churchill was taking his seat in the Prime Minister's map room in the Ministry of Defence – where the first item on the agenda for his Defence Committee was the 'Policy for Chemical Warfare'.

Among those joining him around the table were Lord Cherwell, his scientific adviser, Duncan Sandys, his son-in-law and Minister of Supply (with responsibility for the chemical weapons programme), Rab Butler, Chancellor of the Exchequer, and Antony Head, Secretary of State for War.

The government's policy on chemical warfare had evolved somewhat over the past eleven months. Back in June 1952, in their major policy paper 'Defence Policy and Global Strategy', the British Chiefs of Staff had trumpeted the 'first use' of these weapons of mass destruction.

'The new nerve gases can ... be used tactically to great advantage and would provide the Allies with weapons of real value against an enemy who relies on massed formation,' the report stated.

> The moral objections to chemical warfare can surely be no greater than to atomic warfare ... we consider that the Allies should be prepared to use these weapons in war when they think it to their advantage to do so, and that this should be reflected in their public attitude to the employ-ment of these forms of warfare.[27]

But in requesting the use of chemical weapons at the start of any hos-tilities, Britain would clearly be in contravention of the 1925 Geneva Protocol (drawn up after the mustard gas horrors of the First World War) prohibiting the use of chemical or biological weapons in wartime.

With the Foreign Office leading the charge – unhappy at the pros-pect of Britain reneging on an internationally recognised treaty – the

Defence Committee then altered the policy so that Britain could now use chemical and biological weapons only in a time of war and in the direst of circumstances. 'The Allies should not take up a position which would deprive them of their ability to use chemical warfare in retaliation, if this were to their advantage,' was the new wording of the policy.

What the Geneva Protocol did not say was anything about the development, production and stockpiling of such weapons. Of course, Britain now possessed the number one weapon of mass destruction with her acquisition of the atom bomb in October 1952; but with the Soviet threat still high, Churchill's government was determined to have the biggest possible armoury, so the expansion and testing of biological and chemical weaponry continued apace.

Cost, however, was a major obstacle. Britain's atom bomb project had absorbed a huge slice of defence expenditure and, still in the era of austerity, there was little largesse to be spread elsewhere. The solution, as ever, might lie across the Atlantic. The United States was about to move into mass production of sarin and Churchill and his Cabinet wondered if they could be given a slice of that cake – at little or, under the canopy of 'defence aid', no direct cost at all.

But Duncan Sandys had to tell the Defence Committee on 6 May that America's response had not been favourable. British negotiators had been told that the 2,500 tons of nerve gas they had requested – two-thirds to go to the army, one-third for the RAF – would be available, but they would have to pay for it, at a price of roughly $10 million.[28]

Britain did have her own nerve gas plant, at Nancekuke Common in Cornwall, on the site of the old RAF Portreath station. Secluded and close to the sea – which was convenient for waste disposal – there were few prying eyes around this top-secret establishment.

Nancekuke was already up and running as a small pilot plant and was just waiting for the nod to expand into full-scale production of sarin. But that, Sandys explained, would cost another £4 million.

The minister also pointed out one other complication, and cost. The shells that Britain wanted to use for her nerve gas bombs did not match those provided by America. So, if Britain wanted the weapons, she would have to provide the delivery method, while America provided the actual nerve agent filling.

The prospect of constant toing and froing across the Atlantic with highly dangerous material was not an appealing one. However, there was a possible solution, born of the trilateral cooperation that existed in the chemical warfare field at the time. Under the arrangement, Canada could produce British-designed casings for weapons, which could then be shipped to the United States and filled with sarin, and then these deadly weapons could be shipped to Britain.

There were those around the table that day who were not put off by the American rebuff, who believed that 'this nerve gas would provide a tactical weapon of considerable importance and we should not lightly deprive ourselves of the ability to use it'. The view was expressed that the negotiations with the Americans had so far not been made at a high level, and a further approach to Eisenhower's Cabinet ministers might yet pay off.[29]

Churchill told his colleagues that 'on balance' he thought it would be best if the United Kingdom could remain independent and produce her own supply of nerve gas.[30]

But the Prime Minister wanted time to reflect on the cost of the Nance-kuke project in the light of a forthcoming defence expenditure review. On the approach to the Americans, he thought it worthwhile to press Britain's case with one of his best contacts in the US administration, his old wartime colleague General Walter Bedell Smith, who had recently retired as director of the CIA and was now Undersecretary of State.

* * *

Less than twenty-four hours after leaving the committee room Church-ill learned of the death of Ronald Maddison, a sober reminder if ever there was one of the destructive nature of the poison gas of which he and his Cabinet colleagues had just agreed to produce more.

Duncan Sandys, who broke the news, tried to put the best gloss on it. These tests, he told the Prime Minister, were of 'an exceedingly mild type and are conducted under strict medical supervision'.[31] He said Porton Down had conducted around 13,000 human experiments since the 1920s, including 1,500 tests with nerve agents, and this had apparently been the centre's 'first fatality'.

In the face of very recent evidence (e.g. Kelly's coma just nine days earlier), Sandys disingenuously claimed that Porton's scientists had been 'greatly surprised' by this incident because other subjects had been exposed to large dosages of nerve gas 'without any lasting effects'.[32]

Churchill was unusually preoccupied at that moment. The Coronation was less than a month away and it was taking up a lot of his time and energy. Even more immediate and important, though, was a foreign policy speech he was due to make in the House of Commons in four days' time in which he would make the controversial case for détente with the new Malenkov regime. As with all his big speeches, this would require endless careful drafting and redrafting in the days beforehand.

So he left the Maddison case and its fallout to Sandys and others, encouraging his Minister of Supply to 'fear nought' and simply suggesting that the best course of action would be to 'tell the truth'.[33] However, this was not necessarily advice that was followed to the letter in the coming months.

Sandys informed Churchill that he was placing an immediate temporary ban on the testing of nerve gas on servicemen at Porton Down. He indicated that an inquest would follow, but he warned the Prime Minister that the 'general circumstances' under which Maddison died would inevitably have to be made public – which might well cause 'some stir in the press'.[34]

The Ministry of Supply then prepared a statement for the media

– only to be used if necessary – which read: 'In every case the nature of the test and the anticipated result was described to the volunteer prior to the test so that he could withdraw if he so wished.' From the evidence of Barnes and others, this was certainly stretching the truth.

Home Secretary Sir David Maxwell Fyfe then stepped in to aid Sandys. He told Churchill his department had been in touch with the coroner, and that he was 'proving to be cooperative'.[35]

'I understand he accepted a proposal that the post-mortem examination should be made by Professor Cameron, professor of pathology at University College Hospital. I have ascertained that the coroner has taken evidence of identification and has issued his order for the burial of the body.'

The body might be being buried, but Maxwell Fyfe told Churchill that the coroner could not legally do away with the need for an inquest:

> He has decided to hold it without a jury, as he has the power to do. He also has the power to direct that the public be excluded from the inquest. I have no power to give him any directions; but he has asked my advice whether this is a case in which it would be appropriate for him to exercise this power and I am telling him that in my view it is.[36]

Coroner Harold Dale had now been 'squared'. The inquest was to be held in secret on the grounds of national security. It was duly opened on 8 May in Trowbridge – attended only by Ronald's father John, an ironworker from Consett – before being adjourned for eight days.

In the meantime senior Whitehall lawyers urgently assessed what liability might fall on the government for Maddison's death. Harry Woodhouse, working for Harold Kent, the newly appointed Treasury solicitor, would steer Sandys and Maxwell Fyfe through the legal complexities and ramifications of the Maddison affair in the coming months – his recommendations not always to their liking.

It became clear to Woodhouse that the ministry's advice to reassure volunteers about their tests was out of date, belonging to the era of mustard gas, rather than the present round of experiments, 'more lethal and more uncertain in operation'.[37]

On 15 May 1953 he wrote to the Ministry of Supply taking issue with the wording, which read: 'Tests are carefully planned to avoid the slightest chance of danger.' He suggested this was not an appropriate phrase to use in conjunction with these lethal gases. What it should read, he said, was: 'Tests are arranged so as to eliminate all foreseeable danger.'[38]

Woodhouse's conclusion was that 'it would be difficult to show there had been no negligence' involved in the tests.[39] He recommended that compensation should be paid, and that Sandys should not seek to adopt some system of indemnities or what he described as 'blood chits' – designed to put responsibility on the volunteers.

Woodhouse's advice on the wording would be heeded. Within weeks the notices to future volunteers would now read: 'The physical discomfort resulting from tests is usually very slight. Tests are arranged so as to eliminate all foreseeable danger, and are under expert medical supervision.'[40] More of the truth, if certainly still not the whole truth.

A few months later, following the inquest and a court of inquiry, Woodhouse made it perfectly clear that the government was liable for Maddison's death. Writing once more to the Ministry of Supply, he said that illness or death caused by sarin gas – an 'experimental substance' – was not covered by the relevant section of the Crown Proceedings Act of 1947, which protected the government from claims by servicemen using normal equipment or supplies 'for the purposes of the Armed Forces of the Crown'.

Nonetheless, Woodhouse conceded that if Maddison's lawyers were to lodge a claim for negligence against Sandys, 'it would not be an easy case for them to substantiate'.[41] But his advice was that if such a claim was made, it would be far better for the minister to settle 'rather than to have the whole case ventilated in court'. He proposed paying a pension, arguing that 'this would probably dispose of the case and Maddison's family would probably be satisfied'.

At the resumed inquest, on 16 May, Ronald's father John was again the only relative allowed to attend. He had been escorted to Porton Down to identify his son's body, where officials explained to him about the tests and described to him how his son had died. He was even able to speak to some of the other test subjects.

Outwardly, and no doubt genuinely, Porton officials offered much sympathy to Mr Maddison, as well as a detailed enough explanation of the events leading up to his son's tragic death. But, with the Treasury solicitor also present to gently coax him, the father's acceptance of the country's need for the tests that killed his son would have helped preclude any future claim he might be thinking of making for negligence. He seemingly bought into the line that Ronald had 'died from an unfortunate accident while on duty at Porton'.

At the secret inquest, coroner Harold Dale decided that Maddison died as a result of choking and he recorded a verdict of death by misadventure. The airman was buried in a lead coffin, with the Ministry of Defence paying John Maddison £16 for the undertaker, £4 for catering and £20 for black clothes. He was sworn to secrecy, and told his family that if he told them what he knew they would 'put him in the Tower'.[42]

The court of inquiry was chaired by retired Air Vice-Marshal Thomas McClurkin, reporting to the controller of supplies. Joining him on the panel was an eminent group, including the Home Office's Chief Medical Officer Sir John Charles and leading representatives from the Medical Research Council, the RAF and the legal branch of the Ministry of Supply.

At first their questioning drew some surprisingly frank concessions from the Porton officials. The establishment's chief superintendent,

Stanley Mumford, told the inquiry that the call for volunteers was couched in vague language because 'if you advertised for people to suffer agony you would not get them'.[43]

On the tests themselves, Mumford insisted they were 'planned to avoid risk', but there was 'inevitably a danger of some poisoning'.[44] Any volunteers feeling unwell, however, could be treated with an atropine antidote, he explained.

Thomas Truckle, senior technician in the physiology laboratory, was in charge of the tests for both Barnes and Kelly and then Maddison. He insisted that he told each volunteer that 'the procedure is a dangerous one', but felt the existing safety arrangements were 'quite adequate'.[45] Leigh Silver, the medical officer who attended Maddison, said he had done everything in his power to save the young man's life.

RAF medical officer Adam Muir said that 'warning signs' flashed up on one or two of the tests, and the dosage was then reduced.[46] What he had not forecast was that two layers of cloth did not increase protection but seemingly made the sarin more toxic.

In the end, however, the court of inquiry exonerated Porton Down and its employees of any wrongdoing. The experiment on Maddison and others had been a 'reasonable' one, and the court was 'impressed by the smoothness of the working of the organisation in dealing with the emergency'.[47]

Crucially, the court instead attributed Maddison's death to a 'personal idiosyncrasy'. Either he had an 'unusual sensitivity' to the effects of the nerve gas or the physiological behaviour of his skin 'allowed an unusually rapid absorption' of the lethal liquid.

There was no suggestion from the inquiry that the tests, which were of 'such importance', should be halted. The only change it suggested was the one that Woodhouse had already recommended – that the men's 'terms of employment' should be amended, to protect the authorities against future liability.

Despite all the attempts to cover it up, such a shocking event was never going to go unnoticed. The *Sunday People* was first to find out about the secret inquest, and local newspapers latched on, with front-page headlines like 'Mystery of Dead Airman – Inquest is Kept Secret'.[48]

On 25 May, the *Daily Mail* reported that some MPs were demanding an inquiry into the 'death riddle of airman guinea pig'.[49] Then the *Sunday Dispatch* was the first to identify Ronald Maddison, who had 'died from suffocation in a hush-hush experiment'.[50]

Duncan Sandys knew he had to say something. So on 9 June, a month after Maddison's death, he finally publicly acknowledged it in the House of Commons – by way of a written answer, so there would be no opportunity for MPs to probe further.

He asked the reliable, stalwart backbench Conservative MP for Salisbury, John Morrison, to plant the question 'about the fatal accident which occurred recently at his Department's Chemical Defence Experimental Establishment'.[51]

Sandys's reply was: 'I regret that on 6 May Leading Aircraftsman Ronald Maddison died from the effects of asphyxia after taking part in a trial with war gas.'

The minister went to say that, in addition to the coroner's inquest, he had ordered a full technical investigation into the circumstances of the accident. 'The report', he asserted, 'shows that all the same precautions had been observed as in the many thousands of previous trials carried out over a considerable number of years.'

He did concede, however, that the 'report raises one or two points of a technical character which are being studied. Meanwhile, further trials of this kind have been suspended.'

Tom Driberg, Labour MP for Maldon and a well-known journalist (he had written the 'William Hickey' column in the *Daily Express*), was not so easily put off. He tabled a question two weeks later, asking Sandys how many fatal accidents had occurred at Porton Down since

1945, how many men had been disabled, whether participation by servicemen was compulsory and if the trials were going to be resumed.[52]

Sandys's reply was that there had been no other deaths or long-term disablements, and that all servicemen had been volunteers. As for resuming the trials, he told the House he was waiting for the completion of the technical study he had referred to a fortnight ago.

That technical study was in the surely very capable hands of Edgar Douglas Adrian, electrophysiologist, winner of the 1932 Nobel Prize for Physiology, master of Trinity College, Cambridge and president of the Royal Society. There was something of a conflict of interest here, however, with Adrian's son, Major Richard Adrian, Porton's medical officer, having been heavily involved in the tests – and the first to attempt to assist Maddison following his collapse.

Adrian co-opted Sir Joseph Barcroft, another eminent physiologist, and Gordon Roy Cameron, leading pathologist, both of whom moved – like Adrian – in scientific circles associated with the exploration of chemical warfare agents.

The committee's report was virtually everything that Porton's scientists – and the government – could have wished for. There was no real criticism of the safety precautions. It stated unequivocally that the experiments were vital for advancing chemical science and developing therapeutic cures for soldiers and civilians, and should continue – albeit within carefully prescribed limits.

It recommended that the inhalation of the gas should not go above a maximum (15mg per minute), and for the experiment that Maddison endured – in which the sarin was administered through the skin – the dose should not exceed 5mg. These 'very small doses' of radioactive sarin would allow 'radio labelling', enabling the nerve agent to be tracked in the body.[53]

Of course not a whisper of what the committee did or said was made public. Given the committee members' own positions in it, a clean bill of health for the chemical warfare industry was not surprising. In late September, the government accepted the vast majority of their recommendations – and testing was given the go-ahead once more. It began in early 1954, once each of the military services had approved the resumption.

It was full steam ahead, too, for greater production of sarin in Britain. Negotiations with the United States to acquire stocks had failed, and the idea of transporting the empty shells across the Atlantic, filling them up with sarin and bringing them back was deemed to be too complicated, dangerous and expensive.

In any case, Duncan Sandys told the Defence Committee that relying on America 'would involve the serious military risk of making ourselves entirely dependent for a vital weapon on a distant and uncertain source of supply'.

Nancekuke's time had seemingly now come. The 'unfortunate' death of Ronald Maddison had been a distraction, but the bigger picture for the government was the need for this additional weapon in the armoury against the Soviet threat.

* * *

From the beautiful, rugged coastline of Cornwall to the sandy beaches, crystal-clear lochs and spectacular cliffs of the Isle of Lewis in Scotland's Outer Hebrides. The government's weapons of mass destruction programme was certainly located in some of the most stunning – and, of course, isolated – locations in the British Isles.

In May the latest biological warfare field trials were conducted at a site just off Stornoway, on the Isle of Lewis. HMS *Ben Lomond*, a tank landing ship, was moored up, together with an accompanying 'floating island' – a 200ft by 60ft steel 'spud' pontoon – fitted out with compartments for equipment, disinfectant, changing rooms and cages for the unfortunate rhesus monkeys and guinea pigs that would be the recipients of the deadly pathogens that were being tested.

Over the next three months, Operation Hesperus (in Greek mythology the 'Evening Star') would employ nearly 200 Royal Navy and associated civilian personnel, plus a regular group of fifteen scientists from Porton Down and the Ministry of Supply's microbiological research department. American and Canadian observers, as part of the tripartite collaboration, were also present from time to time.

In the Second World War biological weapon testing was mainly held on the Porton Down range (where ricin was the favoured poison), although Gruinard Island in the Scottish Highlands and Penclawdd on Wales's north Gower coast were both flooded with anthrax. But after the war the testing was done at sea, and Operation Hesperus followed Operation Harness in 1948 to 1949 and Operation Cauldron in 1952.[54]

If the Chiefs of Staff had been keen about the use of chemical warfare in 'Defence Policy and Global Strategy', they could not see biological weapons playing as big a part. 'Research in bacteriological warfare has not yet gone far enough to enable us to decide whether or not it would be advantageous for the Allies to use it.'[55]

Churchill was ambivalent about the use of these weapons of mass destruction. There had been grim times in the past when he was forced to contemplate the use of such weapons, most notably in July 1944, when the V-1 flying bombs were threatening another Blitz-type bombardment of London and other cities.

Then a worried Prime Minister Churchill pondered retaliating with mustard gas. 'I should be prepared to do anything that would hit the enemy in a murderous place,' he wrote to his military secretary, General Ismay.[56] This was also when the Allied troops were fighting their way through France and the outcome of the war was still far from certain. Churchill wanted the matter 'studied in cold blood by sensible people'.

Desperate times bred desperate thoughts. Eight years on, the Prime

Minister was no great advocate for the use of weapons of mass destruction – and he certainly wanted no hint about Britain's chemical and biological programme to reach the general public.

Reacting to the Chiefs of Staff, he declared:

If anything has to be said, either privately or publicly, we could state that we would not use biological warfare unless it was used against us, but obviously we needed to study its methods in order to find a defence against it and be able to retaliate if retaliating became necessary.[57]

There had been a scare in Operation Cauldron in September 1952, when the Fleetwood-based trawler *Carella*, with eighteen on board, had ignored warnings when returning from a trip to Iceland and sailed through a cloud of plague bacteria.[58]

Porton Down scientists worried about a risk of contamination. But the trawler was not stopped for medical examination or disinfection but instead was closely monitored for three weeks by a Royal Navy destroyer and a fisheries vessel. None of the crew reported feeling ill, and under this period of surveillance they even went into Blackpool on shore leave. The First Sea Lord, Admiral Sir Rhoderick McGrigor, and Chancellor Rab Butler, deputising briefly in Cabinet as Churchill and Eden were away, dealt with the matter and ensured no word of it leaked out.

No such incidents occurred during the Operation Hesperus trials. Brucellosis and tularaemia were the agents tested, which were contained in British B/E1 and US E61 bombs. One of the purposes of the trials was to test the downwind travel – and survival – of the weapons and their impact, over very short distances (25 yards) and much longer (up to 1,200 yards).

But very poor summer weather hampered Operation Hesperus. Rain throughout May was followed by a period of dense fog in June.

Even after a break in the trials in July, there was very little improvement, with yet more persistent rain.

'A waste of time and money,' was Rab Butler's verdict when the Cabinet came to assess the trials.[59] Duncan Sandys then suggested that the trials should be moved to the more benign climate of the Bahamas, where the Chiefs of Staff had located a site which was 'probably as good as any in the world'.

Sandys spoke passionately. 'This is a field in which we have a technical lead compared with America. It is worth retaining. If we don't keep ahead of them, it will hardly be worthwhile to go on with it at all.'[60]

He said safeguards could be put in place that would eliminate the risk of an 'unfortunate incident', and asserted that there was very little shipping in the area.

The Bahamas came under the authority of Oliver Lyttelton, the Secretary of State for the Colonies, and a sceptic of biological warfare. 'The favourable conditions for biological weapons testing is just what attracts tourists. [It's] a pity the Minister of Supply can't find any other place in the whole world.'[61]

A week later and the subject was top of the Cabinet agenda. This time, Sandys won the day. One of the Cabinet's 'overlords', Lord Frederick Woolton, was back on duty and seemed to capture the mood of the Cabinet: 'I dislike all research into biological warfare. But the issue was whether these experiments should be made. Much would depend on the presentation to the public. [If] it could be presented as defensive – that [would] satisfy me.'[62]

Lyttelton, so hostile a week earlier, now withdrew his objections, although he 'still had apprehensions about the site'. The enthusiastic Sandys said: '[We] can do in four months in the Bahamas what would take five years in the Hebrides. We can't justify continuing the research if we shrink the trials.'[63]

Churchill, who had taken a back seat in this discussion, did not demur, only quipping that in any formal press release, '[we should] call them "anti-biological warfare trials"'.[64]

A few months later the Chiefs of Staff would formally update the British government's position on biological warfare. 'Should war come', they wrote,

Britain must, as far as possible, be in a position (A) to protect her civil population and service personnel, as well as crops and livestock, against attack by biological methods, and (B) to retaliate by these methods against the enemy should the government of the day decide to adopt this course.[65]

* * *

Winston Churchill's desire to take on the mantle of Cold War peace-maker was growing. At the beginning of April he helped Eden draft a 'thank you' telegram to their old wartime colleague Vyacheslav Molotov, for aiding the release of a group of British diplomats and churchmen held prisoner in Korea. Molotov, Minister of Foreign Affairs in the war, was now Deputy Premier and the third member of the ruling troika alongside Malenkov and Beria.

'Were there', Eden wondered, 'further questions directly rising be-tween our two Governments on which progress might now be made?'[66] Eager to engage in some high-level summitry – with either Malenkov or Molotov – Churchill joked to his Foreign Secretary in schoolboy fashion: 'If it is Mol, you go. If it is Mal, it's me.'[67]

Unfortunately, Eden would not be going to Moscow – or anywhere else – for some time. For some years he had suffered from abdominal pains, and was finally told he required an urgent operation for the re-moval of gallstones. But when it took place, on 12 April in the London Clinic, it very nearly cost him his life.

The surgeon's knife slipped and his bile duct was cut. Eden sustained a high fever and lost a great deal of blood, but he managed to pull through. A second operation on 29 April was necessary, but that went little better than the first. Eden's duct was blocked and he was suffering from jaundice.

Now his fortunes changed, because travelling through London at the time was Dr Richard Cattell, the American surgeon regarded as one of the world's best in complex gall bladder operations. He offered his services and that of his specialist team at the New England Baptist Hospital in Boston.[68]

Churchill was taking a very close interest in Eden's troubles – not just because he was a most-valued colleague, but because his niece, Clarissa, was the Foreign Secretary's wife. He felt that it would not reflect well on Britain's medical profession if the third operation was carried out abroad, albeit in America.

But eventually, on the recommendation of Churchill's own doctor Lord Moran – who advised him that Cattell was 'outstanding in every way' – it was agreed that Eden would cross the Atlantic in early June.[69] The expensive trip would be paid for out of Conservative Party funds.

Churchill now temporarily, but very eagerly, assumed control of the Foreign Office in Eden's absence – the only major office of state that had eluded him in his fifty-year political career. Eden's pragmatic approach to the Soviet Union was all about building up and maintaining the military and economic strength of the Western alliance, while waiting patiently for evidence of real change from the new men in the Kremlin. Foreign Office mandarins and others in Whitehall now looked on aghast at Churchill's increasing belief in 'easement' with the Soviets, and his efforts to rekindle the kind of 'big man' summit he had enjoyed with Roosevelt and Stalin during the war.

Diplomats at home and abroad tried to steer the Prime Minister away from the policy of détente. Sir Alvary Gascoigne, who was just about to complete his tour as ambassador in Moscow, supplied the

Prime Minister with evidence that very little was changing in the behaviour and outlook of the Soviet Union's senior politicians.

A meeting with Andrei Gromyko, deputy minister for Foreign Affairs, left Gascoigne fuming at the unsympathetic approach of the Soviet minister. Gascoigne had been pursuing two historical disputes – one was compensation for a north-east coal conveyor, rammed and damaged by a Soviet 'spy' trawler back in 1946 when on its mission to help map the British coastline.

The other was a cause célèbre – the case of Mrs Clara Hall, the Russian-born wife of a British diplomat, who had been refused an exit visa to join her husband in Ottawa, where he had moved six years earlier to become deputy chief at the British high commission in Canada. This extraordinarily mean act had meant that Alfred Hall had never seen his six-year-old son Nicholas, who was born just after he left Moscow in 1947.

Gascoigne reported back to London: 'Gromyko behaved exactly like a "robot" executing orders from above … this is, I fear, only too good an illustration of the fundamental hypocrisy, inhumanity and utter selfishness of the Soviet system.'[70]

On the Hall case, Gascoigne assured the Foreign Office that he would take it up again, but warned: 'We must let the "dust settle" and hope for the best.' Churchill, now reading all Foreign Office papers in his new role, concurred, writing 'yes' in his purple ink in the margin. He was clearly keen, despite the provocation, to tread carefully with the Kremlin as he pursued a new relationship.

Back in London, the Atlantic Committee of the Cabinet – a group of high-ranking civil servants from across Whitehall who met regularly to discuss NATO affairs – looked sceptically at the 'new look' Malenkov regime. Any conciliatory signs, it warned, 'might well prove more dangerous to Western cohesion … than the bludgeoning xenophobia displayed by Stalin'.[71] 'We must avoid being lulled into a false sense of security,' it concluded.

The Prime Minister was now Sir Winston, having been knighted by the Queen on 24 April and also accepting the coveted Order of the Garter. He had been offered it previously by George VI in 1945, but had declined, famously saying (not to the King): 'How can I accept the Order of the Garter when the people of England have just given me the Order of the Boot?'[72]

He and Clementine had been quite content to remain 'commoners', although Churchill was aware that the father of his great military ancestor, the First Duke of Marlborough, had been knighted, and there was appeal in following in his footsteps. In addition, he still felt guilty at refusing the Garter in 1945. 'Why have you not congratulated me, you pig,' he wrote impishly to Viscount Bracken a few days later.[73] The reply was in a similar vein: 'Dear Sir, recovering from shock. But give me notice of canonisation. Love Brendan.'

With a new spring in his step, Churchill embarked on his mission to 'parley' with the new Soviet leadership. Eden, recovering at home after his near-death operations, could do little to stop him, but telephoned Anthony Nutting, his young junior minister, and pleaded with him: 'Try not to allow too much appeasement of the Russian bear in my absence, dear boy.'[74]

Churchill ploughed on regardless. On 4 May he drafted a letter to Molotov, which he sent to Eisenhower for approval. In it he wrote:

I wonder whether you would like me to come to Moscow so that we could renew our own wartime relation and so that I could meet Monsieur Malenkov and other of your leading men. Naturally I do not imagine that we could settle any of the grave issues which overhang the immediate future of the world, but I have a feeling that it might be helpful if our intercourse proceeded with the help of friendly acquaintance and goodwill instead of impersonal diplomacy and propaganda. I do not see how this could make things worse.[75]

But for John Foster Dulles in particular, such a casual approach would make things infinitely worse. At first, Eisenhower drafted a relatively amenable reply to Churchill, which would have read:

Foster and I foresee no special harm to our country's interests through your carrying out the intention suggested in your cable. We, of course, assume that the procedures followed would preclude any interpretation anywhere that your solitary pilgrimage portended or implied any break in our common front.[76]

But after Dulles had got his hands on the letter, it was turned into a condemnatory reply. When sent on 5 May it read:

Foster and I have considered it deeply and since you sought my views I must say that we would advise against it.

You will pardon me, I know, if I express a bit of astonishment that you think it appropriate to recommend Moscow to Molotov as a suitable meeting place. Uncle Joe used to plead ill health as an excuse for refusing to leave territory under the Russian flag or controlled by the Kremlin. That excuse no longer applies and while I do not for a minute suggest that progress toward peace should be baulked by mere matters of protocol, I do have a suspicion that anything the Kremlin could misinterpret as weakness or over-eagerness on our part would militate against success in negotiation.[77]

It was not just the choice of venue that Eisenhower thought was a bad idea. He suggested it would embarrass him, 'probably infuriate' the French, and undermine the united front and 'mutual confidence among the members of NATO and other free nations'. 'Naturally the final decision is yours,' he concluded, 'but I feel that the above factors are so important that I should in all candor and friendship lay them before you.'

When Churchill's response came two days later, it was that of a somewhat hurt, and chastened, man. 'I am not afraid of the "solitary pilgrimage" if I am sure in my heart that it may help forward the cause of peace and even at the worst can only do harm to my reputation,' he wrote.[78] 'I am fully alive to the impersonal and machine-made foundation of Soviet policy although under a veneer of civilities and hospitalities.'

'Of course,' he continued in more frustrated fashion,

> I would much rather go with you to any place you might appoint and that is, I believe, the best chance of a good result. I find it difficult to believe that we shall gain anything by an attitude of pure negation and your message to me certainly does not show much hope.

Churchill finished by saying that he would consult with his Cabinet on Eisenhower's 'weighty adverse advice', and thanking the President for 'the care and thought you have bestowed on my suggestion'.

In Eden's absence Churchill's occasional 'back-channel' diplomacy with the Soviets increased – much to the fury of Foreign Office officials, if they found out about it. His emissaries on these occasions were invariably Conservative backbenchers Julian Amery and Robert Boothby, who would report back after informal meetings with the new Soviet ambassador to London, Jacob Malik, his chargé d'affaires Georgy Rodionov and second secretary Georgy Zhivotovsky. Jock Colville, Churchill's private secretary, and Christopher Soames, his son-in-law and parliamentary private secretary, also once held private talks with Malik at the Soviet embassy.[79]

In fact Churchill did not discuss his summit initiative with Cabinet, nor did he heed Eisenhower's advice for caution. Instead he decided to unveil his 'easement' strategy four days later in the course of a major foreign policy speech in the House of Commons.

The Prime Minister spent the weekend of 9 and 10 May working on the speech at Chequers, assisted by Sir William Strang, Permanent Undersecretary at the Foreign Office, but was also joined for discussions over lunch on the Sunday by Lord Bernard Montgomery, the wartime victor of El Alamein, who was now NATO's deputy Supreme Allied Commander.

Churchill's normal impatience with the Foreign Office and its wariness did not extend to Strang, whom he liked and trusted. Strang was known (privately if not publicly) as an anti-appeaser in the 1930s and he was also an old Moscow hand, having worked in the British embassy in the same period.

When he returned to London on Sunday evening the Prime Minister asked Strang and Selwyn Lloyd, junior Foreign Office minister, to join him in Downing Street to help put the final touches to the speech. The two men arrived at 10 p.m. and left some time after midnight, with Churchill finally retiring at 2 a.m. – as was his habit.

When he stood up in the House of Commons at 3.32 p.m. on Monday 11 May, it was to deliver his last great speech in that setting. It was a masterly summation of the current international scene, reflecting on the current impasse in Korea, the deterioration of the position in Indo-China, the threat to British interests – and British troops – in Egypt, the future of Europe and the prospects for peace in the Middle East.

For nearly an hour this consummate history lesson was delivered with all the old eloquence, fluency and wit, punctuated by constant cheers and laughter from all sides of the House. Churchill opened by saying that there were many recent precedents for him taking charge of the Foreign Office. 'My knowledge, such as it is, is not mainly derived from books and documents about foreign affairs but from living through them for a long time.'[80]

On Korea – to loud cheers all round – he said he would be 'very content with even a truce or a ceasefire for the moment'. On Egypt, he warned its dictator, General Mohamed Naguib, that if his army, 'aided and trained by Nazi instructors and staff officers in unusual numbers', attacked British troops in the Suez Canal zone, British troops would have no choice but to defend themselves.

'I am advised that we are entirely capable of doing this without requiring any physical assistance from the United States or anyone else', he declared, to resounding cheers from his own backbenchers.

On the future of the continent, he referred to the 'inspiring and unconquerable cause of United Europe'. He noted the birth of the European Coal and Steel Community ('on which I believe we have observers'), and recognised that the much-delayed European Defence Community, which would incorporate German troops into a 'European army', was 'intensely needed'.

But Churchill then spelt out his attitude to a federal Europe:

> Where do we stand? We are not members of the European Defence Community, nor do we intend to be merged in a Federal European system. We feel we have a special relationship to both. This can be expressed by prepositions, by the preposition 'with' but not 'of' – we are with them, but not of them. We have our own Commonwealth and Empire.

Then it was onto the crucial closing passages, when he addressed what he described as the 'supreme event' in the world at present – the 'change of attitude' in the Kremlin following the death of Stalin.

In opposition to the recent speeches by Eisenhower and Dulles, Churchill declared that 'it would, I think, be a mistake to assume that nothing can be settled with Soviet Russia unless or until everything is settled'. Resolving just two of the 'difficulties' between West and East – peace in Korea, an Austrian treaty – 'might lead to an easement in relations for the next few years, which might in itself open new prospects to the security and prosperity of all nations and every continent'.

To loud cheers, he continued on the theme by asserting that 'it certainly would do no harm if, for a while, each state looked about for things to do which would be agreeable instead of being disagreeable to each other'. No desire to reach a 'general settlement of international policy … [should] impede any spontaneous and healthy evolution which may take place inside Russia'.

The Prime Minister then marched on to the real meat of his speech. To strong vocal support – especially from the Labour benches – he advocated a 'conference on the highest level' between the leading powers as soon as possible.

Such a summit meeting, he said, 'should not be overhung by a ponderous or rigid agenda, or led into mazes and jungles of technical details, zealously contested by hordes of experts and officials drawn up in vast, cumbrous array. The conference should be confined to the smallest number of Powers and persons possible.'

In other words, himself, Eisenhower and Malenkov in a Tehran or Yalta setting. 'It might well be that no hard-faced agreements would be reached, but there might be a general feeling among those gathered together that they might do something better than tear the human race, including themselves, into bits.'

Anticipating criticism for his initiative, he asserted: 'I do not see why anyone should be frightened at having a try for it … At the worst the participants in the meeting would have established more intimate contacts. At the best, we might have a generation of peace.'

The British press was united in its praise. *The Times* led the plaudits, describing it as 'magnificent in its broad survey and penetrating in its analysis'.[81] The pro-Labour *Daily Herald* welcomed a top-level conference, but suggested China should be involved.[82] The communist *Daily Worker* described the speech as the 'most pacific and hopeful speech delivered by a British minister in recent years'.[83]

In Moscow, *Pravda* and *Izvestia* merely published brief reports without any editorial comment. From the White House and the US Department of State there was silence. Filling the vacuum was Senator Alexander Wiley, Republican chairman of the Senate's Foreign Relations Committee, who commented: 'I'm for anything that might help the world out of this situation ... but the country should not let any meetings or talk of meetings induce us to let our guard down and invite another Pearl Harbor.'[84]

Editorials in American newspapers contrasted – not always favourably – the old Churchill who fought appeasement, who warned of the aggressive Soviet Union in his Fulton, Missouri, speech, with the new Churchill who promoted 'easement'. But the liberal American journalist Ed Murrow, renowned for his broadcasts from London in the Blitz, advised: 'In considering his proposals it might be useful to remember that this gallant old man has not always been wrong in his assessment of the direction in which the affairs of men and nations move.'[85]

Eden, recuperating at home, was appalled that Cabinet and the Foreign Office strategy had been so flagrantly ignored. Later he would claim that 'it must be long in history since any one speech did so much damage to its own side'.[86] Lord Robert 'Bobbety' Salisbury, Leader of the House of Lords, was equally furious, and in a telephone call Eden had to steer him away from thoughts of resignation.

Harold Macmillan too was contemplating his position. 'I shall not stay if we are now to seek "appeasement" and call in peace,' he wrote in his diary.[87] 'Churchill may know what he is doing, but he has not told the Cabinet as a whole.'

The housing minister worried that

we and the Americans are now in total disagreement ... the President is very naïve and inexperienced; Dulles is ignorant and stupid; some of the old Republicans are hopelessly reactionary – but we have got to get along with them. Malenkov has made a breach in the Anglo-American front such as Stalin never succeeded in doing.

Sir William Hayter, soon to succeed Sir Alvary Gascoigne as the British man in Moscow, thought the speech was a 'disaster'.[88] As he got his shoes under the table in coming months, he saw little profit in reaching out to the new Soviet government. 'It talks of coexistence, but they visualise it as the coexistence of the snake and the rabbit,' he stated.

But there was one man in the British political establishment who was able to have a rare face-to-face meeting with one of the Kremlin's leaders. Harold Wilson, thirty-seven, President of the Board of Trade in the Attlee government until his resignation over the introduction of NHS fees, had already established rare access to the Soviet government.

This came not just from his political role as a trade negotiator but also in his private capacity as economic adviser to Montague Meyer, Britain's biggest timber exporters, who did profitable business with the Soviet Union.

Just two days after Churchill's speech, Wilson set out on a long-planned visit behind the Iron Curtain that took in East Berlin, Prague, Budapest and – for the central part – Moscow. It would be the Labour left-winger's third visit to the Russian capital, and another reason for MI5 to update the file which it had kept on him since his first trip in 1947.

Wilson was the first major British politician to visit Moscow since the Berlin Blockade crisis of 1948 to 1949. He stayed in room 101 at the opulent Hotel National – which contained an intriguing mix of Tsarist furniture and antiques together with socialist realist artwork – which was routinely (for important visitors) bugged with cameras and audio equipment. However, there was nothing in Wilson's behaviour or the company he kept to excite the interest of the MGB.

On Thursday 21 May, accompanied by Sir Alvary Gascoigne, he had five hours of talks at the Kremlin, ninety minutes of which were with Anastas Mikoyan, the Minister of Trade he knew from previous trips, but also an hour with Molotov, one of the new 'big three' Soviet leaders.

The British embassy, mindful of its duty to the government of the day, told journalists that the Labour politician's meeting with Molotov had been purely a 'social call'. But Wilson, revelling in his role as a self-styled 'diplomat-at-large', had much more to say to the newsmen after his trip to the Kremlin.

He told them 'no questions were barred' and that he was able to talk 'freely and frankly' with the Soviet foreign minister.[89] 'Mr Molotov and I discussed the whole range of foreign affairs – in Kipling's phrase, from China to Peru. I had a lot of questions to ask and they were all answered.'

He went on, 'I found the Russians most cooperative and eager to extend trade with Britain, not only in regard to timber.' On the atmosphere in the country, post-Stalin, he observed: 'There does seem to be a little less tension under the new regime and the people themselves seem a lot gayer.'

On the subject of a summit or a 'four-power' foreign ministers meeting, Wilson said Molotov had been a 'little non-committal'. But he gathered the impression that a Soviet reply to Churchill's peace initiative would shortly be forthcoming.

On his way home Wilson stopped off in Budapest, where he pleaded the case of another casualty of the Cold War, Edgar Sanders, who was languishing in jail after being given a thirteen-year sentence in February 1950 on 'charges' of espionage and sabotage. Speaking on behalf of the government as well as the opposition party, Wilson made it clear there was no question of removing the trade embargo on Hungary until Mr Sanders was released.

On his return Wilson was debriefed by Churchill and Foreign Office officials. He certainly impressed his own party when he also gave it a verbal briefing a few weeks later – with Attlee congratulating him on a 'magnificent inside report'.[90]

Not everyone was convinced Wilson's intelligence from his Moscow visit was all it was claimed to be. Backbencher Richard Crossman reck-oned his colleague had done a magnificent job – 'of blowing out his information so that he could tell us everything that was happening in Russia'.

Harold's technique, he said, 'was to start by saying "Of course, I only have 2 per cent of the information necessary to form a judgement, but most of the pundits in Washington have only 1 per cent," and then to go on to give judgements on everything.'

MI5 filed away what information they could acquire about Wilson's visit. The spies would continue to watch the MP for Huyton as his rise to the top of British politics accelerated in the coming years.

* * *

In public Eisenhower and Dulles tried hard to suppress their irritation about Churchill's eagerness for engagement with the new Soviet regime. At one of his regular press conferences on 14 May, the President merely said he 'had no objection to Sir Winston's proposal' but would like to see 'something that would be evidence of good faith all round' before committing himself and his government to a Potsdam-style summit.[91]

In private there were no such inhibitions. In one National Security Council meeting in May the President 'wondered whether Sir Win-ston's faculties and judgment were not deteriorating'.[92] In another, just two days after Churchill's speech, Eisenhower told his colleagues 'our relations with Great Britain had become worse in the last few weeks than at any time since the end of the war'.[93] Even Walter Bedell Smith, Churchill's great friend, acknowledged relations 'were now not good'.

Eisenhower's election victory had been built around the expectation that he would bring an end to the war in Korea – but in May that pros-pect was not on the horizon. Negotiations about a truce were about to restart after a six-month recess, and the possibility of exchanging prisoners of war was being discussed for the first time.

But on the battlefield, after the calm of April, there were signs that the communists were preparing to increase the size and frequency of attacks. Worrying intelligence reports clearly indicated troops were being moved up to forward positions from the northern coastal areas. There were increasing contacts between the 8th Army and enemy reconnaissance patrols on the front line.

At three dramatic NSC meetings on successive Wednesdays in May, a frustrated Eisenhower loosened previous reservations and started to seriously consider using the atom bomb to hasten the war's end. On each occasion he was guided by the NSC Planning Board's Document 147, which offered him six options for fresh action, ranging from a modest increase in military action to a massive full-scale offensive in Korea and an air and naval assault against Manchuria and China. For the latter, the military would need 'authority to use atomic weapons' from the President.

At the meeting on 6 May, General Bradley briefed about the communists' military build-up, pointing out that planes had been reinstated in four airfields in North Korea. Eisenhower wondered whether these would be a good target on which to test the effectiveness of an atom bomb. 'At any rate,' he added, 'he had reached the point of being convinced that we have got to consider the atomic bomb as simply another weapon in our arsenal.'[94] However, Bradley doubted whether those fields would be the best target for an A-bomb.

A week later Eisenhower assessed the financial benefit of using the ultimate weapon. 'It might be cheaper, dollar-wise, to use atomic weapons in Korea than to continue to use conventional weapons against the dugouts which honeycombed the hills along which the enemy forces were presently deployed.'[95]

Bedell Smith was concerned about the reaction of UN allies to a fresh, massive assault inside and outside Korea. He now raised the spectre of a third world war. 'We should not underestimate the severe Chinese Communist reaction ... [and] we must count on a probable Soviet intervention and on the real possibility of general war.'[96]

Vice-President Richard Nixon said any choice they now made must address the long-term problem confronting the West 'when the Soviet Union had amassed a sufficient stockpile of atomic weapons to deal us a critical blow and rob us of the initiative in foreign policy'.[97]

Bedell Smith reckoned that if armistice was the eventual outcome in Korea, 'Congress and the people would begin to tot up the net results of two years of savage fighting, and there would be bitter criticism of the small result ... of this long and costly effort.'

A clearly impatient Eisenhower retorted, 'If people raised hell when they contemplated these results, the thing to do would be to ask them to volunteer for front-line action in a continued Korean war.'[98]

A week later, on 20 May, the same arguments were played out again. Once more, the Joint Chiefs of Staff made it clear that expanding the war outside Korea would require the atom bomb. The conversation then moved from the theoretical to the practical. What would need to be done, asked Eisenhower, for America to be ready to mount this operation, say, in May next year?

General Bradley thought they would immediately have to bring the South Korean forces up to twenty divisions. General Collins said the Marine division, and a regimental combat team from the 82nd Airborne Division, were ready to go. 'In three months,' Collins added, 'we should have to begin the selection and the movement of American forces ... to augment our strength in Korea.'[99]

'The quicker the operation was mounted, the less the danger of Soviet intervention,' Eisenhower averred.[100] 'Everything [...] should be in readiness before the blow actually fell.' But he stressed his worry at the prospect of world war beginning in Manchuria.

The President then turned his thoughts to consulting his key allies, pondering whether Churchill and French President René Mayer should be brought up to speed about America's new plan in 'an informal and exploratory way'.[101]

As the meeting neared its conclusion, Eisenhower fretted that details of the military briefing given by the joint chiefs might leak from the room, and demanded that a record be kept of all twenty-six present.

He finished the meeting by reiterating that the extreme action proposed by the joint chiefs to end the war in Korea – which included the use of atomic bombs – should be accepted as a general guide forward if the negotiations broke down. Still the President's anxieties continued right to the very end. He voiced his concern 'over the possibility of intervention by the Soviets'.[102]

Dewey Short, the Republican chairman of the House Armed Services Committee, came away from a meeting at the White House that week to tell reporters: 'The Reds are stalling … [and] the Eisenhower administration is becoming convinced that the Communists do not want peace in Korea.'[103]

Meanwhile, on the front line, the battle continued. In one notable skirmish, 300 Chinese soldiers smashed through barbed wire and minefields at Chorwon on the western front and charged an Allied outpost, engaging UN infantrymen in a short but savage hand-to-hand battle. Early reports said 100 Chinese were killed and 130 wounded in close fighting and by artillery fire.

Negotiations between the two sides were set to resume on Monday 25 May. But hopes for peace – let alone a truce – were looking forlorn. The possibility of an American atomic assault on the Korean peninsula was moving closer.

Uprising on the streets of East Berlin – the first chink in the Soviet armour.
© Associated Press

CHAPTER 6

'WE GOVERN BY POPULAR WILL'

The rousing sound of William Walton's orchestral march 'Crown Imperial', which had accompanied the exhilarating fly-past by squadrons of RAF Meteor and Royal Canadian Sabre jet fighters, slowly faded away. Television viewers watched the newly crowned Queen Elizabeth II raise a gloved hand to acknowledge the departing pilots, then turn to give a final wave to the thousands of rain-soaked well-wishers on The Mall before leaving the balcony with her family for the sanctuary of Buckingham Palace.

Live coverage of this epic Coronation day on Tuesday 2 June then cut to the woman who had started it all off over seven hours ago. The 27-year-old continuity announcer Sylvia Peters, dressed in a flowery evening gown and pearls, sat alone, but looking assured, before the cameras in the BBC's Alexandra Palace studios in north London. She urged viewers to stay tuned for the evening schedule, which included a speech by Sir Winston Churchill and an interview with mountaineer Raymond Greene (brother of Graham and Hugh Carleton Greene) about the triumph of Edmund Hillary and Tenzing Norgay in climbing Mount Everest.

Sylvia, who had met the young Queen before the big day, suspected she had been chosen to introduce the Coronation coverage in part because she was the same age as the monarch. She was being modest, however, as she was fully qualified for the task, having had six years' experience of broadcasting live, without an autocue and with little or no rehearsal.

A petite brunette with large eyes and a flashing smile, she was very much out of the school of the charming, decorative hostess that the BBC management favoured. Sylvia possessed an excellent memory, which she certainly needed on this occasion as she was only handed the script for the broadcast the night before.

On a simple set, with the map of the Coronation procession route as a backdrop, she had heralded this extraordinary event for the nation at 10.15 a.m. with the words: 'This is a great and joyous day for us all.' Now, at 5.26 p.m. after those many hours of near flawless coverage by the BBC's army of accomplished technicians and its team of polished reporters, led by the incomparable Richard Dimbleby, Sylvia justifiably and proudly declared that this had been 'the greatest day in the history of television'.

The figures alone would back her assertion. It would later be calculated that nearly 8 million people in Britain tuned in at home, with 10 million more crowded into other people's homes, and a further 1.5 million viewing the ceremony in cinemas, halls and pubs. That amounted to 56 per cent of the population – nearly twice as many as listened to it on the radio.[1]

A further 1.5 million in western Europe watched the Coronation too, relayed to them by their local television stations. In addition Operation Pony Express enabled full film recordings of the event – the moment it was over – to be flown over the Atlantic on three Canberra jet bombers to Canada, and then on to America. In all, it was estimated that over 2 million Canadians watched the broadcast, along with a staggering 85 million Americans.

Television, ably supported by radio, had made the Coronation one of the first – if not the first – truly global experiences. Even the Soviets ceased jamming the BBC's General Overseas Service frequencies for the duration of the event, and Politburo chief Molotov was seen to attend a party at the British embassy to celebrate the occasion.

For the *Daily Express*, one of the papers that had campaigned long and hard for full coverage of the Coronation – inside Westminster

Abbey as well as on the streets of the capital – it had been 'Queen's Day – TV's Day'.[2] The BBC had set 'brilliant new standards in linking the crown with the people', wrote correspondent Robert Cannell. Television cameras had 'democratised representations by giving the "ordinary" viewing public access to a state ritual usually reserved for the privileged few'.

The *Manchester Guardian*'s radio critic agreed that the BBC had carried it off with the 'greatest skill and care'.[3] 'It was surprising, even to those who expected it to be well done, to see how clearly the cameras showed all the important movements and passages of the prolonged service, without ever faltering or taking a shot without significance.'

For the people of Britain, still wearing the cloak of austerity, living in industrial towns still scarred by bomb craters and with rationing yet to be completely lifted, it was an uplifting, unifying experience. But the future of this exciting new – or newish – medium was certainly not settled.

Churchill, no great advocate of television – he had had many tussles with the BBC over the years – had ultimately bowed to the clamour of public opinion the previous October. Many bishops, politicians and others in the British elite had not wanted the cameras in Westminster Abbey – 'beyond the west door' – disturbing the intimate, spiritual centuries-old ritual between monarchy and church.

But Churchill told the Cabinet, 'we govern by popular will', having been persuaded by the massive opinion poll surge in favour of the most widespread TV coverage possible.[4] But he and very many in the country's elite were still unsure about what cultural and social part television ought to play in national life when normality resumed after the festivities.

The *Manchester Guardian* kicked off the debate two days after the spectacle. An editorial claimed that radio had already had a 'corrosive effect' on politics by allowing voters to listen to major political speeches in their own homes and keeping them away from candidates' meetings during the campaign.[5] 'With television as an added attraction to armchair politics', it went on, the hard benches in the schoolroom or suburban hall are likely to become even more sparsely filled. When almost all his constituents can see a Prime Minister at home, where is the audience for the local MP? Valuable as it is that millions of people should have a ringside seat at great national occasions, there are undoubted dangers in the withering of national life.

The writer did acknowledge that it might just work the other way, and 'if the competition of great events forces local leadership to try and interpret them more clearly in terms of everyday life, it may be all to the good'.

In the letters column of *The Times*, five 'grandees' issued a plea to the government that while television might now be safe with the BBC, it should not be placed in the hands of other parties. Under the headline 'A Call to Social Responsibility', this cross-party grouping warned of the dangers of commercial television.[6]

The group consisted of Churchill's great friend the Liberal politician Violet Bonham Carter; his wartime Chancellor and atom bomb adviser Lord Waverley (formerly Sir John Anderson); his one-time rival the former Foreign Secretary Lord Halifax; trade unionist and Labour MP Tom O'Brien; and businessman and wartime head of the British Food Mission to the United States Lord Brand.

This eminent group noted that over 1 million viewers now held television licences, with that figure expected to rise by 600,000 a year. 'Before long ... most of the population of Great Britain, including millions of children, are likely to become regular viewers. We believe that the development of this new medium of information and entertainment calls for the highest sense of social responsibility in all those engaged in it.'

They went to say that 'commercialization – now imminently threatened – is fraught with dangers to those spiritual and intellectual values which the BBC has nobly striven to maintain'. They urged the government not to bow to the 'intense pressure' for a commercial channel.

The letter signed off by saying that the group was planning to form a national television council, specifically 'to resist the introduction of commercial television into this country, and to encourage the healthy development of public service television in the national interest'.

Commercial television's case took another blow when it was learned how the Coronation broadcast had been handled by the television stations in the United States. They had undertaken to package the film with 'the greatest dignity and good taste', but there were some lapses, NBC's *Today* show being a prime example.

The programme included advertisements, news items, spot announcements and the occasional interview. A one-minute commercial for a deodorant was played just before the network came back for the anointing of the sovereign. Then just before the crown was lowered onto Queen Elizabeth's head, NBC switched to an advert for Blake's shampoo, which was claimed to 'Make Every Girl Look Queenly'. At one point the show's presenter, Hans von Kaltenborn, asked rhetorically: 'Is this show put on by the British for a psychological boost to their somewhat shaky Empire?'

However, it was the appearance of the show's engaging and hugely popular comic mascot, a one-year-old chimpanzee named J. Fred Muggs, that caused the real furore. The ape was respectfully 'interviewed' in the course of the Holy Communion service by the show's host Dave Garroway, who asked him, 'Do they have Coronations deep in the jungle? Do you have a king and queen, or do you just live and enjoy life?'

Of course the British newspapers, particularly those that were habitually anti-American, had a field day with all this, responding with a mixture of outrage, some serious comment and numerous cartoons. The tone of the coverage in the tabloids was set by the *Daily Express* headline: 'The crowning of J. Fred Muggs'.[7]

Typically, 'Cassandra' in the *Daily Mirror* exploded:

> What they did to our Coronation story is a repulsive and hideous example of squalid big business using the cathode-ray tube ... soup and soaps were

thrust into sacred scenes and an obscene interview with a chimpanzee made a mockery of centuries of our history and tradition, and motor-car salesmen shouted that their cars were the 'Crown Jewels of America'.[8]

It was reported that the BBC had asked its New York office for a full report prior to making a formal protest to the US networks. Ben Gross, columnist for New York's *Daily News*, commented: 'Whether or not we approve of royalty, the fact remains that a Coronation is a solemn religious ceremony – and therefore should not be cheapened. I hate to admit it, but the British have a point.'[9]

Yet despite the undoubted quality of the BBC's coverage that day, juxtaposed with the poor judgement displayed by some US networks, the reality was that British television – without the financial resources – was lagging some way behind its American counterparts. 'The critics of commercial television concede that when American TV is bad, it is the world's worst,' wrote the *Baltimore Sun*'s London bureau reporter.[10] 'But when it is good, it is superb.'

In the relationship between politicians and television, US programmes were innovative in a way that would have horrified most British newspaper editors. On the day after the Coronation, 50 million Americans watched their President act as master of ceremonies in a half-hour live broadcast from the 'Fish Room' in the White House.

This 'folksy panel show', carried on all four national TV networks and radio, saw Eisenhower direct a supporting cast of four Cabinet colleagues who reported on the policies and plans of their respective departments. Quickly dubbed the 'family circle telecast' by newspapers, the President began seated at a table for some introductory remarks. He was then on the move, walking over to a desk where a stack of mail had been placed, illustrative of the 3,000 letters a week received at the White House.

The President read out a letter from a housewife in Pawtucket, Rhode Island, who told him that she was worried about how he was going to balance the national budget, 'with all the money you have

Convicted atom bomb spies Julius and Ethel Rosenberg. Their desperate pleas for clemency were ultimately rejected by President Eisenhower. SOURCE: UNITED STATES LIBRARY OF CONGRESS

The funeral cortège at Leconfield, East Yorkshire, for five of the seven Avro Lincoln bomber airmen shot down by Soviet fighters. They were buried – with full military honours – at St Catherine's Church.

ABOVE Members of the Duke of Wellington's Regiment take a well-earned break during the fierce Battle of the Hook in May 1953, in the closing exchanges of the Korean War.

SOURCE: MINISTRY OF DEFENCE

LEFT Syngman Rhee, the autocratic South Korean leader whose unpredictable behaviour in armistice negotiations infuriated his American allies.

ABOVE The FBI file picture of John Archibald Wheeler. The physicist lost a top-secret H-bomb paper and set off panic in the White House.

SOURCE: FBI, FREEDOM OF INFORMATION ACT REQUEST

LEFT J. Edgar Hoover, who launched one of the biggest ever inquiries in his 48-year tenure as FBI chief into Wheeler's missing paper.

SOURCE: UNITED STATES LIBRARY OF CONGRESS

ABOVE The frigate HMS *Snipe* with thirty-two Royal Marines on board, dispatched to the Falklands to remove the 'invading' Argentinians.

LEFT Captain Jimmy Priestly Robinson, the young US pilot who was killed in the Ivy Mike H-bomb test.

Colonel Frank Schwable,
the American pilot captured
and apparently brainwashed
by the Chinese in North Korea.
SOURCE: USMC MILITARY HISTORY DIVISION

The top-secret Kelvedon Hatch underground nuclear bunker (pictured today) in Essex,
designed to look like an innocent rural bungalow. © ROGER HERMISTON

Melinda Maclean with her boys Fergus and Donald Jr. In September she fled with them to the Soviet Union to be reunited with her husband Donald, the 'missing British diplomat' (and KGB spy).

The mannequin inhabitants of a house in Doom Town in the Nevada desert – about to have the test atom bomb 'Annie' dropped on them live on US television.

ABOVE It was an armistice, not a peace agreement – separate tables for the two sides at the Korean War armistice signing ceremony at Panmunjom in July.

SOURCE: US DEPARTMENT OF DEFENSE

LEFT Winston Churchill and Italian Prime Minister Alcide De Gasperi relaxing in the garden at No. 10 on 23 June – just hours before the former suffered a stroke from which his doctor feared he would never recover.

© HULTON DEUTSCH / GETTY IMAGES

Brendan Bracken, Churchill's great friend and confidant who played a key part in keeping news of his stroke out of the press.

SOURCE: YOUSUF KARSH,
DUTCH NATIONAL ARCHIVES

Mao Tse-Tung. The Chinese leader, worried by the effect the Korean War was having on his five-year plan for industrialisation back home, eventually agreed to an end to the conflict.

to spend for guns and planes. The sums are so huge I really find it impossible to grasp them.'

'I might tell the lady so do I!' Eisenhower told viewers. 'I chose the letter because it brings up this great problem of security and the money that it costs.' Then, acting like a 'principal introducing the teachers on parents' visiting day', he invited his subordinates George Humphrey (Treasury Secretary); Herbert Brownell Jr (Attorney General); Ezra Taft Benson (Agriculture Secretary); and – refreshingly, a woman – Oveta Culp Hobby (Secretary of Health, Education and Welfare) to set out their stall.

This was no spontaneous briefing, more a carefully managed production; the five had undergone not one but two dress rehearsals in previous days. But there were no typed speeches and they talked mostly straight at the camera; only occasionally did eyes flicker from side to side to look at the big cue cards, which bore phrases like those that an orator jots down for an off-the-cuff speech.

The inspiration for this dabbling in 'direct democracy', masterminded by Eisenhower's creative press secretary James Hagerty, came from President Roosevelt's 'fireside chats' broadcast on radio and – in more recent memory – Vice-President Richard Nixon's 'Checkers' speech the previous September.

Roosevelt was a master at talking directly to the people; his warm voice and easy reading style helped insert him right into the heart of the American living room. He had all the devices of a good talker – seriousness, gaiety, sarcasm, humour, vivid figures of speech. 'Daddy's here and everything will be all right' was the impression he sought to give, and it worked brilliantly. Few doubted that he would have been just as relaxed and effective in front of a television camera.

That was radio, however, and the example of how a politician could shape television to his advantage came from Nixon's impassioned defence after being accused of managing a 'secret' campaign fund for his own personal use in the autumn of 1952.

After a vicious newspaper campaign, Nixon's position as Eisenhower's running mate was in grave jeopardy. So he chose to go on primetime TV and fight the charges by talking to 60 million Americans directly. Appearing utterly transparent, disclosing full details of his financial affairs, he also painted in something of his backstory; the patriot from a modest Californian background whose wife had no mink coat but instead wore 'a respectable Republican cloth coat'.

But the climax of the broadcast was a reference to his daughters' new puppy, a cocker spaniel called Checkers, a gift he had received while on the campaign trail. There was barely a dry eye in the house as he told viewers: 'And you know the kids, like all kids, loved the dog, and I just want to say this, right now, that regardless of what they say about it, we are going to keep it.'[11]

Nixon's speech was a landmark moment in the relationship between politicians and television. Like Roosevelt in his 'fireside chats', he had been able to leap over the heads of the media and take his seat in the public's front room. Small wonder then, as Eisenhower's show was dissected, Nixon was given credit as its 'founding father'.

Although a little fidgety and a bit stiff in manner, characteristic of the army man he was, Eisenhower managed an easy conversational style and his broadcast was generally deemed to have been a success. It produced some good news lines too, the best of which came when he declared that there would be 'no new Munich' and that his administration would permit 'no risk of a general war'.

If there was to be one, however, America was well prepared. The day after Eisenhower's broadcast, the biggest atom bomb yet was dropped from a B-36 bomber and exploded on the Nevada Proving Grounds. This was the eleventh and last in the very public spring series of tests known as Operation Upshot–Knothole; the yield of the bomb, dubbed 'Climax', was put at over 60 kilotons, nearly four times as great as Annie, the first atomic bomb detonated live on television back in March.

* * *

At the beginning of June, while the eyes of the world were trained on London, cracks in the Soviet edifice began to emerge. The first was in Czechoslovakia, where on the eve of the Coronation the authorities in Pilsen fought to wrest back control after a day-long show of unrest from workers.

This historic city in western Bohemia, freed from the Germans by General George Patton's 3rd Army at the end of the Second World War, might have avoided the Soviet yoke had it not been for a certain General Dwight Eisenhower. Having to balance military and political objectives, Eisenhower ordered Patton to stop at Pilsen, thus sacrificing Prague to the Red Army – in return for increased cooperation from Stalin in Europe and with the war against Japan. The Moscow-backed communist regime assumed control of Pilsen, and the whole of the country, in the three years that followed.

The story of what had happened in Pilsen – whose citizens still nursed fond memories of the liberating Americans – took a week to filter through to the West. Unconfirmed reports were finally authenticated by the ruling Communist Party's mouthpiece, *Pravda Pilsen*, which admitted workers had torn down and trampled underfoot pictures of Stalin and Klement Gottwald (first leader of the puppet Czech state) and orchestrated a riot 'with the intention of overthrowing the Communist regime'.

The latter comment was a classic overstatement by the communist press. In fact, the Pilsen protests were driven first and foremost by economic not ideological motives, although there were enough manifestations of the latter to suggest that the Czech people were not happy with their lot five years after democracy was stripped from them by the Kremlin.

On 30 May, the regime, in financial trouble, announced a comprehensive devaluation of the koruna ('crown'), erasing nearly all savings and reducing worker living standards by as much as 10 per cent. Rationing of food at subsidised prices was stopped and work quotas increased.

Furious employees at the famous Lenin Škoda arms factory in Pilsen were the drivers of the uprising. Their management had paid their wages for May one week earlier than normal – thus reducing their value by nearly 80 per cent after the currency reform was introduced.

At around 9 a.m. on 1 June, a crowd of around 4,000 began marching towards the City Hall, mainly Škoda workers but also students, office workers and even some rebelling security police and soldiers.[12] The civic building was stormed by a group of 150, who burned documents, ripped down the Soviet flag and waved the US Stars and Stripes, and smashed busts of Stalin, Lenin, Malenkov and Gottwald.

A large portrait of Edvard Beneš, the last democratic President of Czechoslovakia, was displayed from an office window, and some of the protesters managed to broadcast over the city radio slogans such as, 'We want freedom! We demand justice! Down with the communists! We want free elections!'

With the local police and security forces unable to control increasingly unruly crowds, the regional Communist Party called urgently for armed reinforcements. Detachments of the People's Militia together with border and interior guards eventually arrived from Prague in the late afternoon.

Among the pitched battles the most violent took place at gate 4 of the Škoda plant, where – according to some sources – submachine guns were turned on rioters, some of whom had destroyed machinery. Remarkably, there were few – if any – fatalities, although the toll of injured reached several hundred. By the evening the special forces had control and the supposed ringleaders – although this was very much a spontaneous uprising of anger – were in detention.

Many workers in the industrial districts around Ostrava downed tools, as did thirty-two factories in Prague, and there were also stoppages in towns such as Strakonice and Vimperk in southern Bohemia. But the protests receded and President Antonín Zápotocký vowed that the currency reform would go ahead, typically blaming this 'counter-revolutionary putsch' on the 'agents of Western imperialism', while awaiting instructions from Moscow on what kind of retribution should be meted out.[13]

Before he heard from the Soviet authorities, the second, far bigger, uprising in the Soviet bloc had taken place. Pilsen was worrying, but the extraordinary events of Wednesday 17 June in East Berlin constituted the most serious threat to Soviet rule behind the Iron Curtain to date.

As with Pilsen, the catalyst for dissent came from the repressive measures that the regime felt were necessary to step up the pace of industrialisation. This time it was announced that from 30 June, all East German workers would have to improve their production quotas – known as 'norms' – by 10 per cent, without any increase in pay.

The beleaguered East Germans were already weary of the strain on their lives and living standards as a result of the Kremlin's attempt to quickly transform their country into a Stalinist command economy. Alongside the pressures on them to step up industrial and military production came the tightening of political control, and a corresponding crackdown on dissent. The increase in 'norms' was the final straw.

Churchill, now acting Foreign Secretary in Eden's absence, monitored the crisis in East Berlin closely and asked his private secretary Anthony Montague Browne to explain the norms system. In the sort of admirably clear reply the Prime Minister appreciated, he wrote:

If the workers produce less than their 'norms' they are subject to various sanctions, such as fines, cuts in rations, or even imprisonment. If they produce in excess of their 'norms' they are given various advantages. It is a common practice to fix the 'norms' by the output of super-workers or 'Stakhanovites' (named after Stakhanov, a [Soviet] miner who produced unparalleled quantities of coal). This naturally makes for discontent.[14]

Staring at what was, to all intent and purposes, a compulsory pay cut, workers' discontent began to spill over on the morning of Tuesday

16 June. At first there was a degree of spontaneity about the protest as construction workers from two sites, the Hospital Friedrichshain and Stalinallee Block 40 – the latter, ironically, a big new housing block built with great fanfare in honour of the now-departed Soviet leader – put down their tools and marched towards the Socialist Unity Party of Germany (SED) headquarters, the 'House of Ministries' in Leipziger Strasse.

What had been a crowd of 400 swelled to around 3,000 by the time they reached the government building, with more workers and other East Berliners joining the ranks all the time as word of the protest spread. Meanwhile, in other parts of the city, strikes were breaking out at construction sites and industrial plants, and plans were drawn up for a general strike the following day.

At the House of Ministries the shouts went up – 'Decrease production quotas!', 'Lower prices in state-owned stores!', along with chants of 'Down with the government!' and 'We want butter not an army!' The gathering called for SED leaders Otto Grotewohl and Walter Ulbricht to come and address their concerns, but instead two lower-ranking ministers, Fritz Selbmann and Professor Robert Havemann, appeared. However, their appeals for calm were quickly drowned out by the noise of an increasingly fractious crowd.

Inside the building at 2 p.m., the SED Politburo convened for its regular Tuesday afternoon meeting and, shaken by the protests, decided to abandon the forced increase to worker norms. But when the concession was announced to the crowd it was clear that it was too late. Their demands now stretched further, for free elections and the resignation of the government.

With the help of the American-run *Rundfunk im Amerikanischen Sektor* ('Radio in the American Sector' – RIAS) radio station in West Berlin – which could be picked up across most of East Germany – news of the proposed strike spread quickly, and workers in the bigger cities of Dresden, Leipzig, Frankfurt and Rostock were all geared up to play their part.

Now the regime decided to counter-attack. Grotewohl and Ulbricht suddenly emerged in the early evening to give speeches in the Frie-drichstadt-Palast before a commandeered crowd of 3,000, while outside blue-shirted members of the 'Free German Youth' (strikingly akin to the Hitler Youth) flooded the streets and engaged in fierce clashes with the protesting workers and their allies.

Riots continued in parts of East Berlin overnight, and worrying in-telligence was reaching the authorities of plans by the protesters for the following day – not just in Berlin, but in the rest of East Germany. In the late evening, Ulbricht met with his state security chief to discuss the deployment of special units of the Volkspolizei, and he was also in touch with Vladimir Semyonov, Soviet high commissioner for Germany, about bringing Soviet troops and tanks into Berlin in the coming hours.

On the morning of Wednesday 17 June, East Berliners awoke to find the front page of the Communist Party organ *Neues Deutschland* dominated by reports of Ulbricht's speech to party members. Just a small paragraph at the bottom of the page was left to reflect on the real story of the previous twenty-four hours. 'On Tuesday groups of Fascist provocateurs, smuggled in from West Berlin, caused incidents in the democratic sector of Berlin. The population joined the People's Police in opposing the bandits, who were scattered and driven off.'[15]

At 7 a.m. some 10,000 workers set off from Stalinallee, the original home of the revolt, and headed once more to the House of Ministries. Many were construction workers wearing the clothes of their trade – white overalls for masons, black corduroy smocks for carpenters, heavy hobnailed boots and threadbare work suits for labourers. As they marched in the pouring rain, once more the numbers grew, until this crowd was 25,000 strong.

Confronted by one human wall of grey-raincoated Volkspolizei, arms locked elbow to elbow, the huge crowd simply smashed through it, disregarding the thudding truncheons to surge on, past soldiers and armoured cars that had been brought onto the streets.

Emerging from side streets, parks and vacant lots still heaped with wartime rubble were more workers, women and children who drifted into the main march. Other more regimented columns of workers were also absorbed, until the numbers had reached nigh on 100,000.

Truckloads of Soviet infantrymen with tommy guns looked on impassively as the crowds reached the government buildings on Leipziger Strasse and Friedrichstrasse. They chanted 'Freedom!', 'We demand the overthrow of the government!', 'Ivans [Russians] go home!' and 'We don't want to be slaves!' They even broke out into a chant of the forbidden anthem 'Deutschland über alles'.

Some of the protesters hurled bricks, sticks and stones, smashing ministry windows. Rioters within the group broke into a nearby state-run store to loot and destroy. Then the demonstrators charged down to Potsdamer Platz, where the Soviet, British and US sectors converged.

There, before a watching crowd of thousands of astonished Western onlookers, they uprooted sector border signs, tore down propaganda billboards and communist flags and set fire to everything that would burn in the rain. At the historic Brandenburg Gate, once the triumphal arch of the armies of the Kaiser and then Hitler, and now the symbol of German division, two men climbed to the top and to resounding cheers tore down the Soviet flag, tossing it to the ground, where the crowd gleefully set it alight.

One of the men, 23-year-old truck driver Horst Ballentin, went away and returned from a West Berlin shop with the black, red and gold German flag.[16] The crowd watched in awed silence as once more Horst climbed the staircase to the top of the arch and set to work to hang the new flag, with its complicated system of cranks and ropes. Just as he completed the task, machine-gun fire from the nearby Soviet armoured cars spattered the flagpole, but Horst and his friend threw themselves to the floor just in time and fled down the staircase.

There was a different kind of close escape for one senior East German politician, Otto Nuschke, the Deputy Prime Minister who had helped draft the Constitution of the German Democratic Republic. Nuschke and his driver blundered into an angry mob, who recognised him and dragged him from his Tatra car.

Nuschke managed to struggle back into the vehicle, and his driver – with no view as protesters had clambered onto his front bonnet – lost his bearings and inadvertently drove into the American sector. When he stopped to get out, fortunately US soldiers were on hand to guide him away from the angry mob. Nuschke and his driver were detained at a police station, where he was interrogated but released to return to East Berlin two days later.

Just after noon, the carnival mood was shattered as the Soviet soldiers and Volkspolizei began to fire on the crowds. Witnesses in West Berlin reckoned the former aimed above the crowds but believed that the latter fired directly at their countrymen and women. Then an even bigger threat emerged as a dozen T-34 Soviet tanks lumbered down Leipziger Strasse, their 86mm guns pointing into Potsdamer Platz.

The demonstrators hurled bricks and Molotov cocktails at the tanks, some youths clambering onto their turrets, while the soldiers responded with increasing gunfire, often directed straight into the crowds. Parts of central East Berlin started to resemble a battlefield as the women of the Red Cross received scores of bleeding men and women at their emergency aid station, while the constant wailing sirens of West Berlin ambulances sounded as they took away the injured who had been carried to the border line.

Yet more Soviet troops and Volkspolizei were drafted and gradually the sting was taken out of the protest. At 1 p.m. the Soviet commandant of East Berlin, Major General Pyotr Dibrova, declared martial law, warning that any group of more than three people in the streets would be fired upon. All train and tram traffic in the sector was halted.

Although the main demonstration was dispersed by now, sporadic fighting continued throughout the afternoon and into the early evening. Outside Berlin, martial law was declared in 167 out of 217 districts throughout East Germany. In some 560 towns and villages there had been demonstrations, with the industrial centres of Magdeburg, Merseburg, Halle, Jena, Görlitz and Brandenburg rising up with particular vigour.

An armoured battalion with tanks was deployed to the city of Görlitz, where a crowd of 30,000 destroyed SED offices, stormed the prison and released inmates. The protesters around the country, just like their counterparts in East Berlin, had all extended their workplace grievances to call for free elections and greater democracy.

Three hundred miles away in the West German capital Bonn, Chancellor Konrad Adenauer addressed the Parliament following an emergency Cabinet meeting. He was determined to tread carefully at this stage, to avoid any inflammatory statements and watch the revolt play out.

So on the one hand, to loud cheers, he declared that the uprising was a 'great demonstration of the will for freedom of the German people of the Soviet zone and of Berlin' and assured the demonstrators that his government was 'with them in heartfelt solidarity'. But on the other he warned that the people should not be 'carried away by provocation into committing rash acts which could endanger their lives and liberty'.[17]

With their headquarters under assault earlier in the day, Ulbricht, Grotewohl and the other SED leaders had been forced to flee to the sanctuary of the Soviet headquarters in Karlshorst. This was now entirely a Soviet-run operation, and their troops, aided by the Stasi (East German secret police), moved around the streets of East Berlin overnight detaining thousands of people.

One of the 'ringleaders' they had already picked up was Willi Karl Göttling, a 35-year-old unemployed truck driver. Married with two young daughters, Ingeborg, who was seven and Renate, who was six, Willi had been out of work for two years because of a weak heart.[18]

At 9.30 a.m. on Tuesday 16 June, he left his two-bedroomed flat in Reinickendorf, in the French sector – which his family shared with his sister and brother-in-law – for his weekly trip across the city to the labour exchange on Sonnenallee in the district of Neukölln, in the

American sector. There he would pick up his meagre benefit cheque of 36 marks, hoping to be back in time for his favourite lunch dish, meatballs with cauliflower.

Willi's journey necessitated crossing briefly through the Soviet sector on the elevated portion of the U-Bahn (subway). On this morning, as he was on his way home, he got stranded in the Soviet sector after subway workers joined the protests and stopped the trains running. Piecing together exactly what happened to Willi after that point is more difficult.

Some reports suggested that he was detained by the Volkspolizei in a wave of arrests on Tuesday 16th, held overnight and then released. On Wednesday 17th, as the uprising reached its height, one eyewitness placed him at the main demonstration at Leipziger Strasse. Later that day, at Stasi headquarters in Lichtenberg, a student named Gottschling recalled encountering a man fitting Göttling's description wearing a bandage on his head, his face clearly badly beaten.

Then at 4 p.m. on Thursday 18 June, East German radio broadcast this statement: 'It is hereby announced that Willi Göttling, a citizen of West Berlin, who was acting as a foreign spy, and who was an organiser of the disturbances in East Berlin, has been condemned to death by shooting. The sentence has been carried out.'

Time magazine's correspondent reported that Willi had been marched onto a field not far from the Brandenburg Gate and executed by a Soviet firing squad. A notice to that effect was pinned up on one of the main government buildings.[19]

Shock at Willi's killing reverberated around East and West Berlin, and spy agencies scrambled to see if there was any truth in the accusation that he was one of their agents. It quickly became clear that it was not. Cecil Lyon, director of the US high commission's office in Berlin, telegrammed Dulles three hours after the broadcast of Willi's death to report that he had canvassed the high commission, the US Army's Counter-Intelligence Corps (CIC) and the Department of Army

Detachment (DAD – the cover organisation for the CIA). '[They] have no (repeat no) knowledge of him.'[20]

Göttling's grieving wife testified that his only real interest was his local church. 'My husband was always very quiet, very reserved. We had been married for twelve years, he lived only for his family, his children were everything to him.'[21]

Yet the pretence that Göttling was a Western provocateur continued to be perpetrated by the Soviets, in private as in public. At 5 p.m. when Colonel Ivan Fadeikin, acting Interior Ministry chief in Berlin, reported to Marshal Vasily Sokolovsky, Chief of the Soviet General Staff, it was to tell him that the situation in the country was 'improving' and that the 'workers' strikes in the overwhelming majority of the GDR cities are over.'[22]

On Göttling, Fadeikin claimed the West German had been recruited by American intelligence on his way to the labour exchange on 16 June and asked to take an active part in the planned riots. The ministry chief went on to say Göttling attacked a Volkspolizei vehicle calling for an end to the strike, throwing the driver and announcer out of the car and 'brutally assaulting them', before picking up their loudhailer and 'urging the crowd to attack police and Soviet troops'.

It was nonsense, of course. Göttling had simply been in the wrong place at the wrong time, an innocent bystander, but he proved an easy scapegoat for the under-pressure East German government and their Soviet masters. He may have been the first to be executed, but he was not the last – it is thought that sixteen more protesters around East Germany faced the firing squad in that and subsequent days. Thousands more were imprisoned, and some would eventually be transported to the Soviet Gulag.

The Allied commandants of Berlin formally denied that Willi was an 'agent provocateur' in the service of one of their intelligence agencies, and declared that 'his execution, on an empty pretext' was an act of brutality 'which will shake the conscience of the world'.[23]

Five days later Willi's widow, weeping helplessly, would take her place with her two young children alongside 200,000 other mourners in West Berlin's Rudolph Wilde Platz. In seven coffins in the centre of the square lay the bodies of men killed in the uprising: an empty eighth space, banked with red and white carnations, was left for Willi, whose body the Soviet authorities had refused to return.

The crowd heard Konrad Adenauer voice their grief:

> Those dead we honour today gave their blood for freedom. They were victims of tyranny … a people can be beaten down with weapons but the will not to bow cannot be torn from their breasts … we swear here we are not forgetting and we shall not rest until you in East Berlin and East Germany are free – until the whole of Germany is united.[24]

The Mayor of West Berlin, Ernst Reuter, who was standing beside Adenauer, stated that the 17 June uprising was 'the greatest event which has happened in our history for a long time. We all know this uprising has shaken the world.'

The Kremlin had been stunned by the uprising. But the West seemed uncertain as to how to grasp the opportunities it presented. Eisenhower and Dulles had indulged in enough rhetoric about 'liberating' eastern Europe, a goal they claimed would replace the Truman administration's 'passive' containment policy. Now that the moment had arrived, would they consider military help or even contemplate direct intervention, or would their response all be about encouragement for the dissidents via a propaganda campaign?

The National Security Council met on 18 June, and the tone of the meeting clearly moved towards the latter course. First up, CIA chief Allen Dulles emphasised immediately that the 'United States had had nothing whatsoever to do with inciting these riots'.[25] Reflecting on both the Czech and the East Berlin disturbances, he said 'the people of the satellites … obviously felt bolder now that Stalin's hand was no longer there'. But he was unsure what should be done: 'It pose[s] a very tough problem for the United States to know how to handle.'

The consensus was that any idea of a 'four-power' conference to map a way out of the Cold War was now redundant. How could any such talks take place, argued Dulles, 'without inevitably providing the [Russians] with some degree of moral support of their tyranny and of depriving the dissident people of the satellites of all hope'?[26]

Eisenhower said the uprisings had given his administration 'the strongest possible argument to give to Mr Churchill against a four-power meeting'.[27] He added that there could be no such conference 'until the Russians have withdrawn their armies from East Germany, at which time we would withdraw our armies from West Germany'.

It was 'desirable', the President added, that West Germany should be rearmed 'rapidly'. He knew that Adenauer was completely opposed to any idea of a national German army, so he declared we must 'throw all our weight behind' a European army with a German contribution – the proposed European Defence Community.

There was discussion about other diplomatic moves, including putting pressure on the Soviets through the United Nations. But it was the propaganda route that easily commanded a consensus, and the President's propaganda chief C. D. Jackson was ordered to come up with policies and actions that could be taken in the next sixty days to exploit the unrest in East Germany and Czechoslovakia.

Over in London, Frank Roberts, senior Foreign Office diplomat and an old and wise Russia hand, had been in regular touch with Churchill as the crisis enfolded. He was surprised at the Prime Minister's reaction.

> I expected that he would be rather attracted by the idea of brave men standing up for freedom. On the contrary he was deeply worried – quite rightly … that if the demonstrations continued, there would be demands for support from the West … which it would be too dangerous to meet.[28]

Churchill's unwillingness to criticise the Soviet response to the uprising was because he could now see a potential road ahead to a face-to-face meeting with Malenkov – and wanted nothing to knock that off course.

At the suggestion of the French premier, René Mayer, a 'Big Three' – or 'three-power' as it was called – summit between America, Britain and France had originally been set for 17 June in Bermuda, a British colony with an American base. The downfall of Mayer's short-lived Radical Socialist government put paid to that, but with a new Prime Minister, Joseph Laniel, due to take office, and on board for the summit, it was now rescheduled for 7 July.

Discussion of the new regime in the Kremlin would of course be top of the agenda. In this relaxed, informal setting, man-to-man, Churchill was planning to make his case for 'easement' with Moscow – and to put himself forward, once more, as the West's emissary in future talks.

All of this lay behind his inclination to give the Soviet army the benefit of the doubt. When he cast his eye over a telegram sent from Berlin on 18 June, he underlined – in his now familiar purple ink – a passage which stated that the Russian troops had throughout acted 'with marked restraint and moderation and have clearly been under instructions to use minimum of force'.[29]

The Prime Minister was then angered by a joint communiqué issued by the three West Berlin commandants – Thomas Timberman (US sector), Charles Coleman (British) and Pierre Manceaux-Démiau (French) – to counter communist allegations that the Allies were in some way provoking the disorders.

The communiqué expressed the commandants' 'grave concern' and condemned the 'irresponsible recourse to military force which had as its result the killing or serious wounding of a considerable number of citizens of Berlin'.

Churchill complained to Sir William Strang, his Permanent Secretary at the Foreign Office. 'I am surprised that they should have issued this protest without informing us beforehand,' he wrote.[30] 'Is it suggested that the Soviets should have allowed the Eastern Zone to fall into anarchy and riot? I had the impression that they acted with considerable restraint in the face of mounting disorder.' He also wondered why Sir Ivone Kirkpatrick, British high commissioner, was still on holiday in Austria at 'such a critical moment'.

Two days later, on 21 June, still clearly irritated, Churchill himself wrote to British commandant Charles Coleman to issue a reprimand.

If the Soviet government, as the occupying power, were faced as you have described with widespread movements of violent disorder they surely have the right to declare Martial Law in order to prevent anarchy, and if they acted – in your [earlier] words – 'with marked restraint and moderation' this [was] no reason for making the statement (communiqué).[31]

Churchill concluded: 'We shall not find our way out of our many difficulties by making, for purposes of local propaganda, statements which are not in accordance with the facts.'

In the continuing absence of Anthony Eden, who was recovering from – finally – a successful operation on his gall bladder in Boston, Lord Salisbury and Selwyn Lloyd were the Prime Minister's junior ministers in the Foreign Office. Salisbury cautioned – as did Churchill – that the Americans might interfere rashly in the shaky new situation behind the Iron Curtain. 'There is a new and more dangerous American tendency ... to advocate new, although, unspecified measures to encourage and even promote the early liberation of the satellite countries. It is my intention to resist American pressure for new initiatives of this kind.'[32]

On 22 June, Selwyn Lloyd offered Churchill suggestions as to his public response in the course of a penetrating four-page analysis of the fallout from the uprising. 'Germany is the key to the peace of Europe,' it began.[33]

A divided Europe has meant a divided Germany. To unite Germany while Europe is divided, even if practicable, is fraught with danger for all. Therefore everyone – Dr Adenauer, the Russians, the Americans, the French and ourselves – feel in our hearts that a divided Germany is safer for the time being. But none of us dare say so openly because of the effect upon German public opinion. Therefore we all publicly support a united Germany each on his own terms.

Until a united Germany was feasible, it was the task of the Allies to ensure that the Germans in the Soviet zone and East Berlin should not become the loyal subjects of the Russian communists. 'Since the Berlin Blockade, we have done all we can to sustain their morale and resistance to communism, at the same time as avoiding any provocation to violence.'

Now, Selwyn Lloyd concluded, it was clear that the puppet regime in East Germany was 'completely discredited'. 'This is a great triumph in the Cold War, perhaps the greatest since the defection of Tito.'

It was a relief, he went on, that the Soviets 'do not appear to have been provoked by these events into contemplating any attack upon our militarily precarious position in West Berlin'. On the other hand, they had shot Willi Göttling 'almost out of hand', rolled three mechanised divisions into Berlin, and severed communications between West and East Berlin.

Selwyn Lloyd recommended that Churchill should write to Adenauer reaffirming that Germany 'would not be let down', reminding the Prime Minister of the words of his foreign affairs speech of 11 May when he declared, 'Western Germany will in no way be sacrificed or cease to be master of its own fortune within the agreements we and other NATO countries have made with them.' He urged the Prime Minister to make a statement on Wednesday 24 June, with questions already on the order paper that day about events in Berlin.

Over at the White House, propaganda chief C. D. Jackson had come up with a string of varied suggestions for Eisenhower on how to undermine the faltering East German regime and to 'nourish resistance to communist oppression throughout satellite Europe' – short of fomenting 'mass rebellion', and 'without compromising its spontaneous nature'.[34]

Police leaders, pilots and Soviet military personnel would be actively encouraged to defect. Western trade unions would be asked to denounce Soviet repression and demand an investigation into workers' economic and labour conditions. 'Black' radio intruder operations to induce defections should be launched. At the United Nations, as well as condemning the actions of the Soviets in the uprising, someone should be briefed to call for a Red Cross investigation of conditions in the USSR.

Jackson also wanted to encourage Konrad Adenauer to build a Bundestag, a West German Parliament, in Berlin on the grounds of the destroyed Reichstag. One of its features would be a 'hall of heroes' in which Willi Göttling would be the first to appear. 'Göttling', wrote Jackson, 'might also be the very handy martyr for the International Conference of Free Trade Unions to latch on to.'

But there were some more controversial elements of Jackson's plans. He wanted to 'encourage the elimination of key puppet officials'. He was also keen to bring back to the table the notion of a 'Volunteer Freedom Corps' (first mooted in Truman's presidency), a kind of 'Cold War foreign legion' of combat battalions composed of willing émigrés displaced from eastern European countries after the Second World War.[35]

Trained by the US Army in West Germany and Austria, this corps would have its own distinctive identity with shoulder patches, insignia and flags. The volunteers would develop paramilitary and espionage skills for future deployment behind the Iron Curtain and, in the event of war, they would fight under American officers as part of a US infantry division.

In an early NSC meeting, Eisenhower had proposed an 'army of 250,000 stateless, single, anti-Communist young men from countries behind the Iron Curtain'.[36] He believed such a corps would induce desertions from the Soviet Union's satellites, while providing America with fighting men at low cost. He also suggested that successful service in the corps might later qualify soldiers for United States citizenship.

Jackson and Eisenhower faced hostile opposition from Europe for this kind of plan. Diplomats had already warned the President that by organising and arming refugees, the Volunteer Freedom Corps would only increase fear and suspicion in European countries. They believed it would give the USSR ammunition in portraying America as war-mongering, and it could be a very provocative step that might lead to all-out war. In addition, it was felt it would detract from the task – already proving a difficult one – of establishing a regular European army – the European Defence Community.

Eisenhower pursued the idea of a Volunteer Freedom Corps throughout the summer and autumn, but it would never see the light of day. Nor did the vast majority of C. D. Jackson's psychological ploys. It took an inquisitive reporter at a press conference held by John Foster Dulles on 30 June to kickstart an idea that the administration had put on the backburner after consideration earlier in the year.

Dulles was asked what steps Western nations might take to capitalise on the unrest behind the Iron Curtain. 'I'm not prepared to say,' he responded. But when asked whether America might consider sending food to the impoverished East Germans, Dulles replied, 'That's an idea worth exploring.'[37]

Food aid for East Germany quickly became a policy priority, and it was the remarkable Dulles family that shaped it. John Foster passed on the idea that very day to the Psychological Strategy Board, and when it met the following day, brother Allen advanced the idea and won agreement for it to be actively pursued.

Then the baton passed to their sister, Eleanor Lansing Dulles, who ran the State Department's Berlin desk. She had just returned to Washington having witnessed the uprising at first hand, and the idea of food aid was already uppermost in her mind. She quickly put together a committee with CIA, agriculture, treasury, defence and other representative agencies on it and got to work on a detailed plan.

The idea was that the food shipments would come from the United States agricultural surpluses, including grain, soy bean oil, lard, sugar, skimmed milk and some meat. Army 'C' rations available in Europe could also be added to the pile. In all, $15 million of food would be sent.

To its creators, the beauty of the food aid plan was that it combined political propaganda with humanitarianism. It pleased the Cold War warriors like C. D. Jackson who wanted, at the very least, to keep the psychological war going and continue to sow greater discord among disaffected East Germans. But it also satisfied US officials on the ground, like James Conant, the US high commissioner in Germany, and Cecil Lyon, director of the high commission's Berlin office, who had witnessed the 'pitiful' day-to-day standard of living of many in the Soviet sector.

Another objective of the food plan was to bolster the position of Adenauer, who was facing crucial elections in September. So the formal, public offer of food aid came after a carefully choreographed exchange of letters between Adenauer and Eisenhower, with the latter's made public on 10 July. 'I am anxious to ... aid the people of East Germany in this hour when many of those demonstrating are demanding more food,' the President wrote.[38] 'I sincerely hope that this effort on our part to relieve the plight of the people ... will be welcomed by the Soviet Government.'

Of course Eisenhower did not expect Moscow to react favourably, and he would not be disappointed. Molotov responded indignantly the next day by way of Elim O'Shaughnessy, US chargé d'affaires in Moscow. The decision to send the $15 million was made 'even without asking the opinion of the Government of the German Democratic Republic.'[39]

'Such manners at [the] present time', Molotov averred, 'would insult even [the] population of a colony, to say nothing of [the] German people and its legal Democratic government.' Clearly, he went on, the 'USA has not shown any sort of solicitude re food supply [for] German people, but has decided to resort to a propaganda manoeuvre[s] having nothing in common with concern for [the] real interests [of the] German population'.

Britain and France were none too enthusiastic about the food aid, regarding it as unnecessarily provocative in the new climate of the Cold War. Churchill would later grumpily tell Lord Salisbury: 'I always thought Eisenhower's move was an ill-timed act of charity and in line with what he told you about "harrying the Communists wherever possible".'[40]

But the food programme would get underway on 17 July when the first shipment of 45,000 tons of foodstuffs, such as milk, butter, bread and cheese, left New York for Hamburg, followed by two more on 20 and 21 July. Distribution centres opened on 27 July at various points in the western sectors of Berlin, and there was an immediate, tremendous response from East Germans.

With the RIAS radio station pumping out continuous reminders about the scheme, by the end of day one 103,743 parcels had been issued, and by the third day, over 200,000 packages were being distributed daily. East Germans waited patiently in long queues, some up to fourteen hours, to receive their food.

'No matter where one turns in Berlin one sees the streets swarming with miserably dressed people carrying suitcases, crates, haversacks, and paper boxes filled with food,' James Conant reported back to Washington. 'As late as 1 or 2 in the morning groups heavily laden with food are on the streets of West Berlin waiting for transportation back.'[41]

The SED leadership, still struggling to re-establish authority after 17 June, was well and truly on the back foot. It ramped up its own propaganda, referring to the 'Ami bait' of the Americans and the 'provocative acts of the American and British warmongers'. The regime began to suspend the sale of train tickets to West Berlin and all freight and bus traffic to West Berlin was halted by the end of the month.

Back in the Kremlin the recriminations over 17 June led to the first major casualty in the ruling elite. Just over a week after the uprising, at a performance of the opera *The Decemberists* at the Bolshoi Theatre, the box with the usual line-up of governing oligarchs on show had a notable absentee – Lavrentiy Beria.

The feared First Deputy Premier, head of the secret police and close ally of Malenkov, had been allocated the blame for the East Berlin uprising and arrested very publicly and humiliatingly at a meeting of the Presidium of the Supreme Soviet. Now Moscow and Berlin had to get to work to counter the American propaganda coup – and bolster their increasingly shaky control of East Germany.

* * *

Even as he grappled with the East German crisis, there was another weighty matter grabbing the world's front-page headlines that demanded Eisenhower's immediate attention – the cause célèbre of the Rosenbergs, who were now facing imminent execution.

Husband and wife Julius and Ethel Rosenberg, convicted back in April 1951 of 'conspiracy to commit espionage' for their roles in a Soviet atomic spy ring, had been sentenced to death and were finally due to go to the electric chair in the Sing Correctional Facility, New York, on Thursday 18 June. But nothing had been straightforward in this, the most controversial criminal case of modern times, and there was still a final twist in the tale.

On Monday 15 June, after all the appeals against the conviction and sentencing, after all the urgings for clemency, it had looked to be finally over for the Rosenbergs. A last petition to the Supreme Court for a stay of execution was denied – albeit by a vote of five to four – and the court, its job done with apparently no further recourse to it, then went into recess until October. But the following day the friends of the Rosenbergs played one final card.

Two new lawyers, Fyke Farmer and Daniel Marshall – on behalf of the National Committee to Secure Justice in the Rosenberg Case – entered the legal battleground with a novel point of law. They argued that the penalty provisions of the Atomic Energy Act of 1946 – specifically the requirement that no death sentence be imposed in a case involving atomic espionage without the consent of a jury – superseded the Espionage Act of 1917, under which the Rosenbergs had been indicted and sentenced to die by Judge Irving Kaufman alone.

They managed to win a hearing and put this argument to one of the justices of the Supreme Court who had stayed in Washington while his other colleagues set off on vacation – William O. Douglas, a strong civil libertarian, who had, however, voted against the stay of execution on the Monday.

Douglas spent twelve hours alone in his study pondering the application. In eventually giving his opinion, Douglas made it clear that the nation must be secure 'against the nefarious plans of spies who would destroy us'.[42] But he did declare doubts about the imposition of the death penalty, ordered an indefinite stay of execution and stated that the Rosenbergs should be given the chance to test Farmer and Marshall's argument in the 'District Court and Court of Appeals'. Incredibly, dramatically, he seemed to have thrown the condemned couple a lifeline.

There was now a sense of panic in the White House and among Douglas's colleagues. Attorney General Herbert Brownell Jr telephoned John Foster Dulles to tell him that he was 'amazed' by Douglas's decision. Brownell immediately petitioned Chief Justice of the US Supreme Court Fred Vinson to bring back all his colleagues from their holidays and deliberate immediately once more, on the grounds that the penalty clauses of the Atomic Energy Act did not constitute a 'substantial question'.[43]

Douglas had by now set off on holiday. Vinson duly summoned him back, and authorised special flights for the other members. So on Thursday 18 June all the justices of the Supreme Court were back in Washington again, set for an extraordinary two-day session; it was only the third time in its 164-year history that the court had been re-convened from a recess.

By now, with all this legal turmoil, together with the backdrop of significant protests in most European capitals and pleas for clemency all the way up to Pope Pius XII, the President was starting to get twitchy about the whole affair.

Whether to grant executive clemency to the Rosenbergs had been one of the first major decisions to await Eisenhower after he entered the White House in early 1953. On 11 February he consigned them to the electric chair, saying that their spying 'involves the deliberate betrayal of the entire nation and could very well result in the deaths of many, many thousands of innocent citizens'.[44] 'By their act,' he went on, 'these two individuals have in fact betrayed the cause of freedom for which free men are fighting and dying at this very hour [in Korea].'

But there was nothing cold and calculated about his decision, as Eisenhower revealed in letters to friends and family as the execution day approached. Writing in response to an old Columbia University friend and colleague, Clyde Miller, he admitted it was 'extremely difficult to reach a sound decision in such instances. Not all the arguments are on either side.'[45]

Miller warned the President that the communist propaganda machine would make the most of the situation, and that 'America's name' would no longer be 'associated with justice and mercy'.[46] Eisenhower countered that communist leaders believed that free governments – America in particular – were perceived as weak and fearful, and 'consequently subversive ... activity can be conducted against them with no real fear of dire punishment on the part of the perpetrator'. It was vital to counter this contention.

The fate of Ethel Rosenberg, the mother of two young children, preyed on his mind. 'It goes against the grain to avoid interfering in the case where a woman is to receive capital punishment,' he told his son Johnnie in a letter on 16 June.[47] But he considered Ethel 'the strong and recalcitrant character … the leader in everything they did in the spy ring'. There was another crucial argument for putting her to death, as Eisenhower explained: 'If there would be any commuting of the woman's sentence without the man's, then from here on the Soviets would simply recruit their spies from among women.'

What Eisenhower made of a desperate letter Ethel wrote to him from her prison cell, left by her lawyer Emanuel Bloch at the White House gate, is not known. Her death sentence, she wrote, was an 'act of vengeance'.[48] 'What single action could more effectively demonstrate this nation's fealty to religious and democratic ideals, than the granting of clemency to my husband and myself.'

'I approach you on the basis of mercy,' she went on, 'and earnestly beseech you to let this quality sway you rather than any narrow judicial concern … I ask this man, whose name is one with glory, what glory there is that is greater than the offering to God of a simple act of compassion.'

While the Supreme Court entered the second day of its hearing, on 19 June, Eisenhower's Cabinet – for the first time – had an extended discussion about the Rosenberg case. The volume and passion of the correspondence he had received from the public had clearly affected the President:

I must say I'm impressed by all the honest doubt about this expressed in the letters I've been receiving. Now if the Supreme Court decided by, say, five to four or even six to three, as far as the average man's concerned, there will be doubt – not just a legal point in his mind.[49]

But the Attorney General was determined to stiffen his resolve. 'Well, who's going to decide these points – pressure groups or the Supreme

Court?'[50] He asked Eisenhower to consider one of his own key arguments in turning down the plea for clemency: 'In terms of national security, the Communists are just out to prove they can bring enough pressure, one way or another, to enable people to get away with espionage.'

Finally, Brownell reminded the President about the evidence of the Rosenbergs' guilt coming from the successful Venona project, the painstaking codebreaking by the US Signal Intelligence Service of messages sent by the Soviet spy agencies to their agents in America. Julius Rosenberg was clearly identified in these decrypts, codenamed successively 'Antenna' and 'Liberal', while Ethel was mentioned too.

The US intelligence fraternity did not want any hint to reach the Soviets that their 'unbreakable' cipher system had been cracked, so using this material in court against the Rosenbergs had not been an option for prosecutors. 'I've always wanted you to look at evidence that wasn't usable in court showing that the Rosenbergs were the head and centre of an espionage ring here in direct contact with the Russians – the prime espionage ring in the country,' Brownell told the President.[51]

Persuaded that his doubts were unwarranted, Eisenhower now replied: 'My only concern is in the area of statecraft – the effect of the action.' He and his Attorney General now awaited the final verdict of the Supreme Court.

The worldwide campaign to stop the execution had mobilised for one final effort, encouraged by the late stay of execution by Justice Douglas. As the Supreme Court reconvened on the morning of Friday 19 June, thousands rallied in western European capitals, the biggest crowds on Paris's Place de la Concorde, Milan's Piazza del Duomo and London's Piccadilly Circus. US consulates all around the globe were ringed by protesters.

At 11 a.m. the nine black-robed judges parted the wine-red velvet drapes behind the bench and took their seats in the courtroom on the second floor of the 'Marble Palace', the Supreme Court's neoclassical building at 1 First Street, Washington DC. A hush fell over the chamber, which was crowded with spectators and lawyers.

Chief Justice Fred Vinson pulled out his glasses and began reading the court's opinion – a majority one – in a low voice. After outlining the issue before them – whether the provisions of the Atomic Energy Act of 1946 overrode the Espionage Act of 1917 – he came to the decision.

> We think the question is not substantial. We think further proceedings to litigate it are unwarranted. A conspiracy was charged and proved to violate the Espionage Act in wartime. The Atomic Energy Act did not repeal or limit the provisions of the Espionage Act. Accordingly, we vacate the stay entered by Mr Justice Douglas on 17 June 1953.[52]

The vote had been passed by six to three. Justice Douglas, whose judgment three days earlier had given the Rosenbergs some hope, now read his minority opinion. 'No man or woman should go to death unless lawful sentence ... I know in my heart that I am right on the law, and knowing that, my duty [was] clear.'[53] Justice Hugo Black, a fellow dissenter, added his voice, saying that 'it was unlawful for a judge to impose the death penalty for unlawful transmittal of atomic secrets unless such a penalty was recommended by the jury trying the case.'[54]

Emanuel Bloch and Fyke Farmer rose to their feet to ask to submit new motions, and the Chief Justice instructed them to put them in writing immediately. This they did, in longhand, sitting at tables in front of the bench, while the justices filed out for a recess.

When they returned, the motions were rejected in an instant. The justices then left the courthouse in different directions to try to evade the demonstrators and press pack. Justice Black departed in a 'windowless laundry van', but the lawyers for the Rosenbergs managed to follow him home, hoping to speak to him and persuade him to make a final intervention. In tears, Black told a member of his family to send the lawyers away.

Emanuel Bloch also managed to get a request through to Justice Harold Burton, who had voted with the majority but had shown some sympathy for the Rosenberg motions. But he refused to push for yet another stay of execution. Now the only hope left for the Rosenbergs was a last-minute presidential pardon.

Over in London, once the verdict of the Supreme Court was known, a deputation from the 'Save the Rosenbergs' campaign called at 10 Downing Street to lobby the Prime Minister – only to be told he was at his country house, Chartwell, for the weekend. The group's leaders – Reverend Stanley Evans, the 'backstreet pastor' who had given a glowing memorial service for Stalin, and Professor John Bernal, the renowned physicist – jumped in a car and headed off to Kent.

When they arrived in the lane outside Churchill's home, they found sixty supporters of the National Rosenberg Defence Committee already there. Evans and Bernal scribbled a note addressed 'Dear PM' asking Churchill to appeal direct 'to President Eisenhower over the Transatlantic telephone immediately'.[55] In reply, a typewritten note was brought out to the crowd which read: 'It is not within my duty or my power to intervene in this matter. Winston Churchill.' The gates of Chartwell were then closed for the night.

Just before 8 p.m. Eisenhower issued a statement from the White House rejecting a final plea for clemency. He said that he was 'not unmindful ... of the grave concern both here and abroad in the minds of serious people'.[56]

But he repeated what he had said back in February, if anything, in stronger language.

I can only say that, by immeasurably increasing the chances of atomic war, the Rosenbergs may have condemned to death tens of millions of innocent people all over the world. The execution of two human beings is a grave matter. But even graver is the thought of millions of dead whose death may be directly attributable to what these spies have done.[57]

To spare religious feelings, the executions were brought forward three hours before the setting sun heralded the Jewish sabbath. Julius was first in the chair, at 8.04 p.m.[58] It took three massive charges of electricity to kill him; he was pronounced dead at 8.06 a.m. and his body removed. Ethel followed him into the chamber at 8.11 a.m., but her death was less straightforward. It required five shocks to kill her and the whole process took four and a half minutes.

The Rosenbergs were the first American civilians to be put to death for conspiracy to commit espionage. Even during the Second World War, soldiers who deserted and fought with the Nazis, and individuals convicted of treason, only received sentences of life in prison – or less. Of the spy ring to which they had belonged, Klaus Fuchs, primary physicist on the Manhattan Project, was jailed for just fourteen years, and David Greenglass, Ethel Rosenberg's brother, was given fifteen years.

Evidence of Ethel's treachery was always tenuous. The couple were doomed because of the febrile political climate of the time. With the Korean War still raging, the influence of Joe McCarthy showing no signs of waning and the Soviet threat still perceived as being very real, most Americans – if reluctantly – assented to the deaths as an example to those who might follow.

Churchill in the doorway at Chartwell for his first public appearance after his stroke.
© Keystone Press/Alamy Stock Photo

CHAPTER 7

THE EMERGENCY
GOVERNMENT

As an old man who had led such a rich and varied – but very demanding – life, Churchill understandably worried about his mortality. Earlier in 1953 he had asked his solicitor Anthony Moir to study the actuarial tables and calculate his current life's chances. 'A man aged seventy-eight, in good health, has 5.926 years expectation of life,' Moir wrote back, perhaps less optimistically than the Prime Minister had hoped.[1]

Despite an outward appearance of vitality for someone of his age, Churchill's health record – largely kept concealed from the public – was not a reassuring one. In all the stresses and strains of the war he had succumbed to two bouts of pneumonia – one, at Carthage, was near fatal – while he also had a heart 'disturbance' on a trip to Washington.

Then in August 1949, while holidaying at Lord Beaverbrook's villa in the south of France, he suffered his first stroke, down his right-hand side, after which he explained to Eisenhower that 'for a good many days I was unable to sign my name'.[2] Again, only his inner circle was aware of the seriousness of his illness – he had merely 'caught a chill' was the word put out to the press.

Jock Colville was noticing a definite deterioration. In November 1952 he observed: 'He is getting tired and visibly ageing. He finds it hard work to compose a speech and the ideas no longer flow.'[3] Yet on good days, like 11 May when he made his 'easement' speech in the House of Commons, it was clear he could summon up the energy and brilliance of the best of times.

Churchill had undertaken an unusually hectic schedule in late May and early June, dealing with the Coronation, trouble in East Berlin, and discussions with allies over the armistice talks in Korea – while shouldering the burden of being both Prime Minister and Foreign Secretary in Eden's absence.

So at 9.30 on the morning of Tuesday 23 June, Churchill's doctor Lord Moran and his ophthalmologist Edgar King arrived at 10 Downing Street to give him a check-up. It was clear he was not in the best shape. 'I thought his speech was a little slurred and a little indistinct. Twice I had to ask him to repeat what he had said,' Moran observed.[4]

The doctor told Churchill he was unhappy he was proposing to carry the burden of the Foreign Office until the autumn. 'He said he must … grunted and picked up some papers.' Before leaving Downing Street, Moran went to find the Prime Minister's private secretary David Pitblado to tell him his concerns about his patient's health.

After lunch Churchill went to the House of Commons, where he seemed in good spirits, answering questions on the forthcoming Bermuda summit, joking with his old sparring partner, that 'extreme Tory from a vanished age' Sir Waldron Smithers, MP for Chislehurst.

On returning to Downing Street, he held informal talks in the Cabinet Room with the Italian Prime Minister Alcide de Gasperi, in Britain on a two-day visit, whose Christian Democratic Alliance – a bulwark against the Italian Communist Party – had just been returned to office. On a beautiful sunny day the two men went out to pose for photographs on chairs in the garden, with Churchill, dressed in striped trousers, waistcoat and spotted bow tie, with cigar in hand, looking relaxed enough, if somewhat tired.

Then in the evening Churchill and his wife Clementine hosted a dinner party at Downing Street in honour of Signor Gasperi. Among the thirty-eight guests were Cabinet members Lord Salisbury, Rab Butler, Lord Alexander and their wives. Also around the table were Churchill's son-in-law and daughter, Christopher and Mary Soames, Mr and Mrs Clement Attlee, Jock Colville and his wife and Sir Kenneth Clark – former director of the National Gallery and now Arts Council chairman – and his wife Jane.

Churchill, who had struggled to maintain conversation in French with Madame de Gasperi, who sat on his right (she spoke no English and he no Italian), eventually rose to his feet at the end of the meal to deliver a typically witty, sparkling speech about the Roman conquest of Britain.

Afterwards, when the men got up to follow the ladies into the drawing room, Churchill made it only as far as the first chair before slumping heavily into it. Lady Jane Clark sat beside him to assist, and as he grasped her hand he said, 'I want the hand of a friend. They put too much on me. Foreign affairs…' and then his voice faded away.[5]

It was clear something serious had happened. 'My father looked unhappy and uncertain and was very incoherent,' Mary Soames observed.[6] Her husband told her to 'guard' Churchill from the other guests, while he explained to them that his father-in-law was 'over-tired'. No doubt some put it down to him having had a little too much to drink.

Once the guests had been ushered away, Churchill was helped upstairs to bed, where he seemed to revive a little. Attempts to contact Lord Moran proved unsuccessful, although eventually a woman on the No. 10 switchboard reached the doctor at 12.30 a.m. to ask him to come and see the Prime Minister early the following morning.

Visiting Churchill in his bedroom at 9 a.m. on Wednesday, Moran observed that the left side of the Prime Minister's mouth sagged, a condition even more noticeable when he spoke. The doctor strongly suspected a stroke – it looked similar to the 1949 incident, albeit on the other side of his body – although at this stage there was no apparent loss of feeling in his left hand or leg, and he was able to walk, albeit unsteadily.

Moran urged Churchill not to attend that morning's Cabinet meeting, due downstairs at No. 10. He said he would return later, bringing with him neurologist Sir Russell Brain. But once the doctor had left, Churchill got up and got dressed, and was escorted by Jock Colville to his usual chair under the fireplace in the Cabinet Room for an 11.30 start.

'I had felt sure the tell-tale droop of his mouth on the left side and his slurred speech would betray the secret,' Colville recalled.[7] But Churchill told none of his colleagues of his trouble, and after greeting them sitting down, went ahead and took the meeting.

In introducing the first item, about continued fighting in Korea, he recommended instructions should be given to a brigade stationed in Hong Kong to move to Korea if the situation needed it. Later on he briefly summed up a discussion on colonial welfare, relayed a message from German Chancellor Adenauer about the recent uprising in East Berlin, concluded a debate about army pay, and summed up in discussion about the possibility of a commercial television channel.

Rab Butler noticed nothing particularly amiss, except that Churchill was quieter than usual, and signalled some items with 'an introductory wave of the hand to the minister concerned'.[8] Harold Macmillan thought Churchill looked 'very white'.[9] 'He spoke little, but distinctly. I remember that he called to me, "Harold, you might draw the blind down a little, will you?"' But George Mallaby, acting secretary to the Cabinet, felt 'it was clear at once … that he was exhausted or ill'.[10]

Churchill still seemed determined to fulfil his weekly appearance at Prime Minister's Questions the following day, asking Colville to bring them to him so he could prepare a final time. But Lord Moran told him there could be serious consequences if he went to the House of Commons, and Christopher and Mary Soames repeated the warning at luncheon.

Clementine and Mary had been due to watch a day's play at Wimbledon, but cancelled it and awaited the arrival of Sir Russell Brain at 6.30 p.m. After being examined by him and Lord Moran, Churchill dined at 8 p.m. with his wife, and then worked a little in his room before going to sleep.

On Thursday it was clear the Prime Minister's condition had worsened considerably overnight. Lord Moran saw that 'his speech was becoming blurred and more difficult to follow ... he is, if anything, more unsteady in his gait'.[11] Frustrated, Churchill told the doctor, 'I don't feel like managing the world, and yet never have they looked more like offering me it.'

Mary was 'painfully struck by his appearance, and found him very despondent'.[12] Churchill now recognised the gravity of his illness and declared, 'I'm going to Chartwell.'[13] There he could hopefully recover – while protecting his privacy. Colville accompanied him in the car to Kent, while Jane Portal, his 23-year-old secretary, the niece of Rab Butler, followed on behind in a police car, ready to set up his office in the country home.

It was on that journey to Chartwell that the first move in a stratagem to conceal the Prime Minister's illness was made – by the man himself. Churchill instructed Colville to let no one know what had happened, and to 'ensure that the administration continued to function as if he were in full control'.[14] On arrival, he was just about able to walk up the steps to the front door unaided, and then took the lift up to his bedroom.

Colville now got to work to inform a select group of Churchill's friends and vital political allies – and the Queen – about his master's serious condition. He telephoned the Queen's secretary, Sir Alan

Lascelles, and then wrote personal letters to Clarissa Eden (Anthony was still recovering after his bile duct operation), colleagues Butler, Lord Salisbury and Lord Alexander, and great friends (and newspapermen) Brendan Bracken (founder of the *Financial Times*), Lord Camrose (owner of the *Daily Telegraph*) and Lord Beaverbrook (owner of the *Daily Express*).

He said to Beaverbrook:

> With sorrow I write to tell you that Winston is seriously unwell. After a dinner he gave to De Gasperi on Tuesday, he was stricken by what is either an arterial spasm (in which case it may pass off) or an arterial clot, which would be far more serious. Although his mind is still clear and good, his articulation is difficult and he finds great trouble in moving.
>
> There is a possibility of a miraculous change in the next forty-eight hours, but it is unlikely I am afraid. He thinks of resigning in the near future. His courage is only matched by an astounding humility which has come over him, and Lady C is no less heroic.
>
> He asks if you will come down to have luncheon with him on Sunday … I have written to Brendan and Camrose; but nobody else knows the truth, whatever the rumours may be. Yours sadly, Jock.[15]

The Queen wrote to her stricken Prime Minister on Friday to say, 'I am so sorry to hear from Tommy Lascelles that you have not been feeling too well these last few days. I do hope it is not serious and that you will be quite recovered in a very short time.'[16] Churchill was 'thrilled' by the letter, and was able to dictate one back, being quite frank about his condition.

But the truth was that on Friday 26 June things were now very serious indeed – he was losing the entire use of his left arm and leg. 'I do not like this, the thrombosis is spreading,' Moran noted.[17] The doctor, who was dean of the medical school at St Mary's Hospital, Paddington, phoned and urgently requested an experienced nurse, Sister Mary Big-more, to come and give personal care to the Prime Minister.

Churchill managed, however, to make it to the dining room for luncheon, where – after a fashion – he relayed his views about future government business with his guests Rab Butler and Lord Salisbury. But on that Friday there was tremendous concern in the household. Moran, watching the sharp decline in his patient, sought out Colville, who was busy in the library drafting out his series of letters. 'Moran told me he did not think Winston would live over the weekend.'[18]

By now it was clear that there had to be a statement of some kind – particularly because Churchill was due to leave for Bermuda in four days' time for his much-anticipated summit with Eisenhower and the French Prime Minister, Joseph Laniel. On the Friday, Lord Moran – with Sir Russell Brain's assent – drafted a medical bulletin that could be given to the public.

It read:

> For a long time the Prime Minister has had no respite from his arduous duties and a disturbance of the cerebral circulation has developed, resulting in attacks of giddiness. We have therefore advised him to abandon his journey to Bermuda and take at least a month's rest. Sir Winston had a similar attack in August 1949 at Cap d'Ail.[19]

There was consternation in the Churchill circle over the relative frankness of this bulletin – and the reference to the previous, covered-up stroke. Grim as the position was at present, they were still holding out hope of a recovery. It seems most likely that Colville, a pivotal figure in all this, then took soundings from Bracken, Beaverbrook and Camrose (who between them controlled a fair proportion of the British press), while Butler and Salisbury – presented with the draft bulletin that Friday at Chartwell – consulted with the influential secretary to the Cabinet, Sir Norman Brook.

What emerged from a flurry of deliberations on Friday and Saturday morning was a completely different bulletin, utterly bland, revealing nothing of the truth of Churchill's illness. It was released at 3 p.m. on Saturday 27 June and read: 'The Prime Minister has had no respite for a long time from his very arduous duties and is in need of a complete rest. We have therefore advised him to abandon his journey to Bermuda and to lighten his duties for at least a month.'

The plot was now well and truly hatched. Meanwhile, Churchill was struggling badly. On Saturday, Jane Portal recorded, 'He is definitely weaker physically and fell down today. In fact he cannot really walk at all and his swallowing is bad.'[20] Mary felt 'wretchedly gloomy' about her father's condition.

On Sunday, Sister Mary Bigmore recorded that the situation was still 'extremely worrying', with her patient paralysed down the left side and unable to speak.[21] She needed additional support, so contacted St Mary's Hospital to ask them to send a colleague, Sister Gammon, who could look after the patient on the night shift.

On Monday, the three newspaper barons – Beaverbrook, Bracken and Camrose – all gathered at Chartwell to agree a plan to keep the story out of the papers. 'As I looked out of my office window at the front of the house I could see these three men pacing up and down the lawn with Jock, pondering how they could keep the matter from the public,' Jane Portal recalled.[22] Bracken and Camrose were adamant about suppressing the news, Beaverbrook less so, telling Churchill, Moran and Colville he believed that 'all Fleet Street knows what happened'.[23]

Camrose, in the meantime, instructed his editor Colin Coote to bring Churchill's obituary up to date and to have an editorial prepared, should the worst happen. The former, headlined 'Winston Churchill – The Record of a Brilliant Career', would begin: 'The world has lost a great figure, and Britain one of her greatest sons. In one sense his task was done. Like Chatham, he had had his "*annus mirabilis*". Like Pitt, he had guided England to "save herself by her exertions and Europe by her example".[24]

The editorial was no less effusive. Headlined 'Great Leader in War and Peace', it read:

Men and women in many lands will mourn the passing of Winston Leonard Spencer-Churchill, for they know well that if he had never lived they might not be alive today. Never was more justified the saying of Pericles that 'the whole earth is the sepulchre of the renowned, and their memorial is written not on tablets of stone but on the hearts of men'.[25]

A betting man on Friday and Saturday might have put money on those articles being published. But on Monday there were small signs of improvement and Churchill was bolstered by the arrival of his actress daughter Sarah and her photographer husband Anthony Beauchamp. He was even able to receive a few telephone calls.

At noon back in London on Monday, Rab Butler chaired the first Cabinet meeting in Churchill's absence. The Churchill circle had made it clear to him when he visited Chartwell on Friday that Eden was the rightful deputy, but with the Foreign Secretary still recovering from his operation, the 'tacit understanding' was that Butler would, for the moment, function as head of the government.

Butler first delivered a brief account of his and Lord Salisbury's visit to Chartwell on Friday, thus giving the Cabinet the first real details of Churchill's illness. Harold Macmillan felt the Chancellor handled it 'with the greatest tact and the lightest of touches' – while not specifically describing it as a stroke.[26] 'It was a terrible shock to us all, although revealed so discreetly. Many of us were in tears, or found it difficult to restrain them.'

However poor his condition, Butler said, the Prime Minister would continue to receive 'the more important papers', and decisions on major questions of policy would be referred to him. Selwyn Lloyd, the junior minister, would handle the day-to-day business of the Foreign Office, while Lord Salisbury would assist, all the while liaising with Churchill.

In Parliament that afternoon, Butler, after being forced to trot out the mantra about the Prime Minister merely needing a 'complete rest', faced some probing questions.[27] First the Labour leader Clement Attlee wanted to know precisely how the Foreign Office would be run in Churchill's absence.

> While I entirely appreciate the qualities of the Lord President of the Council [Lord Salisbury], I should have thought that if the Prime Minister wanted a complete rest he should be free from coming to many decisions on foreign affairs ... it seems to me that the Lord President of the Council, in the position as stated, is in a very semi-detached position.[28]

Could not junior ministers give the kind of 'authoritative lead' required, Attlee asked.

Butler assured him that Lord Salisbury had 'plunged straight into the foreign situation ... which he was well versed in before taking on the extra duty of assisting the Prime Minister'.

Labour MP James Callaghan pointed out that there were now only eight Cabinet ministers who could answer to the House of Commons. Butler meekly replied that 'every possible consideration will be taken into account by the government in order to serve the House to the best of our ability'.

Attlee's questions had rattled the government and clearly greater clarity was needed. So after some phone calls to Chartwell, it was announced publicly that Lord Salisbury had been appointed 'acting Foreign Secretary'.

While Jock Colville was the principal orchestrator of the 'cover-up', he was receiving valuable help from his fellow principal private secretary, David Pitblado, and the controller of the Central Office of Information, Thomas Fife Clark. On that Monday, Clark wrote to Lord Swinton, the Commonwealth Secretary – who was also in charge of the government's PR – with his latest thoughts about strategy.

Up to now, Clark wrote, despite some 'political mischief-making by the *Daily Mirror*', no media outlet anywhere had suggested that the Prime Minister was suffering from any specific ailment.[29] 'So far we have got by with a medical report which does not contain any sort of medical reference,' he observed. 'But it is clear if a second medical report is issued, it must be in medical terms. The aim must be to hold this back at any rate while the situation is static.'

Clark admitted that there were worrying reports emanating from Paris and other places that Churchill had had a stroke. 'No reference of this kind has yet been published here, and we must try to hold the line for as long as we can.'[30] He told Swinton that to put the newspapers off the main scent it was important 'that each day we should have a small amount of news which I can give to the press informally and of course without quotation … small points daily about mild activity at Chartwell'.

In the next few days that strategy was clearly working as headlines began to appear which talked of 'Premier's Rest Cure Showing Results', 'Churchill Benefiting From Rest' and 'The Gentleman in the Country'.[31]

Churchill's slight improvement continued on Tuesday 30 June, helped by visits from Lord Cherwell and Sir Norman Brook, the latter sent away with the final proofs for Churchill's wartime memoirs, *Triumph and Tragedy*. Beaverbrook rang up and lobbied for a more honest health bulletin to be released, but was persuaded otherwise.

On Wednesday morning, 1 July, the consensus was that the invalid was much better. 'You're going to get quite well,' Christopher Soames suggested.[32] 'Yes, but I don't know how much difficulty I'll have getting back my position,' Churchill replied. He felt well enough to dictate a long reply to Eisenhower, responding to the letter of concern the President had sent him.

'I am so sorry to be the cause of upsetting so many plans,' he told Eisenhower.[33] 'I had a sudden stroke which as it developed completely paralysed my left side and affected my speech.' Referring to his previous stroke in 1949, he said:

As I was out of office I kept this secret … I am therefore not without hope of pursuing my theme a little longer but it will be a few weeks before any opinion can be formed. I am glad to say I have already made progress. I have not told anybody these details which are for your eyes alone.

He used the letter to continue to bang the drum for a summit with the Soviets, taking exception to a Republican senator's comments that the perceived change of policy in the Soviet Union was only due to 'fear among a trembling remnant of gangsters and felons cringing in the Kremlin'.

'I am anxious that before we reject all hope of a Soviet change of heart we should convince our peoples that we have done our best. After all, ten years of easement plus productive science might make a different world,' he went on.

Finally, he finished the letter by telling Eisenhower that he was sending Bedell Smith the final chapters of his war memoirs, 'which refer to you and to some divergence of views between us. They will probably be published in October though whether I shall still remain in office is unpredictable.'

Churchill was taking the time during his recuperation to delve into the parliamentary novels of Anthony Trollope, starting first with *Phineas Finn*. The book was propped up on a desk for him, or a stand placed next to his wheelchair. 'In those early days he couldn't move his left-hand side and his right was difficult too, and his speech was still affected, so Liz (Elizabeth Gilliatt, his other secretary) and I helped,' recalled Jane Portal.[34] 'When he got to the end of the page he would blink and I would turn it over.'

Harold Macmillan was the guest at dinner on Wednesday 2 July, and Churchill managed to talk to him 'with great animation' about the Housing Minister's successful speech on school buildings in the Commons the previous day.[35] 'At dinner he talked so much at the beginning that he slobbered over his soup. He poured out some champagne with a steady hand and cried out "you see, I don't spill precious liquor!"'

Churchill claimed his arm was nearly restored and his leg much improved. 'There were times I thought he was putting on an act ... but it was a jolly brave one,' Macmillan wrote. But he felt the atmosphere was 'gay', and added: 'It was a kind of conspiracy we were all in – and it was rather fun to have such respectable people as Salisbury, Butler and co. as co-conspirators.'

A few days later, despite the Beaverbrook–Bracken–Camrose axis working effectively to cover up the story in Fleet Street, that conspiracy was nearly blown apart by the efforts of a diligent provincial newspaperman.

Trevor Lloyd-Hughes, political correspondent of the *Liverpool Daily Post*, was standing in the members' lobby in the House of Commons early on the evening of Wednesday 8 July when a Conservative MP, an old and trusted friend, walked by. Without stopping, the MP whispered to the reporter: 'Churchill's had a stroke: he's going to retire.'[36]

After receiving confirmation of the story following further calls to contacts, Lloyd-Hughes was given permission by his editor to go ahead and write it up for the following morning's paper. But he was still not permitted to tell the full story because nowhere in the published front-page article did it mention that Churchill had suffered a stroke. However, cautious though the piece was, it was certainly a startling piece of news – and on the right track.

'Churchill Planning to Retire' was the headline, with Lloyd-Hughes writing that he would step down within the next three months, to be succeeded by Anthony Eden.[37] 'The Prime Minister has taken the decision with extreme reluctance and only because of serious warnings from his doctors. His retirement will have tremendous international implications and, in the opinion of experts, may postpone indefinitely a Big Four meeting with Russia.'

Lloyd-Hughes cautioned his readers: 'For this reason, and also because of possible effects upon the Conservative Party, there might be an official denial that the Prime Minister is contemplating resignation. In fact I understand that this step is in his mind at present.'

Remarkably, the story wasn't followed up in any of the big national papers. The only titbits of information that had emerged were of the kind that appeared in the *Manchester Guardian* on 1 July – a short story, with the headline: 'Beginning to Benefit from Rest?' Churchill's friends had done their job utterly effectively and the rest of the British press was effectively muzzled.[38]

The core of Britain's clandestine government for much of the summer of 1953 was as follows: Rab Butler and Lord Salisbury were effectively joint acting Prime Ministers, running Cabinet and being its 'public face' on the big matters of the moment – talks with Russia, the aftermath of the East Berlin uprising, tensions in Egypt and the future of television. Commonwealth Secretary Lord Swinton's prime task was to smother any stories of ill-health.

But the nitty-gritty, day-to-day work of this emergency government was in the hands of the unflappable Cabinet Secretary Sir Norman Brook, supported down at Chartwell by Jock Colville, Churchill's trusted private secretary, and his son-in-law Christopher Soames, who cleared the daily red boxes.

Soames, aged thirty-two, MP for Bedford since 1950 and Churchill's parliamentary private secretary, was not supposed to view Cabinet papers or secret documents. But that principle was waived as he made himself indispensable in this crisis. 'The shrewdness of his comments, combined with his ability to differentiate between what mattered and what did not, was of invaluable help in difficult days,' an appreciative Colville later recalled.[39]

Throughout July the Prime Minister's mood was up and down, and while there were obvious improvements in his condition, there were also setbacks. On 8 July, Moran recorded 'some strength of the left foot and an obvious improvement in his "attitude to life"'. Three days later he could lift his left arm above his head and switch on his reading lamp. He was also able to walk a little unaided around the pond, feeding the goldfish.

The *Liverpool Daily Post* story about him planning to retire was only the half of it. On bad days Churchill contemplated giving up, but mostly the urge to recover and return to office was strong. After he had made it through the first week, he set himself the target of reappearing at the party conference in October. 'Margate was the goal,' recalled Jane Portal.[40] 'He had already begun dictating the speech he might make. It was like writing a book, he would go over it again and again, perfecting it. He spent those three months writing the Margate speech.'

In the week beginning Monday 20 July, Colville began to plan a carefully orchestrated photo opportunity to demonstrate that his master, after the prescribed 'month's rest', was recovering from his 'overstrain' and on the road to recovery. The idea was that Churchill, en route to Chequers, would stop off in Downing Street so he could be seen – albeit very briefly – back at the seat of power.

'Would you like me to arrange for two trusted press photographers to be outside the front door so as to photograph you as you leave the building?' Colville asked Churchill.[41] 'It would be the first photograph taken since your illness and would clearly be of great interest to the press.' Churchill was clearly nervous at the prospect. 'Do nothing until

I tell you. If photographed at all it will be inside the garden and standing still.'[42]

On Wednesday 22 July, Moran found him in 'poor form', walking badly with his speech slurred.[43] Yet the following day he demonstrated to his doctor that he could get out of bed, walk across the room and climb onto a chair. 'What do you think of that?' he asked defiantly.

So Colville continued to work on his plan, and briefed Fleet Street editors that the Prime Minister would be in Downing Street on Friday 24th. He suggested to Churchill that first of all some photographs could be taken in the garden – with Sir Russell Brain, the Prime Minister's neurologist, 'asked to come by the side door in the garden at the 11 Downing Street end'.[44]

I suggest that you should leave by the front door for Chequers – otherwise it will be thought there were special reasons for your not doing so. If you paused on the doorstep to acknowledge the welcome of the crowds the photographers in the street would all take photographs of you doing so. You would then only have to walk three or four yards to the door of the car, and we would take such steps as are possible to prevent your being photographed getting into the car. If you walked using your ordinary walking stick with the gold top I am sure that nobody would notice that you were not walking perfectly normally.

In the end, however, the Downing Street plan was considered too risky and instead the photo opportunity was staged at Chartwell prior to Churchill's continuing rehabilitation at Chequers. One of those 'trusted' cameramen Colville referred to, Eric Greenwood from *The Times*, was invited to come and take a picture for release to the general press.

So after lunch with Colville, who reckoned he was 'amazingly restored', Churchill posed at the front door of Chartwell, wearing a summer suit and fedora, with the gold top stick in his right hand and the obligatory cigar in his left.[45] He was able to walk unaided to his car, pausing on the way to admire a lime tree in the yard.

'Churchill had a fine photograph of himself, looking very well, in all the papers on Saturday,' noted Macmillan.[46] The *Times* headline was 'Great Benefit from Month's Rest', quoting the statement put out by Downing Street to accompany the picture.[47] The American news agencies speculated – correctly as it turned out – that the Prime Minister would be heading to the south of France for 'further rest' in August or September. 'He will be in closer touch with British state affairs than was possible at his own country estate at Chartwell,' reported United Press.[48]

Churchill was now starting to immerse himself more closely in day-to-day government business. First, though, he invited Eden and his wife Clarissa to luncheon with him and Clementine on Monday 27 July. The Foreign Secretary, returning from America after his operation, had had his own photo opportunity with reporters on Sunday, looking well, if somewhat thinner as he had lost one and a half stone.

It could have been a tricky discussion about whether Churchill was willing to hand over the reins of power to his perennial successor, but in the event the conversation was kept to foreign affairs. There was much to ponder, especially on Russia, with the arrest of Lavrentiy Beria having just been reported in the Soviet press – which Eden believed had been a setback for the moderates in the Kremlin.

'Anthony was very outspoken to Winston about his Russian get-together, Aunt Clemmie agreeing with Anthony,' noted Clarissa. Eden also defended Eisenhower, about whom Churchill declared, 'He is a nice man, but a fool.'[49]

Easement with the Soviet Union continued to be the subject most on Churchill's mind as he re-engaged more fully in the early weeks of August. He told Colville he was depressed by Eden's attitude, which 'consigns us to years more of hatred and hostility'.[50] He was also perturbed by Lord Salisbury's report of his recent discussions with Eisenhower and Dulles in Washington.

'Lord S says he found Eisenhower violently Russophobe ... and believes the President to be personally responsible for the policy of useless pinpricks and harassing tactics the US is following against Russia in Europe and the Far East.'[51]

Not everyone at the Foreign Office welcomed Churchill's revived interest. 'We are trying to conduct our foreign policy through the PM who is ... always in the bath or asleep or too busy having dinner when we want urgent decisions,' wrote a frustrated Evelyn Shuckburgh, Eden's principal private secretary.[52] 'He has to be consulted about drafting points in the reply to the Soviets; about every individual "intelligence" operation (which he usually forbids for fear of upsetting the Russians).'

Keen to return to the political fray, Churchill now told Beaverbrook he had 'not absolutely excluded the idea of going to Washington in the last fortnight of September if progress continues good. There are a lot of things I might say in a talk with Ike.'[53]

Certainly normal life was beginning to return. He was playing croquet, and walking round the garden at Chequers. Sir Norman Brook was a regular visitor to run through government business, while Denis Kelly, his assiduous researcher and editor, worked with him in the afternoons on his war memoirs.

On Wednesday 12 August, on his way from Chequers to Chartwell, he stopped in at 10 Downing Street to be examined by Sir Russell Brain, who told him he had made 'considerable progress'.[54] Privately, to Lord Moran, Brain said, 'In a month's time he will be as well as he will ever be ... [but] I doubt whether he will ever be able to re-enter public life.'

But Churchill's inner circle was starting to think differently, heartened by the advances he had made. 'Bless him. He now thinks that the fractional measure of moderation induced by illness has well-nigh renewed his youth,' Bracken wrote to Beaverbrook on 14 August.[55] 'Retirement is not in his vocabulary. Such defeatist trash is not for him!'

There were still the moments of doubt. Churchill told Colville on 15 August that 'he was coming round towards resignation in October' and that 'he no longer has the zest for work and finds the world in an abominable state. Greatly depressed by thoughts on the hydrogen bomb.'[56]

If the British press had been dutiful – or merely ignorant – about Churchill's stroke, that was not the case with the American correspondents. Brothers Joe and Stewart Alsop, sharp Washington insiders and renowned columnists on the *New York Herald Tribune*, had published – by and large – the full story in early August, which was then syndicated to papers all around America.

'The facts are these,' Stewart Alsop wrote. 'In the last week of June Churchill suffered a stroke, caused by a partially blocked artery which resulted in an interference of the blood supply to the brain ... doctors believed, at best, that Churchill would be a semi-invalid confined to a wheelchair for a long time.'[57]

Alsop then reported – his one error in the article – that Churchill had 'prescribed for himself an unconventional course of treatment, designed to restore his circulation. To the astonishment of the doctors, he was able very soon to leave his wheelchair. He now walks about, although for brief periods and with some difficulty.'

On 17 August, the *Daily Mirror*, seizing on the *Tribune*'s story, was belatedly stung into action. 'What is the Truth About Churchill's Illness?' it roared.[58]

Is there any reason why the British people should not be told the facts about the health of their Prime Minister? Is there any reason why they should always be the last to learn what is going on in their own country?

Must they always be driven to pick up their information from tittle-tattle abroad?

To Moran, Churchill reacted disingenuously. 'Five million people read that. It's rubbish, of course, but it won't help at Margate.'[59] But he need not have worried – there was no real follow-up in Fleet Street to the *Daily Mirror* story. His stroke, now known about by millions of Americans, still remained hidden from the British public.

Churchill was now determined to pass the next milestone, returning to take charge of Cabinet once more, and he duly reached it at 5 p.m. on Tuesday 18 August. He had been driven up from Chartwell in the morning, and saw Sir Norman Brook and Lord Moran before taking luncheon in bed.

Word had got out about his surprise return, and ministers arriving in the late afternoon were greeted by an unusually large crowd in Downing Street, applauding them as they arrived. Churchill, accompanied by Clementine, stood on the steps of No. 10 to acknowledge the cheers, looking pale and leaning on a stick, but jauntily doffing his hat.

In the meeting, which lasted just under two hours, he was, according to Harold Macmillan, in 'tremendous form, full of quips and epigrams.'[60] He chipped in when the latest diplomatic moves over Egypt were discussed, and then sanctioned the sending of two more battalions to trouble-torn Kenya. On disputes over constitutional reform in different areas of Nigeria, he quipped: 'They are divided. We come in as umpire, as well as ruler.'

On rioting in Colombo, Ceylon, following a general strike by communist parties, he commented: 'It's a bit hard to us to be asked to come in when we have been turned out. Why can't they maintain adequate forces to preserve law and order.' But he was happy to sanction the sending in of UK naval landing parties. 'Teach them a lesson. Would do them good.'[61]

After it was over Sir Norman Brook, who took the minutes, thought the Prime Minister had allowed other ministers to talk more than usual. But he observed Churchill had walked to his seat as he normally did, and no one would have noticed anything amiss with his speech. 'He has dipped his foot in water, and it wasn't cold; he wants to go on.'[62]

A trip to Lord Beaverbrook's villa in the south of France now beckoned, where the Prime Minister could relax and – hopefully – do some painting. All the while he would be thinking, dictating passages, planning for his next milestone – the leader's speech at the party conference on 10 October. His future as Prime Minister would depend on the success of this address.

* * *

The war in Korea had entered a dangerous phase. With the National Security Council having effectively authorised – as a final option – the use of atomic bombs, the United States set out to warn her enemies of that perilous consequence. American diplomats in the relevant capitals began to leak contents of those meetings in the spring when the Joint Chiefs of Staff recommended tactical nuclear weapons should be in the armoury for use in North Korea and across the border in China.

In late May, Secretary of State John Foster Dulles had travelled to New Delhi, where he used the neutral Prime Minister of India, Jawaharlal Nehru, as a conduit to the Chinese leaders. He told Nehru – to tell Mao – that 'if the armistice negotiations collapsed, the United States would probably make a stronger rather than a lesser military exertion, and that this might well extend the area of conflict'.[63] In other words, atomic bombs could be dropped on Manchuria.

A few days later, General Mark Clark wrote to North Korean leader Kim Il-sung and his army commander General Peng Dehuai to emphasise that the negotiations had reached their final stage and the

UN would no longer 'engage in prolonged and fruitless repetition of arguments'.[64]

Then on 3 June it was the turn of the Soviets to get the message, when the new US ambassador in Moscow, Charles Bohlen, hammered home to Soviet Minister of Foreign Affairs Vyacheslav Molotov 'the extreme seriousness and importance' of the final US negotiating position.[65] The nuclear threat, coded or otherwise, had now been relayed to all three enemy parties.

But in any case, for different reasons, Peking, Moscow and Pyongyang had little appetite for continuing the war in Korea. In December 1952, Premier of the People's Republic of China Zhou Enlai had announced that the government would accelerate its industrialisation programme with its first five-year plan in 1953. There was an urgent need to divert spending away from the military – which had taken 48 per cent of the national budget in 1951 – towards consumer and export industries.

Whether the threat of atomic attack worried Mao unduly anyway was a moot point. Famously, a few years earlier the Chinese leader had described nuclear weapons as 'paper tigers' and declared that the 'outcome of war is decided by the people, not by one or two types of weapons'.[66] He believed that a nuclear attack against his undeveloped, rural country with its vast – and widely dispersed – population would be ineffective.

The morale of the North Koreans was also starting to crack. In May 1953, the UN air force had elected to target irrigation dams and rice fields, washing away lines of communication – roads and railways – and destroying crops to cause famine and unrest in the countryside. Humanitarian concerns had prevented this sort of attack until now, but in mid-May five dams were struck, including Toksan, near Pyongyang, and seventy nearby villages were submerged. National income had diminished by more than one-third and inflation was destroying incomes across the war-ravaged country.

As for the Soviet Union, after Stalin's death there were a mixture of economic and political motives for wanting the curtain to be brought down on this war. The new leadership wished to spend less on military hardware and concentrate a little more on providing better consumer goods for their hard-pressed people, who had already been through four of the five-year plans the Chinese now envisaged. In addition, Malenkov, in his speech to the Supreme Soviet on 15 March – and elsewhere – had given out enough signs to show he was interested in a different kind of relationship with America, possibly even one of peaceful coexistence.

Whatever the reason – US threats, or self-interest, or a mixture of the two – the North Korean and Chinese negotiators were less intransigent in late May and early June. Talks proceeded smoothly, and on 8 June there was a major breakthrough with an agreement on the voluntary repatriation of prisoners of war. On 15 June, the military leaders worked out an agreed demarcation line between the two armies, and General Peng Dehuai ordered all Chinese and North Korean forces to cease offensive operations the next day. It looked like the war, in its thirty-sixth month, might be over within days, not weeks.

But there was one major stumbling block – the acerbic, prickly, obstinate President of the Republic of South Korea (ROK), Syngman Rhee. The 78-year-old ex-émigré, who lived for many years in the United States and Hawaii before returning to South Korea after the Second World War, should have been the ideal placeman and partner for the Truman and Eisenhower administrations.

He had established his credentials as a fighter for Korean independence over half a century, his badge of courage earned by a period of torture and imprisonment at the hands of the Japanese. This Harvard graduate spoke fluent English and conversed with authority with the American politicians, businessmen and military officers who were helping sustain his new country.

His single-minded devotion to his homeland should have been a strength. But the US Department of State, in many dealings with him between the wars, had identified him as a stubborn personality and a 'dangerous mischief maker'. Now, in the role he had wanted all his life, he quickly displayed disturbing authoritarian tendencies. The National Assembly of the Republic of Korea was disbanded if it showed any signs of having a mind of its own, and elections were thoroughly rigged. Opposition leaders were intimidated or arrested by a ruthless security police, usually accused of being communists.

Indeed, Rhee was the most virulent of anti-communists. 'It is perfectly clear to me that communism can only be defeated by war,' he told a correspondent from *Time* magazine.[67] 'What we must bring about is the one event that the Soviet system cannot survive – a setback, a defeat … our only chance of escaping a third world war is to inflict such a defeat in one of the "little" wars, perhaps this war.'

It was this attitude that he still carried with him in the summer of 1953, just as the United Nations, led by America, was seeking a compromise in order to end the war. Rhee still countenanced nothing less than the expulsion of all Chinese forces from Korea, and the complete unification of the north with the south. So on 18 June he deliberately sought to sabotage the delicate armistice agreement when he authorised the release of 25,000 anti-communist North Korean prisoners of war who had been in the custody of ROK forces.

The UN forces recaptured only around 1,000 – the rest melted away and merged with the local population. Having broken the prisoner exchange contract, UN commanders were now worried that Rhee might do further damage on the battlefield. His South Korean troops held two-thirds of the UN front lines where combat had been suspended. If Rhee ordered his soldiers to attack the communist forces, a counterattack would most likely wipe out the ROK forces and along with them the adjoining American and UN forces in the remaining third of the front line. There was no knowing where this might end.

Eisenhower and Dulles were at the end of their tether. 'It is impossible to attempt to recite the long list of items in which Rhee has been completely uncooperative, even recalcitrant,' the President reflected.[68] It was at this moment that America gave serious thought to activating Operation Everready, drawn up a year earlier and designed to overthrow Syngman Rhee in circumstances like this when he wilfully obstructed the UN mission.

In May, General Mark Clark had spelt out what would happen in Operation Everready. 'President Rhee would be invited to visit Seoul or elsewhere – anywhere to get him out of Pusan' (the temporary capital of South Korea), he wrote in a memo to the US Department of the Army.[69] 'At an appropriate time, the UN commander would move in to the Pusan area and seize between five and ten key ROK officials who have been leaders in Rhee's dictatorial actions … and take over control of martial law through the ROK Chief of Staff until it is lifted.'

Clark said that Rhee would then be urged to sign a proclamation lifting martial law, permitting the National Assembly freedom of action and to establish freedom of the press and radio 'without interference from his various strong armed agencies', and that 'if Rhee would not agree to issue the proclamation he would be held in protective custody, incommunicado'.

Churchill was on board for Operation Everready, whenever the Americans saw fit to launch it. On 19 June the Prime Minister noted in a letter to Eisenhower: 'There will be a lot of trouble if the war goes on while Syngman Rhee is in office.'[70] Eisenhower agreed, ruefully observing, 'It is remarkable how little concern men seem to have for logic, statistics, and even, indeed, survival; we live by emotion, prejudice and pride.'[71]

Churchill responded by affirming his support for the removal of Rhee if Eisenhower thought the time was at hand, and offered him an extra British brigade for the task. On 21 June, the British ambassador to Washington, Sir Roger Makins, sent back a top-secret handwritten letter, which included Eisenhower's response.

I saw the President this morning and gave him your message. On Rhee, he sympathises with your desire but said emphatically that any change must come or appear to come from within. He felt strongly that the Western powers that had intervened in Korea to uphold freedom and democracy must not be seen to be setting up a puppet government. He had given much thought to this.[72]

Makins added that the President 'entirely agrees that the matter should be kept in closest secrecy. Any hint that such a thing was under discussion could have [a] most serious effect.'

The ambassador added that he 'understood confidentially' that Eisenhower and some of his advisers 'have, in fact, already discussed at length ways and means of dealing with Rhee and that there are also unconfirmed indications that a military coup in Korea is being prepared'.

But if Churchill felt it would be legitimate to remove the stubborn Rhee for the sake of peace, his acting Foreign Secretary certainly did not. On 3 July, as Churchill's recovery from his stroke was just getting underway, Lord Salisbury wrote a stern and cautionary note to his stricken Prime Minister.

I do not at all like the idea of the United States or us embarking on wars both with Rhee and the Chinese communists, and greatly hope things will not come to that. It would be likely to cause bewilderment to those whose sons are fighting in Korea and also to earnest supporters of the United Nations. The alternative of the United Nations forces clearing out is not very attractive either, especially for the Americans, who have had 130,000 casualties in defending the country.[73]

At lunch with NATO deputy commander Lord Montgomery two days later, Churchill voiced his frustration when asked what Britain's policy was in Korea.

If I were in charge I would withdraw the United Nations troops to the coast and leave Syngman Rhee to the Chinese. But the American public would not swallow this.

I'd never heard of the place till I was seventy-four. Its importance lies in the fact that it has led to the rearming of America. That may have saved the peace of the world.[74]

The Prime Minister's musings while ill may not have represented his considered opinion when fit and well. However, as it turned out, there was no need for Operation Everready. Slow and painstaking diplomacy would eventually bring round the unpredictable Rhee – much of the credit going to Walter Robertson, America's assistant secretary of state for Far Eastern affairs, who had been specially dispatched by Dulles from Washington.

The 'quiet, softly-spoken' Robertson effectively acted as Rhee's counsellor in those first few days. 'He brought the fanatic South Korean President down to earth by sitting with him in a room for several days and listening patiently and sympathetically while Rhee talked steadily about his grievances,' noted Sherman Adams, Eisenhower's Chief of Staff.[75]

Then Robertson patiently made sure Rhee understood America's position, that the United States would not go to war to unite his country, but on the other hand would not leave South Korea without economic aid and military support after the truce. On 12 July, Robertson was able to fly to Tokyo with a letter from Rhee to Eisenhower agreeing not to obstruct an armistice.

In return, Rhee would eventually gain a US–South Korea mutual security treaty, a lump sum payment of $200 million as the first instalment of a long-term economic aid programme for his country and the expansion of the ROK army to twenty divisions.

But Rhee's reckless act on 18 June only encouraged the communists to try to take advantage of the apparent disarray on the UN side – to teach Rhee the lesson that he could still lose the war, and warn him not to hinder the armistice negotiations. It would cost thousands of lives in the final five weeks of the war.

In July, a series of ferocious, if short-lived, offensives were launched against the ROK lines. On 13 July, 80,000 soldiers from the Chinese People's Volunteer Army struck the east-central Kumsong ('bulge') sector, the brunt of their attack aimed at four ROK divisions. The Chinese broke through the main line of resistance along 21 miles of the front, and the South Koreans were forced to withdraw 19 miles to avoid encirclement. However, the new ROK army – more resilient than at any time in the three years of the war – counter-attacked after 16 July and even pushed the communists back 5 miles.

The end result of these encounters was probably a narrow points victory for the Chinese. But the terrain they had recovered was relatively useless, and both sides were wearying of this attritional warfare. Negotiations – with Rhee now onside – continued apace in the third week of July, and 27 July was the day finally set for signing an armistice.

The final military demarcation (or 'armistice') line, agreed on 23 July, showed precious little difference from the 38th parallel which had divided the nations at the start of the war. It would meander in an east–west fashion across Korea, connecting the East Sea with Gyeonggi Bay, 148 miles away on the peninsula's west coast. A 2.5-mile-wide fortified 'buffer' zone was also established between North and South Korea.

The build-up to the signing ceremony in Panmunjom was in keeping with much of the diplomacy of the past year – scrappy, argumentative and acrimonious. Communist negotiators insisted that newspaper correspondents from the ROK and from China should be barred. General Clark said he would not be party to a ceremony with that and other 'such strings tied', and threatened to boycott Panmunjom and have the armistice documents flown to Tokyo for him to sign.[76] He was persuaded by Eisenhower to stay and sign on Korean soil – and give way on the issue of the newsmen.

The communist side, concerned with the symbolism of the event, had provided only one entrance in the original plans for the simple pinewood pagoda that was to be constructed for the ceremony – a door facing north, provocatively requiring the United Nations delegation to cross into communist territory to enter.

General Clark successfully argued for a southern entrance for his commanders so that they would not have to pass through the enemy area. He had also insisted on the removal of two communist 'peace dove' propaganda symbols – created by Pablo Picasso and familiar throughout the world from communist-led peace demonstrations – from the pagoda.

So, promptly at 10 a.m. on 27 July, in an atmosphere of chilly politeness, the two chief actors entered from their opposite sides of the building for the stark, underplayed ceremony. General William Kelly Harrison Jr, the UN senior delegate, tieless and without his many Second World War decorations, sat down with calculated casualness at his table and methodically began to sign for his side with his own ten-year-old fountain pen. The North Korean military commander General Nam Il, wooden-faced and sweating profusely in his heavy tunic, took his seat at another table to sign for the communist side.

Each man signed eighteen copies of the main truce documents (six each in English, Korean and Chinese), which aides carried back and forth. Meanwhile, the rumble of artillery still rolled through the building. Flashbulbs blazed and cameras whirred as the two chief delegates silently wrote.

When they had finished, Harrison, a direct descendant of the 9th President of the United States, and Nam Il, a schoolteacher in uniform, rose and departed without a word to each other, or even a nod or a handshake. Outside, a correspondent asked a British officer whether the Commonwealth Division would celebrate with the traditional fire-works. 'No,' said the Briton, 'there is nothing to celebrate. Both sides have lost.'[77] It was a view echoed by the leader writer of *The Times* that morning, whose piece was headlined 'Fought to a Draw'.[78]

The ceasefire was in place, so the document said, only 'until a final peaceful settlement is achieved'. Article IV (Paragraph 60) of the armistice agreement called for a political conference to be held within three months to strive for a permanent solution.

So, thirty-seven months and two days after the Soviet-trained North Koreans attacked across the 38th parallel, the war – a devastating struggle, laced from the start with glory, agony, triumph and frustration – came to a halt. The countries involved suffered a total of more than 4 million casualties, of which at least half were civilians – a higher percentage than in the Second World War.

A total of 36,940 Americans lost their lives in the Korean theatre; some 92,134 were wounded in action, while 8,176 were reported as missing. Casualties among other UN allies totalled 16,532, including 3,094 dead. A million South Korean civilians were killed, together with 217,000 soldiers. On the North Korean side, 600,000 civilians died, along with 406,000 troops. It was calculated that around 900,000 Chinese soldiers lost their lives in combat.

Lord Salisbury announced the armistice in the House of Lords, claiming that the United Nations action – the organisation taking up arms for the first time in collective resistance to aggression – had been successful. In August 1950, he told their lordships, the total evacuation of UN forces from Korea seemed to be almost inevitable. 'Since then … the forces of aggression have been driven back beyond the line from which they started.'[79]

More than 1,100 British servicemen had been killed in the war, with 2,600 wounded and over 1,000 missing or taken prisoner. 'The contribution of this country and of the Commonwealth … has been one in which we can take pride,' Lord Salisbury said.

On the eve of the armistice signing, President Eisenhower had spent the day at the White House in contemplative mood, painting and – a favourite pastime of his – re-reading some of Abraham Lincoln's famous speeches.

He chose the closing lines from his hero's second inaugural address to conclude his press statement on the ending of the war:

> With malice toward none; with charity for all; with firmness in the right as God gives us to see the right, let us strive on to finish the work we are in … to do all which may achieve a just and a lasting peace, among ourselves, and with all nations.[80]

The last remaining act of the Korean War – the repatriation of all remaining prisoners of war, dubbed Operation Big Switch – would be played out between August and December. In those months the UN Command transferred 75,801 captives into Chinese and North Korean hands, including about 450 women and twenty-three children. The communists for their part handed over 12,773 prisoners to the UN, including 3,326 Americans. That left about 23,000 in UN hands to be moved to the Neutral Nations Repatriation Commission in the Korean Demilitarized Zone, where they could make a final choice concerning their future place of abode.

Only 137 of those 23,000 wanted to go home to North Korea or China: most chose resettlement in South Korea or Taiwan. Of the 359 prisoners who had been in communist hands, ten – two American and eight Korean – elected to return home. But 325 Koreans, twenty-one Americans and one Briton chose to make their future in a communist country.

The US public was shocked. How could these soldiers have been so brainwashed that they would choose a life of rice and cotton suits in preference to a return to Jersey City or San Francisco? At a time when American political self-confidence was under such strain from

McCarthyism, was this not clear evidence of the ability of the communists to make conversions even amid the brutality of a prison camp regime? Seeds of fear and doubt were sown that would not be easily rooted out.

Up until the last minute the UN Command spokesmen tried to persuade the defectors to change their minds, broadcasting from a van just outside the barbed wire perimeter of the pro-communist prisoners' compound. But seventeen of the Americans and the sole Briton crowded against the wire and responded by singing 'The Internationale' and other songs, and danced a community dance, while their South Korean comrades played music and shouted a loud 'No' in concerted efforts to deny themselves the opportunity of hearing the appeals.

One of the twenty-one, Corporal Clarence Adams from Memphis, Tennessee, an African-American, cited racial discrimination in the United States as a reason for refusing repatriation. While a prisoner, Adams had taken classes in communist political theory, and afterwards lectured other prisoners in the camps.

The sole Briton not to return home was Andrew Condron, a Glaswegian from 41 (Independent) Royal Marine Commando. 'Right up until the last minute I had no thought other than to come home,' he recalled later.[81]

> But I had been quite impressed by the friendly behaviour of the Chinese in the camps, and I was interested in the Marxist ideas they put forward as an answer to man's problems. I knew of course that this was theory, and it wouldn't necessarily be followed through by the practice. So I thought that I would like to go to China for a year, and see if the practice matched the theory.

In fact, Condron would stay in China until 1960, when he eventually decided to return to the United Kingdom because of growing xenophobia under Mao. He received an honourable discharge from the Royal Marines and began work selling the *Encyclopædia Britannica* door-to-door.

* * *

A gathering of Whitehall's finest met in conference room A at the Cabinet Office on Wednesday 29 July 1953 to ponder the United Kingdom's prospects in the event of a future atomic war. The vivid report they had in front of them must have felt at times like something out of the pages of the bleakest kind of dystopian novel.

The group sitting down that afternoon was the Home Defence Committee, chaired by Cabinet Secretary Sir Norman Brook, who had himself set it up five months earlier. Among those joining him at the table – civil servants and military leaders – were the 'big beasts' from the Treasury, Home Office and the Ministry of Fuel and Power – Sir Thomas Padmore, Sir Frank Newsam and Sir John Redcliffe-Maud.

All of these men would have crucial roles to play if the state of affairs envisaged by the author of the report should ever come to pass. The document was named 'The Initial Phase of the War', and it was compiled by Robert Hall, director of the economic section of the Cabinet Office, and his committee, the 'National Economy in War Working Party'.

Hall's committee had taken as its brief the words of that influential paper of a year ago, 'Global Strategy and Defence Policy', which had warned that when World War Three arrived, it would begin with a Soviet atomic-led attack on the United Kingdom of 'unparalleled intensity', which would ensure 'terrible damage'. It had been the job of Hall and his colleagues in the past four months to calculate what kind of destruction would be wrought on the country, and what kind of civil defence – if any – could be mounted in the face of it.

The grim scenario Hall was invited to consider went like this. It is mid-September 1956, and the United Kingdom is at war. There has been a warning of an attack and up to 9 million people – 5 million organised – have fled the towns and cities. But in just a few mass raids in the opening days of the war, Soviet planes have penetrated UK defences, dropping 132 Nagasaki-type atomic bombs, which burst at a height of about one-eighth of a mile. They have fallen at night, and all terrified citizens can do – with few adequate air-raid shelters – is to take cover at home as best they can.[82]

The bombs have struck vital targets, destroying seats of government, ports and dockyards, railway centres, oil installations and big centres of population; thirty-five have landed in the London area. In addition, forty more bombs have been dropped on atomic air bases and atomic energy establishments, while a further twenty-eight remain in reserve, ready to complete the devastation of precision targets not taken out in the first wave.

How many Britons would survive? What conditions would they live in, and what resources would be available to them? Would any kind of government – national or regional – remain and would it be able to manage a ravaged country? These were the questions that Hall and his colleagues had to address.

Hall, a dapper, modest Australian-born economist, had been at the heart of planning and execution of Treasury policy in his day-to-day work. He had played a vital part in the big financial controversy of 1952, when he was one of those leading the opposition to ROBOT, Rab Butler's attempt to solve Britain's balance of payments by allowing sterling to 'float' and to be convertible.

But now, given a less dry subject to explore on paper, he used striking imagery and story-telling to support his usual masterful analysis, presenting a very clear picture of a post-apocalyptic country.

The casualty count alone was frightening. Hall calculated that

1.378 million people would be dead after those early attacks, and 785,000 seriously injured. In the first days of an atomic war there would be more casualties than there were – military or civilian – in both world wars. Ten million people would be left homeless.

In Hall's scenario, only 300,000 hospital beds were left to accommodate those 785,000 seriously injured – and a quarter of these would be taken up by the 'ordinary sick'. With a severe shortage of surgeons, only one-sixth of the 200,000 who were critically ill could be operated on. 'The rest must presumably be left to die – with what effect on public morale may only be imagined.'[83]

The demand for emergency feeding was 'overwhelming and long-lasting' for the homeless, 'huddled around the edge of the bombed-out areas'. The Ministry of Food might be able to handle this problem, but only if enough vans and petrol are available, if there is any water left for baking and cooking, and if they can make it through the rubble.

As for fuel and power, generating stations supplying about two-fifths of the electricity of the country have been shut down and three-fifths of the nation's gas has been lost. There is plenty of coal at the pithead, but whether any transport is available, or any roads open, to transport the coal to the gas works and electricity stations is doubtful.

Hall identified one or two 'bright spots in this bleak panorama'. A quarter of normal railway working is possible, rising to a half in a fortnight – although London has just one terminus in action. Half of the industrial capacity of the country is undamaged – although factories will be difficult to run without many workers and managers, who have either been killed or have disappeared to look after their homes and families.

What about the survivors? Take John Smith of Labernum Villa, Stoke Newington in London as an example. 'His house has been badly damaged; but a couple of rooms downstairs can be made weatherproof with blankets and tarpaulins, and John Smith is a conscientious sort of person who would like to stay put and get on with his job for as long as possible.'[84]

But there are severe difficulties.

He has no electricity and gas to cook by, and the coal delivery has not got through. Apart from the tins in the store cupboard, the family has to rely for its food on the emergency feeding centre a mile away. Even worse, there is no water until a meagre supply comes through by lorry – if indeed these supplies do get through at all and are enough to go round. John Smith would like to go to his job, which is essential work, but does not even know if the factory is standing.

There are at this stage no newspapers and no current for his all-mains receiver, so he cannot even find out from the wireless what the Government would like him to do.

It has become clear that London is unworkable, and it is no longer possible for the central government to function in the destroyed capital.

'Consider the explosions everywhere,' Hall imagined,

the nerve-wracking effects of [the] blasts, the fires raging everywhere, the sight of the injured whom no one can reach – above all, perhaps, the dread of the unknown and the terror of radioactive effects. It is a shattering prospect, and it is a bold man who would deny the probability of a mass flight, set off by the instinct of self-preservation, and the possibility of serious panic, especially in a congested area such as the East End of London.

So Hall's overall conclusion, if not quite in these words, was that the United Kingdom was hopelessly ill-prepared for surviving an atomic attack. More hospital beds and doctors would be needed; larger stocks of food and fuel near the target area; much greater numbers of lorries and other vehicles to work around the ravaged areas; building supplies for repair on a huge scale; and the better protection of communications systems.

Authority would collapse in Hall's scenario. He had not been asked to make recommendations, but nevertheless he made a major one. Britain could survive a nuclear attack, only after a fashion,

> but a sufficient number of key people concerned at all levels of government, local, regional and central, must be so placed that they survive the disaster and are able to exercise immediate and effective control and leadership. There must be adequate means of communication between the central Government, the Regions, and the local areas, and some means of communication with the people as a whole. Unless these conditions can be met, any detailed plans which may be made in advance are likely to break down.

Sir Norman Brook's committee – judging from its relatively brief minutes – seemed stunned by what they had read. Admiral Sir Rhoderick McGrigor, First Sea Lord, reflected that

> it was clear everything should be done to prevent such an attack taking place. This emphasised even more than before the importance of the Allies building up a powerful deterrent. The Russians ... must be made to realise that the effect of atomic attack on their ability to fight a war or even survive might be worse than on the United Kingdom.[85]

Sir William Dickson, Chief of the Air Staff, looked ahead to a time when the Soviet Union, if not matching America in her atomic stockpile, would have enough to mount an effective counter-attack. 'The point would [then] be reached when for either side to initiate atomic warfare would be a form of mutual suicide.'[86]

That was for the future. Right now, the United Kingdom was the first target in the Soviets' sights, and Brook's committee took on board Hall's recommendation that much more was needed to ensure the country had a functioning government of sorts when the atomic bombs started to fall.

The baton now passed from Hall to Sir Thomas Padmore, who had been heading a Committee of the Redistribution of Government Staff in War since the late 1940s. He had to consider how many ministers and civil servants could safely remain in London – or whether a widespread dispersal of day-to-day government operations to the countryside would work better.

In the Second World War, Churchill and his colleagues had remained in the heart of the capital in the underground Cabinet War Rooms. They had another option, codenamed 'Paddock', which was a vast subterranean complex built directly beneath the Post Office Research and Development Station in Dollis Hill, Willesden. But Churchill disliked the damp, oppressive atmosphere of 'Paddock', and used it just twice for Cabinet meetings in the whole of the war.

The Whitehall system of linking bunkers had been further developed since the war. But now, in the atomic age, the requirements would be very different. Padmore would contemplate keeping just 7,000 to 8,000 central government staff in London, so he needed to find an alternative seat of emergency government for the Prime Minister and his staff in – ideally – a massive, secluded rural site.

At this early stage there was already a frontrunner – the huge, 240-acre Spring Quarry underground complex at Corsham, in north Wiltshire. Spring Quarry had already done war work – Churchill and Beaverbrook sanctioned its conversion in 1940 into the largest underground factory in the world, producing Centaurus radial engines for the Bristol Aeroplane Company. Padmore began to draw up tentative plans for the new use of Spring Quarry, giving it the codename 'Subterfuge'.[87]

There were, as ever, lessons to be learned from America. The White House was well advanced with its own secret programme to ensure continuity of government in the event of nuclear attack, building communication sites, personnel bunkers and command and control posts, ranging from southern Pennsylvania all the way to North Carolina.

In July, the 'Big Daddy' of them all was nearly ready. Work on the Raven Rock Mountain Complex near Blue Ridge Summit, Pennsylvania, was all but complete, two and a half years after being authorised by President Harry Truman. 'Site R', also dubbed the 'underground Pentagon', was an underground nuclear bunker which had emergency operations centres for the US Army, Navy and Air Force.

It was actually more of a mini city. Sat half a mile inside Raven Rock and another half a mile below the mountain's peak, Site R had power stations, underground water reservoirs, a small chapel, clusters of three-storey buildings set within vast caverns, and enough beds to accommodate 2,000 high-ranking officials from the Pentagon, the State Department and the National Security Council.

Money had been no object in the building of 'Harry's Hole', as the locals liked to call it. Eisenhower dispatched National Security Advisor Robert Cutler one Sunday to inspect the project, and in his briefing to the President that evening he mentioned that the cost would be $37 million. But, repeating his report to the full National Security Council the following morning, Cutler put the expense at $47 million.

'That's not what you told me yesterday,' the President exclaimed. 'I know, sir,' Cutler replied. 'This banker's face is red. I added the figures again last night and found I was $10 million off.'[88] The NSC members, Eisenhower along with them, broke into laughter. With the final touches being put to Raven Rock, the President could now be satisfied that his administration's plans for Doomsday were all in place.

Georgy Malenkov – Stalin's protégé and successor,
who brought the Soviet H-bomb project to fruition.

Mohammad Mossadegh – Iran's eccentric premier, a constant thorn in Britain's side.

CHAPTER 8

JOE 4

Stalin's successor had much to prove when he stepped onto the podium beneath the imposing statue of Lenin in the lofty, columned Great Hall of the Kremlin on Saturday 8 August 1953. The serried ranks of the uniformly grey-suited 1,300 members (virtually all men) of the Supreme Soviet had travelled from all corners of the USSR to listen to their new leader's vision of the future – to hear if it would be any different to the man whose coat-tails he had so firmly clung to over the past quarter of a century.

Georgy Maximilianovich Malenkov, aged fifty-one, was an unprepossessing-looking individual. Short – around 5ft 7in, the same height as Stalin – and fat, he had a head like a bull with a pale, pudgy, strangely cherubic face, with thick, bushy eyebrows and a full crop of stiff black hair. Smiling did not come easy to him, and when he broke out into a grin, it had an unfortunately petulant, even sinister air. A Western diplomat quipped that his picture was the 'best anti-Communist propaganda I know'.[1]

Malenkov was born in Orenburg in the Urals on the boundary of Europe and Asia, nearly 1,000 miles from Moscow. His father was a wealthy farmer and his mother the granddaughter of an Orthodox priest – bourgeois and religious connections he was not especially keen to linger over when establishing his proletarian credentials in later years.

Malenkov was too young to take part in the 1917 revolution but gave up his university studies to fight with the Red Army in Turkestan in the Civil War. Joining the Communist Party in 1920, he first completed his education and graduated as an engineer in 1925. His big break came in the same year when Stalin took notice of his diligent party work and recruited him to his group of secretaries.

From then on, as the dictator's protégé, his rise was meteoric; head of the party for the Moscow region five years later and then, at thirty-two, landing a big job on the Central Committee of the Soviet Communist Party. There he perfected a system of personnel card indexing, a ready reference of comprehensive, minute information on his master's friends and enemies. He knew the bodies – and where they were buried.

Indeed, Malenkov played his part in the Great Terror of the 1930s, personally supervising regional purges of the Communist Party in Kazan, Belorussia and Armenia in 1937.

By the time of the Second World War Stalin had made him a member of his inner five-man circle, and Malenkov was given the responsibility of aircraft production, increasing it to the point where the Soviets were turning out 40,000 planes a year. During the war years too, he often acted as Stalin's spokesman.

He was resented by others in the Politburo who regarded him purely as Stalin's creature, a man with no regional party base. To Khrushchev, Malenkov was a 'typical office clerk and pen-pusher' while in similar vein Molotov derided him as 'Telephone Man'.[2]

This was sheer jealousy in the top ranks. Malenkov, aside from his proven organisational and administrative roles, was actually one of the more intellectually minded members of the Politburo. His all-round skills, as much as Stalin's backing, had enabled him to reach the summit.

But he had had little or no experience of the world outside the Soviet Union. His only visit abroad was in 1947 to Warsaw, to help form the Communist Information Bureau (Cominform) there. Ideologically, this trip was like a short walk to a Moscow suburb.

The Kremlin public relations machine got to work to bolster Malenkov's image. *Pravda* published a photograph showing him with Stalin and Mao Tse-Tung – just the three of them. In actual fact, this was a dismemberment of a picture taken three years earlier at the signing of the Sino-Soviet treaty; in the original, some fifteen other Soviet leaders, including Beria and Molotov, had been present – but they were now removed from the photograph and Malenkov moved nearer to Mao.[3]

But there had been enough clues in the previous five months to suggest that the new Soviet administration would not be dominated by one strongman, and Malenkov would instead be '*primus inter pares*'. Who the '*pares*' were now, no one was entirely certain – but Malenkov's speech was about to make it a little clearer by ruling out one of the candidates.

Dressed in his tightly buttoned, greenish khaki tunic – Stalin's uniform of choice – and clutching a black folder, the chairman of the Council of Ministers began to speak just after 8 p.m. Moscow Radio was carrying the speech live, and big crowds gathered in the public squares in the capital to hear it broadcast through loudspeakers.

Old habits die hard and the first half of Malenkov's speech, delivered quickly and quietly, was a dull recitation of a seemingly interminable list of statistics to prove that the latest five-year plan was on track – 38 million tons of steel produced so far that year, more than double the 1940 figure, over 320 million tons of coal, 93 per cent more than in 1940, 5,300 million metres of cotton textiles, 34 per cent more than at the start of the Second World War.[4]

Yet amid the blizzard of figures there were signs of a new economic strategy, a loosening of the traditional Stalinist straitjacket. First there was an announcement of the halving of a punitive tax on collective farms, which was greeted warmly by the delegates. Then Malenkov outlined his plan to allow an increase in consumer goods and farm produce at the expense of heavy industry.

Despite spectacular claims of economic success for his five-year plans, Stalin had continued to neglect the overall living conditions of the Soviet man in the street, which remained inadequate. Malenkov was determined to improve them, so much so that he had not even bothered to consult the Central Committee – the usual forum for important change.

He wanted to increase production of clothes and shoes, as well as put more meat, fish and sugar on the tables of Soviet citizens. He also wished them to enjoy less 'essential' items like bicycles, watches, sewing and washing machines, radios and televisions.

He was prepared to bring in much greater quantities of food and consumer goods from abroad – with one-third coming from outside the 'people's democracies'. 'The Soviet people are right to demand of us ... durable, well-finished and high-quality articles,' he asserted.[5]

Malenkov's address then picked up pace when he turned to the international situation. Loud applause greeted his assessment of the Korean armistice as a 'victory for the peace-loving forces', the 'camp of peace and democracy'.[6] Raucous laughter from the deputies then echoed around the hall when the Premier mocked the fate of the 'interventionists' in Korea.

'Having suffered great losses in manpower and equipment, having had their military prestige badly tattered, they were forced to renounce their aggressive plans. This is, indeed, as the popular saying goes, a case of setting out to get wool and coming back shorn of their own.'

That Malenkov had asserted his pre-eminence in the Kremlin hierarchy became clear when he confirmed the downfall of one of the inner circle. Observers of these occasions would note that in Stalin's time Malenkov and Beria would usually sit together, often whispering and exchanging notes during the interminable speeches.

Since March, however, friends had become rivals, and Beria's 'liberal' policies had been blamed by the Politburo for the recent troubles in East Germany. The delegates would have been aware of Beria's arrest weeks earlier through the pages of *Pravda*, but – as was the way in these big set-piece communist leaders' speeches – confirmation of his purging was quietly slipped into a passage about the enemies of the Soviet Union.

The downfall of his former ally did not demonstrate 'weakness' in the Soviet state. 'The enemy of the people, Beria … the rabid agent of imperialism … has been unmasked and rendered harmless,' Malenkov announced to stormy applause.[7]

Then came the pivotal moment of the speech, the one that would make the headlines in newspapers all over the globe, the moment that profoundly startled the Western world.

> We know that abroad the warmongers for a long time cherished illusions about the United States monopoly in the production of the atomic bomb. History has, however, shown that this was a profound delusion. The transatlantic enemies of peace have recently found a fresh consolation. The United States, if you please, is in possession of a weapon still more powerful than the atom bomb and has the monopoly of the hydrogen bomb. This, evidently, could have been some sort of comfort for them had it been in keeping with reality. But this is not so.

Pausing for effect, he then delivered his punchline to a cheering audience: 'The government deems it necessary to report to the Supreme Soviet that the United States has no monopoly in the production of the hydrogen bomb either.'

The audience erupted into loud, prolonged applause. Malenkov smiled, waited for the cheers to die down, then concluded: 'As you see, convincing facts are shattering the wagging of tongues about the weakness of the Soviet Union. Those, however, who indulge in such chatter prefer to deal not with facts, but with fiction and inventions.'

The veracity of Malenkov's assertion that the Soviet Union now possessed the H-bomb was immediately called into question by American politicians. Senator Edwin Johnson, a Democrat member of the Joint

Committee on Atomic Energy, scoffed at the Soviet Premier's claim. 'I feel he's manufacturing propaganda to impress his satellite empire, and particularly Communist China,' he told reporters in Denver.[8] Republican Senator Alexander Wiley, singled out for attention in Malenkov's speech, said it was likely intended 'to divert the attention of the free world from the moral, spiritual and economic weaknesses behind the Iron Curtain.'[9]

But the scientific community was prepared to believe that the Soviet leader was not lying. Lewis Strauss, chairman of the Atomic Energy Commission, tersely accepted the blow. 'We have never assumed that it was beyond the capability of the Russians to produce such a weapon. That is the reason why more than three years ago it was decided to press forward with this development for ourselves.'[10]

The Times captured the mood of foreboding in its editorial on the Monday: 'It is a dreadful reminder of the facts of power in the world, and as far as it dispels any illusion about Communist strength, the effect may even be salutary.'[11]

In fact, Malenkov was jumping the gun by four days, because it was not until the morning of Wednesday 12 August, at the Semipalatinsk Test Site, on the steppe in north-east Kazakhstan, that the Soviet Union successfully exploded her first thermonuclear device.

The test had been prepared under the direction of legendary Soviet nuclear weapons developer Yuli Khariton and his brilliant young protégé Andrei Sakharov. The intense preparations included the placement of 1,300 scientific instruments, along with camera equipment housed in special protective casing, on a massive 7,000 square mile site (roughly the size of Wales).

Just as in America's A-bomb tests on the Nevada Proving Grounds, the Soviets had built an even more extensive mock 'city', complete with industrial and administrative buildings, to measure the destructiveness of the device's impact. Tens of thousands of people were evacuated beforehand from the zone where fallout was deemed possible (and only returned to their homes seven months later).

Codenamed 'RDS-6' (although the Americans would later dub it 'Joe 4'), it had a yield of 400 kilotons – thirty times the power of the Hiroshima bomb. Dropped from a tower, its intensely bright explosion could be seen as far as 60 miles away from the test site, while its deafening roar could be heard even further away.

Most of the buildings within a 2.5-mile radius were instantly levelled by the shockwaves, while radioactive contamination rendered the use of the rest impossible. A gigantic, glowing mushroom cloud measuring half a mile in diameter rose over Kazakhstan.

At the heart of RDS-6's operational principle was Sakharov's '*Sloika*' or 'Layer Cake' design, named after a favourite Russian puff pastry. The spherical atomic charge was covered by alternating layers of thermonuclear fuel and uranium-238 and 'crimped' from above with a chemical explosive. The bomb used lithium-6 deuteride as its thermonuclear fuel, which produced tritium, another thermonuclear fuel, during the explosion itself.

The official announcement came on 20 August. 'A few days ago in the Soviet Union one of the types of the hydrogen bomb was exploded for experimental purposes,' it read.[12] 'As a result a thermonuclear reaction of great force was set off.' At the end of the communiqué was a claim that the USSR still sought international agreement – within the framework of the United Nations – to 'ban the use of atomic weapons and other types of weapons of mass annihilation'.

In the weeks that followed, a US panel, headed by Hans Bethe (the designer of America's first thermonuclear device Mike), assessed the radioactive material gathered by reconnaissance aircraft after the Kazakhstan test – and argued that it did not constitute a 'true' hydrogen bomb because the fusion reactions in the device were responsible for no more than 20 per cent of its power. But although Joe 4 produced a significantly smaller yield than Mike, the Soviets argued that their weapon was ready for immediate use as it could be delivered by a bomber.

Soon afterwards the 32-year-old Sakharov became the youngest person elected to the Soviet Academy of Sciences and received the first of three 'Hero of Socialist Labour' titles – the Soviet Union's highest civilian award for heroic and distinguished achievements.

In America's scientific community, there was a mixed reaction to Sakharov's device. Edward Teller, 'father' of the hydrogen bomb whose 'alarm clock' design had influenced it, recalled: 'The Soviets were making rapid progress, indeed, but with two competing laboratories in the United States, and with seemingly unanimous support from the Atomic Energy Commission, I was not worried.'[13]

Elsewhere, though, there was great apprehension. The *Bulletin of the Atomic Scientists* was an organisation founded in 1945 by the men who built the first atom bomb at Los Alamos, but who now 'could not remain aloof of the consequences of their work' and lobbied using both technical and humanist arguments against the savage new power they had unleashed.

The *Bulletin* had devised a crude guide for the public's benefit to estimate the up-to-date danger of nuclear annihilation, calling it the 'Doomsday Clock'. Midnight would be when the world was obliterated after a nuclear war – or even just an episode – between the superpowers.

When it was first established in 1947 – the year of the Marshall Plan for aid to the ravaged economies of Europe, but also the development of the Truman Doctrine of military aid to countries threatened by communism – the clock was set at seven minutes to midnight. Then in 1949, when the Soviet Union successfully tested her first atomic bomb, the hands moved to three minutes to midnight.[14]

Now, in August 1953, the clock edged ever closer to Armageddon – to two minutes to midnight. The explanation for the move was given by co-founder of the *Bulletin* Eugene Rabinowitch, the Russian-born former senior chemist and section chief on the Manhattan Project.

In an article entitled 'The Narrowing Way', Rabinowitch argued that the thermonuclear explosion by the Soviet Union 'means that the time, dreaded by scientists since 1945, when each major nation will hold the power of destroying, at will, the urban civilization of any other nation, is close at hand'.[15]

The Kazakhstan explosion may have been 'weak' compared to 'Mike' but Rabinowitch predicted that a full-scale Soviet H-bomb would follow without much delay. 'The British, if they so decide, undoubtedly will be able to produce one, also,' he remarked.

His conclusion was fearful.

The continued existence of the urban, technological Western civilization will soon hang in a precarious balance, resting almost entirely on a highly irrational and unreliable fear. Elimination of atomic weapons from national arsenals through an international control mechanism, substituting mutual interdependence for mutual fear, had a slight chance of success in 1945 or 1946. It has none now and will not until the cleavage of the world into two sharply opposed power camps disappears.

Churchill, in his recovery at Chequers, mulled over the Soviet announcement with his dinner guest Oliver Lyttelton. 'I was depressed, not only about myself, but about the terrible state of the world,' he told Lord Moran.[16] 'That hydrogen bomb can destroy 2 million people. [But] it is so awful I have a feeling it will not happen.'

With Parliament in recess, and Britain's 'emergency government' ticking over at half-pace in the late summer, there was little if no official political reaction to the Soviet H-bomb. 'It made little impact on opinion except to underline the terrible dangers into which the world was drifting,' recalled Harold Macmillan.[17]

Over at the White House, however, it was a different matter. An agonised Eisenhower turned over and over in his mind the idea of launching a nuclear strike against the Soviet Union before it was too late. On 3 September, Robert Cutler told Dulles: 'The new H-bomb development was on his [the President's] mind ... he had doubts, he said, about how much we should poke at the animal through the bars of the cage.'[18]

Then five days later Eisenhower responded to a note from Dulles – outlining the Secretary of State's concerns about collective security policies – with a long, considered memorandum of his own. In the course of it, he asked whether 'our own preparation could no longer be geared to a policy that attempts only to avert disaster during the early "surprise" stages of a war, and so gain time for full mobilization'.

'Rather', he went on,

we would have to be constantly ready, on an instantaneous basis, to inflict greater loss upon the enemy than he could reasonably hope to inflict upon us. This would be a deterrent – but if the contest to maintain this relative position should have to continue indefinitely, the cost would either drive us to war, or into some form of dictatorial government.[19]

Bleakly, Eisenhower wondered if 'in such circumstances we would be forced to consider whether or not our duty to future generations did not require us to *initiate* war at the most propitious moment that we could designate'.

Two weeks later, at a National Security Council meeting, the President once more voiced his thoughts about a pre-emptive strike on Moscow. 'It looked … as though the hour of decision was at hand, and that we should presently have to face the question of whether or not we would really have to throw everything at once against the enemy.'[20]

Eisenhower told colleagues he had 'raised this terrible question because there was no sense in our now merely shuddering at the enemy's capability' – particularly when it was not known if Moscow had one nuclear weapon or a thousand. 'We were engaged in the defense of a way of life and the great danger was that in defending this way of life we would find ourselves resorting to methods that endangered this way of life,' he admitted.

While their politicians faced such stark dilemmas, the reality of the situation was hammered home to already anxious Americans in newspaper and magazine articles. The respected science writer Michael Amrine, in his syndicated column headlined 'US Could Suffer a New Pearl Harbor', concluded that 'not since the British burned the White House in the war of 1812 has Washington and the whole of America been in such danger from a foreign power'.[21]

The hydrogen bomb was, he wrote,

> purely and simply a city killer ... and America has the most concentrated cities and the most densely packed industrial areas in the world ... the Russians have heavy bombers in mass production and there is no doubt that they can deliver atomic bombs upon virtually any American city, since our civil defense is almost non-existent, except in a few progressive communities.

Back in October 1951, *Collier's*, the popular US weekly news and current events magazine, devoted an entire issue to describing events in a hypothetical third world war – the story was entitled 'Preview of the War We Do Not Want – an Imaginary Account of Russia's defeat and Occupation, 1952–60'.[22]

Twenty of America's finest writers contributed pieces; Ed Murrow imagined himself as an embedded journalist on a B-36 bomber, dropping nuclear weapons on Moscow. In this 'war', in which the United Nations was ultimately victorious over the Soviet Union, nuclear weapons were extensively used but did not have apocalyptic effects. In a second wave of attacks, Detroit, New York and Hanford were all hit – but suffered fewer casualties than before, having built up their civil defences.

Collier's printed a record 3.9 million copies to satisfy nationwide interest in the story. Now, on 21 August 1953, it returned to the subject of nuclear attack on the nation and the prospects of effective civil defence – and its outlook was much gloomier.

Val Petersen, the former governor of Nebraska whom Eisenhower had appointed as director of the Federal Civil Defense Administration, had been a keen observer of all those nuclear tests in the Nevada desert in the spring and early summer. In a special article for this edition of *Collier's* entitled 'Panic: The Ultimate Weapon', he outlined his current thinking on America's readiness in the event of an atomic strike.

With a heavy focus on the problems presented by widespread panic, Petersen's piece was a horrifying glimpse into a futuristic world of death and destruction. Mock headlines blazed: 'A-Bomb Destroys Downtown Buffalo – 40,000 Killed', and '203,000 Killed As A-Bomb Hits Bronx: County is Rushing Aid'.[23]

'You have just lived through the most terrifying experience of your life,' imagined Petersen.

An enemy A-bomb has burst 2,000 feet over Main Street. Everything around you that was familiar has vanished or changed. The heart of your community is a smoke-filled desolation rimmed by fire. Your own street is a clutter of rubble and collapsed buildings. Trapped in the ruins are the dead and wounded – people you know, people close to you. Around you, other survivors are gathering, dazed, grief-stricken, frantic, bewildered.

The message was clear:

War is no longer confined to the battlefield. Every city is a potential battleground, every citizen a target. There are no safe areas. Panic on Main Street can be as decisive as panic in the front lines. Just as a single match can burn a dry forest, so a trivial incident can set off a monstrous disaster when the confusion and uneasiness of the population have reached tinder point.

It was a depressingly bleak assessment from the man charged with protecting the United States against nuclear attack. What Petersen chose to offer as some slight compensation were some handy tips on how not to panic in the face of this catastrophic onslaught. There was a huge self-test to determine how 'panic-proof' the reader was; on a scale of 'I'm not bothered' to 'I blow up' it asked questions such as, 'How do you feel when you're alone and your doorbell and telephone ring simultaneously?', or 'How do you feel when you see a picture of bodies after a fatal accident?' Under a sub-heading of 'How Panic-Proof Are You?', *Collier's* readers were invited to 'set an alarm clock ringing continuously on a table near you. Then count the crosses in a circle without using a pencil to assist you.'

Finally, Petersen included a handy guide called 'Panic Stoppers: How to keep from being a victim of panic'. Citizens were advised to buy a battery-powered AM radio, keep a three-day emergency supply of food and water, and even build a home bomb shelter.

'Don't be afraid of being scared,' the article concluded.

> If an attack comes, you will be scared and so will everyone else. It is *what* you do when you are afraid that counts. Fear can be healthy if you know how to use it; it can make you more alert at a time when you and your neighbors must act to protect yourselves.

Just two days after this edition of *Collier's Weekly* was published came a newspaper report that rounded off this summer of apprehension. United Press International reported that an even more terrifying weapon than the A-bomb or the H-bomb was now on the horizon – the C-bomb, or cobalt bomb.

'C-Bomb Latest Way for World to End Itself' was just one front-page headline, in New York's *Daily News*.[24] The agency quoted an unnamed 'British scientist' who said that while only an idea at present, the operation of a cobalt bomb was based on 'simple and well-established' principles which would certainly make it feasible.

He said that the C-bomb could be made in three parts, beginning with an A-bomb in the centre. This would act as a detonator for a hydrogen bomb. The whole contraption would then be encased in a thick shell of cobalt, which would be blasted into a fine dust giving a 'penetrating radiation lasting for at least a year'.[25] The scientist estimated that approximately 10,000 tons of cobalt would be enough to unleash a radioactive dust that would settle everywhere on the planet, both indoors and outdoors, suggesting that 'it might wipe out the human race at one shot'.

The notion of a cobalt bomb had first been introduced by Hungarian-born theoretical physicist Leó Szilárd, advocate of the nuclear chain reaction and an instrumental scientist in setting up the Manhattan Project, which produced the first atomic bomb. Szilárd outlined the concept of the C-bomb in a radio programme in February 1950 – not to recommend that it should be built, but as an illustration that nuclear weapon technology would soon reach the point where it could end all humanity.

'How much horror can there be in the world?' an editorial asked in California's *Hanford-Sentinel*.[26]

> We have travelled the entire gamut of terror … it appears that here again, as with gas (in the Second World War), the salvation for the world lies only in the hope that the weapon is so terrible neither side will dare to use it. If this is not true, the Biblical prophecies of many religions may come true in our time.

* * *

On the afternoon of Tuesday 25 August, Churchill chaired the second Cabinet meeting since his return to No. 10 following his stroke. After discussions about the Mau Mau rebellion in Kenya, building up the military strength of NATO and the agenda for a possible 'four powers' meeting on the future of Germany, his acting Foreign Secretary took the floor to introduce item four on Persia – as many in Whitehall still liked to call it, although the country's name had formally changed to Iran in 1935.

Six days earlier the nationalist Prime Minister of Iran, Dr Mohammad Mossadegh, had been driven from power by what had been widely reported as a military coup d'état. Lord Salisbury expressed relief at the outcome, telling colleagues that if General Fazlollah Zahedi, the former Minister of the Interior, had not taken over, 'a Communist coup would have followed in two or three days'; even now, he added, not all of the communist leaders had been rounded up.[27]

'This was a spontaneous uprising out of loyalty to the Shah and dislike of Mossadegh,' Salisbury declared. 'It is in our interests that this government should survive – communism is now the only alternative.'

But Salisbury was telling nowhere near the real story. Far from being a spontaneous revolt, this had been an unparalleled coup, long orchestrated by the intelligence services of the United States and Britain – the CIA and MI6 – and sanctioned by Eisenhower and Churchill. The Americans had given this covert toppling of the democratically elected Iranian Prime Minister the code name Operation Ajax or, more formally, TPAjax (TP indicating that it was carried out in Iran), while the British called it Operation Boot.

What was more, it was the British who had conceived of the idea, intelligence officers mostly taking the lead but senior diplomats and politicians following willingly in their wake. Only in the past six months had the Americans come fully on board, ultimately taking responsibility – with their superior resources – for planning and executing the series of events that led to Mossadegh's downfall.

Salisbury was partly right about one thing – the fear of communism. This had been the Eisenhower administration's principal concern, that Iran, with her long border with the Soviet Union stretching from the Caucasus to central Asia, would succumb to her giant neighbour's influence and go the way of eastern Europe. But for Britain – and for Churchill in particular – it was mostly about Iran's oil, to which the Prime Minister had an emotional attachment as well as economic and political imperatives.

* * *

The origins of how Britain came to be initiating a coup d'état in the Middle East could be traced back to 1908, when a giant oilfield was discovered in the Khuzestan region of Persia during an expedition by Devon-born William Knox D'Arcy, an exotic millionaire who had made his fortune from gold prospecting in Australia.

The Anglo-Persian Oil Company (APOC, later the AIOC), with D'Arcy – who had been rescued from bankruptcy after discovering the oil – as a director, was formed to handle the bounty. In 1913, in its first year of production, the Abadan refinery produced 33,000 tons of the 'black treasure'.

Churchill, as Lord of the Admiralty, was persuaded that oil would be the key to the fortunes of Britain's warships. It burned hotter than coal and produced steam faster, which enabled a ship to accelerate more rapidly and rely on fewer boilers. So in 1914, on the eve of war, he persuaded MPs to back his plan to pay £2.2 million (£250 million in today's prices) to acquire for the government a controlling 51 per cent stake in APOC. He told the House that the cheap, abundant Persian supplies would provide the Admiralty with nearly half of the navy's oil requirement.

'Fortune brought us a prize from fairyland beyond our wildest dreams,' Churchill would say later, 'mastery itself was the prize of the venture'.[28] In the coming decades Britain's whole standard of living was enhanced by the oil from Iran. British cars, lorries and buses ran on the cheap supplies from Abadan, and factories throughout the country were fuelled by it.

Britain and the Soviet Union carved up Iran in the Second World War, but after they pulled out their troops winning greater control of this precious national asset became a rallying cry for Iranian politicians of all hue. Ernest Bevin, Labour's Foreign Secretary, recognised an ideological inconsistency. 'What argument can I advance against anyone claiming the right to nationalise the resources of their country?' he asked Chancellor of the Exchequer Hugh Dalton. 'We are doing the same thing here with our power in the shape of coal, electricity, railways, transport and steel.'[29]

The Iranian oilfield yields were outstripping those in Saudi Arabia, but the government in Tehran was receiving less than half than its counterpart in Riyadh in direct payments from the AIOC. Bevin proposed scrapping the earlier oil treaty signed in 1933 and setting up a new company owned 50/50 between the AIOC and the Iranian state – but the company rejected it. A 'supplemental oil agreement' was instead agreed, which would have seen royalties eventually increased to a maximum of 30 per cent.

However, before this agreement could be signed, the Arabian-American Oil Company (Aramco) agreed to its deal of a 50/50 split of profits between it and the Saudi government. Once it got wind of this in November 1950, the Majlis (the Iranian Parliament) refused to consider anything less than the same.

The scene was now set for all-out confrontation, led by surely the most eccentric, yet one of the most charismatic, politicians of the post-war world. Sixty-eight-year-old Mohammad Mossadegh came right out of Iran's social and political elite; his mother was a princess of the Qajar dynasty that ruled Persia until 1925, while his father, a wealthy landowner, was Minister of Finance for thirty years.

Despite being educated in France and Switzerland, Mossadegh was turned against the West by the secret Anglo-Persian 'agreement' of 1919 (it was never ratified) which would have effectively made his country a British protectorate. It hardened his thinking into a simple 'Persia for the

Persians' slogan. After the war he held a variety of political roles – governor general of the important Färs province, Minister of Finance and then briefly Minister of Foreign Affairs in the government of Shah Reza Khan.

His opposition to the increasingly dictatorial Shah led Mossadegh into internal exile, then imprisonment (when he thought he would be executed), and then house arrest. But Khan's removal by the British and Soviets had paved the way for Mossadegh's return to the heart of Iranian politics, and, having gained a seat in the Fourteenth Majlis in 1944, he set about fighting for Iran's political and economic independence – in particular leading the campaign for the nationalisation of oil.

In March 1951, the Prime Minister, General Haj Ali Razmara – who had resisted the calls for nationalisation – was assassinated by a member of a fundamentalist group. A week later the Majlis voted to 'accept the principle that oil should be nationalised throughout Iran'. The following month Mossadegh – against all expectations – was elected Prime Minister, and he immediately passed the formal bill to nationalise the AIOC.

'We are nationalising the AIOC because it has systematically over several decades refused to engage in a constructive dialogue with us,' Mossadegh declared.[30] 'Working hand in glove with the British government, it has trampled on our national rights. Their conduct was one of unspeakable arrogance.'

The man who had dared to take on Britain was, despite his high society background, essentially humble and ascetically minded. His office on the second floor of Tehran's Majlis building was as bare as a hermit's cell:

Furnished with a sagging cot, a few dinghy chairs, a foot locker, and a small table on which rested a half-used box of Kleenex, a bottle of ink, and a key ring with three keys. The only spot of color in this drab room was supplied by a bright blue enamel chamber pot under the cot.[31]

Mossadegh's frail body was surmounted by a great elongated head, his expressive face enveloped in loose parchment-like skin, with large eyes and a big drooping nose, giving him the appearance of Grock, the Swiss 'king of clowns' of the 1950s. Mossadegh may have been a figure of fun to some in the Western media, but he was alternatively billed as 'an incorruptible fanatic, rather like an elderly Robespierre'.[32] In fact, he was in fragile health; for most of his life he had suffered from a nervous illness that affected him at times of difficulty and stress.

This contributed to an already passionate, theatrical personality, and would lead to fainting fits or floods of tears, often at critical moments in the Majlis. Most episodes were genuine, but he was also quite capable of hamming it up for effect when required.

Mossadegh's eccentric behaviour did not end there. He undertook nearly all his work as Prime Minister from home, meeting colleagues and foreign diplomats while in bed – something that he shared in common with Churchill. Unlike Churchill, though, he would also conduct Cabinet meetings from his old iron bedstead, dressed only in a pair of grey woollen pyjamas – lying horizontal apparently aided his illness – while chairs for his colleagues were arranged all around, together with little tables on which they would be served cups of tea.

Disputing Mossadegh's nationalisation, Bevin's successor as Foreign Secretary, Herbert Morrison, took Iran to the International Court of Justice in The Hague in May 1951, where he accepted a ruling that the AIOC should temporarily be run by a board of five – two from Britain, two from Iran plus a neutral third – while the legal question was resolved. But Mossadegh and his ministers turned this down flat, saying that the court had no jurisdiction over the matter.

Morrison then became increasingly belligerent in Cabinet and even in public. He asked his military planners to prepare two lines of action – Operation Midget, which would evacuate all 4,500 British citizens from Abadan and the AIOC facilities, followed by Operation Buccaneer, the army's seizure of Abadan. But the British Chiefs of Staff were sceptical; there were few troops available to cope with Khuzestan's fierce summer climate and harsh terrain, and moving a battalion from Egypt could risk nationalists seizing the Suez Canal.

By early autumn neither side had budged, so the AIOC withdrew all but a handful of staff. With their own people unable to run the refinery, Iran's oil exports dropped to virtually nil. The Attlee government also arranged for a major boycott of Iranian oil and reinforced their warships in the Persian Gulf.

Mossadegh enhanced his international reputation when he took his case to the United Nations in New York in October 1951, bringing up the question of 'colonial exploitation' and allying Iran with the 'hundreds of millions of Asian people' in India, Indonesia and elsewhere who had recently gained their independence.[33] *Time* magazine would make him their Man of the Year.

But from 26 October 1951 the whole dynamic of the Britain–Iran crisis changed, because Churchill's Conservative government was returned to power with a parliamentary majority. The new Prime Minister scolded his predecessors 'who had scuttled and run from Abadan when a splutter of musketry would have ended the matter'.[34]

But Churchill was not about to invade. Instead, as 1952 developed, he utilised both overt political pressure and covert activities to try to unsettle the Mossadegh government and recover the oil he had helped bring to Britain.

*　*　*

The covert work to bring about Mossadegh's downfall had already begun under Morrison's stewardship of the Foreign Office. At MI6 headquarters at 54 Broadway, the Middle East desk was run by George Kennedy Young, a fierce red-haired Scotsman with decidedly right-wing political views.

Young believed that spies should be proactive, and he was the leader of the MI6 group of so-called 'firebreathers' whose swashbuckling instinct was to take the Cold War to the enemy. Plotting to remove the Mossadegh regime was just the opportunity he was looking for.

Small steps first, however, and the Foreign Office sent out two leading scholars of the region to Tehran to begin the planning, to make assessments of Mossadegh's strengths and weaknesses and to make contacts among politicians, military and the wider society.

The first was Ann (Nancy) Lambton, aged thirty-nine, a reader in Persian at the School of Oriental and African Studies at the University of London. Lambton was unrivalled in the breadth of her knowledge of the country, its language, its religion and its people, born of academic study but also of personal experience, having completed her doctorate in 1939 after a year of field work in Iran, and then spending the war years as press attaché in the British Legation in Tehran.

The austere, patrician Lambton quickly decided it was 'impossible to do business' with the stubborn Mossadegh, and recommended courting dissident politicians and stirring up opposition 'from the bazaars upwards'. She also urged the Foreign Office to send out Robert Zaehner, a quixotic Oxford don and former intelligence agent, to join her and start to put together a network of disgruntled opponents of Mossadegh.

Zaehner, a fluent Persian speaker whose cover was as 'acting counsellor' at the British embassy, cultivated some important contacts. One was Ernest Perron, the Shah's former tutor and personal friend, and the other – more importantly – was a family of wealthy and influential merchants, the Rashidian brothers – Seyfollah, Asadollah and Qodratollah. With a monthly stipend of £10,000 from British sources (worth about £320,000 today) these three were able to bribe politicians, government officials, clerics, newspaper editors – anyone with influence in Iranian life and society.

But the spy who would play the crucial role in Operation Boot was a scholar and adventurer who might have stepped straight out of the pages of a John Buchan novel. The 34-year-old Christopher 'Monty' Woodhouse had graduated from Oxford in 1938 with a first-class degree in classics and was almost immediately recruited by the Special Operations Executive (SOE), shortly afterwards leaving London to join the Greek resistance in their fight against the German occupiers.

When he first arrived in Tehran in the late summer of 1951, his objectives – on behalf of his MI6 employers – were clear. 'Forestall a Soviet-backed takeover by the Communists, remove Mossadegh from power, establish a pro-Western government, and undo so far as possible the damage done to Britain's oil interests.'[35]

But it was not a propitious start. He found the Shah – Mohammad Reza Shah Pahlavi, son of the ousted Reza Khan – 'behaving like a mesmerised rabbit, Soviet agents encouraging Azerbaijani secessionists and at the same time supporting Mossadegh, and the Tudeh (Communist) Party, though illegal, openly active'.

Woodhouse knew cooperation with the Americans was vital, and was encouraged by the attitude of the new US ambassador Henry Grady and the CIA representative Roger Goiran. Together with his MI6 deputy Norman Darbyshire, he began financing and strengthening the organisation of the Rashidian brothers and improving intelligence on the communists' plans and those of the Prime Minister.

By the time Churchill was back in office, Mossadegh had consolidated his grip on power. He had persuaded the Majlis to give him the power to rule by decree, at first for six months but then extended in August to a whole year. The man who had made his reputation in Iran as a democratic politician, a constitutionalist, was starting to take on the trappings of a dictator.

Britain had been getting her oil from alternative sources – principally Saudi Arabia and Kuwait – but Churchill knew a permanent loss of revenue from Abadan would be a serious addition to the balance of payments problem. So he first sought America's help to put together a deal that Mossadegh might accept.

A joint proposal offered $10 million in immediate American aid; suggested the International Court of Justice could adjudicate on the amount of compensation the AIOC should receive for Iran's nationalisation; promised the AIOC would pay for oil stored in Iran; and offered negotiations for the renewed flow of oil. Mossadegh promptly turned down the proposals, instead setting out counter-proposals he knew would be unacceptable.

The Churchill and Truman offer having now been rejected by Mossadegh, the contingent of British spies, assisted by Sam Falle, the resourceful oriental secretary at the British embassy, stepped up plans for a possible coup. But Mossadegh's agents were at work too, and the amount of activity the British were undertaking was becoming more obvious.

So the Iranian premier put a stop to it on 22 October 1952 when he severed all diplomatic relations with the United Kingdom. However, Monty Woodhouse was not worried. 'Our preparations were almost complete for launching a coup d'état against him,' he recalled later.[36] 'But these were only technical preparations; no policy decisions had been taken, nothing had been said to the Shah or the Americans, both of whom would have to approve.'

Woodhouse and Falle then flew to Washington to try to bring the CIA fully on board. Meanwhile, throughout the autumn British embassy officials had been putting their government's case for a coup in a series of meetings with the US State Department. On 26 November, Henry 'Hank' Byroade, assistant secretary of state for Middle East affairs, wrote a lengthy memorandum to his superior, Harrison Freeman Matthews, Deputy Undersecretary of State, bringing him fully up to date with developments.

The document was headed 'Proposal to Organize Coup d'état in Iran and Oil Problem.'[37] Byroade set out first what he described as the 'Problem'.

The British Foreign Office has informed us that it would be disposed to attempt to bring about a coup d'état in Iran, replacing the Mossadegh

government by one which would be more 'reliable', if the American government agreed to cooperate. British and American intelligence agencies
have had very tentative and preliminary discussions regarding the practi-
cability of such a move but cannot go further unless the State Department
is prepared seriously to consider it a matter of policy. The intelligence
representatives have requested a definite statement on this point.

Byroade told Matthews he had met Bernard Burrows, head of Chancery
at the British embassy in Washington, the previous day when Burrows
had informed him that his government, after previous doubts, had
concluded 'a coup d'état might well be within our capabilities and is
probably our best chance to save Iran'. Burrows and his colleagues
had not settled on any specific candidate to replace Mossadegh –
an 'old guard' politician or a moderate nationalist leader – but 'the
organization with which they are in contact is equally flexible in its
views about a leader'.

Byroade believed the British desire for a coup was now

much more immediate and definite, and seems to require serious attention at a high level … At the moment, we are called upon to say whether
we are willing seriously to consider the suggestion, so that the covert
operating agencies may know whether it is worth their while to get into
detailed study of the technical aspects.

The British wanted an answer by 1 January 1953 as the 'covert agencies
say next April would be the last time to make the move and about four
months of preparation would be necessary'.

Byroade advised Matthews there would need to be definite assurances that any American involvement in a coup would be kept secret.
'[The] CIA believes that the project is probably feasible and that it
could probably be handled in such a way that the British and American
connection with it could never be proven.'

But 'many things could go wrong … The general trend in Iran has been so steadily against the West that any sudden change brought about by unusual methods would look fishy to world public opinion.'

Byroade was concerned that all this talk of a coup came at a time when America was still trying to broker an oil settlement with Mossadegh. But despite his general scepticism, he suggested that Matthews should meet the British team face to face the following week.

So on Tuesday 3 November, Sir Christopher Steel, deputy head of mission at the British embassy in Washington, and Bernard Burrows sat down with Paul Nitze, director of policy planning at the State Department, Harrison Freeman Matthews and John Jernegan, assistant secretary of state for Near East affairs.

'British Proposal to Organize a Coup D'état in Iran' was the heading of the record of the meeting.[38] In fact the British contingent, knowing of the State Department's reluctance, trod carefully. Steel said his government was by no means decided on promoting a coup but 'did think it should be seriously considered' and wanted the Americans 'to be thinking about it'. Of course the plans had elements of 'uncertainty and danger'. But Steel and Burrows – playing to the main American fear – insisted 'it might be less dangerous than continued reliance upon the Mossadegh government as a barrier against Communism'.

Paul Nitze wondered if the organisers of the coup could have a trial run by undertaking a campaign against the troublesome (to the West) cleric Ayatollah Kashani and the Tudeh Party – without, at this stage, displacing Mossadegh. But Steel said it would be impossible to do anything against the Tudeh Party unless the machinery of government was fully controlled.

'I said we would not want to dismiss the idea of a coup, but we did feel that at least one more effort should be made to arrive at an oil settlement with Mossadegh,' Matthews recorded. 'I also observed that the present administration is not in a good position to take serious decisions of this kind since it will be going out of office so soon.'

Both parties agreed to 'keep the suggestion in mind', and that the CIA and MI6 should halt their discussions on the matter until further notice. Burrows said the MI6 officers would be returning to London – and in any case, it was preferable that further 'technical discussions' should be held in the Middle East.

While elements of the CIA had consistently favoured a coup, Truman and Acheson had always been reluctant. But they were now yesterday's men, and the British were hopeful that Eisenhower and the Dulles brothers, determined to roll back communism, would soon provide new impetus to the project.

In the early months of 1953, however, despite his country's economic situation looking increasingly parlous, Mossadegh appeared to be at the height of his popularity. He was emboldened to introduce legislation reconstructing the Iranian Parliament to be more compliant, he extended his own powers and he began to limit the powers of the Shah. He then began expropriating some of the Shah's estates.

Anthony Eden was arguably more qualified than anyone to assess the mood in Iran and how to deal with 'Old Mossy', as he called him (Churchill derisively dubbed him 'Mussy Duck').[39] At Oxford he had studied Persian, which he referred to as 'the Italian of the East'. He was a junior minister at the Foreign Office during the time of negotiations over a new oil treaty in 1933, and had been to Iran and visited Abadan.

But whatever his affection for the great culture of the country and the character of its people, he had made up his mind that Mossadegh was a devious character devoid of reason because of his antagonism to the British. 'Interviews with Mossadegh, whether in bed or out of it, affable or corrosive, did not advance us one jot,' he recalled.[40]

He was not averse to Woodhouse's project, but as the meetings of his officials in late 1952 illustrated, he felt it was vital that America should come on board. The British coup plotters now felt their project had stalled. 'Everyone was waiting for somebody else to strike the first blow, Woodhouse recorded.[41] For a while he kept his operational planning running, as well as contact inside Iran with vital agents like the Rashidian brothers – but he was about to stand it down. 'Then by the middle of April, we heard that Bedell Smith and Allen Dulles (the CIA's outgoing and incoming chiefs) were becoming eager for action and would deplore the liquidation of our organization.'

Eisenhower and John Foster Dulles, with their new administration now firmly bedded in, were also eager for something to be done about Iran. In its updated intelligence estimate, the CIA advised them that 'the Iranian situation has been slowly disintegrating ... and a Communist takeover is becoming more and more of a possibility'.[42]

At a National Security Council meeting on 4 March, John Foster Dulles suggested that if Iran fell there was 'little doubt' that neighbouring areas of the Middle East – with 60 per cent of the world's oil reserves – would succumb to communist control as well.[43] The Secretary of State admitted, 'We do not have sufficient troops to put into the area ... to prevent a Communist takeover, and the Soviets ha[ve] played their game in Iran very cleverly and with a good sense of timing.'

Vice-President Richard Nixon cast even further into the gloom. With Stalin on his deathbed at that moment, he forecast greater, rather than less, hostility from the Soviet Union to the West. 'It was quite likely', he declared, 'that they would increase their pressure in Iran to secure its control as rapidly as possible by a coup d'état. Such a course of action might constitute the miscalculation, which we all dreaded, which would cause the beginning of world war three.'[44]

A despairing-sounding Eisenhower wondered why 'we seemed unable to get some of the people in these down-trodden countries to like us instead of hating us'. His instincts were still to use America's largesse to prop up Iran's fading democracy.

'If I had $500 million of money to spend in secret, I would get $100 million of it to Iran right now, he declared, to which Harold Stassen, his mutual security secretary, replied that he could probably find

'$5 million, $10 million, $40 million – if Secretary Dulles believed he could make headway by the use of such funds'.

Stassen added that he wished he could read reports about mobs in Middle East states rioting and waving American flags, to which C. D. Jackson responded abstrusely that 'if the President wanted the mobs he was sure he could produce them'.

Towards the end of the meeting Robert Cutler read a four-point record of 'possible action' by the NSC, including 'an attempt to explore with the British the possibility of unilateral United States action in Iran' (quite possibly the coup project). Eisenhower replied that 'it certainly seemed to him about time for the British to allow us to try our hand'.

The US administration was finding it impossible to broker an agreement that would satisfy Iran but not upset the British. Eden and Rab Butler were in Washington for talks in early March, and an anxious Foreign Secretary once again demanded that William Alton Jones – a leading US oil executive hired first by Truman as an intermediary between Iran and the West – and his technicians should not return to Abadan and give Mossadegh the credibility in negotiations that he wanted.

During March 1953 a key figure in pushing Eisenhower and Dulles towards covert action was General Walter Bedell Smith, now Undersecretary of State having just stepped down as director of the CIA. In January he exploded at Kermit Roosevelt, the CIA's top officer in Iran, asking him: 'When is this goddamned operation going to get underway? Pull your socks up and get going. You won't have any trouble in London. They'll jump at anything we propose. And I'm sure you can come up with something sensible for Foster to OK. Ike will agree.'[45]

With the Iranian premier's increasing dictatorial and volatile behaviour, any lingering doubts the administration had about sponsoring a coup were being erased. On 6 April, Allen Dulles approved a budget of $1 million to be used by the CIA's Tehran station 'in any way that would bring about the fall of Mossadegh'.[46]

Twelve days later a report entitled 'Factors Involved in the Overthrow of Mossadegh' was completed.[47] It identified General Fazlollah Zahedi, former Minister of the Interior who fell out with Mossadegh over the latter's tolerance of the Tudeh Party, as the potential new Prime Minister. He would have the best chance of winning the backing of the Tehran garrison and would be popular enough to get the mobs – a crucial factor in Iran's street politics – out on the streets.

The coup was now definitely on, and the Americans assumed full control. If it had been Operation Boot up to April 1953, from hereon in it was definitely Operation TPAjax. The next few months were spent finessing the project, primarily in Nicosia (at the MI6 station) and Beirut (at the CIA station), with final meetings to sign off the plan at MI6 headquarters at 54 Broadway in mid-June. Woodhouse and Darbyshire were among the MI6 officers present at some – if not all – of these meetings, but the real movers and shakers were now the CIA's Kermit Roosevelt and Donald Wilber, in close collaboration with the US ambassador in Tehran, Loy Henderson – who had earned the trust of Mossadegh through countless bedside chats since he became ambassador in 1951.

The CIA's head of station in Tehran Roger Goiran and his colleague George Carroll – a paramilitary warfare expert who would deal with the military planning – were also present. Goiran would later pull out of the project to be replaced in Tehran by Joe Goodwin, a former Associated Press correspondent.

The TPAjax plan stated in its introduction that 'the policy of both the US and UK governments requires [the] replacement of Mossadegh as the alternative to certain economic collapse in Iran and the eventual loss of the area to the Soviet orbit'.[48] The cost of the operation was put at $285,000 – of which $147,500 would be borne by the CIA, and $137,500 by MI6.

In the fortnight before the coup, the strategy was to create 'public hostility, distrust and fear of Mossadegh and his government'. With

$150,000 to spend on this initial phase, a massive propaganda campaign would target the Prime Minister, ridiculing and undermining him through cartoons, articles in the press, and pamphlets. CIA artists prepared a giant wall poster showing General Zahedi, the new leader, being presented to the Iranian people by the Shah.

The Shah's role was crucial, and for this the spies considered Princess Ashraf, 'his forceful and scheming twin sister', to be most likely to remove the monarch's 'pathological fear of British intrigues against him'. Ambassador Henderson would also play a vital role in cajoling him to approve the coup.

If the Shah could remove Mossadegh, quasi-legally, by issuing a *firman* (royal decree) naming Zahedi as Prime Minister, this would be the easiest course. Deputies in the Majlis would be bribed to ensure a successful vote in the Parliament. If that course failed, a military coup 'must follow within hours'.

The crucial body in the coup was what the plotters called the 'military secretariat', comprising a very tight group of capable senior officers who would liaise at all times with the CIA field station. They would have to organise the immediate seizure of the army's general staff headquarters, Radio Tehran, the telephone exchange, the Majlis and its printing press and the national bank and its printing press.

The secretariat would also round up key figures in the Mossadegh government, key army officers, and newspaper editors – and, of course, Mossadegh himself. The CIA and MI6 plotters were most worried about a 'violent reaction' from the Tudeh Party, and 'must be fully prepared to meet it with superior violence'. It would not be possible to neutralise Tudeh until Mossadegh had been overthrown, and then at least 100 party and front group leaders needed to be arrested – most of them coming from a list of eighty recently prepared by MI6.

Every effort would be made to persuade religious leaders to 'spread word of their disapproval of Mossadegh … stage political demonstrations under religious cover, and reinforce the backbone of the Shah'.

Contacts in the bazaar would be primed to spread anti-government rumours.

All this and more were presented to the two governments in late June and early July. Of the two principal architects of the coup plan, Donald Wilber was the CIA's leading expert on the Islamic world and the one driving the psychological warfare. A student of ancient and modern Middle East at Princeton University, he spent much time in the region in the 1930s – especially Egypt – on archaeological excavations.

Wilber was an inveterate note-taker and a talented writer, observing everyone and everything on his travels; key attributes of the successful spy. He was recruited by the CIA's predecessor, the Office of Strategic Services, in the war and ran operations in Iran, using a position in the Iran–America Society as his cover. There he monitored the German and Soviet presence in the area, and he stayed on to track Soviet activities as the Cold War began.

The 37-year-old Kermit Roosevelt – grandson of the 26th President (Theodore) and a cousin of the 32nd (Franklin Delano) – had also worked for OSS in the war and, like Wilber, spent time in Iran and Egypt, while also helping to plan the Allied invasion of Italy. Quiet, unassuming and courteous, he was – as Kim Philby (MI6's counter-intelligence chief turned Soviet agent) who encountered him in Washington in the early 1950s observed – 'the last person you'd expect to be up to his neck in dirty tricks'.

But Roosevelt was as much at home with tribal leaders, potentates and kings as he was in the corridors of Capitol Hill. He preferred to be called Kim after Rudyard Kipling's character who played the 'Great Game', and his sense of adventure would stand him in good stead for this assignment. Politically, he was a passionate Arabist who wanted the region to shake off its colonial past and embrace democracy and free markets.

Roosevelt, head of the CIA's Middle East desk, was now the undisputed chief of the coup project and his critical meeting, to gain the administration's final approval, was held on Thursday 25 June. Among those hearing his presentation at the State Department were John Foster Dulles, brother Allen, Bedell Smith, Byroade, Matthews, Charles Wilson (Secretary of Defense) and – crucially – the man on the ground in Iran, Ambassador Henderson.

The coup could only be delivered with the initial 'confident, enthusiastic leadership' of the Shah, Roosevelt emphasised.[49] Once he had dismissed Mossadegh and named Zahedi as the successor, it was essential there was immediate military and popular backing to render 'any resistance from Mossadegh and his ally, General Taghi Riahi, absolutely hopeless. And if that can be done, the Russians also will find it hopeless – impossible to intervene.'

Loy Henderson told the gathering that he did not like doing things this way at all. 'But we are confronted by a desperate … situation and a madman who would ally himself with the Russians. We have no choice but to proceed with this undertaking.'[50]

Finally, John Foster Dulles rose to his feet and declared: 'That's that, then; let's get going.'[51] Churchill would sign off on the plan on 1 July when recovering from his stroke at Chartwell, while the final, vital authorisation – Eisenhower's – was given on 11 July.

On 19 July, Roosevelt slipped into Iran from Iraq at the Khanaqin border crossing, his fake passport bearing the name of an American traveller 'James Lockridge'. Armed with his stash of money, he worked from a villa on the outskirts of Tehran with the CIA's Joe Goodwin and George Carroll, together with two undercover British intelligence officers. When he had downtime, 'Lockridge' would play tennis on the Turkish embassy court or that of the French institute.

Bringing the nervous, suspicious Shah on board proved far from easy. Princess Ashraf, his twin sister, who was in exile in the south of France, was bribed with gifts of a mink coat and a large amount of cash to fly home and try to convince her brother to authorise the coup.

She achieved something of a reconciliation, but ultimately failed to persuade him.

Then it was the turn of General H. Norman Schwarzkopf, who had developed a friendship with the young monarch when he had headed up the US military mission to the Iranian Gendarmerie in the 1940s. Again, Schwarzkopf made progress, but left Tehran with the Shah's position still in the balance.

Roosevelt had long and inconclusive discussions with the monarch, warning him that a failure to act would mean a communist Iran and a divided country like Korea. The Shah demanded proof that the British and American administrations – at the highest level – had authorised the coup, so coded messages had to be provided.

For the British, it was arranged for the BBC Persian Service to broadcast the code. At the close of the broadcasting day instead of the usual ending 'It is now midnight', the BBC announcer would declare: 'It is now *exactly* midnight'. As for the Americans, the Shah had his proof when President Eisenhower veered from his script when giving a speech to the state governors in Seattle on 4 August and slipped in a passage about the dangers of Soviet expansion in the Middle East and communism in Iran.

The Shah was seemingly satisfied by these messages. But the CIA team endured a further anxious delay when on 11 August the monarch promptly left the capital for Kelardasht, his favourite holiday home, near the Caspian coast. However, putting himself over 100 miles from the rumours and intrigues of the capital seemed to settle his nerves, and – probably with a final exhortation from his wife, Queen Soraya – he put pen to paper and signed the *firmans* appointing General Zahedi in Mossadegh's place and calling on army officers to support him.

Everything was now set for Operation Ajax – but it would begin disastrously, very nearly fatally. Roosevelt and his team temporarily lost contact with General Zahedi and his 'military secretariat', and there was a two-day delay in beginning the action, which was enough time for Mossadegh's spies to uncover the basic information about the plot.

It was all supposed to start smoothly with Colonel Nematollah Nasiri, commander of the Shah's Imperial Guard, proceeding to Mossadegh's house, presenting him with the *firman* removing him from power, and arresting him. But when the colonel arrived at the Prime Minister's home just before midnight on Saturday 15 August with two truckloads of soldiers, he was immediately surrounded by a bigger contingent of troops loyal to Mossadegh, who promptly arrested him.

Loyalist units secured army headquarters and other strategic locations around Tehran, and disarmed the Imperial Guard. The military secretariat's network began to collapse, with many of its key officers refusing to carry out assigned tasks; General Nader Batmanghelich 'lost heart and went into hiding', while Colonel Abbas Farzanegan fled and took refuge in the US embassy compound. Mossadegh allies who had been earlier arrested were now released.

Radio Tehran went on air with news of the aborted coup at 5.45 a.m. on Sunday 16 August. A despondent Shah and his wife fled to Baghdad, where he told the US ambassador, Burton Berry, that he would head for Europe and then eventually America, where 'he would be looking for work shortly as he has a large family and very small means outside of Iran'.[52] There was calm on the streets, tanks and troops loyal to Mossadegh ringed his residence and the royal palaces, and it appeared the coup had failed.

General Zahedi moved from safe house to safe house to evade Mossadegh's police and troops. In the afternoon of 16 August his son Ardeshir invited two US correspondents, Donald Schwind of the Associated Press and Kenneth Love of the *New York Times*, to the family home in the hills north of Tehran to view the Shah's *firmans*, in the hope that news of them would be widely distributed throughout the city.

'Shah Flees in Iran Coup' was the headline in Schwind's report the next day.[53] He wrote that 'aged Premier Mohammad Mossadegh held supreme power in Iran today after crushing a bloodless attempt to unseat him by supporters of Shah Mohammad Rez Pahlevi'.

Schwind described how 'the mob of Communist and Mossadegh supporters – more than 100,000 strong' – had packed the capital's main Parliament Square the night before, howling for the ruler's blood. Banners demanded 'Death to the Shah' and 'End the dynasty'.

Mossadegh, who had jailed leaders of the opposition and dissolved the remnant of the Majlis, now felt that he was safe and told his supporters to return to their homes and carry on their lives as normal. It appeared all over so CIA headquarters ordered Roosevelt to cease the operation and leave if he felt his life was in danger.

In the State Department there was dismay. Bedell Smith sent a memo to Eisenhower explaining that the

> move failed because of three days of delay and vacillation by the Iranian generals … we now have to take a whole new look at the Iranian situation and probably have to snuggle up to Mossadegh if we're going to save anything there. I daresay this means a little added difficulty with the British.[54]

But Roosevelt had other ideas. He ignored the instructions of his superiors and regrouped with his team undeterred. 'Our studies convinced us that if you could bring about a clear-cut unmistakable confrontation between the Shah on one side and Mossadegh on the other, the army and the people would throng to the support of the Shah,' he later wrote.[55]

But Roosevelt had some work to do to stage-manage that confrontation. First, he had copies of the decree dismissing the Prime Minister plastered around Tehran. Then he ordered his vast network of paid informants and pliable newspaper editors to spread rumours that the failed revolt was in fact all about Mossadegh wanting to seize power from the monarchy, rather than the other way around. Then the military secretariat was asked to bring in more troops from outlying regions of Iraq to bolster the coup effort.

Roosevelt knew the mobs of Tehran's streets and bazaars held the key, and he got his agents like the Rashidians to mobilise them on the Shah's behalf. By the morning of 19 August they were out in force, led by a frightening-looking cadre of Iranian weightlifters, the Zurkanehs. Trucks and buses loaded with Bakhtiari tribesmen and other civilians, funded by the CIA, were bussed in from outlying areas to swell the crowd. Surging through the streets, they broke windows, beat up bystanders and shot their guns in the air, shouting 'Long live the Shah!'

Mossadegh's advice to his supporters to go home on 16 August clearly backfired. The marching column first seized control of the central cable office, closely followed by the foreign and defence ministries and army headquarters. Radio Tehran's transmitter was shut down soon after 2 p.m.; when it reopened a few hours later, it carried the voice of General Zahedi reminding the Iranian people that he was the newly appointed Prime Minister of the Shah.

The final showdown was at Mossadegh's house, when loyal troops fought pitched battles with Zahedi's troops for many hours, reducing the building to rubble and leaving scores of people dead. The Prime Minister had long since fled, but he surrendered personally the following evening to General Zahedi in the latter's office at the Officers' Club in Tehran.

Schwind reported that an 'eyewitness saw him clad in pink pyjamas … pale, barely able to walk and visibly depressed as he weakly returned the salutes of Zahedi's guards as he limped into the club'.[56] He would be taken to a military jail and later put on trial, when he would be sentenced to three years' solitary confinement in a military prison. Many of his associates would not be so lucky – some were tortured, tried and imprisoned and some were executed.

The Shah returned in triumph three days later. He delivered a radio address which assured his people he 'nursed no grudge in his heart' and 'would extend clemency', while at the same time hinting darkly that 'the law must be carried out' to those who had 'violated the constitution'.

The following day, Sunday 22 August, Roosevelt was invited to the Shah's palace and sipped vodka with him in his lavishly appointed sitting room. The Shah raised his glass and told the young CIA officer: 'I owe my throne to God, my people, my army – and to you!'[57] The two men drank silently, savouring their success.

Before heading back to CIA headquarters at Langley, Roosevelt stopped over in London to brief senior MI6 officers, acting Foreign Secretary Lord Salisbury – and the Prime Minister. After a long lunch at the Connaught Hotel with the former, he was taken by taxi to Downing Street.

Roosevelt was ushered into a downstairs room, a living room which had clearly been converted into a bedroom. There he saw Churchill, still recovering from his stroke, propped up by pillows in the middle of the bed. 'We met at your cousin Franklin's, did we not? I thought so. You have an exciting story to tell – I'm anxious to hear it,' he told him.[58]

But the CIA officer found it difficult to hold the Prime Minister's attention over the course of the next two hours. 'Quite often he interrupted with questions, and quite often he would doze off for a few minutes. He was, it seemed, consumed alternately by curiosity and sleepiness.'

The Prime Minister became fully alert when Roosevelt described the activities of the influential Qashqai tribal chiefs, previously supporters of Mossadegh who had been unwilling to succumb to CIA blandishments. 'Never could trust those damned Qashqai. They screwed us up in World War One as well as in the Second World War. A treacherous bunch.'

Finally Roosevelt quoted the Shah's words about owing his country to God and some others – including him. Churchill grinned and said:

'Young man, if I had been but a few years younger, I would have loved nothing better than to have served under your command in this great venture!'[59]

Eisenhower, too, was equally impressed by Roosevelt when personally briefed by him a few days later. He wrote up his thoughts about the meeting in his private diary seven weeks later:

Our agent there [Roosevelt] worked intelligently, courageously and tirelessly. I listened to his detailed report, and it seemed more like a dime novel than an historical fact. When we realize that in the first hours of the attempted coup, all element of surprise disappeared through betrayal, the Shah fled to Baghdad, and Mossadegh seemed to be more firmly entrenched than ever before, then we can understand exactly how courageous our agent was in staying right on the job and continuing to work until he reversed the entire situation.[60]

The President was worried that details of the CIA–MI6 coup would leak out. 'The things we did were "covert"', he wrote. 'If knowledge of them became public, we would not only be embarrassed in that region, but our chances to do anything of like nature in the future would almost totally disappear.'

For the moment at least, the real story behind the events of 16 to 19 August 1953 remained secret. At the second Cabinet meeting since Churchill's stroke on 25 August, when Salisbury was somewhat economical with his account, Churchill was desperate to take advantage of the improved position.

He was at odds with the Chancellor over offering the new Iranian government a short-term 'rehabilitation' loan. 'I suggested it to Rab without getting any encouragement,' he said.[61] 'He would sooner see the US do it. It would be a pity if they collared our long-established position in Persia for a small sum down. [These are] big stakes for us.'

Butler replied: 'We don't want to prejudice our case on compensation for oil nationalisation ... we are always refusing development money, even to Dominion territories.'

Churchill wished to know whether the government was losing £60 million from oil revenue a year because of the loss of Abadan. Butler said that was the case initially, but that loss had now been offset by developing other resources.

But the Prime Minister was not to be deterred, again emphasising that the 'political advantages of a loan should be kept in mind ... [even] a very small loan might bring very large benefits'. Eventually the argument was brought to an end, and it was simply agreed that Salisbury and Butler should find out what America's intentions were.

Who would now reap the benefits of Iranian oil – the Iranian people themselves, the British, the Americans, the rest of the world – would be a matter of tough negotiation. For the moment, Churchill and Eisenhower, and their spies, would bask in the success of a unique joint enterprise.

Cheddi and Janet Jagan – the left-wing couple swept to power
in British Guiana's first proper democratic elections.
© Associated Press

CHAPTER 9

OVERTHROW

To all intents and purposes the trail of the 'missing diplomats' – as the press liked to call them – remained decidedly cold by the autumn of 1953. Nearly two and a half years on from their dramatic late night disappearance on the cruise ship SS *Falaise* from Southampton docks, no solid information had been presented about the whereabouts of 'Foreign Office' officials Guy Burgess and Donald Maclean.

Associated Press, quoting diplomats in Berlin, reported that the two men were languishing in the MGB's Lubyanka prison in Moscow. *The People* claimed that Burgess had been spotted attending a conference in the Chinese province of Guizhou. FBI reports even suggested they may have fled to Buenos Aires disguised as women. The sightings had grown ever more fanciful the longer time passed with no hard news.

Unusually, not a word had appeared in the Kremlin's mouthpiece *Pravda* trumpeting the success of an MGB coup to whisk them out. It was universally accepted in Whitehall that they were Soviet agents and now in the care of their employers somewhere behind the Iron Curtain. But for exactly how long they had passed secrets to Moscow, and how much damage they had done to British intelligence and the British state, was by no means clear.

What seemed very likely – but again by no means yet proven – was that they had been part of a wider Soviet spy ring in the United Kingdom. MI5 had spent many hours the previous year interrogating the prime suspect Kim Philby, former head of Soviet counter-intelligence at MI6, without being able to force a confession from him. Now there was a lull in this investigation, but MI5 'watchers' continued to keep close surveillance on him.

The other man under suspicion was art historian Anthony Blunt – Surveyor of the Queen's Pictures – a wartime employee of MI5 and a good friend of Guy Burgess. Intelligence agencies on both sides of the Atlantic were keeping an eye on him in 1953; the FBI knew he was planning a trip to America in the autumn, and were giving 'consideration to the advisability of interviewing Blunt if he actually arrives in the country'.[1]

The torrent of speculation about Burgess's and Maclean's roles and influence – then and now – continued unabated. Hermann Giskes, the head of German intelligence (Abwehr) in Holland in the war, had published a book called *Englandspiel* ('The English Game'), revealing how he had caught dozens of SOE agents and then used them to send back disinformation to London.

It was one of British intelligence's biggest wartime disasters, and left-wing Labour MP Arthur Lewis wondered whether the betrayal had come from inside the ranks of SOE or MI6. He put down the following question in Parliament: 'What position was held by Mr Guy Burgess in connection with the operations when a number of British Secret Service agents were parachuted into German hands in Belgium?'[2] 'None', was the briefest of replies from junior Foreign Office minister Anthony Nutting.

Then came the remarkable headline in the *Daily Express*: 'Missing Diplomat in Peace Moves'.[3] In a front-page story, the newspaper carried the startling view of David Lawrence, an American political commentator, that Donald Maclean was now helping to shape the peace overtures of the new Malenkov regime.

The evidence, Lawrence claimed, came from *Pravda*'s unusually full coverage of Eisenhower's big speech in April 1953. 'It indicated that an

Anglo-Saxon mind is in Moscow advising on propaganda. That would be someone who knew that the publication of the President's speech would appeal to Western visions of "fair play" – notions which Russia has hitherto ignored.'

Lawrence also suggested that the Soviets' part in the exchange of prisoners in the Korean War showed 'they realized how sentimental we are about the return of a few people who have been sick and wounded. That is another example of how they have suddenly seen our vulnerabilities on the propaganda side.'

He was convinced all the evidence pointed to Maclean, the former head of the American desk in the Foreign Office. 'Every recent move the Russians have made is the kind of move an Anglo-Saxon would make if he were sitting in Moscow.'

In the highly unlikely scenario that Maclean had become a key adviser in the Kremlin, he was doing it from the grey, closed city of Kuybyshev on the Volga, 500 miles from Moscow, where he and Burgess were living in an apartment guarded by their MGB minders. Maclean, who had accepted treatment for his alcoholism, had now been allowed to take up a job teaching English in a local school. Burgess, who never made any effort to learn Russian, had no gainful employment, but enjoyed greater freedom to roam the bars of the city.[4]

Although enduring something of a spartan existence compared to their lives in England, life in the Soviet Union had started to improve for the two men. While Stalin was alive, with Beria by his side, the suspicion that they were not in fact MGB agents, but rather double agents planted by MI6, still persisted in some quarters of the Kremlin. Now, in the more relaxed atmosphere after the dictator's death and the arrest of his secret police chief, those doubts had been erased.

Then in September the newspapers finally had a real story about Maclean to get their teeth into – only this time it was about his wife, Melinda. The 37-year-old American-born wife of the missing diplomat had been an object of both pity and fascination in the previous two years as she attempted to ride out the public furore over her husband's disappearance.

Melinda had been forced to suffer constant door-stepping from journalists. Locals in her village of Tatsfield on the border of Kent and Surrey were offered huge sums of money for information – Sylvia Streatfield, Melinda's daily help, was told she would receive £250 for 'any good story'.[5] Journalistic ethics went out of the window as far as Melinda was concerned, and Churchill's good friend Violet Bonham Carter wrote to *The Times* to complain on her behalf, after the *Daily Express* ran a front-page 'interview' with her when she had put down the phone to them without commenting.

Her two boys, Fergus, eight, and Donald Jr, six, had been followed to school and questioned about their father, even though they had not yet been told by their mother about his disappearance. Melinda herself had to undergo bouts of questioning from MI5, who were convinced her husband was a traitor and that she was planning to join him.

They were right about the latter. When Donald Maclean fled the country on that night in late May 1951, Melinda was about to give birth to a daughter, also called Melinda ('Mimsie'). Once the baby was born, and the scandal blew over, it was her intention to re-join him wherever he had gone behind the Iron Curtain.

To that end, her husband's MGB handler, Yuri Modin, first contacted her one day in the late summer of 1952, after she had dropped the boys off at school. In a rendezvous by the side of a secluded country road, Modin confirmed his identity by producing one half of a postcard. Melinda then reached into her bag to produce the other half – left to her by Donald, with instructions that she should not trust anyone who could not produce its match.

Modin recalled another clandestine meeting with one of his colleagues a few weeks later, this time in London, but Melinda told him it would be impossible to get out of England unnoticed, especially with her three young children in tow, and asked him to come up with a solution to her dilemma.[6]

Then in September 1952 Melinda took matters into her own hands. After finishing a holiday in France, she elected to move to Geneva, where she could escape the endless gossip and speculation, and put Fergus and Donald into the International School.

Living in a 'small, dark apartment' in the Rue des Alpes, albeit with a view of the lake, Melinda seemed depressed with her new life as a single mother in a foreign country.[7] When Donald's brother Alan visited her in October and asked if she would join her husband if she had the opportunity, she replied 'firmly' that she would not.[8]

Then in the summer of 1953 friends noticed a change in her mood. She seemed distracted, and was not keen to leave the flat for long just in case she missed someone or something. She announced she was going on holiday to Majorca, Spain, but at the last moment changed her mind and took Fergus and Donald on a five-day trip to the remote Alpine town of Saanenmöser – a likely place for a meeting with a Soviet agent.

She then rebooked the Majorca trip for 23 July. While there, she gave away a lot of her clothes to the maid of a family she was staying with. The boys told a child they met on a beach that the photos he had taken could not be forwarded to them 'as we are going away and we don't know where we are going'.

On Thursday 10 September, on her return to Switzerland, she told her mother, Melinda Dunbar, that she had run into an old friend in the local market who had invited her and the children to stay with him for the weekend in his villa at the other end of Lake Geneva.

The following day she cashed a substantial cheque, bought daughter Mimsie some new clothes and settled an outstanding garage bill. Then she drove off in her black Chevrolet with the children. When they had not returned by Sunday night, Mrs Dunbar was frantic with worry. The next day she notified the British consulate in Geneva.

It would later transpire that Melinda had driven to Lausanne, where she parked the Chevrolet in a garage next to the railway station, saying she would pick it up in a week's time. The attendant, Marcel Micheli, observed 'that the lady seemed extremely nervous and impatient ... and she had no luggage whatsoever'.[9]

In fact, her luggage and tickets had already been left for her in a station locker. Melinda and her children took the next train to Zurich, where they changed and took a train to Schwarzach in Austria. There, a porter recalled taking their luggage to a waiting car which had Salzburg number plates, then watching as it drove off towards Vienna.

Halfway there, they switched cars and drove to a small airport in the Soviet zone of Austria. There they were met by MGB officials, and they boarded a small military-type aircraft, which flew them to Moscow to be reunited with Donald.

By 17 September 1953 the Geneva police had a fair idea about the route Melinda had taken. They also had in their possession a telegram from Melinda to her mother, which had been handed in the day before at the post office in Territet, a summer resort next to Montreux, frequented mainly by the British. It read: 'Terribly sorry delay in contacting you. Unforeseen circumstances have arisen. Am staying here longer. Please advise school boys returning about a week's time. All extremely well. Pink rose in marvellous form. Love from all. Melinda.'[10]

The telegram was a ruse, designed to put Interpol off the scent. Melinda was certainly not by the shores of Lake Geneva, but ensconced at the Sovetskaya Hotel, near the Dynamo football stadium, on the road from Moscow airport, where she had been reunited with her husband.

Yuri Modin was one of a 'sizeable drove' of MGB officers present for that reunion. It was the first time he had met Donald Maclean and he found him 'just as I had imagined: cold, distant, supercilious and thoroughly aristocratic'.[11] As for the meeting between husband and wife, he found it 'curiously unemotional'; Donald remained distant, even with his sons, and barely embraced his wife'.

Whatever the state of their marriage, the truth of the matter was that Melinda had known Donald was a Soviet agent right from the start of their relationship in 1939. 'You have got two lives to lead, I only have one,' she once wrote in a letter.[12] It was Melinda who had encouraged Donald's flight with Burgess in 1951, and ever since then she had been waiting for the right moment to join him.

* * *

On 23 January 1901, the day after Queen Victoria's death, 27-year-old Winston Churchill accepted a wager on the future of the British Empire. A Minneapolis industrialist named James C. Young had hosted him to dinner, and towards the end of a lively evening – lubricated generously with brandy and cigars – he bet the young MP for Oldham £100 (£12,000 today) that Britain's position in the world would drastically wane within the following decade.

The betting note written by Churchill recorded that the wager was over whether 'the British Empire will be substantially reduced ... and will lose one quarter of India, or of Canada, or of Australia before ten years are gone'.[13] There is no firm evidence as to whether he ever collected his winnings.

Fifty-two years on and Churchill and the British government still presided over thirty-five colonies, with a total land mass of 2 million square miles, and a population of 74 million. The process of decolonisation was certainly underway – India had gone six years earlier – but Churchill's passion for the Empire remained undimmed.

In setting out his geopolitical strategy to the Cabinet in November 1951 he emphasised that 'our first object is the unity and consolidation of the British Commonwealth and what is left of the former British

Empire'.[14] He was not inclined to hasten moves towards independence – and if he thought a crown colony was imperilled by a foreign power, or even merely by foreign influence, he would not hesitate to threaten, or even use, military force.

Such had been the case with the Falkland Islands back in February, when a territorial incursion by the Argentinians and Chileans was seen off with a warship. Now, in early October 1953, again in the Latin American orbit, came the problem of British Guiana. Once again a warship – and many soldiers – were deployed, this time because Churchill's government was convinced that the colony's newly elected government was aiming to turn the country into a communist state.

Lying on the northern coast of South America next to the Atlantic Ocean, British Guiana was sandwiched between Venezuela to the west and Suriname to the east, with another border to the continent's biggest country, Brazil, to the south. It was Britain's only colony on the continent, acquired from the Dutch in 1831 when three separate territories – Berbice, Essequibo and Demerara – were united into the single political entity of British Guiana.

Like the Dutch before them, the British used the colony to grow sugar cane for Europe's exploding consumer markets. After slavery was formally abolished in 1833, the planters of the crop were forced to import huge numbers of contract labourers – mainly from India – to work the fields. When cane sugar prices fell in the late nineteenth century, there was a shift towards rice farming, forestry and mining – especially of bauxite, which became the second most important staple of the Guianese economy.

But in 1953 sugar cane was still by far the biggest resource, with 28,000 out of the country's working population of 100,000 employed in the industry.[15] Nearly all the plant was grown on seventeen large plantations owned by private companies, and one of these – Britain's Booker Brothers, McConnell & Co. – had a controlling interest in the majority of them. In fact, Booker's influence on the economy of the country was so great – with its separate companies involved in shipping, import and export trade, and the wholesale and retail sale of consumer goods – it earned the sobriquet 'Bookers Guiana'.

As for bauxite, British Guiana's exports now accounted for one-fifth of world production. Ninety per cent of the colony's output was in the hands of the Demerara Bauxite Company, a subsidiary of the Aluminium Company of Canada. Together, sugar and bauxite made up 90 per cent of British Guiana's exports. The country was therefore effectively controlled by Britain in alliance with two multinational companies.

But while these industries flourished for the benefit of Britain and the world's other rich nations, the profits were clearly not trickling down to the workers. As the winds of nationalism blew through Africa and the Caribbean, the squalor and poverty in British Guiana, with the glaring contrast between rich and poor, was encouraging the political parties of the left.

If Whitehall was not alive to the problem, the new governor, Sir Alfred Savage, certainly was. He identified the sugar estates as the crux of the problem:

> It is there that the extremist is well supported. It is easy for him to point to the dreadful housing and social conditions which exist (and to ignore the improvements) and compare them with the comfortable quarters and the neat compounds and the recreational facilities of the staff who are predominantly European.
>
> It is also easy for him to allege unfair profits being transferred to absentee landlords and to blame, as is done, the British Government for the conditions which exist.[16]

Savage also noted the racial discrimination exhibited by the ruling British. '"White" clubs are a threat to security. One of these clubs recently blackballed a worthy Chinese citizen. There is very little social contact between white people and others. At the Coronation Ball at Government House a group of "whites" left early after a "Paul Jones".'

Exploiting this simmering atmosphere of discontent extremely effectively were a charismatic young political husband and wife duo, Cheddi (thirty-three) and Janet (thirty-two) Jagan, who headed British Guiana's left-wing People's Progressive Party (PPP). As far as Churchill and his Colonial Secretary Oliver Lyttelton were concerned, they had now gone from a mere inconvenience to being a real and present danger to British authority in the colony.

The couple had met as students in Chicago in 1940. Cheddi, an East Indian from British Guiana, was studying dentistry at Northwestern University, while Janet, a second-generation American of Jewish descent, was a student nurse at Chicago's Cook County Hospital. They married in 1943 and returned to Cheddi's native country, where Janet helped him set up his dental practice in the capital, Georgetown.

Quickly they set about invigorating British Guiana's political scene. Janet, a former graduate of the US Young Communist League, started the colony's first women's political group, tramping through the canebrakes to demand better housing for the poorly paid sugar workers. Journalists dubbed her 'The White Woman in White' because of the white sari she wore when lecturing in the fields.[17] Meanwhile, the waiting room of Cheddi's dental practice became the meeting place for the discontented, especially those who sought Guianese independence.

Cheddi won a seat in the legislature and quickly built a reputation as a highly effective organiser, a politician with a tenacious and incorruptible character. Janet helped her husband set up the PPP, became general secretary and went from village to village making speeches and organising protests. The Jagans helped spark a bitter strike on the big Enmore plantation in June 1948 when five workers were killed after government police shot into a crowd of demonstrators.

Janet Jagan's speeches were rousing affairs, often opening with an uplifting account of the Berbice uprising of 1763, when 5,000 oppressed African slaves seized the plantations of their Dutch masters and held on to the region for nearly a year.

She would urge the blacks and Indians in her audience to stay united and not succumb to Britain's strategy of dividing and ruling them. She would highlight the conditions of the women in the rice fields, 'slaving from morning to night in water which reaches their waist' for just four dollars a week, and that because workers earned so little, 'in the Colonies old age is a time for fear – no one looks forward to it in peace and quietness'.[18]

When interviewed, Janet always maintained that she had shed her former communist connections, and both she and her husband were careful instead to burnish their credentials as democratic socialists. But MI5 – who had the responsibility for dealing with subversion in the colonies – had been keeping a close eye on them.

MI5 had known them to be – at the very least – communist sympathisers since 1947, when Cheddi was first spotted making contact with the Soviet embassy in Washington. A year later MI5 watchers observed a meeting Cheddi had in London with two prominent British communists, Michael Carritt and David Ainley. From then onwards, as the Jagans grew in influence in British Guiana, their phones were tapped, their letters intercepted and they were constantly watched, at home and abroad.

MI5 had a senior liaison officer (SLO) in the region based in Port-of-Spain, the capital of Trinidad and Tobago, and he kept a close watch over events in British Guiana, visiting periodically. Such was the interest in the Jagans that Sir Percy Sillitoe, the director general of MI5, and especially Milicent Bagot, assistant director of section E1 – which dealt with international communism – were kept personally briefed.

Bagot, aged forty-six, was a trailblazer, one of the first women officers and the very first to reach senior rank. She joined MI5 from Special Branch in 1931, and since then had built a formidable reputation as an expert on Soviet espionage and counter-subversion; in particular she had an encyclopaedic knowledge of all the leading personalities in the Communist Party of Great Britain.

MI5 found it very hard to prove that the Jagans and the PPP were out-and-out communists under the control of Moscow or Peking and receiving direct financial support from them. They could find no real proof of direct affiliation with communist parties around the world.

There was only circumstantial evidence, through the receipt of communist literature like *Soviet News* and *Soviet Weekly*, from the Jagans' participation in international far-left conferences, and from meetings with leading British Communist Party officials. But the couple were careful to say nothing incriminating at the latter (knowing their phones or rooms were often bugged), and when asked by journalists about their status, would usually describe themselves as 'progressive Labour'.

In 1951, the MI5's SLO in Trinidad, in a lengthy memo to Sillitoe, charted the growing impact of the Jagans. 'They have continued unabated their disruptive action,' he wrote, detailing their opposition to the colony's budget proposals, their 'fomenting' of a strike among sawmill workers, and their effective organisation of mass demonstrations against a commission sent over to advise on the redrafting of the constitution.[19]

They had personally encouraged the crowds to chant 'Class rule, property and income qualifications must go!', 'Get off our backs!' and 'Down with colonial slavery!', while at the same time distributing copies of the Soviet weekly magazine the *New Times*.

The MI5 officer also reported the large and receptive crowds that PPP executives – especially Janet Jagan – had drawn in tours round the country and detailed the 'remarkable achievement of the party' in relation to its organisation and its literature sales. The circulation of *Thunder*, the official party magazine established in January 1950 (and edited by Janet), had reached 4,000 copies by the end of July 1950. But by the end of January 1951, it was selling 8,000 copies every month.

Yet by February 1953 it appeared to MI5 that the influence of the Jagans could be waning. The first proper general election in British Guiana under a new constitution was due in April, and the SLO in

Trinidad, after a three-day visit and a consultation with the acting governor, reckoned 'personalities will count for a lot and [Cheddi] Jagan will not have many candidates who have much popular appeal'.[20]

'Further, there has been an encouraging increase in public opposition to the more communist activities of the PPP, and Mrs Jagan's recent defeat in the Georgetown municipal election has emphasised this'. He did, however, sign off with the caveat that 'the Acting governor does not underrate the organising abilities of the Jagans and their followers ... and it is not wise to make dogmatic forecasts'.

The PPP fought the 27 April election on a programme of complete independence for British Guiana; federation within the Caribbean; nationalisation of the major industries; abolition of the governor's reserved powers; and big health, education and housing programmes. The party defied all expectations and stunned the world with an overwhelming victory, winning eighteen out of twenty-four seats in the new legislature, which entitled it to six ministries and the ability to enforce Cabinet policy decisions. But although the PPP now had a major voice in running the colony, under the terms of the new constitution ultimate power still rested in the hands of the governor.

The PPP's electoral victory was viewed as the first openly pro-communist government ever to hold power in the British Empire. '"Near Commies" Win Landslide in Br. Guiana' and 'Communist-led Party Wins' were some of the headlines in North American papers.[21] The *Manchester Guardian* went even further: its first report labelled the PPP triumph as a 'Communist Victory in British Guiana'.[22]

The Queen sent her good wishes for the 'success of the new constitution'.[23] Oliver Lyttelton hoped the new administration would build up a 'tradition of obligation to the interests of the people of orderly debate and good government'.[24] From the headquarters of the British Communist Party came the simple message from leaders Harry Pollitt and Rajani Palme Dutt: 'Congratulations on splendid election victory'.[25]

The US Department of State exchanged frantic cables with the

Foreign Office over the result, outlining its fear that communism might spread throughout the British West Indies, threatening the vital American lifeline through the Panama Canal. In the Second World War the United States had built an airbase on British Guiana – Atkinson Field, 25 miles from Georgetown – which was used as a refuelling stop for thousands of American-built lend-lease aircraft. That base had been reduced to 'housekeeping status', but in some corners of the administration there was now talk of reactivating it.

Churchill, as shocked as anyone, wondered whether he had to accept the result. He told Oliver Lyttelton: 'We ought surely to get American support in doing all we can to break the Communist teeth in British Guiana.'²⁶ He added, jokingly, that 'perhaps they could even send Senator McCarthy down there'.

Lyttelton reassured the Prime Minister that the governor was not worried because the PPP's policies were 'no more extreme than that of the Opposition here'.²⁷ What was concerning was the Jagans' overseas trips to communist countries.

Sure enough, shortly after the election Janet Jagan, flushed with success and her new reputation on the world stage, left her four-year-old son Joe with her husband and first went to Denmark to address the Copenhagen congress of the (far-left) Women's International Democratic Federation. She then went on to Romania for further appearances.

She also travelled to London, where MI5 bugged the room where she held a meeting with Rajani Dutt and Idris Cox from the executive of the British Communist Party. 'We'll be glad to do all we can to help,' the officers listening in heard Dutt tell her.²⁸ Cox advised her to 'raise issues in such a way that will arouse people to struggle, and from their own experience begin to realise what an obstacle the constitution was'.

At the first meeting of the new legislature, governor Sir Alfred Savage ushered in the new political era with some warm words, saying British Guiana has been described as 'the land of six peoples' – in reference to the multi-ethnic population – and that a 'most heartening feature of the recent elections was the absence of racialism'.[29] But he cautioned, 'to those who feel that El Dorado has now been discovered I would say you must not expect too early or too easy a solution to your problems'.

Savage was soon in conflict with the PPP – and in particular Janet Jagan. He assented to the repeal on a ban importing 'subversive' literature – but ministers responded by bringing in stocks of communist material. More seriously, sugar workers came out on strike seeking official recognition for their union, with some setting cane fields aflame and destroying 236 tons of sugar. Short sympathy strikes sprang up involving dockers, sawmill and timber workers and government and factory employees.

Savage identified the Jagans as orchestrators of the unrest, and his State Council passed a resolution regretting that 'certain ministers of the Crown have been actively engaged in promoting and sustaining the strike' and this was 'the negation of good and responsible government'.

Throughout July and August 1953 Savage was in regular contact with the Colonial Office assistant secretary Norman Mayle about ensuring the effectiveness of the local police force and its backup volunteer force, should likely disturbances and riots break out. However, by the end of the summer he was starting to get very anxious about the extent of the civil unrest.

'I regret to say the situation has deteriorated,' he wrote to Lyttelton on 2 September.[30]

All estates on the east bank of the Demerara are now on strike … in Berbice, Skeldon and Rose Hall are on strike as a result of agitation by Mrs Jagan and Adjodha Singh (MP for the Berbice River), who are now doing everything possible to spread the strike to the rest of the area.

Savage said the commissioner of police felt that he could control the situation even if all sugar workers went on strike, but added that if other industries and ports were significantly affected 'outside assistance may be required to maintain order'.

MI5's security liaison officer in Trinidad, C. A. Hubert, had also been receiving reports from one of his agents about the PPP's encouragement of political activism among the youth of British Guiana. 'The Pioneer Youth League held a record number of meetings, at all of which the speeches have been markedly anti-British and pro-Communist.'[31]

It was Hubert's opinion that while the PPP was making 'little effort to redeem its more constructive election promises, the left-wing element, led by Mrs Jagan, is going right ahead in an effort to expand its membership and the membership of its front organizations'.

In early September, the governor of Barbados, Timothy Luke, paid a visit to British Guiana and was startled by what he saw. 'Senior officials are completely disheartened and pessimistic; the public service is approaching demoralization: the business and commercial community are embittered and frightened … and a run has started on the Government Savings Bank.'[32]

Luke had no doubt that Janet Jagan was the prime mover behind the disorder. 'Whether or not she is a member of the Communist Party, she is thoroughly trained in Communist tactics and is in addition an exceptional, able, ruthless and energetic woman.'[33]

By now Lyttelton's patience was running out. He had received intelligence reports that the sales of kerosene and petrol in small quantities – to men and women without cars – was growing rapidly. He was even led to believe there was a plot to burn down the wooden capital of Georgetown.

As for the PPP government, he told Savage on 24 September: 'It is clear they have no intention of working the present constitution in the interests of the people of British Guiana as a whole, but are seeking a one-party totalitarian control of the country and a link-up with Russia which we obviously cannot contemplate.'[34]

Savage was now worried that he could not even rely on local police and volunteers to keep any kind of order. 'It is possible at least 50 per cent of both forces would refuse to accept full duty,' he telegrammed

Lyttelton on 29 September.[35] 'It [is] imperative that the proposed operation should commence without delay ... it cannot be ruled out that the PPP leaders may be planning a coup to take over the government.'

Lyttelton now acted swiftly. On 4 October the Home Secretary, Sir David Maxwell Fyfe, and the senior legal assistant to the Commonwealth Relations Office, Sir Sydney Abrahams, made a 1,000-mile round trip to Balmoral to see the Queen on her summer retreat. For them she duly signed a special order in council that would enable the governor to suspend the constitution, remove Chief Minister Cheddi Jagan from office and declare a state of emergency.

In the meantime the Colonial Secretary had his chiefs of staff launch the military operation codenamed Operation Windsor, which saw the cruiser HMS *Superb* and frigates HMS *Burghead Bay* and HMS *Bigbury* dispatched to Georgetown, carrying a battalion of 700 troops from the Royal Welch Fusiliers and a small contingent of Royal Marines. The aircraft carrier HMS *Implacable*, with 600 troops from the Argyll and Sutherland Highlanders on board, was also ready to set sail from Devonport as backup if required.

At a Cabinet meeting Churchill and Lyttelton debated whether America should be told of Britain's military action. Churchill was sure that 'in the United States anti-communism will offset anti-colonial feeling', but asked whether the Americans should be told in advance.[36] Lyttelton advised not: 'Tell Canada twenty-four hours in advance. Don't tell India. Tell the US the situation is worsening – not the action we intend to take.' The Prime Minister made the following recommendation: 'Safety in overwhelming force. Have enough troops: and use teargas.'

To Churchill's irritation, the surprise element of the operation was blown by the *Times* correspondent in Jamaica, who had observed HMS *Superb* leave Kingston after embarking and refuelling, and reported that it was heading into the South Atlantic on 'emergency duty'. Lyttelton was forced to make a public statement about the forthcoming action, saying: 'Her Majesty's government is not willing to allow a Communist state to be organised within the British Commonwealth.'[37]

The ratings on board HMS *Superb*, which lay off the coast while the two frigates disembarked the Royal Welch Fusiliers, were given a somewhat mixed message about their mission. Jon Willsher, who was on board, recalled:

> We were told that we were going to remove the Government since they were Communists, and if we did not do so, the US would intervene. We were also given a secondary reason, it being that the Jagans were of Indian extraction and the native population would not accept them.

When the British troops landed in Georgetown on Thursday 8 October and began to fan out across the city to occupy key sites, they were surprised by the air of calm, with people peacefully going about their normal activities. At the stadium in the Bourda area of town an international cricket match was taking place between British Guiana and Trinidad, in which Gerry Gomez, the visitors' talented batsman, excited a large crowd with a cultured innings of 148.[38]

Once the troops had secured the capital, Savage took to Radio Demerara to justify what some were labelling a 'coup'. 'Why has this been necessary? It is because over recent months there has been a planned and continuous programme of strengthening links with communist countries with a view to making British Guiana a servile state where people are compelled, under intimidation, to give up those freedoms we cherish.'[39]

Savage denied he had taken no interest in the plight of the sugar workers. 'Do you remember my visits to the estates some weeks ago when my wife and I met many of you and I undertook to do all I could to help, particularly on the question of housing and land?' On the run on the Savings Bank, he told his listeners $2.5 million had been withdrawn, many by people with small savings, and he urged them to put the money back.

The governor said a new interim government 'with which Guianese will be fully associated' would be set up and a commission of inquiry would follow. 'I realise that I have a very heavy task in front of me,' he concluded. He then issued a draconian emergency order giving himself widespread powers; a police officer could arrest – without a warrant – anybody 'he had reasonable ground for suspecting to have committed an offence against the Order'.

The six PPP members on the Executive Council were all dismissed. At this stage there would be no arrests of ministers, although senior civil servants who had shown loyalty to the government were dismissed.

The PPP leadership did not react for the first couple of days. MI5's C. A. Hubert in Trinidad noted with quiet satisfaction that 'it was obvious that the PPP leaders had no idea that the constitution would be suspended or that they might be arrested'.[40] Then the party sprang to life and issued a document entitled 'A Call to Action', in which it condemned the 'invasion of the colony by foreign troops' and urged 'a policy of non-cooperation with the present regime', declaring a general strike and a boycott of all goods and supplies coming from the United Kingdom.

But the presence of the British troops had its effect and an uneasy peace prevailed. At the Cabinet meeting on the day of the troops' arrival, Lyttelton proclaimed that the troops had 'landed with the response of cheers – contrary to the governor's forecasts'.[41]

Churchill warned that the PPP 'know how to play constitutionally. Don't therefore put ourselves in the wrong by acting prematurely. [We] can't yet defend the arrests of individuals.' But Lord Salisbury countered: 'The world will be watching us. Suppose ex-Ministers flout the law, promote strikes etc – they should be arrested. We should look weak to leave them at large.' Sir Norman Brook scribbled a note to

Anthony Eden which read: 'This will keep our troops there longer and be a Communist success.'

A week later a big left-wing meeting in London's Beaver Hall condemned the government's 'disgraceful and unparalleled action.'[42] Fenner Brockway, Labour MP for Eton and Slough, asked: 'Has a single gun been found, any arms seized, any plot for a coup d'état uncovered? There is not a whiff of evidence to justify this gunboat diplomacy.'

But in the debate in Parliament that followed a few days later – with the dismissed Cheddi Jagan given leave to come and watch from the Strangers' Gallery – the Labour Party leadership provided little effective opposition to Lyttelton, seeming to reluctantly accept his action. The Colonial Secretary gleefully hammered home his central argument with relish, stating:

> Here is a colonial crisis which could become as serious as Mau Mau terror in Kenya. But unlike the leaders of Mau Mau, the men and women round Dr Jagan are cool, sophisticated politicians operating with full knowledge of all the weapons in the Communist armoury. That is the menace in British Guiana.[43]

Over in Washington there was appreciation for the British action at the weekly National Security Council meeting. The economic motives for Britain's move were considered almost as important as the political; after pointing out that communist influence in the colony had grown since the April elections, Allen Dulles also reminded Eisenhower that the colony was a major source of the world's supply of bauxite.

In the coming days John Foster Dulles would instruct his ambassadors throughout Latin America to justify the British action and promote the issue as the threat of communism in the western hemisphere, not British colonialism.

The President's Undersecretary of State Walter Bedell Smith was even more blunt when dealing with the sensitivities of India – the ancestral homeland of the majority of the Guianese. In a telegram to New Delhi he wrote: 'Total evidence leads us to conclude a definite plan existed to establish a Commie bridgehead in the colony with the idea to make it a Commie centre at least for the Caribbean and possibly more general Western Hemisphere operations.'[44]

Like Iran, the overthrowing of a democratically elected government in British Guiana had dual objectives. For oil in Iran, read sugar and bauxite in British Guiana. Fear of communism was the common thread between the two, as it had been throughout the year.

The success of these two missions would embolden the Eisenhower administration. A few days later, in countering protests to the British action by the increasingly left-wing government of Jacobo Árbenz Guzmán in Guatemala, assistant secretary of state for inter-American affairs John Cabot gave a clear pointer to a future regime change operation. 'Guatemala was openly playing the Communist game,' Cabot told the UN General Assembly, 'and could not expect any positive cooperation from the United States.'[45] The next target had been fixed.

* * *

In late September 1953 Churchill was on the French Riviera, staying in Beaverbrook's villa La Capponcina at Cap d'Ail, across the bay from Monte Carlo. He had brought his easel and paint brushes as always, but along with his daughter and son-in-law, his secretary Jane Portal joined the party to help him work on the speech that he would deliver to the Conservative Party conference in Margate on 10 October.

This would be his political comeback, the real test of whether his physical and mental capabilities were back to something like normal following his stroke in June. It would be the critical moment in deciding whether he wanted to continue as Prime Minister – and whether his party felt that he was up to it.

The holiday started off badly. 'Papa is in good health – but alas, low spirits,' his daughter Mary observed in a letter to her mother.[46] 'He feels his energy and stamina to be on an ebb tide – he is struggling to make up his mind what to do.'

Jane Portal told her uncle Rab Butler that 'the PM has been in the depths of depression. He broods continually whether to give up or not. He was exhausted by Balmoral and the Cabinets and the journey.'[47]

Churchill's mood was not helped by his inability to paint. Albert Nockels, Beaverbrook's faithful butler of thirty-two years, who was helping the PM, recorded a distressing incident in a letter home to his master.

'He woke up in a very bad temper this morning, and when his valet took him his breakfast he burst into tears. Walter [Meyer – Churchill's valet] asked him if anything was the matter and he replied "I can no longer paint – my arms won't let me".'[48]

After a couple of days Churchill's spirits lifted, helped by the arrival of Jock Colville and his wife Margaret, and by some other stimulating guests. Somerset Maugham and his close friend the portrait painter Sir Gerald Kelly, who were staying at the writer's Villa Mauresque at Cap Ferrat just a few miles along the coast, came for lunch on Sunday 20 September.

Unable to paint effectively, Churchill read – first Benjamin Disraeli's political novel *Coningsby*, then *All Quiet on the Western Front* by Erich Maria Remarque; the latter he described as 'a grisly book, all about concentration camps … like taking refuge from melancholy in horror.'[49]

But by 21 September the Prime Minister had dictated to Jane about 2,000 words of a possible speech for Margate, and when finished, planned to give it an outing to a 'select audience'. Meanwhile, he was still plagued by doubts, telling Clementine: 'I still ponder on the future and don't want to decide until I am convinced.'[50]

His conversation at Cap d'Ail was of 'little else' but Margate, Colville observed, along with the constant refrain that he and Eden should meet Malenkov and Molotov face to face.

Back in London, however, quite a few of Churchill's senior colleagues were unconvinced that he had a political future much beyond the party conference. In between their holidays over the parliamentary recess, the Conservative Party's 'wise men' – Rab Butler and Lord Salisbury, together with party chairman Lord Frederick Woolton, Chief Whip Patrick Buchan-Hepburn and Harry Crookshank, Leader of the House of Commons – gathered to try to plot a way forward without the 'Old Man'.

The latter two were now convinced Churchill must set a date for his departure. Crookshank had felt the first Cabinet meeting that Churchill had attended after his stroke had been unnecessary, and arranged purely so the Prime Minister could demonstrate to colleagues – and the world – that he was fit enough again.

'Harry still feels – and very strongly – that Churchill ought to resign,' Harold Macmillan noted in his diary.[51]

For over a year he has, in fact, been unable to perform his functions properly … [yet] Harry feels unhappy that history will accuse us all – Rab, Bobbety [Salisbury], and the politicians in the cabinet – of weakness and cowardice. We know the Emperor has no clothes, and we dare not say so.

Buchan-Hepburn, who had visited Chartwell repeatedly in July and August, was increasingly frustrated, and 'blew up' when at dinner with Crookshank about Churchill's reluctance to even contemplate retirement.[52]

As for Woolton and Salisbury, they had something of an unusual, conspiratorial conversation in a room at Buckingham Palace while they waited for separate audiences with the Queen – Woolton to be sworn in as the new Minister of Materials, Salisbury for the regular weekly audience (in Churchill's absence on holiday).

'Bobbety' first bemoaned the lack of 'youth' in the Cabinet and suggested that he himself, at the age of sixty, might retire and go back to

Hertfordshire to look after his estates. He had first offered his resignation – perhaps half-heartedly – on the grounds of age on 6 September, saying that most of the Cabinet were over seventy and keeping out young talent would ruin the party.

Salisbury then revealed to Woolton that Churchill intended to go on for two more years. The Prime Minister still had a 'mission', feeling that he was the only person who could bring peace to the world by dealing with the Kremlin.

Woolton was sceptical: 'I remember so well him telling me that he thought he could manage Stalin and that he would bring him to London. Roosevelt suffered under the same delusion.'[53] As for Churchill's plan to go on and on, Woolton believed 'the only thing that will save the party from disaster at the next election is for Churchill to go, to hand over to Eden and to let the latter form a new Cabinet.'

Churchill arrived back from holiday on Thursday 1 October. Lord Moran gave him the political gossip, 'but I do not think he took it in; his mind was on the conference'.[54] He said he had now completed 4,000 words of his speech, enough for an hour-long address. 'I suggested fifty minutes would do, and he did not demur,' recorded the doctor.

In the evening Churchill hosted an awkward dinner with Salisbury, Butler and Eden – the latter having just returned from a recuperative cruise around Greece. The Prime Minister and his Foreign Secretary had some sharp words over the former's 'easement' speech earlier in the summer. 'W didn't like my lack of enthusiasm for his May 11th speech,' Eden recorded in his diary that night.[55] 'He kept emphasising its popularity to which I replied that I was not contesting that.'

Perhaps Churchill had received intelligence of some of the meetings the senior Tories had held about his future in previous weeks. 'At one point Salisbury pulled him up very sharp – even angrily – when the former thought his loyalty to W had been impugned.'

As the talk moved on to the possibility of high-level talks with the Soviets, Churchill pointed to the success of the free-flowing discussions between himself, Stalin and Roosevelt in the war. Eden responded that it was 'not true that to meet without an agenda was the best method with the Russians ... They liked to have an agenda which they could chew over well in advance.'

The dinner did not end well as far as Eden was concerned. 'The important question was "what next?" On this W appeared to have no ideas. A depressing evening.'[56]

The day after, Eden made a welcome return to Cabinet after his six-month absence. As if to make amends for the dinner the night before, Churchill wrote to him afterwards to say, 'It was a great pleasure to see you in your place today.'[57] He went on to observe that 'for some time I have been watching it, and have had the feeling that we are getting into a smoother period in international affairs'. Churchill asked Eden if he could show him a draft of his own planned speech at the party conference 'so as to shape my own remarks accordingly'.

Macmillan thought that Churchill had 'excelled himself' at Cabinet – 'in control of the situation, and in showmanship'.[58] In the following week in the run-up to Margate, Churchill was in close contact with Oliver Lyttelton over the crisis in British Guiana. But his main preoccupation remained the party conference speech, drafting and redrafting, swapping notes with Eden and running it over with Norman Brook and Lord Woolton.

On Thursday 8 October, in Downing Street, Churchill staged a dress rehearsal. At noon he consumed a dozen oysters, two mouthfuls of steak and half a glass of champagne. An hour later he took a dose of the powerful stimulant amphetamine that Lord Moran had prescribed for him. Then at 2 p.m. he got to his feet and, with wife Clementine looking on, gave the speech in thirty-six and a half minutes without a pause. 'I had not the stimulus of an audience. But I know now that I can stand [all] that time. I feel it is all right,' he told Moran.[59]

Churchill was highly nervous about the forthcoming ordeal, as were the members of his close circle. But forty-eight hours later, with another dose of amphetamine, and with his throat having been sprayed by his otolaryngologist Charles Wilson, he stood up to deliver the speech he had been thinking about, and working on, almost as soon as he had started to recover from his stroke back in early July.

Christopher Soames sat behind the Prime Minister – to his right – on the rostrum in the Margate Winter Gardens, and anyone watching him rather than the speaker would have seen a face absolutely taut with anxiety throughout the fifty minutes. Only in the moments of levity – and there were a few – did his expression alter with just a glimmer of a smile, before resuming a countenance of grim concentration.

But he need not have worried. As *The Times* described:

> The old fighter and sage was back. The flashes of wit, the love of re-sounding phrase, the zest for the party struggle, the manner of shaping policy by what seems to be private soliloquy and, above all, the gift for capturing and transmitting the thoughts of the British people on the great questions of peace and war – all these were there.[60]

Perhaps he moved a little bit more stiffly and slowly than before. He kept to his script more closely than usual, but his mental alertness and imagination were clearly on show, along with all the old mannerisms – the pretence of pausing to search for the exact word, the delighted childlike glow that came over his features as he neared the punchline of a joke.

As for the substance of the speech, nearly all the headlines the next day reflected the passage where, once more, he pressed the case for an informal summit with the leaders of the USSR. 'No one can say it is dead,' he said of the initiative he first broached back in May.[61]

> I still think that the leading men of the various nations ought to be able to meet together without trying to cut attitudes before excitable publics or using regiments of experts to marshal all the difficulties and objections,

and let us try to see whether there is not something better for us than tearing and blasting each other to pieces, which we can certainly do.[62]

He was cheered when he announced the success of the military operation in British Guiana. 'It is always a difficult problem to decide at what point communist intrigues menace the normal freedom of a community, but it is better to be in good time than too late.'

On the domestic front, he trumpeted the improvement in the economy. 'Two years ago we were sliding into bankruptcy and now at least we may claim solvency.' He also hailed the fulfilment of one of his key election pledges: 'We persevered and now this second year 300,000 houses to sell or let will actually be built.'

And while he was still on figures, he proclaimed – to great cheers – that in the first two years of Tory government

the British nation had actually eaten more meat, including red meat, than they did in the last two years of the socialist administration. That at any rate is something solid to set off against the tales we are told of the increasing misery of the people – and the shortage of television sets.

What of his own future? 'One word personally about myself,' he concluded.

If I stay on for the time being, bearing the burden at my age, it is not because of love for power or office. I have had ample share of both. If I stay it is because I have a feeling that I may, through things that have happened, have an influence on what I care about above all else, the building of a sure and lasting peace.

Thunderous applause rang out in the hall. Going to congratulate him in the green room afterwards, Jane Portal found him in tears. 'I've done it,' he simply said. 'We were all weeping by then,' she recalled.[63]

'How would Churchill come through? The answer was really magnificent,' recorded Harold Macmillan.[64]

He spoke for fifty minutes in the best Churchillian vein. The asides and impromptus were as good as ever. His voice seems sometimes weak, and once or twice flagged. But this happens to everybody in the course of a long speech. Altogether, the old man has triumphed once more by sheer persistence.

The delegates were no less impressed. 'He is not a bit changed, after all; he is in good shape,' said one, while another remarked: 'I guess the Old Man will be with us next year.'[65]

Relaxing back in Downing Street that evening, Churchill told Lord Moran: 'I think it went very well, they all said so. I have never, Charles, taken so much trouble over a speech before … I knew from the beginning this was the hurdle I had to surmount.'[66]

Reading the first editions of the Sunday papers was a pleasurable experience. 'The delegates have acclaimed him as their future leader – that must surely put an end to all speculation,' was *The Observer's* verdict.[67] Only the *Sunday Pictorial* hinted at the physical problems: 'There appears to be a slight twist on the right side of his face which became more marked as the speech progressed.'[68]

At 5.30 p.m. on Monday 12 October, the Chief Whip arrived at No. 10 for a meeting with the Prime Minister to plot the way forward for the party after the latter's triumph two days earlier. But first Patrick Buchan-Hepburn came across an extraordinary scene in the Cabinet Room, where he saw a four-month-old leopard cub sat on the table among all the ink stands and blotting paper, surrounded by a group of officials – and Churchill.

The leopard, Buchan-Hepburn gleaned, was a present to Churchill from Colonel Sabah As-Said, the general manager of Iraqi Airways (and son of the Iraqi Prime Minister), and had stopped off en route to its new home at London Zoo. Stroking its head, Churchill asked the two zoo keepers, 'Is it a boy or is it a girl?'[69]

They looked dumbfounded. They had thought of all the questions but not that one! The leopard was duly rolled on its back for a technical check-up, and while the lady secretaries tried to look unconcerned, it was pronounced to be a boy. Then the No. 10 black cat was seen to be advancing with its hackles up, so the leopard was hastily returned to its cage, amid murmurs of wonder and appreciation.

With the drama over, the leopard gone and the crowd dispersed, Churchill was able to tell Buchan-Hepburn the good news that he had received that morning – he had just been awarded the Nobel Prize for Literature. The citation would acclaim him for 'his mastery of historical and biographical description as well as for the scintillating oratory in defending exalted human values'.[70]

Churchill asked a secretary to get Eden – who was in Paris – on the line. 'Is that you Anthony? How are you? I thought you would like to know that I have just been awarded a Nobel Prize.'[71] Buchan-Hepburn heard a pause for effect, then Churchill's inimitable chuckle. 'But don't worry – it's for literature, not for peace!'

Eden himself was due to meet John Foster Dulles and French Minister of Foreign Affairs Georges Bidault for the so-called 'Big Three' peace talks in four days' time. Churchill meanwhile, buoyed by his conference success, was not yet willing to give up on his hopes for a one-to-one with Georgy Malenkov.

Frank Olson – the American bacteriologist who fell to his death in mysterious circumstances.

Sidney Gottlieb – mastermind of the CIA's MKUltra programme and developer of 'truth drugs'.
Courtesy of the CIA

CHAPTER 10

'AN EXTREME MEASURE'

The first alert – the yellow warning – that enemy planes had been spotted approaching the coastline of America was issued to President Eisenhower in the White House at 9.10 a.m. on Thursday 5 November.

For the next fifty minutes, he and his staff continued with business as normal. Then, precisely at 10 a.m., James Rowley, chief of the President's Secret Service detail, hurried into the Oval Office, interrupting the conference that Eisenhower was holding with National Security Council members.

Rowley notified the President that the red warning alert had just sounded, which meant that an attack was now imminent. Flanked by his special counsel Bernard Shanley, Eisenhower promptly left his office in the East Wing, walked swiftly through the Rose Garden and followed Rowley into a subterranean bomb shelter. Mrs Eisenhower, who had come from the second-floor living quarters of the White House, hurried to join them underground along with 170 other staff members.

The eerie rise-and-fall wailing of more than 100 sirens sounded out all over Washington DC, and some half a million government workers and schoolchildren flocked to designated shelter areas in their buildings. If the expressions on their faces were of excitement rather than anxiety, it was because they were certain – or almost certain – that this was not a real assault on their city, but merely a drill for a mock air attack. Thankfully, two Soviet planes were not about to drop their payload of A-bombs onto the capital.

However, it was Washington's first major war emergency exercise since the Soviet Union announced two months earlier that she possessed the hydrogen bomb. Civil defence officials estimated 'casualties' of 150,000 if one bomb was dropped over downtown Washington several blocks from the White House and another about 2,500ft south of the Pentagon.

Part of the fascination for reporters was that, for the first time, they were allowed to view – and give some details of – the secret $1 million presidential bomb shelter, first dug in the Second World War, which had been substantially improvised and improved in recent years.

Newsmen were not allowed to disclose the exact location of the shelter, but they could relay some details – if not all – of what was inside. So their readers learned that the brightly lit rooms, all painted pale green, could easily accommodate 200 people. They were told they were designed to repel poisoned gas and atomised radiation particles, and possessed decontamination equipment.[1]

The bunker had a self-contained power plant, and an 'elaborate' communications system, for conversation both internally and, vitally, with the outside world. Within minutes of the President's arrival, he was able to conduct official business, with US Army Signal Corps experts patching him through to all government departments and establishing teletype contact with the Western Union office in New York (the latter on the assumption that the Washington office of the telegraph system had been knocked out by one of the bombs).

At 10.18 a.m. it was all over. The all-clear sounded and the President, with a solemn look on his face, escorted his wife back to her quarters. US civil defence had been sharpened by the exercise and the lucky ones who would remain after an A-bomb attack – primarily those at the heart of government – would know what to do and where to go.

* * *

Protecting the main organs of government from nuclear attack was one thing. But under what circumstances America was prepared to use her stock of tactical A-bombs remained a constant source of discussion in the National Security Council in the autumn of 1953.

The armistice in Korea was holding, although Eisenhower and Dulles were exasperated at the behaviour of President Rhee, who was treating the Indian delegation heading the prisoner repatriation programme with contempt. General John Hull, commander of Far East Command, was especially nervous about the behaviour of the South Korean President, who still showed no real appetite for a political conference and continued to talk darkly about his ultimate goal to advance to the Yalu River and unify Korea by force if necessary.

'Trying to save South Korea is a little bit like trying to defend the basic rights of someone in court who insists on behaving in such a fashion as to earn the contempt of the judge, the jury and all of the spectators,' Eisenhower confided to his diary.[2]

Britain's senior military staff, in their latest estimation of the likelihood of war with the Soviet Union, calculated that everything that had happened since Stalin's death – the change of government, riots in East Germany, the Korean armistice and Malenkov's accent on consumer goods production – suggested that the Kremlin wished, despite their recent testing of the hydrogen bomb, to avoid a general war. In addition, they believed that 'temporarily at least, they [the Soviets] will be more careful than before not to run the risk of precipitating [an] unintentional war'.[3]

US war planners more or less assented, but would also have agreed with the conclusion of the British Chiefs of Staff that 'there remains the possibility that unresolved problems in the Far East might lead to a war in that area which sooner or later might involve the USSR and develop into general war'. It was that kind of scenario – the Chinese or North Koreans breaking the armistice – that encouraged the National Security Council to debate once more the deployment of atom bombs on the battlefield.

In the meeting on 13 October, Admiral Arthur Radford, the new hawkish chairman of the US Joint Chiefs of Staff, demanded to know whether he could count on the use of atomic bombs if the armistice was broken. Eisenhower said he believed 'we should use the bomb in Korea if the aggression is renewed' – but he worried that using the weapon unilaterally 'would cause a dangerous breach in allied solidarity'.[4] Dulles replied that he would be happy to discuss the matter with Churchill and Eden when he met them in London the following week.

At the NSC meeting two weeks later, Eisenhower reiterated that 'it was agreed we would use atomic weapons to meet the situation'.[5] He asked Dulles if their allies had been informed about America's stance on the use of nuclear weapons in Korea – to which the Secretary of State replied that he was certain that they had been, though no 'formal consultations' had taken place.

In fact, Dulles had not talked about the use of the A-bomb to the Prime Minister and Foreign Secretary during his visit to London on 16 and 17 October. But Eden certainly knew his views – indeed, he had been quite startled by them when he visited Washington earlier in the year, prior to the first of his gall bladder operations.

On that occasion, in a meeting in the State department, Dulles had declared that it was wrong to attach the 'stigma of immorality' to any particular weapon. He then launched into a folksy account of warfare down the ages.[6]

Doubtless the first wild animal that was killed by a man armed with whatever weapons, be it club or stone, felt man had taken unfair advantage of it. One could not stop inventiveness nor the improvement of weapons. The problem was how to deal with these improvements and how to use them if necessary. Immorality attached to the launching of aggressive war, not to the means that might be used for waging it.

At that time Eden had wanted a public reassurance that the British government would be consulted if America wished to use her bases in the UK for an atomic attack. He also wanted Eisenhower to give Churchill a private assurance that the President would not launch an atomic weapon anywhere without consulting the Prime Minister.

Dulles was content to affirm the administration's consent to the former – but as to the latter, he was rather more non-committal: 'To the extent that time and circumstances permitted, the United States would of course wish to consult with the UK on situations that may arise which would lead to general war.'[7] But as for a personal commitment from the President – 'this of course was a matter which could be decided only by the President himself'.

So the matter of whether to consult Britain – and other allies – about the plan to launch a nuclear attack was yet to be decided. But the place of nuclear weapons in the US armoury was now formally approved in a brand-new, wide-ranging security policy document entitled 'NSC 162/2'. Paragraph 39(b) – the language of which Eisenhower had closely shaped – read: 'In the event of hostilities, the United States will consider nuclear weapons to be as available for use as other munitions.'[8]

Emboldened by this clarity, the Joint Chiefs of Staff now lobbied for the right to take far swifter action if war was resumed on the Korean peninsula. Back in May, the planning was for a nine- to twelve-month build-up of forces before operations could begin against the communists. But now the generals wanted no delay, and the ability to launch swift and severe retaliation.

As Radford and his colleagues stressed, to achieve victory would mean 'employing atomic weapons ... and conducting large-scale air operations against targets in China, Manchuria and Korea'.[9] His very first action would be to 'obtain the necessary presidential authority to enable the immediate employment of nuclear weapons in sufficient quantity to insure success'.

Britain's atomic bomb programme had just reached its own landmark. The country's first operational nuclear weapon, a 10,000lb freefall bomb named 'Blue Danube', had been assembled at the dedicated storage and maintenance facility for nuclear weapons at RAF Barnham in Suffolk.

Now it was delivered to the Bomber Command Armament School at RAF Wittering on the border of Cambridgeshire and Northamptonshire. There was, as yet, no aircraft equipped to carry it, although the 'V' bombers – Valiants, Vulcans and Victors – were soon expected off the production line.

While the weapons were becoming ever more advanced, one element of manpower that many British MPs saw now as an anachronism remained. The Home Guard – 'Dad's Army' to many – had performed a valuable, if somewhat symbolic, role in the Second World War. On returning to power in 1951, Churchill, fearful of the prospect of 20,000 Soviet paratroopers landing on the British Isles, announced that he wished to revive the disbanded citizens' militia.

Recruitment began in April 1952, with a target of 175,000, but by November only 31,000 had enrolled, with a further 25,000 on the reserve list – figures that palled alongside the 285,000 men and women who had joined the Civil Defence Corps. There were doubts whether the Home Guard had any real role to play in the atomic age, and the Labour MP Woodrow Wyatt, himself a former junior defence minister, complained in Parliament that this 'farce' should be brought to an end, questioning, 'Surely it is a waste of enthusiasm and energy to keep in being a force to which there has been no response?'[10]

Churchill and his colleagues were having none of it. At Cabinet,

War Secretary Antony Head, presenting the case for the guard's continuance – at a cost of £1 million a year – admitted that it might seem 'anomalous' when substantial reductions might have to be made in the main army.[11]

He believed the Home Guard would be 'an aid to civil power under atomic attack'. But he admitted that a 'strong lead will be necessary if we are to avoid a rundown'.

The Prime Minister seemed happy to be the one who backed the initiative. 'No doubt. Continue it. And announce it with determination,' he said.[12] So the Home Guard had a stay of execution.

It was clear that enthusiasm remained in the current ranks. A week or so later the 4th Derbyshire Battalion announced it was forming the very first mounted section of the Home Guard. Commanding officer Colonel J. L. Lycett said he had applied for permission because much of the area that he would have to defend in time of war was rough, hilly ground, unsuitable for any form of transport except horses.

The animals would be hired from the High Peak Hunt, farmers and riding schools, and members of the section – stationed at Matlock and Bakewell – would receive riding breeches, spurs, peaked caps rather than berets and other special equipment.

* * *

In October, the New York-based publishing house Ballantine Books – in only its second year of existence – brought out a startling novel by Ray Bradbury, America's most widely known contemporary author of science fiction. The curious title, *Fahrenheit 451*, referred to the temperature at which book paper catches fire and burns.

In the dystopian world created by Bradbury it was firemen who now had the crucial role, for it was no longer their job to put out fires; instead it was their duty to start them. The Bradbury world was one in which books and independent thought were forbidden, and the possession of books was punished by burning not just them but also the place which housed them, and, ultimately, their owner.

The novel's main character, Guy Montag, is a fireman who never questions his destructive role until a chance encounter with his eccentric, free-spirited young neighbour Clarisse. With his eyes opened by her, he recognises the folly of destroying knowledge, quitting his job and pledging himself to the preservation of literary and cultural writings.

Fahrenheit 451 undoubtedly struck a chord with thinking Americans through its atmosphere of paranoia and suspicion and the fearful sense it conveyed of a world rushing towards a nuclear holocaust. And away from those central themes, its depiction of a future high-tech society where big-screen televisions and mood-altering pills combined to atrophy people's minds was – with hindsight – remarkably prescient.

'It was conceived out of Hitler's burning of the books, and is all the timelier now because of the fortunately ill-fated American venture on a similar path,' wrote the critic August Derleth in the *Chicago Tribune*. 'It is a gripping and, in implication, a terrible reading experience, since it points so clearly the direction in which many Americans, who seek to suppress freedom of thought and of the press, are traveling.'[13]

Derleth – and Bradbury – were of course pointing the finger at Joe McCarthy, and the campaign led by his acolytes Roy Cohn and David Schine against the US State Department's libraries in Europe and Asia, which had been accused of harbouring communist or pro-communist literature.

Earlier in the summer it had seemed that Eisenhower, until now fearful of McCarthy's influence over the Republican Party and the country generally, was at last prepared to confront the Wisconsin senator, and he would do so by getting involved in the raging argument around book censorship and book burning.

It came by way of some impromptu remarks that the President uttered to 10,000 students and their families at a commencement service at Dartmouth College in New Hampshire. The central theme of his address was courage; the courage to confront and help correct the things wrong in American society. 'Don't join the book burners,' he told the graduates.

> Don't think you are going to conceal faults by concealing evidence that they ever existed. Don't be afraid to go in your library and read every book, as long as that document does not offend our own ideas of decency. That should be the only censorship.
>
> How will we defeat communism unless we know what it is, and what it teaches, and why does it have such an appeal for men, why are so many people swearing allegiance to it? It is almost a religion, albeit one of the nether religions.
>
> And we have got to fight it with something better, not try to conceal the thinking of our own people.[14]

There was no doubt in the minds of the press the next day – 'Eisenhower's blistering attack on "book burners" stirred speculation in Washington that he may be preparing for a test of strength with Senator McCarthy', reported United Press International.[15]

However, when questioned by reporters four days later at his weekly press conference, Eisenhower denied he had aimed his remarks at McCarthy and said he 'did not deal' in personalities. He then extended his time by half an hour to go on and give an often thoughtful exposition of the flow of ideas in a democratic society.

He told the journalists: 'The United States was strong enough to expose to the world its differing viewpoints – from the man with Socialist leanings to the man who is so far right that it takes a telescope to find him.'[16] He recalled that Americans had criticised themselves after the Second World War for having failed to read Hitler's *Mein Kampf*; if they had, the Führer's whole strategy would have been laid out clearly in front of them. By the same criteria of 'know thine enemy', he had no problem with libraries stocking Stalin's *Problems of Leninism*.

However, he said that US government information libraries overseas should not stock communist works: it would be the 'acme of silliness for America to be a party to its own self-destruction'. No one should get the impression that 'he was attempting to propagate communist beliefs by use of government money', and if the State Department was burning a book that was 'an open appeal to persons in foreign countries to be communists, then the department could get rid of it in any way it pleased, as far as he was concerned'.

It was a nuanced response, almost a lecture on freedom of speech, but it still provoked the following headlines the next day: 'Ike Has No Objection to Burning of Propaganda Books', led the *Albuquerque Journal*, while the *Knoxville Journal* went with 'Ike OK's "Propaganda" Book Burning'.[17] And having raised hopes that through the book debate he might be prepared to confront McCarthy's wilder excesses, Eisenhower was perceived in many quarters as backing away again. McCarthy himself responded blithely: 'He couldn't very well have been referring to me. I have burned no books.'[18]

McCarthy's own public standing wavered from time to time, but his message got through. For communism there was widespread public repugnance; in a Gallup survey, 81 per cent of Americans thought that the Soviet Union sought world rule, 66 per cent did not think that even ex-communists should be allowed to teach in colleges and universities, while 67 per cent would not allow a pro-communist to give a speech in their city.

Eisenhower was always alive to public opinion. So rather than confront the often poisonous atmosphere McCarthy had created, he sought the senator's – and America's – approval of his own efforts to stamp out communists in government. The first show of virility on this front came on 23 October when the White House put out an announcement that 1,456 employees had been removed from the government's payroll between May and September under Eisenhower's loyalty-security programme.[19]

Under Truman, a government employee could not be removed from their job unless there was 'reasonable doubt' about their loyalty. But under Eisenhower, dismissal could happen if the head of a government agency alone decided the employee was 'not reliable or trustworthy' – even though their loyalty was not in question.

Pressed on the figures, Eisenhower's press secretary James Hagerty commented that those fired were not all spies or communists, but they were all 'security risks'. All this was of great encouragement to McCarthy, who went on television to assert – completely without foundation – that 90 per cent of the 1,456 had been dismissed 'for a combination of communist activities and perversion'. It proved his long-held contention, he said, that the Truman administration had been 'crawling with communists'.

Indeed, it was now the recently retired President who would be the next target in this new round of communist bashing. Eisenhower had no love whatsoever for his predecessor – he had been hurt by Truman-approved attacks on him in the 1952 presidential campaign, particularly the sensitive charge that he had been politically involved in deals at Yalta and Potsdam that had 'given' East Germany, Poland and China to the communists.

So when Attorney General Herbert Brownell Jr came to him with a plan that would brand Truman as soft on communism, while at the same time embellishing the administration's anti-communist credentials – and remove 'some of the glamour of the McCarthy stage play' – Eisenhower authorised it, without asking for all the details. It was a decision that would backfire on him.

Brownell's political bombshell – timed to coincide with congressional elections – was dropped onto an audience of Chicago business executives on 6 November, when he accused the former President of being flagrantly weak on communism by citing the case of Harry Dexter White, an assistant secretary to the Treasury Department whom Truman appointed US director of the International Monetary Fund (IMF) in 1946.

White had been a powerful figure in the Roosevelt administration, one of the architects of the post-war world economic order through his leadership at the Bretton Woods conference. Brownell, however, accused Truman of appointing White to the IMF job despite having received two warnings – in December 1945 and then three months later – that White was a Soviet spy.

'When no attention was paid to so great a danger as the espionage activities of Harry Dexter White you can imagine how little notice was given to Communist Party members, Communist propagandists and Communist fellow travelers in government,' Brownell declared.[20]

The allegations about White were well known. They had surfaced in 1948 when he was named by Elizabeth Bentley and Whittaker Chambers – themselves Soviet agents – and had been forced to appear before the House Un-American Activities Committee. White denied all ties to communism and accusations of espionage in front of the committee, but three days after his appearance, he died of a heart attack.

The reality was that Truman had dismissed the second FBI report on White – he never accepted he had been given the first – as evidence offered by 'a crook and a louse' (Bentley and Whittaker), and had been unconvinced by accusations of White's 'friendliness with Russia' during the war.[21] He had seen no good reason not to promote him.

A ferocious political spat developed in the wake of Brownell's speech. Harold Velde, the Republican chairman of the House Un-American Activities Committee, subpoenaed Truman to appear before the committee. 'This is the most incredible, insulting un-American thing I've encountered in my twenty-one years in Congress,' responded the ranking Democrat Francis Walter.[22] In any case, the former President declined to appear, citing the constitutional separation of powers.

Events rapidly spiralled out of control for Eisenhower. Dismayed by Velde's action, he then had to face an uncomfortable press grilling on the Brownell speech five days later. He was asked: 'Do you think the administration's action in virtually putting the label of traitor on a former President is likely to damage our foreign relations?' To which he replied tamely: 'I reject the premise ... I would not answer such a question.'[23] He admitted knowing Brownell was going to talk about Truman and White – but not that White would accuse Truman of having knowledge of the FBI reports. Eisenhower also said he personally would not have summoned Truman to appear before the HUAC, although he was not telling Congress how to run its business.

Then Truman, fed up with these Republican 'snollygosters' (a southern word for 'a man born out of wedlock'), decided to go on national TV to give a full explanation of his role in the Harry Dexter White affair.

Sat in a small studio in Kansas City, flanked by the American flag and wearing an American Legion pin in the lapel of his suit, his 'tell-all' raised as many questions as it answered. Truman said that he knew White had been accused of disloyalty but had decided to retain him in order not to endanger an intensive FBI investigation into spies in the US government. Firing White would have tipped off the others in his 'team' who were also under surveillance.

Truman lashed out at Brownell, saying the Attorney General had 'degraded his office and deceived his chief as to what he proposed to do', and in saying 'Harry Dexter White was known to be a communist spy by the very people who appointed him' he had lied to the American people.[24]

But there was much more.

It is now evident that the present administration has fully embraced, for political purposes, McCarthyism. I am not referring to the senator from Wisconsin – he is only important in that his name has taken on a dictionary meaning in the world. It is the corruption of truth, the abandonment of our historical devotion to fair play … it is the use of the big lie and the unfounded accusation against any citizen in the name of Americanism or security. It is the rise to power of the demagogue who lives on untruth; it is the spread of fear and the destruction of faith in every level of our society.[25]

If Brownell, with Eisenhower's backing, had hoped to upstage McCarthy with his revelations about White, it failed. Truman's outburst brought the senator from Wisconsin right back to centre stage. A furious McCarthy, who had remained largely in the background while the White affair raged, now demanded a right of reply on television with equal air time to respond to Truman's withering comments. He was duly granted half an hour at primetime across all networks, and a week later his vitriolic response, although aimed principally at the former President, also encompassed the current one.

'Tonight I shall spend little time on Harry Truman,' he told America in a calm, modulated voice. 'He is no more important than any other defeated politician.'[26] In fact, McCarthy spent some moments lambasting what he called 'Trumanism' – 'the placing of your political party above the interest of the country, regardless of how much the country is damaged thereby'. On Truman's definition of McCarthyism, he said it was 'identical, word for word, comma for comma, with the definition adopted by the communist *Daily Worker*, which originated the term'.

Then McCarthy turned to the Eisenhower administration, declaring that the 'raw, harsh, unpleasant fact is that communism is an issue and will be an issue in [the] 1954 [congressional campaign]'. He attacked the State Department for retaining John Paton Davies Jr, a career diplomat whom he accused of pro-Chinese leanings; he condemned the White House for failing to take stronger action over American prisoners in Korea; and he criticised it for refusing to cut off aid to allies – like Britain – who still traded with China. Current foreign policy was, in the senator's estimation, just 'whining, whimpering appeasement'.

Some of Eisenhower's aides were convinced this dual attack on Democrat and Republican administrations was also about McCarthy positioning himself to run for President in 1956. Propaganda chief C. D. Jackson was particularly incensed. 'Listening to Senator McCarthy last night was an exceptionally horrible experience,' he wrote to Eisenhower's Chief of Staff Sherman Adams.[27] 'Obviously the President cannot get down in the same gutter – but neither can he avoid a question, if not several questions, at the next press conference.'

Jackson then urged a strong response:

I hope this flagrant performance will open the eyes of some of the President's advisers who seem to think the senator is a really good fellow at heart. They remind me of the people who kept saying for so many months that Mao Tse-Tung was just an agrarian reformer. If every egghead can rise to a fever pitch when Brownell talks about Truman, can't a single Republican work up some temperature when McCarthy refers to Eisenhower as he did?

It fell to John Foster Dulles to launch something of a fightback a week later. With a voice filled with emotion, he unusually opened his weekly news conference with a carefully prepared statement designed to answer McCarthy's attacks – but without mentioning the senator by name. 'Since I met with you last week,' he told reporters, 'there has been a widely-publicized criticism of this administration's foreign policy. The burden of that criticism was that we spoke too kindly to our allies and sent them "perfumed" notes, instead of using threats and intimidation to compel them to do our bidding.'[28]

Dulles said he preferred treating America's allies as 'friends, not satellites', adding – in a clear reference to McCarthy – 'we do not propose to throw away those precious assets of mutual respect and friendship by blustering and domineering methods'. The military bases America shared with friendly powers were vital for use in defence against the Soviet Union's 'rapidly mounting power'.

In his own press conference the following day, Eisenhower declared he was in 'full accord with the statements made yesterday by Secretary Dulles'.[29] But his only direct response to McCarthy's speech was to say that 'by next fall I hope that the public, no longer fearful that communists are destructively at work within the government, will wish to commend the efficiency of the administration in eliminating this menace to the nation's security'.

So the White House was still, to a large extent, dancing to McCarthy's tune. The following day, the senator from Wisconsin cleverly and deferentially acknowledged: 'President Eisenhower is an honourable man. I think he will follow the will of the American people as that will is made known to him.'[30]

But that will, he went on, was right behind his own campaign to stop trade with 'Red China', and he asked 'every American who feels as I do about this blood trade to write or wire the President and tell him how they feel'.

Over 50,000 telegrams and letters would eventually be received by the White House – the vast majority supporting the crackdown on Chinese trade – the second largest campaign since 'Save the Rosenbergs' in the spring.

Over the late summer McCarthy's Permanent Subcommittee on Investigations held public hearings into supposed security leaks at the Government Printing Office, a big operation whose clients were Congress and its executive agencies. The committee then turned its attention to communist infiltration of the United Nations, with American television viewers able to watch the inquisition of Julius Reiss, a clerk employed by the Polish delegation of the UN, who had been a well-known Communist Party leader. There was also a probe for subversives in the United Electrical, Radio and Machine Workers union, which organised workers at General Electric and Westinghouse plants.

But McCarthy had even bigger fish to fry. Having married his long-time aide Jeannie Kerr, the couple were honeymooning in the West Indies when he received an urgent call from his aide Roy Cohn, reporting news of likely communist infiltration in the US Army – specifically, the Signal Corps.

McCarthy cut short his honeymoon and returned to Washington. The Signal Corps had numbered 350,000 officers and enlisted men at its wartime peak, although that figure had shrunk to just over 50,000 in the early 1950s. At its headquarters at Fort Monmouth in New Jersey, it employed some of the country's brightest scientists and engineers, working on highly sensitive programmes, such as new power systems, guided missile controls and ground radar stations.

Worries about security and espionage at Fort Monmouth pre-dated McCarthy's committee. Joel Barr and Alfred Sarant, two probable Soviet agents who fled the country in 1950, had spent time there. Julius Rosenberg had worked for the Signal Corps at Fort Monmouth until his suspension in 1945; now McCarthy set out to prove that Rosenberg had created a spy ring that had outlasted his death in the electric chair.

It was Fort Monmouth's commander, Major General Kirke Lawton, who had tipped off Cohn and his colleagues to the possibility of sub-version at his facility, and a few days before the public hearings Lawton suspended forty-two Fort Monmouth employees as security risks. (All but two would later get their jobs back.)

In classic McCarthy style, five days of closed-door hearings in Oc-tober 1953 generated a spate of sensational headlines: 'Executed Spy Bared as Head of Radar Ring'; 'Espionage in Signal Corps for Ten Years is Charged'; and 'Rosenberg Called Radar Spy Leader – McCarthy Says Ring he Set Up "May Still be in Operation" at Monmouth Laboratories'.

The hearings were held at the Federal Courthouse in New York City – the same building where the Rosenbergs had been tried, convicted and sentenced to death. Early on in the Signal Corps inquiry, David Greenglass, Julius's brother-in-law, who was convicted of espionage as part of the spy ring but spared execution, looked as if he had provided McCarthy with some compelling evidence.

From his prison cell in Pennsylvania, Greenglass testified to the subcommittee that there had been a spy ring at Fort Monmouth. One highly classified project at Fort Monmouth had been work on the 'proximity fuse', an electronic device that used a tiny radar to detect its target and detonate a bomb in flight. In his deposition, Greenglass claimed that Julius Rosenberg had been an inspector at one of the firms the US Army had contracted to work on the fuse – and that he had subsequently stolen it, put it in his briefcase and eventually handed it on to his Soviet contact. Greenglass also claimed that the Rosenberg spy ring was still in operation.

However, Greenglass's claims soon faded away without any other corroboration. McCarthy then alleged the Communist Party had organised a special cell, called the 'Shore Club' unit, to infiltrate Fort Monmouth. Once again, no substantial evidence emerged in the hear-ings to prove this organisation had ever existed.

McCarthy and his assistants Roy Cohn and David Schine hauled before them a large number of mostly former Signal Corps employees who had left the service at the end of the war. The majority refused to testify, citing the Fifth Amendment's protection against self-incrimination. McCarthy made it clear that they were just hiding behind the Constitution and this was as good as an admission of guilt. Increasingly frustrated, he and his sidekicks responded with some of their most hectoring questioning yet.

One such victim was Marcel Ullman, a television repair man who had worked at the Signal Corps laboratories until 1948. He had to endure three appearances before the committee, invoking the Fifth Amendment when asked whether he had belonged to the mythical Shore Club, or had connections with convicted spies Rosenberg, Alger Hiss and Morton Sobell (an electrical engineer who passed secrets to the Soviets). Ullman was somewhat startled to be asked whether he knew Dean Acheson, Truman's Secretary of State.

Eventually McCarthy lost patience and told him bluntly:

All of the evidence indicates that you have been active over just as long a period of time as Julius Rosenberg and involved in the same type of filthy activities against your country, the country which has treated you rather well. Rosenberg has been executed, and you are walking the streets free. Do you not feel that if Rosenberg was properly executed, you deserve the same fate?[31]

Cohn and McCarthy had lost some of the clarity and the edge that characterised their investigations earlier in the year. Cohn was always brash and smug, but now he was pompous and petulant, and his questioning rambling and repetitive. McCarthy was impatient, overly aggressive and excessively dramatic, overplaying things for the TV audience.

The tide was beginning to turn against McCarthy. After the hearings adjourned in mid-December, newspapers in the Fort Monmouth area were the first to condemn him. The *Asbury Park Press* said the charges were 'ridiculously thin accusations', while the *Long Branch Daily Record* spoke of 'McCarthy's reckless charges, his masterful dissemination of half-truths, insinuations and innuendos ... his callous disregard of American citizens who have never been convicted of anything, much less accused'.

A more natural foe, the *New York Times*, published a series of articles saying that security had already been tightened at Fort Monmouth before McCarthy's investigation began. The paper would urge its readers to view his charges sceptically, suggesting that 'Senator McCarthy's shameless scramble for publicity has never been exposed more clearly than in the Monmouth case'.

There were signs too that the administration was just starting to push back. US Army secretary Robert Stephens infuriated McCarthy when he announced the results of his own inquiry into the army in mid-November; it concluded that there were no suspected spies among the suspended Fort Monmouth employees, and no 'current case' of subversion. For good measure, he added that he did not believe there had been any espionage there during the Second World War.

Brutal, clumsy and unconvincing though they were, it appeared that the army hearings had not, as yet, damaged McCarthy in the eyes of the public. A Gallup poll in December 1953 asked: 'What is your opinion of Senator Joseph McCarthy – Favourable or Unfavourable?' Fifty per cent said favourable, 29 per cent unfavourable, with 21 per cent undecided.[32] The favourable response was up 18 per cent from the summer.

Eisenhower continued to reject calls from those he trusted outside the White House, including his own brother Milton, for a public showdown with McCarthy. He used his Vice-President Richard Nixon as an intermediary to try to stop him pushing the Monmouth investigation too hard. He even invited him to lunch – with other leading

Republicans – at the White House. The senator from Wisconsin would have to be left to self-destruct on his own.

*   *   *

In the summer of 1953, two US senators had sought to open up the Central Intelligence Agency to scrutiny – but for completely different reasons. The first, unsurprisingly, was Joe McCarthy in his role as the nation's communist hunter-in-chief.

The object of his initial interest was CIA official William P. Bundy, the son-in-law of former Secretary of State Dean Acheson (who was himself a favourite McCarthy target). The Wisconsin senator wanted to subpoena Bundy so his committee could question him about a $400 contribution he had supposedly made to Alger Hiss's defence fund.

Ultimately, McCarthy hoped this would be the start of a full-scale investigation of the CIA, having been persuaded by colleagues that Soviet agents had successfully infiltrated the agency. But director Allen Dulles was having none of it, and Eisenhower had also made it known that he would not allow the CIA to be examined in public – or in private.

Vice-President Richard Nixon, once more the peacemaker between the White House and McCarthy, duly stepped in and, over a lunch with the Wisconsin senator and his fellow committee members, persuaded them that the CIA was an inviolable body and that the level of opposition – even among conspiratorial Republican right-wingers – would be too great.

McCarthy reluctantly agreed not to table Bundy's subpoena, and in a statement to the press said he was prepared to hand over his information to Allen Dulles, who could study it and act if necessary. McCarthy told the press this was 'neither a victory nor a defeat', but in truth it was a setback – the first his committee had suffered. A gleeful *Washington Post* deemed it 'his first, total, unmitigated, unqualified defeat'.[33]

The other senator wanting oversight of the CIA was Mike Mansfield, the Democratic freshman senator from Montana. Newly elected, Mansfield was from a small state and had yet to build his reputation and influence. But he was a keen advocate of the oversight of key government bodies, and as a result, he quickly turned his attention to the CIA.

Mansfield believed the CIA had to maintain its secrecy to be effective, to encourage clandestine sources of information. But he argued that there was a

> profound difference between an essential degree of secrecy to achieve a specific purpose and secrecy for the sake of secrecy. Once secrecy becomes sacrosanct, it invites abuse. If we accept this idea of secrecy for secrecy's sake we will have no way of knowing whether we have a fine intelligence service or a very poor one.[34]

Mansfield had witnessed McCarthy's debacle over the CIA, and wanted Congress to be able to examine the agency's work in a more responsible way. So he introduced a resolution for the establishment of a Joint Congressional Oversight Committee for the American Clandestine Service. Mansfield envisaged this committee being similar in structure and size to the Senate's Joint Atomic Energy Committee – the focal point for the scrutiny of America's nuclear weapons and power programme. It would be a disciplined body with a professional staff and the ability to keep secrets.

He won support from another freshman, 32-year-old Stuyvesant Wainwright II, congressman from New York's first district, and also from Peter Frelinghuysen Jr, a Republican from New Jersey. But that was about as good as it got. Mansfield's efforts to open up the CIA foundered at first base, facing implacable opposition from such influential figures as Senator Leverett Saltonstall, chairman of the Senate Armed Services Committee.

Then there was Eisenhower. The President knew Wainwright a little, because the young congressman had served on the Supreme Headquarters Allied Expeditionary Force in the war. Eisenhower was furious at the prospect of oversight, telling Wainwright that 'this kind of a bill would be passed over his dead body'.[35]

So there were no watchers for the watchmen. If there had been, then the events following the death of a government employee who fell from a tenth-floor hotel bedroom in New York on Saturday 28 November may well have been very different.

For this man was one of the first casualties of MKUltra, the CIA's covert programme exploring the use of mind-altering drugs. He was not one of those troubled members of society who had been co-opted as human guinea pigs – the psychiatric patients, the prostitutes, or the homeless. He was instead one of the agency's own employees.

Associated Press reported in an evening dispatch that earlier that day Dr Frank Rudolph Olson, forty-two, of Old Braddock, a bacteriologist at Camp Detrick, 'fell or jumped' to his death from a tenth-floor room at the Hotel Statler.[36]

According to the story, Olson had been in New York with a friend, Robert Lashbrook, a 'Defense Department chemist', to see a doctor, and they had planned to return home that day. However, in the early hours, Lashbrook woke up to see his companion crash through the window shade and glass. Olson, clad only in his underwear, struck a fourth-floor ledge and then landed on the sidewalk.

The report added that Olson, a former captain with the US Army Chemical Corps, 'had been despondent over ill health', according to friends from his home town. He left a wife, Alice, thirty-eight, and three children: Eric, who was nine; Lisa, who was seven; and Nils, who was only five.

The *Iron County Miner* paper based in Hurley, Wisconsin – where Olson went to university – hinted at something more when it wrote that he 'was engaged in the chemical warfare phase of our defense program'.[37] But barring a brief report of his funeral in Olson's local paper, the Maryland-based *Frederick Press*, there would be no further coverage of this mysterious death. The CIA wanted it that way.

But the clues that there might be a bigger, more sinister story behind the bald coverage were there in the Associated Press report, in the words 'bacteriologist', 'Army Chemical Corps', 'Camp Detrick' and 'Defense Department chemist'.

The complete story and the facts behind Olson's death have never fully come to light. His personal story went something like this. After obtaining a degree and PhD in bacteriology at the University of Wisconsin, he was recruited to work at the US Army Biological Warfare Laboratories at Camp Detrick in Maryland during the war. By then the US government was vigorously pursuing secret chemical and biological warfare experiments, primarily to counter Japan, which was the leader in this field at the time.

In the late 1940s, Olson began working as a CIA employee on the organisation's technical services staff, run by Sidney Gottlieb and his deputy Robert Lashbrook. Olson was involved in experiments aimed at producing poisons and germ strains that would be useful in interrogating or assassinating people.

While his colleagues devised poisonous paper, fountain pens and lipstick, Olson specialised in developing bacteria to be used in aerosol delivery systems. He co-authored a 220-page study entitled 'Experimental Airborne Infections', which described experiments with 'airborne clouds of highly infectious agents'.[38]

But by 1951 Olson was starting to express moral misgivings about his work to his wife and a few of his colleagues. Those concerns were only heightened through his involvement with the CIA projects named 'Bluebird', 'Artichoke' and 'MKNaomi', which were all interrogation programmes using the biological agents that Olson had helped to develop. He is believed to have been present at brutal interrogations at Camp King in Germany, and been horrified by what he witnessed.

Then came the CIA's obsession with LSD, the magic espionage weapon that could unlock the minds of homegrown traitors and Soviet agents. Operation MKUltra was born not long afterwards, and Olson was quickly assigned to work on the project.

The outlandish Sidney Gottlieb, who ran MKUltra, took LSD and mescaline himself, and would urge his colleagues to do likewise to gain first-hand experience of the drugs. So it was that on 18 November, Gottlieb and Lashbrook gathered together a group of CIA officers at a weekend retreat at Deep Creek Lake, three hours' drive from Camp Detrick.

Olson believed that they were there to discuss joint projects on biological warfare and drugs for mind control. In fact, as they settled down in the cabin's living room for drinks after a hearty dinner, Sydney Gottlieb served Olson and others a bottle of Cointreau that had been laced with LSD.

His 'trip' was a disastrous one for Olson, leaving him paranoiac and full of self-doubt. A week later he went to see the chief of the CIA's special operations division, Vincent Ruwet, and told him he wanted to pull out of the germ warfare work and devote his life to something else.

The CIA sent him to New York City to consult one of their physicians, Harold Abramson, an allergist and paediatrician, who was helping the agency with the psychotropic research into the effects of LSD. Abramson 'treated' Olson with bourbon and the sedative Nembutal – a highly dangerous combination – and then recommended that he should be sent to a mental institution to recover.

Lashbrook, who had accompanied Olson to New York, booked them into a room on the tenth floor of the Hotel Statler on the evening of 27 November. At 2.30 a.m., Lashbrook claimed he woke up to see Olson run across the room and jump through a curtained and closed window. The glass shattered and Olson crashed down to the street below; he died within minutes as a result of his severe injuries.

Lashbrook immediately began to cover the CIA's tracks. His first phone call was not to a hospital or the police, but to Sidney Gottlieb. When the police arrived, Lashbrook told them he was with the Defense Department and implied that Olson might have killed himself because of job-related stress. New York detectives fared little better in unearthing the truth. In their files, they recorded the theory that Olson had killed himself because of a homosexual lovers' quarrel with Lashbrook.

The background as to how and why Frank Olson met his death would not start to emerge for a quarter of a century. The CIA connection would never find its way into the papers in 1953. MKUltra's secrets were safe.

It was no doubt pure coincidence, but in December a highly classified manual was made available to read at the CIA entitled 'A Study in Assassination'.[39] It stressed that 'assassination is an extreme measure not normally used in clandestine operations' and 'can seldom be employed with a clear conscience ... persons who are morally squeamish should not attempt it'.

Having then gone on to detail various killing techniques, the author then wrote: 'The most efficient accident, in simple assassination, is a fall of 75 feet or more onto a hard surface.'

* * *

In November 1953, America's other principal intelligence agency was on the trail of the country's best-known scientist. Robert Oppenheimer was about to travel to London to deliver an address as part of the prestigious Reith Lectures, and the FBI had been detailed to watch his every move.

The charismatic wartime head of the Los Alamos Laboratory had spent much of 1953 warning of the dangers of nuclear proliferation and arguing fiercely for a system of international arms control. But his opposition to the hydrogen bomb – out of practical as well as ethical reasons – had stirred up enmity in the hierarchy of nuclear scientists, and his influence on key bodies such as the Atomic Energy Commission was waning.

Lewis Strauss, head of the Atomic Energy Commission, was Oppenheimer's most powerful enemy. Strauss began a campaign to curb the influence of America's foremost scientist and ultimately destroy his reputation, enlisting a young acolyte, William Borden (staff director on the Joint Committee on Atomic Energy), to draw up a substantial dossier on Oppenheimer's supposed communist sympathies and links.

Through his contacts in the media, Strauss planted unfavourable articles about Oppenheimer in *Time*, *Life* and *Fortune* magazines. He was also able to call on the services of the FBI through his friendship with J. Edgar Hoover, so that throughout the summer Oppenheimer's phone was invariably tapped wherever he travelled.

In that febrile period, with McCarthyism showing no signs of waning, Oppenheimer knew that he was vulnerable to accusations of past communist association. In the 1930s, at Berkeley, he was sympathetic to communist goals, although he never joined the American Communist Party – even though his brother Frank did. In 1942, on a Manhattan Project security questionnaire, Oppenheimer half-jokingly wrote that while he had never been a communist, he had 'probably belonged to every communist-front organization on the West Coast'.

But most concerning was the knowledge that in early 1943, soon after being named director of the Manhattan Project, Oppenheimer was approached by Haakon Chevalier, a Berkeley professor of French and an old friend from within the communist movement. Chevalier told Oppenheimer that he knew of a way to pass information to the Soviets. Oppenheimer rejected Chevalier's offer, but also did not report it for another eight months.

That error of judgement over Chevalier would now come back to haunt Oppenheimer, and would be high on the list of charges in the document that Borden was drawing up for Strauss. While Borden was finishing compiling their dossier, Strauss asked Hoover's men to enlist the help of MI5 to monitor Oppenheimer's movements in the UK.

So in advance of Oppenheimer's trip, Philip O'Brien, under his FBI cover title of assistant legal attaché at the American embassy in London, contacted Brigadier Bill Magan, a senior MI5 director based at the service's Leconfield House headquarters. 'Prior investigation has reflected that Oppenheimer formerly associated with known and suspected Communist Party members,' O'Brien wrote.[40] 'His wife Katherine and his brother Frank have admitted prior Communist Party membership. Allegations have been received indicating that Oppenheimer has been responsible for delaying the development of the hydrogen bomb.'

O'Brien had discovered Oppenheimer's itinerary, which included brief visits to France and Denmark after his time in England. 'It is requested you advise this office of any pertinent information concerning the subject's activities and contacts, while abroad, that may come to your attention.'

Oppenheimer and his wife travelled by boat from New York, docking in Southampton on Tuesday 10 November. In London they booked into Claridge's Hotel for the duration of their three-week stay. Bill Magan delegated the watch on Oppenheimer to a junior, Philip Ray, who in turn wrote to the commander of Special Branch, saying that he 'would be grateful if you will kindly let us know if he comes to your adverse notice in any way'.[41]

During his visit Oppenheimer delivered a lecture at the Harwell Atomic Energy Research Establishment, and afterwards went to dinner at Christ Church, Oxford, where he dined with guests including Sir John Cockcroft, the Nobel Prize-winning physicist, and Professor Hans von Halban.

Halban, a German-born physicist and a friend of Lord Cherwell, was someone of interest to the US authorities. He had worked at the

Montreal Laboratory – part of the Manhattan Project – in the war, but was now *persona non grata* in the United States for supposedly divulging atomic secrets to the French.

But there was nothing untoward for Special Branch to pass on, no indiscreet talk, and Oppenheimer did not associate with anyone who held communist views. O'Brien said he was 'under pressure' from Washington to report on Oppenheimer's activities, but Ray replied that, 'on present information, we had no justification for taking any special surveillance action'.[42]

Oppenheimer's six Reith lectures were delivered under the title 'Science and the Common Understanding'.[43] There was some excitement over his second lecture, entitled 'Science as Action: Rutherford's World', in which he told his audience that scientists splitting the atom had discovered 'mysterious particles' that flashed for a millionth of a second before changing into something else.

This new family of particles had taken scientists to a new level in working out the laws of the sub-atomic world, and opened up a new frontier, 'where discovery is as uncharted as it was in the new world in the fifteenth century when Columbus discovered America'.[44]

On the whole, though, Oppenheimer's lectures were for the cognoscenti rather than the layman. One critic wrote that 'his glittering rhetoric held his listeners in a web of absorption that was often less attentive than trance-like'. Lord Cherwell, himself a master at simplifying science and making it accessible, described the talks as 'somewhat incomprehensible'.[45]

It was when Oppenheimer left London for a brief visit to Paris that his naïvety – for such an intelligent man – revealed itself again. Or perhaps it was because he just did not care. Whatever the case, FBI agents in the French capital tracked him to a flat near the Sacré-Coeur, where he was meeting his old friend Haakon Chevalier and his wife for dinner.

Chevalier was still on the watchlist of the French intelligence services, suspected of being a Soviet agent, so Oppenheimer's visit – however harmless – was just another piece of information for Strauss to add to his dossier.

Matters came to a head in early December. Eisenhower held no great animosity towards Oppenheimer; he may have disagreed with his analysis of the arms race and his desire for government openness, but the President greatly respected him as a scientist and as a man. However, when a report from J. Edgar Hoover – including a lengthy letter from chief accuser Borden – landed on his desk on Wednesday 2 December, the President reluctantly felt duty-bound to act.

That day Eisenhower had first taken a call from Charles Wilson, in which the Secretary of Defense said he had read the FBI report and felt that it carried 'the gravest implications that Dr Oppenheimer is a security risk of the worst kind ... Some of the accusers seem to go so far as to accuse him of having been an actual agent of the communists.'[46]

Wilson, thinking back to the events of January when John Archibald Wheeler had lost the 'secrets' of the H-bomb, had even discussed with Hoover whether Oppenheimer and Wheeler might have been co-conspirators in a spy ring.

In fact, the exact words of the report's startling conclusion was that 'more probably than not he has ... been functioning as an espionage agent; and more probably than not, he has ... acted under a Soviet directive in influencing United States military, atomic energy, intelligence and diplomatic policy.'[47]

Eisenhower noted that the 'new charges' against Oppenheimer, after a 'long, exhaustive and careful analysis' of his beliefs and associations stretching back to 1931, 'presented little new evidence.'[48] He was supposed to have contributed money to the Communist Party; he had a 'pattern' of communist associations; his wife and brother were party members; and, at various times, he had attempted to thwart American development of the atomic and hydrogen bombs.

'The overall conclusion has always been that there is no evidence that implies disloyalty on the part of Dr Oppenheimer,' the President recorded.[49] 'However, this does not mean that he might not be a security risk.'

After discussions with Wilson and his National Security Advisor Robert Cutler, Eisenhower felt he had to play it by the book and take immediate action against Oppenheimer. So he ordered that a 'blank wall' be placed between Oppenheimer and any government material 'of a sensitive or classified character', pending a full hearing of the case against Oppenheimer by the Atomic Energy Commission.[50]

The figure of Joe McCarthy had loomed large over Eisenhower's decision. The Wisconsin senator had been itching to summon Oppenheimer before his committee, and if he had failed to order an investigation the President would have been vulnerable to a McCarthy charge that he was shielding a potential security risk.

Strauss had achieved his initial objective – removing Oppenheimer from the orbit of government and stifling his influence. It was the first step on the road to blackening his rival's reputation and, ultimately, bringing him down.

The Big Three in Bermuda – Joseph Laniel, Dwight Eisenhower
and Winston Churchill at the Mid Ocean Club.
© Keystone Press/Alamy Stock Photo

CHAPTER 11

'WINSTON'S BABY'

Bermuda, even in winter, fits many people's idea of paradise. A collection of seven main islands and scores of delightful islets, it is warmed by the Gulf Stream and the sun's rays, yet free of the relentless heat of the tropics. Its beaches are filled with fine pink sand, its calm waters dazzle an iridescent turquoise, its untouched coral reefs bring forth a kaleidoscope of colour and its winding roads are flanked by a profusion of fragrant oleander, hibiscus and bougainvillea.

In his dying days, the great American humorist Mark Twain, who adored the place, quipped: 'You go to heaven if you want to – I'd rather stay here.'[1] This seemingly tranquil island, the oldest and most loyal of British colonies, was surely the perfect place for the new 'Big Three' – Eisenhower, Churchill and the latest French premier, Joseph Laniel – to unwind, reflect on a turbulent year, think imaginatively and prepare to act generously in plotting the way forward.

This was the summit that would have taken place in July had it not been for Churchill's stroke. In most people's eyes it was 'Winston's Baby', the last chance for the Prime Minister to press his case, face-to-face with fellow Allied leaders, for a policy of 'easement' with Moscow.

The Prime Minister was certainly buoyed by the prospect, even scenting the opportunity of some creative 'down time' away from the meetings. 'My Dear Friend,' he wrote to Eisenhower, 'I'm so glad that it is all fixed … I am bringing my paint-box with me as I cannot take you on at golf. They say the water is 67 degrees which is too cold for me.'[2]

A round at the immaculate Mid Ocean Club, where the delegates would be staying, was very tempting for the President, but he anticipated headlines accusing him of frivolity. 'I do not know that I shall bring along my golf clubs, but I do hope that the entire period will not be one of such exhausting work that we shall be denied time for any recreation to say nothing of a bit of thinking.'[3]

Bermuda held fond wartime memories for Churchill. He had flown there in January 1942 from Virginia aboard the state-of-the-art British Overseas Airways Corporation flying boat 'Berwick', having spent several weeks in Washington conferring with President Roosevelt, who had just brought the United States into the war after the catastrophic Japanese attack on Pearl Harbor.

It was the darkest of times for a beleaguered Prime Minister. On Boxing Day he had suffered a mild heart attack shortly after addressing a joint session of Congress. As for the conduct of the war, Rommel was in the ascendant in Africa, while the Japanese were closing in on 'Fortress Singapore'.

But in his 24-hour stopover, Churchill's spirits were lifted by the rapturous reception he received from the Bermudians, delighted by his surprise visit and breaking blackout regulations to come out and greet him. The Parliament building in the capital Hamilton where he gave his address was thronged with Assembly members, high-ranking United States officers (America now had an air and naval base on the island) and colonial officials, while many others crowded onto a gallery outside the building and peered through open windows.

The Prime Minister duly delivered one of his classic wartime speeches, praising the 'valiant resistance of the Russian armies and peoples', sympathising with an America 'now set upon by those same villainous powers … with every circumstance of treachery and malice', and hailing the recent agreement of twenty-six nations, 'who would now march forward in comradeship until those who have sought to trample upon the rights of individual freedom are finally overcome'.[4]

He made the 3,300-mile trip back to Plymouth, audaciously, in the flying boat, travelling by night to avoid the German bombers. Now, eleven years on, with an entourage of ministers, officials, secretaries, and his doctor Lord Moran – who had also been with him back in 1942 – he would return in another advanced, if rather more comfortable aircraft, the Boeing Stratocruiser 'Canopus'.

The British party touched down at 2 p.m. on Wednesday 2 December at the US Kindley Air Force base, where a guard of honour was provided by the Royal Welch Fusiliers – the same regiment that had recently been sent to stabilise the situation in British Guiana – accompanied by their mascot, a beautiful white Kashmir goat named Gwilym. Churchill dined quietly that evening with Anthony Eden and Sir Norman Brook.

Churchill and Eden greeted the arrival of the French party the following morning, then, after lunch, the Prime Minister met the governor Sir Alexander Hood and the Speaker of the House of Assembly of Bermuda Sir John Cox, to ensure there would be no repeat of the embarrassment of the previous week when the Queen and Prince Philip visited the island.

The royal couple had arrived in Bermuda on the first leg of a scheduled twelve-country tour, spanning six months, of the Commonwealth. But Sir Alexander and his officials had generated dreadful headlines for the young monarch's visit when they left off the guest list for the main banquet the only two black members of the Bermudian Parliament.

Sixty-five per cent of Bermuda's population was black, emphasising the non-representative way in which the country was governed. This was adding insult to injury for black Bermudians, and the inadequate explanation given for their absence from the royal dinner was that the guest list was drawn up 'according to precedence'.

'Will Our Officials Never Learn?' raged the *Daily Mirror*.[5] 'For precedence read the authority of the closed mind and the dull head. The Queen is journeying to meet her peoples. In the name of the awakening

Commonwealth – let her.' The *Daily Herald* in its editorial called it 'gross ill manners ... [when] one of the moral pledges by which the Commonwealth is held together is that the colour bar should be utterly destroyed as speedily as possible'.[6]

Churchill's cautionary words to Hood ensured that MPs Edward Trenton Richards (who would later become Bermuda's first black government leader) and George Williams were on the guest list for a banquet the following night for the summit leaders. 'Big 3 Dinner Makes up for "Color" Controversy' would be a typical headline the day after.[7]

But there would still be much more to be done for the British rulers to make up for once the red carpets were rolled away. Everywhere – in schools, surgeries, on transport, in social clubs and restaurants – rigid racial segregation was still very much the norm, as much as anything to suit the hordes of American tourists who descended on the island each summer to bolster Bermuda's economy. Black and white were equally under the sway of the 'first families' of Bermuda, the so-called 'Forty Thieves', a self-perpetuating oligarchy of bankers and businessmen who controlled most of the political and economic power on the islands.

Property qualifications meant that only 5,000 out of 35,000 inhabitants could vote in elections. All of this made up the darker side of Bermuda, which was described vividly in a series of eve-of-conference reports by the renowned Canadian journalist Jack Scott. 'Most of us here soft pedalled the story in deference to the occasion of the Queen's visit and to the first impact of Bermuda's physical beauty ... but this is the shabby backdrop on the stage dominated for the moment by the leaders of the West's most powerful democracies,' he wrote in the *Vancouver Sun*.[8]

On Thursday Churchill and Eden had a whole day to prepare for the arrival of Eisenhower and Dulles and the start of the summit the next day. The view from the Foreign Secretary's camp was not encouraging. 'A. E. has spent [the day] trying to get the Old Man's mind into some kind of order,' recorded Evelyn Shuckburgh, his private secretary.[9] 'He hardly listens to argument and constantly reverts to wartime and post-war analogies. I was at part of one of those meetings in his room and was shocked how old, weary and inconsequent he seemed.'

Churchill admitted at dinner that night, 'I have become torpid in the middle of the day ... This old carcass of mine is a bloody nuisance.'[10] But Jock Colville felt the 'PM got going well', although he turned gloomy when the conversation moved to the arms race and reflected on 'the demoralisation which the scientists have caused'. But he believed it was 'not in Russia's interest to make war' and he was confident about 'building for peace' in a meeting with Malenkov.

After Eisenhower's arrival on Friday morning, the Big Three took little persuading to pose for photographs in wicker chairs on the veranda of the Mid Ocean Club. After a brief discussion with Churchill about who should sit in the middle, the President took centre stage, just as Roosevelt always did in the wartime summits.

The conference had been given real focus by a Soviet 'note' of 26 November, which had included an agreement to hold a four-power (USA, Britain, France and the Soviet Union) meeting in Berlin – at foreign minister level – to discuss disagreements over the future of Germany and Austria. The Kremlin had also suggested a five-power meeting (adding China) to discuss wider matters of 'tension' – but Eisenhower and Dulles were never going to agree to that, having no desire to even recognise the communist regime of Mao Tse-Tung.

Dulles welcomed the Kremlin's initiative, but, as ever, cautioned: 'Are the Soviets willing to have any fresh breath of freedom touch any part of the area now behind the Iron Curtain? If they say no, then I don't see the chance of getting anywhere.'

For Churchill, the note was a move in the right direction, but he still hankered after a face-to-face meeting with Malenkov. The day after the Soviet announcement, the US ambassador to London, banker and naval hero Winthrop Aldrich, gave Dulles his assessment of Churchill's mood on the eve of Bermuda. 'His remarks in [the House of] Commons on 3 November seemed to show a tempering of his optimism expressed in May, although not [the] abandonment of [his] dream,' Aldrich wrote.[11]

> We consider chances better than even that Churchill will not press a specific suggestion for any chiefs of state meeting. It must always be borne in mind, however, that he is imaginative, unpredictable, firm in the belief of his own genius, and apparently determined to attempt one last crowning act on [the] world stage.

Aldrich had read Churchill's mind well, because when the Prime Minister took his opportunity to address the subject of the Soviet Union in the latter part of the first plenary session on Friday 4 December, he did his best, at this stage anyway, to rein in his enthusiasm.

Following a perceptive, if slightly worthy, contribution from the French Foreign Minister Georges Bidault, it was Churchill's turn to address the gathering in the heightened atmosphere, which had been made more dramatic by the deployment of candles and hurricane lamps around the antique conference table as all the lights had fused.

At first Churchill put his oratorical flourishes to one side and simply tried to calmly convince the Americans and the French that the 'new look' strategy of the Kremlin was not one to be feared, or ignored. He believed steadfast opposition from the United States and her allies had played a part in provoking this different attitude, but the enemy's mindset was changing for practical, economic reasons, because the 'hopes of a communist utopia which had been dangled before the eyes of millions had not been borne out. At the disposal of the Soviet leaders at any moment were enormous opportunities for improving the material situation of their population.'[12]

The Prime Minister was willing to believe that 'a definite change in Russian policy and outlook [had developed] which may govern their actions for many years to come ... Let us make sure we do not too lightly dismiss this possibility.' He cautioned the many sceptics around the table that their own people 'must be convinced ... that no *bona fide* movement towards a "détente" or effort for improvement had been rebuffed and cast aside without consideration'.

There was no mention this time of a big summit meeting. Instead Churchill put the case for more contacts, more trade, greater 'infiltration' and a reassurance that 'they would not have another dose of Hitler'. Yes, the West should continue to make it clear it did not tolerate the subjugation of the Soviet Union's satellite countries, but it certainly did not intend to start a third world war to free them.

'Encourage, encourage the world,' Churchill concluded in an optimistic peroration, 'by stimulating prosperity and getting people in a more agreeable state of mind. This might carry us through a period of years to a time when a much better scene will come.'[13]

But then the atmosphere in the room turned around completely when Eisenhower had his say. The gathering was shocked by the President's brief response: violent and vulgar, he came down on Churchill 'like a ton of bricks'. If he understood correctly, he said, 'Sir Winston had no quarrel' with Russia's supposed 'new look' strategy.[14] But in a crude analogy Eisenhower proceeded to liken the Soviet Union to a woman of the streets. She might be bathed and perfumed and wearing a new dress, rather than the usual old patched one, but she was still the same old whore. And America intended to 'pull the old girl off the main street and put her on a back alley'.

The President was not convinced

there had been any change in the Soviet policy of destroying the capitalist free world by all means, by force, by deceit or by lies. This was their long-term purpose. From their writings it was clear there had been no change since Lenin. If he had misinterpreted the Prime Minister, he would be happy if Sir Winston would correct him.

Eden broke the stunned silence by asking the President when the next meeting would be. 'I don't know. Mine is with a whisky and soda,' he replied and with that he got up and abruptly left the room.[15]

It was a remarkably tetchy start to the conference, and Eisenhower's mood would not improve much in the coming days. His response to Churchill was indicative of how he had come to regard his old wartime friend. Outside of the conference room he found him, as ever, stimulating and engaging company; inside, on the real political business of the moment, he was increasingly frustrated with what he regarded as his anachronistic attitudes.

'Winston is a curious mixture of belligerence and of caution, sometimes amounting to almost hysterical fear,' he reflected.[16]

When he really wants to do something, he pooh-poohs and belittles every word or hint of risks involved … he cannot help thinking he himself is the world's only statesman today; it is almost impossible for him to see anyone else proposing an idea of any general importance to the world.

Eisenhower believed that Churchill was deliberately using his deafness as a ploy 'to avoid hearing anything he does not want to hear'. Beyond his disability, the President no longer bought into the notion of the special relationship in the same way that the Prime Minister did: 'He gives me a lecture on the might, the power, the majesty of the two great nations of the United States and the United Kingdom marching before these little trembling dictators.'[17]

Eisenhower seemingly kept his feelings well hidden, for Churchill's perspective on their relationship was much different. 'Things are very easy between us,' he told Lord Moran, 'I think he trusts me.'[18] But as the conference progressed the Prime Minister came to the conclusion that it was Dulles who was the driving force in American decision-making.

'It seems that everything is left to Dulles. It appears that the President is no more than a ventriloquist's doll ... This fellow preaches like a Methodist minister, and his bloody text is always the same – that nothing but evil can come out of a meeting with Malenkov.'[19]

The 1,500 journalists holed up in the luxurious Castle Harbour Hotel down the road from the Mid Ocean Club were thrown a juicy bone on that first night when Jacques Baeyens, head of press at the French Ministry of Foreign Affairs, could not resist leaking the full contents of the first plenary session – including the frank remarks made by Eisenhower. Such was their bluntness that even the world's media sought to tone them down a little in their reports the following morning.

On day two the focus was on the French. First, Prime Minister Laniel retired to his bed with a fever and a temperature. Then Churchill administered a 'bawling out' to the French delegation for the leaking of the previous day's session.[20] 'The press had had a full account of what happened,' and 'been able to reprint whole passages that had been spoken around the table', he complained to chairman Eisenhower.[21] 'It was a very serious matter if people were talking of confidential matters to the press,' he concluded.

Eisenhower was less worked up, but agreed it was 'serious', and asked each delegation to nominate a member so that a collective account could be written up immediately after each session finished and then distributed to the press. It would prove effective enough in stifling any leaks – but of course the off-the-record chats between politicians, advisers and journalists still went on in the bars of the Castle Harbour Hotel.

The thorny subject of the European Defence Community – or a 'European army' as many preferred to call it – dominated the latter stages of the big plenary session on day two. With Laniel in bed, Foreign Minister Bidault had to put his government's case – and attempt to withstand a withering attack from a grouchy Churchill.

The idea of a European army followed hard on the heels of the establishment of NATO in late 1950 – and was to come under its supreme command. America insisted West German rearmament was an essential ingredient in strengthening European security and combatting communism. It would also enable Washington to begin to scale down its huge commitment to the continent. But the French, with vivid and painful memories of the war and military occupation, were deeply fearful at any prospect of German rearmament.

Instead they proposed the Pleven Plan (after the then French Minister of Defence René Pleven) for a European Defence Community, into which national contingents would be integrated at the level of the smallest possible unit. So there would be no German army, but German battalions sprinkled among European brigades. The 13,000-strong force would come under a common budget, with common arms, centralised military procurement, a minister of defence and an overseeing European Defence Council of Ministers. The EDC treaty was signed in May 1952 and was supposed to last for fifty years – but it needed ratification by all the participating European countries.

Churchill had never shown any great enthusiasm for the EDC, labelling it from the off as a 'sludgy amalgam'. Nothing had really happened in the last eighteen months to change his stance, but, mindful of America's desire for it – and her veiled threat to pull out of NATO if it did not happen – it was his government's policy to back the plan and try to chivvy the French along. But with the recent bewildering turnover of governments in Paris, the EDC had yet to be approved in the French Parliament.

The Prime Minister was tiring of all the arguments and used the session to lambast the French and promote his now preferred option – for a 'good strong' German army under NATO control, where it would be properly constrained and controlled so its dreadful deeds of the century's two world wars could not be repeated.[22]

But Eisenhower stuck to America's guns, saying that 'to resort to a national army was a second choice so far behind the EDC that there could be no comparison'.[23] In any case, he added, the last time he had spoken to Chancellor Adenauer he had been 'unalterably opposed to the idea'.

Bidault spoke generously and eloquently, saying France would never forget the part Sir Winston had played in 'restoring freedom, liberating territory, returning France to independence and the world to dignity'.[24] He spoke of the 'heavy parliamentary battle' he and Laniel were waging against the Gaullists and the communists and he maintained they had 'done what they could and their efforts were not yet over'.

To 'federate' an army was not an easy thing. There had been encounters which were marked on the flags of France and Germany for centuries. Bidault asked those around the table to try to understand the 'moral psychological and national drama of this problem for the countries situated on the western edge of the continent'. He concluded: 'The first phase of the battle has been hard, and help is needed for the second phase.'

With no fixed agenda and no conference secretariat, the summit began to drift. General Hastings Ismay, NATO Secretary General, observed that 'as a result, all kinds of important delegates spend hours cooling their heels and twiddling their thumbs without knowing whether they are wanted ... or not'.[25] And after the indiscretions of Monsieur Baeyens on the first day, the reporters now fretted about their sparse communiqués, which contained little or no solid news lines.

But one vital subject that dominated much of the American and British discussions away from the big plenary sessions was atomic power – and the use of atomic bombs. Both Eisenhower and Churchill had brought with them their key advisers – Lewis Strauss, head of America's Atomic Energy Commission and the man who had just engineered Oppenheimer's downfall, and Lord Cherwell, Churchill's trusted scientific guru.

In an early meeting of these four Churchill seized the opportunity to press – as he had done all year – for the United States to share intelligence and cooperate scientifically on all atomic matters. Sir Roger Makins, Britain's ambassador to Washington, had warned the State Department on the eve of the conference to be prepared for this, as 'the Old Man' was in a 'bitter frame of mind' over what he saw as broken agreements.

First Churchill informed Eisenhower and Strauss about the recent delivery of Blue Danube, Britain's first operational atomic weapon. But its use was some way off, and he pointed out that British planes were now being built with no real knowledge of the specifications – weight, dimension and ballistics – of America's atomic weapons, if called upon to deliver them.

That sort of information, the Prime Minister emphasised, had to be shared. Then, in a *coup de théâtre*, he pulled out a photostat of the original copy of the 1943 Quebec Agreement signed by himself and Roosevelt, and read it to the President. Now was the time, he said, to publish this and other related documents which demonstrated the historic close collaboration between the countries in the civil and nuclear field.

A startled Strauss retorted that Quebec had been superseded by the Blair House Agreement of January 1948. This had re-established some areas of collaboration between the two countries following the punitive – for the British – McMahon Act of 1946, but still ruled out the sharing of secrets over the making of nuclear bombs.

In the end the two Americans conceded that greater transparency on this subject would benefit relations between the two countries, and Eisenhower asked Strauss to prepare a white paper to that end, with Cherwell's help.

A small victory for the British, but on the central question of when to deploy atomic bombs there was no meeting of minds. Eisenhower had told the first plenary session that 'the world was in a rather hysterical condition about the atomic bomb'. Now as Dulles and Eden entered these nuclear discussions over the next few days, it became crystal clear to Eisenhower that both the Prime Minister and the Foreign Secretary – naïvely in his view – still looked on the possible use of the A-bomb 'as the initiation of a completely new era in war'.[26]

> They apparently cling to the hope (to us fatuous) that if we avoid the first use of the atom bomb in any war, that the Soviets might likewise abstain. Our thinking, on the other hand, has come a long way past this kind of conjecture and hope. Specifically, we have come to the conclusion that the atom bomb has to be treated just as another weapon in the arsenal.

Churchill and Eden said the use of the A-bomb would be 'morally repugnant' to the world. If at all possible, they would want public opinion to develop – 'which it probably would do very quickly' – before any response to a Soviet strike.

But Eisenhower scorned this equivocation. He made it absolutely clear that he was willing to strike first, if it came to it, rather than merely respond to such a punitive attack from the Russians. 'I gave my conviction that anyone who held up too long in the use of his assets in atomic weapons might suddenly find himself subjected to such widespread and devastating attack that retaliation would be next to impossible.'[27]

Eden had listened to Dulles stripping away the distinction between conventional and atomic weapons earlier in the year, so he cannot have been surprised by the American approach. Nonetheless he was depressed by these conversations. 'The prospects are too horrible for the human mind to contemplate,' he told Evelyn Shuckburgh.[28] To his wife Clarissa he wrote: 'Conference is very hard going now and I am sad and tired, not so much about details as about this poor world and what I fear lies ahead.'[29]

But there was some optimistic news on the atomic front. Eisenhower disclosed that he planned to leave Bermuda earlier than the other leaders in order to deliver an address at the United Nations entitled 'Atoms For Peace'. This speech had sprung from Operation Candor,

Eisenhower's attempt to better explain and if possible reassure his country – and the world – about developments in the arms race.

He told Churchill and Eden that he would tell his UN audience that the tremendous destructive power of the American and Soviet weapons – which were now thermonuclear too – left little hope for survival in a future war. Nuclear technology would only grow cheaper and atomic weapons would clearly become available to more countries. Devastating surprise attacks by nations would become a distinct possibility.

The 'awful arithmetic' of the atom had to be turned into a note of hope for peace. One solution could be for the three nuclear powers to agree to an international stockpile of fissionable material, a sort of 'uranium bank', which would be put under the supervision of the United Nations for the study and exchange of peaceful uses of atomic energy. One of the purposes would be to diminish the Soviet stockpile as well as America's – so for example, the US might put in 1,000kg, the USSR 200kg and the UK 40kg. After that, details could be worked out between the interested parties as to how much could be made available to the scientists of the world to use for practical purposes.

Eisenhower enthused about the future use of atomic energy. America had a ship ready to run on it, and it could have great capabilities in the medical field and in agriculture. In his speech he would pledge the United States' 'determination to help solve the fearful atomic dilemma – to devote its entire heart and mind to find the way by which the miraculous inventiveness of man shall not be dedicated to his death, but consecrated to his life'.[30]

Churchill and Eden were shown the full draft of the speech and the Prime Minister applauded its idealism. 'I think it will help towards the "easement" of which I have sometimes spoken … it is a great pronouncement and will resound through the anxious and bewildered world.'[31]

The Prime Minister did, however, suggest that Eisenhower dropped one phrase that did not reflect well on Britain – a reference to the 'obsolete colonial mould' – and asked him to substitute the 'United States being free to use the atomic bomb' for the 'United States reserves the right to use the atomic bomb'.[32] The President duly obliged.

Churchill could make no real headway with the Americans when it came to Egypt, where Britain still maintained 80,000 troops in the Suez Canal zone at massive cost guarding the flow of oil, while facing increasing threats from an aggressive military government. He desperately wanted American military and financial support, but Eisenhower and Dulles – always unimpressed in any case by Churchill's 'imperialistic' attitude in the Middle East – were reluctant to give it, having other strategic plans for the region.

Churchill used the final plenary session on Monday 7 December to give his 'easement' policy with the USSR a final outing. He said he was 'anxious' to find something that would please the Russians.[33] Of course, he acknowledged, 'they have treated us so badly in the last few years, [but] he still thought one ought not to fail to do for them what was just or express willingness to do it'.

In the draft communiqué he had counted 'nine notes of strength and unity for a strong front'. Could we not, asked the Prime Minister, strike just one note 'which, at any rate, would give the sense that we wished them no harm and would feel it our duty to help them if they were maltreated or assaulted, that we would instantly play our part on their side as intended if they were right?'[34]

This was a variation on the Locarno Pact scenario he had briefly outlined in his 11 May speech – whereby if one country violated another's agreed borders, neutral countries would step in to enforce them militarily. But Dulles responded by arguing that such a guarantee would single out the Germans by name as the Soviet Union's future aggressor, and castigate them as 'some sort of moral and political inferior' – just the sort of thing that had 'helped Hitler to power'.[35] Although he sounded unimpressed, he thought 'some general formula' might accomplish what Churchill wanted, and this might be 'discussed by the experts in Paris'.

Churchill had coined the phrase 'Iron Curtain' in his famous speech in Fulton, Missouri. Now his 'final mission' to be the man to try to start to draw that curtain down was stalled in the face of implacable American opposition, softly aided and abetted by his own Foreign Office. He was unlikely to be sitting down face to face with Georgy Malenkov any time soon.

In the blandest of bland final communiqués, the only worthwhile initiative recorded was the approval of a joint text by the three allies, accepting the Soviets' offer of a meeting of the foreign ministers of the four powers, probably in Berlin in January 1954. The hope was that this meeting will 'make progress towards the reunification of Germany in freedom and the conclusion of an Austrian state treaty – and thus towards the solution of other major international problems'.[36]

There was little else in the communiqué apart from warm words about 'unity of purpose', and assurances that the three countries would 'remain resolute in maintaining our solidarity and vigilance against efforts to divide us'. On a European army, there was merely the 'reaffirmation that the EDC is needed to assure the defensive capacity of the Atlantic community of which it will be an integral part'.

However, matters descended into farce on the night the communiqué was discussed as Eden – joined by Evelyn Shuckburgh – had to leave the conference and go and sit patiently by Prime Minister Laniel's bedside to persuade him to agree to the mildest of sentences about 'European unity'.

'The French advisers all in despair: "*Nous ne pouvons pas rien*"', observed Shuckburgh.[37] But Eden succeeded in his mission and the text was signed. 'Anthony is so very good with other people,' Churchill acknowledged to Moran that night.[38] 'His voice is so smooth and his manner, so quiet, so persuasive.'

But Dulles was not so emollient when he visited Laniel's sickbed the following day on the eve of his departure. His lecture – for that is what it effectively was – started off well enough, with the Secretary of State fondly recalling the many cycling trips he had made with his father through the French countryside, and then his period studying at the Sorbonne. He had always been a friend of France, but he explained that he had to speak 'very frankly'.[39] Leadership required

> the facing up to responsibilities and realities … [and] the world would not stand still while France continued to postpone facing up to the decision on the EDC which involved the basic question of European unity … If France could not act when the situation required it, all the friendship in the world would not be able to support or sustain a position of leadership for France.

Laniel feebly replied that he 'would continue to do his best' and hopefully a pro-EDC majority would emerge in the new French Assembly.[40] Dulles, his message clearly understood, said he did not want to tire Monsieur Laniel and bade him farewell.

Tempers had frayed all round by the end of the summit. The struggle to commit some form of consensus to paper convinced Eisenhower that a 'final communiqué destroys the intimacy and value of informal talks'. He was adamant that he would never again come to one of these summits unless it was publicly announced beforehand, in all three capitals, that there would be no final document.

If there was one subject at Bermuda where there was unanimity it was over Indo-China, where the seven-year war against Vietminh forces was taking a heavy toll on France, the colonial power. Eisenhower's government had committed financial assistance and military advice to stop the further spread of communism. Churchill's support was merely moral, but he applauded the French for 'her valiant effort to preserve her empire and the cause of freedom in Indo-China'.

The final communiqué insisted the three allies 'recognised the vital importance' of the struggle to protect the independence of Cambodia, Laos and Vietnam' and pledged to 'continue to work together to restore peace and stability in this area'.

The communiqué, such as it was, received bad press. 'An extraordinarily anaemic document', wrote the *Manchester Guardian*'s diplomatic correspondent, 'composed largely of platitudes and pious hopes'.[41] *Le Monde* said it had a 'rare vagueness', while the *Ottawa Journal* described it as a 'masterpiece of concealment, telling us little more than we knew all along'.

The British contingent stayed on in Bermuda for a couple of days after the departure of the Americans and the French. Eden, 'slightly pickled' as he relaxed with a drink in the company of Cyrus Sulzberger, the *New York Times* foreign correspondent, dismissed it as 'Winston's conference ... It had no real use.'[42] Too much time, he complained, had been devoted to the reply to the Russians on the four-power meeting, and to 'Ike's speech' at the United Nations.

But Sulzberger thought Eden looked 'rather healthy, full of energy and with good colour' following his operations earlier in the year. It was generally accepted that the Foreign Secretary had been one of the better performers at Bermuda, and what had also been notable was the blossoming friendship between him and Dulles. They got into the habit of strolling down to the sea together in the mornings and swimming, followed by lengthy conversations on the beach, and this cosy informality caused some consternation among their aides.

After a trip around the island with the governor followed by an inspection of the Bermudian troops, Churchill finished his current book, *Death to the French* by C. S. Forester, and moved on to a new historical novel, *Royal Flush* by Margaret Irwin. But his mood turned when he was told about the House of Commons' allocated time for debates the following week – two days for television, and only one for foreign affairs and atomic war.

Furious, he summoned a secretary to take down a note – only to discover that there were none, as his entourage had all headed off for a moonlight swim. The patient Eden, who had remained behind at the Mid Ocean Club, volunteered to take down a telegram at the Prime Minister's dictation while Jane Portal was found. 'We were all clearly in great disgrace,' private secretary Shuckburgh noted. 'Poor Jane … got the brunt of it. The old boy kept repeating to her, "You left me all alone."'[43]

Jane Portal's qualities were well known. But it was the presence of another outstanding woman in the British government group that saw at least one kind of a breakthrough at Bermuda. The 33-year-old Caroline 'Joan' Petrie, who had entered the Foreign Office six years earlier, was the only female diplomat in any of the delegations at the summit.

Petrie's presence had allowed the British newspapers to indulge in some frivolous reporting. Apparently, according to the *Daily Mirror*, 'green-eyed Joan' was taking a swimsuit in the hope she might get the time 'for a dip in the warm Caribbean'.[44] Atticus, in the *Sunday Times*, commented on the government's decision to 'introduce a beautiful girl on the British side of the table at Bermuda'.

Once the conference had got underway, it was noticed that the President's perpetual doodling in moments of boredom – and there were quite a few in Bermuda – took in pencil sketches not only of Churchill, but of Miss Petrie too.

* * *

Even if Churchill had been able to make the trip to Moscow to push for détente, it was now not entirely clear whom he would be meeting. Back in September, Malenkov's grip on power appeared to have been loosened when it was announced that Nikita Khrushchev had been appointed First Secretary of the Communist Party.

The post of First Secretary was always understood to be a vital – if not *the* vital – role in the Kremlin hierarchy, enabling its occupant to build up a power base in the party and become, effectively, the real ruler of the Soviet Union.

Malenkov's name seemed to be still first and foremost in all *Pravda* pronouncements, but Kremlinologists believed that the first major shift in the post-Stalin power struggle had taken place, and Khrushchev, a 59-year-old stocky, unsophisticated son of a Ukrainian coal-miner, was now challenging for pole position.

Yet *The Times*, in its assessment of the appointment, believed – as did everyone – that Khrushchev was cut from the same cloth as Stalin's successor. 'By temperament, party experience and drive, reticent manners, and fear of contact with foreigners, Khrushchev is of the Malenkov type, the communist department chief who believes in and works for the speedy transition to communism.'[45]

Western politicians fervently hoped that Khrushchev might have a fresh approach that would bring about a thaw in the Cold War. But at this stage there was no great optimism in the corridors of power in Whitehall and Washington.

On 23 December, another member of Stalin's old gang took a more precipitous fall. Moscow Radio announced that the hated Lavrentiy Beria, the former head of the secret police, who had been dismissed and not seen in public since his arrest in June, was to be tried for high treason and anti-Soviet activities by the Supreme Court of the Soviet Union.

The text of the announcement revealed a litany of alleged offences. Beria had 'subverted the collective farm system and created food difficulties in the country'; he had 'acted as a traitor to the motherland, having sold himself to foreign intelligence services'; and he had carried out 'treacherous acts, attempting to weaken the defence capacity of the Soviet Union'.[46]

In among the other charges against Beria, it was curious to note that back in 1919, in Azerbaijan, he had supposedly been an MI6 agent, working to assist the so-called 'Mussavitist' movement against the rampaging Bolsheviks. A far-fetched notion perhaps – 'agent of Western imperialism' was a commonly used description of Soviet 'traitors'.

The investigation also unearthed crimes testifying to 'his profound moral degradation'. In short, the state prosecutor concluded, Beria and his six accomplices – including army general Vsevolod Merkulov – were the 'most evil enemies of the Soviet people'.

Some speculated that the man who for fifteen years ran the dreaded Soviet secret police and headed up his country's atomic programme and who, as Stalin's lieutenant, held the power of life and death over millions of Soviet citizens, might already be dead. After all it was six months since he was first arrested.

In fact, Beria was still alive, and in the middle of an eleven-day hunger strike, having refused to admit any guilt of any sort. His trial took place on Wednesday 23 December, when he and six of his associates were inevitably found guilty and the judge ordered the death sentence to be carried out that very day.

General Pavel Batitsky was given the job of Beria's executioner. It took place in the grim surroundings of the basement of the Lubyanka jail, the MGB's headquarters.

Beria went down on his hands and knees begging to be spared, leaving Batitsky unmoved. 'In all that you have done, so loathsome, mean and nasty, can you not find enough courage in yourself to accept your punishment in silence?'[47] After stuffing a towel in Beria's mouth to stifle his wailing, he shot him through the forehead.

* * *

As 1953 drew to a close, of all of the problems facing the Western allies the war in Indo-China was perhaps the most intractable. It had been dragging on since 1946, fuelled by a combination of French intransigence towards decolonisation, the corruptness of the local rulers in Vietnam, Laos and Cambodia and the ferocious desire for independence determinedly waged by the Vietminh, backed by increasing military support from China.

What had started as a classic nationalist, anti-colonial revolt now had the stamp of communism about it. The messianic political leader of the Vietminh, 63-year-old Hồ Chí Minh, ironically claimed to have learned the meaning of revolution after spending time in Paris in the 1920s. His Marxist credentials would be later honed in Stalin's Russia, at the Communist University of the Toilers of the East.

Hồ's military lieutenant was a 42-year-old political economy graduate, General Võ Nguyên Giáp, who had waged guerrilla war against the Japanese when they took over the country during the Second World War and now employed it against the French, whom he had every reason to hate. Not only had Giáp been imprisoned by the French, but his sister had been executed by the French, and his wife, sentenced to hard labour for life, had died in a French prison.

These men were the kind of unflinching opponents the French faced. The war had so far cost France over 75,000 nationals, together with 58,000 Indo-Chinese. Since the politicians refused to send national servicemen to Indo-China, it was the cream of the French regular officers that bore the brunt; every three years the war consumed an entire class from Saint-Cyr, the elite military academy akin to Britain's Sandhurst or America's West Point.

The French public had long wearied of this brutal colonial conflict being fought in their name 6,000 miles from home. This was the 'slandered war', 'the dirty war' – '*la sale guerre*' – and few could see what sort of vital French interest prevailed in the region any more.

But there was a vocal and passionate minority within the political and military establishment who wished to pursue the conflict to its bitter end. And as French Foreign Minister Georges Bidault told Eisenhower and Churchill at Bermuda, despite the offer of an armistice and negotiations from Hồ and his Vietminh on 27 November 1953, France was determined not to abandon the other, more amenable associated states of Indo-China: Laos and Cambodia. 'This was a point of honour. The French would never abandon their comrades in battle. They would never abandon them under any conditions and nothing would be done without their agreement.'[48]

But of course Indo-China had long since ceased being a purely French affair. After Mao's succession in China and the communist aggression in Korea, the fear in Washington in particular was of other countries in South East Asia and the Far East going the same way. This was the 'domino' effect, which Vice-President Richard Nixon illustrated on his return from a ten-week trip of Asia and the Middle East in mid-December 1953.

'If Indo-China falls, Thailand is put in an almost impossible position. The same is true of Malaya, with its rubber and tin. The same is true of Indonesia,' Nixon told his nationwide radio audience.[49]

If this whole part of South East Asia goes under communist domination or communist influence, Japan – who trades with this area in order to exist – must inevitably be orientated towards the communist regime. That indicates to you and to all of us why it is vitally important that Indo-China not go behind the Iron Curtain.

With the Korean War over, there was now a real worry that China – known to be training, equipping and supplying the Vietminh – would be free to send in the People's Liberation Army to help defeat the colonists. Then there was the legacy of Munich, which hung heavy over the deliberations of Eisenhower and Dulles. For the Nazi menace of the 1930s now read the communist threat of the 1950s – this was the sort of language used on Capitol Hill. Right-wing Republicans like Joe McCarthy had constantly baited President Truman for 'losing China'; Eisenhower did not want to run the risk of appeasing, and then losing, Indo-China.

So American treasure, if not yet blood, poured into Indo-China.

There was a small Military Assistance Advisory Group comprising thirteen officers and forty enlisted men to monitor the US hardware that was being used in the country and observe and lend advice to French forces. In September 1951, when the French effort looked in danger of collapse, Washington shipped to the battle zone 130,000 tons of equipment, including 53 million rounds of ammunition, 8,000 trucks and jeeps, 650 fighting vehicles, 200 aircraft, 14,000 automatic weapons and 3,500 radios.[50]

By the end of 1953 the Eisenhower administration was paying 75 per cent of the cost of the war; US assistance had risen from $10 million in 1950 to a massive $1 billion by 1954.[51] At Bermuda the President had attempted to bolster the spirits of the French, paying tribute to the 'magnificent campaign they had waged so long and at such cost'.[52] He told Foreign Minister Bidault that another aircraft carrier, *Arromanches*, would be handed over in the next few days, along with twenty-five more aircraft and some more helicopters. The US commitment was still strong.

As for Britain, she was preoccupied with fighting her own battle with communist guerrillas in Malaya, further south. The Cabinet turned down a French request for transport aircraft in May, but a few weeks later – at the urging of Colonial Secretary Oliver Lyttelton, who feared that if Indo-China fell the situation in Malaya might deteriorate – it endorsed a policy of encouraging further American aid.

Eden contrasted the relative success that Britain was having in her colonial battles by employing her own hardened native-born troop units in the jungles of Malaya and the forests of Kenya, whereas the French used only their volunteer forces.

Although he had no desire for Britain to get involved in Indo-China, Churchill's colonial instincts had shone through at Bermuda. From his first-hand experiences in North Africa and Tunisia, he had been struck by the 'wonderful manner in which the French cherished and nourished the civilisation they had implanted ... Dark days lie ahead in

Asia as a result of those who thought they could do without the guidance and aid of the European nations to whom they owed so much.'[53]

Wistfully, he promised 'he would say no more on this subject. He knew it was not a popular thing at present but he had done his utmost for it all the days of his life.'

Eisenhower and Dulles professed to abhor French and British imperialism and backed self-determination for their subject peoples. Yet if there was a choice between accepting – or promoting – an independence movement, or confronting it, if there was just the mere hint of communist affiliation, they would plump for the latter.

Bogged down, the constantly rotating French troops faced not just the Vietminh, but mosquitos, fever, amoebic dysentery and the weakening effect of fighting in a hot climate. The French troops found it difficult to distinguish between the peasant in his rice paddy and the enemy who had just laid his submachine gun in a ditch. Meanwhile, it was clear from intelligence reports that the roads leading to the Chinese frontier had been rebuilt and the French might at any moment find themselves facing aggression in the air or an avalanche of land forces.

A new, radical military initiative was required to break the deadlock and General Henri Navarre, commander of French forces in Indo-China since the end of May, was about to provide it. His strategy was aimed at relieving the pressure on Laos, while inflicting a major defeat on the Vietminh before the expected extra Chinese aid materialised.

The plan was straight out of the Saint-Cyr textbook. Tired of chasing, and being chased, by General Giáp's versatile guerrilla force, Navarre would instead lure the Vietminh forces into the open for a proper set-piece battle, and then crush them with superior firepower and equipment.

It was to happen at the isolated village of Dien Bien Phu, deep in Vietminh territory and thus cutting off Giáp's main communications with China. It was in the largest valley in the area – too big to be easily sealed off – and another major advantage was that it had an airstrip, which was built by the Japanese in the Second World War. Navarre would make his garrison at Dien Bien Phu into a fortress in case events turned against him and he had to withstand a siege.

The initial operation to land paratroopers, codenamed Castor, began at nightfall on 20 November when 2,200 troops from the elite of the French Expeditionary Force were dropped into the valley north and south of Dien Bien Phu. They comfortably defeated the few Vietminh that they encountered and began improving the airstrip and establishing defensive positions.

The local commander at Dien Bien Phu, a flamboyant cavalryman, Colonel Christian de Castries, then started to establish the fortress by setting up seven satellite positions, each, it was alleged, named after his former mistresses – Anne-Marie, Beatrice, Claudine, Dominique, Elaine, Françoise and Huguette.

By December, the French had 4,500 men in the valley. But they were entirely dependent on air supply from a small number of transport planes, and 200 miles from their bases around Hanoi they would be operating at extreme range. The air power de Castries would call upon consisted of forty-eight Martin B-26 Marauder and Privateer bombers, and 122 Bearcat and Hellcat fighter-bombers.

Navarre and de Castries knew General Giáp had artillery, but hitherto he had used nothing bigger than Japanese and Chinese 75mm field guns, and he had possessed few anti-aircraft weapons. Navarre's intelligence officers calculated too that Giáp's primitive supply system over the tortuous jungle trails would leave him unable to provide anything more than 25,000 shells for his guns – or with sufficient rice to eat.

But throughout December Giáp's troops set about improving route 41 leading to Dien Bien Phu, enabling the road to handle trucks and artillery pieces. The Chinese were starting to supply bigger and better weapons – howitzers, mortars and 37mm anti-aircraft guns.

Perhaps most crucially, a general mobilisation call had gone out for thousands of labourers – 'the people's porters' – to carry this improved weaponry to Dien Bien Phu across hundreds of miles of Asia's most inhospitable terrain. A new slogan – 'The land to the peasants!' – would spur them on their gruelling way.

On the final day of the year, Larry Allen, the Associated Press correspondent in Hanoi, reported that the Vietminh had attacked three French strong points in northern Laos and were 'closing in on the fortress of Dien Bien Phu further north in neighboring Vietnam'.

'The Vietminh troops have already cut Indo-China in two by driving from the seacoast of central Vietnam through the narrow waist of Laos to the frontier of Thailand. There are signs fighting is going to spread like a prairie fire.'[54]

The American administration looked on with some trepidation. John Foster Dulles was watching closely to see if the Chinese were not only supporting the Vietminh with trucks and weapons, but sending the People's Liberation Army in to help them finish the job. Ever suspicious of Peking, Dulles had not ruled out the Chinese resuming hostilities in Korea.

So in his final weekly press conference of the year Dulles issued a veiled threat. American reaction to either of these scenarios would 'not necessarily be confined to the particular area the Communists choose to make the theatre of their new aggression'.[55]

Dulles was signalling that he was prepared, if necessary, to use sea and air power, conventional or nuclear weapons, against communist China. This was all in keeping with a new military doctrine he would unveil in a few weeks' time, with the threatening title 'Massive Retaliation'.

The fate of Indo-China still hung in the balance at the close of 1953. If this had been a year of maximum danger in the Cold War, 1954 promised to be more of the same.

POSTSCRIPT

Winston Churchill's 'final mission' to talk face to face with Georgy Malenkov – his 'solitary pilgrimage' – was never fulfilled. To his chagrin, it was a Labour Party delegation led by Clement Attlee and Aneurin Bevan who were granted the first official Western audience with Malenkov and his inner circle during a tour of China and the USSR in August 1954.

The sheer novelty of simply meeting and talking with Stalin's successor outweighed any significant development that the Labour leaders were able to report towards easement with the Soviet Union. Malenkov, all 'feline charm', presented his dinner companion, Labour Party chair Dr Edith Summerskill, with a bunch of carnations – but declined to commit himself to a visit to London.[1]

A peeved Churchill thought Attlee's visit might give Labour a 'vague, sloppy initiative in the direction of peace' at the next election, so he sought to undermine it with a withering, sporting comparison at his party conference speech.[2] 'I am sorry that Mr Attlee did not have more success in his trip abroad, but even our football team came a cropper in Moscow,' he told delegates – a reference to Arsenal's 5–0 defeat at the hands of Dynamo Moscow four days earlier.[3]

It would be left to Churchill's successor Anthony Eden to meet the new men in the Kremlin on home turf – but not until April 1956. By then Malenkov had been fully eased from power and succeeded by Nikita Khrushchev, who made the trip to the United Kingdom with his right-hand man, Nikolai Bulganin. Khrushchev had already begun the debunking of the Stalin myth with his famous denunciation of the Soviet dictator in his speech to the Twentieth Congress of the Soviet Communist Party in February 1956.

On the first day of 1953, Churchill, presciently, had told Jock Colville that if he lived to his normal life span he would 'assuredly see eastern Europe free of communism'.[4] Colville died, aged seventy-two, in November 1987 – two years before the Berlin Wall came down. Might the Cold War have been shortened further if Churchill had had his summit meeting with the Soviet leaders? He was an Old Man in a hurry, his vanity and ambition derided by allies and friends, and viewed with suspicion by foes. But he had clearly perceived that the over-extended Soviet empire in the East could not last, and that the attraction of the communist ideal was starting to diminish. There would be practical evidence of Soviet retreats soon after 1953, from Austria in 1955, and from Finnish naval bases in 1956.

To the continuing exasperation of his heir apparent – and most of the senior members of his Cabinet – Churchill determinedly soldiered on as Prime Minister, despite his stroke and the obvious ravages of old age, until April 1955. On his final night in Downing Street he confided to Colville: 'I don't believe Anthony can do it.'[5]

Surprisingly, given all his experience on the world stage, Eden's downfall came via a foreign adventure. After over seventy years in Egypt, British forces – over 80,000 of them – finally started pulling out of the Suez Canal zone in March 1955 following the agreement that had been concluded six months earlier with the new Egyptian leader, Colonel Gamal Abdel Nasser. The last unit to depart was the 2nd Battalion Grenadier Guards, which left on 24 March 1956.

Four months later Nasser announced the nationalisation of the Suez Canal, to which Eden responded with fury, orchestrating a secret invasion to seize it back, only to be rumbled and left abandoned by

America. He resigned on grounds of ill-health – but really in ignominy – in January 1957, to be succeeded by Harold Macmillan.

Seventy years after it started, the Korean War is still, technically, in progress. The armistice of July 1953 held, and for fifty days in 1954 all the main protagonists gathered in Geneva to try to thrash out a proper peace agreement. They failed, and the demilitarised zone along the 38th parallel simply hardened into an international border.

Inter-Korean relations have waxed and waned, as has the interest of various American administrations. In January 2018, the hands of the Doomsday Clock moved to two minutes to midnight for the first time since 1953 when the 'hyperbolic rhetoric and provocative actions' of both President Donald Trump and North Korean leader Kim Jong-un – now the ninth holder of nuclear weapons in history – reached their climax.

At the Geneva peace conference of 1954 where the Korean talks failed, there was some success in bringing the war in Indo-China to an end. The French 'fortress' of Dien Bien Phu had fallen to the Vietminh on 8 May after a bloody 55-day siege, and the French power had no choice but to sue for peace.

But no one was happy with the 'accords', such as they were. Much like Korea, the country was divided between north and south, along the 17th parallel, the communist government of Hồ Chí Minh with its capital Hanoi in the north, and the nationalist, 'State of Vietnam' French puppet government under Emperor Bảo Đại with its capital Saigon in the south. Laos and Cambodia were recognised as independent countries.

Elections were supposed to follow within two years to elect a President and reunite the country. But of the nine participating countries, the United States refused to be bound by the agreements, as did the South Vietnamese. The final declaration also remained unsigned by them all.

Eisenhower's administration was convinced that the national elections in 1956 would result in a crushing victory for Hồ Chí Minh, the scourge of the French colonialists. So America moved quickly to establish a strong capitalist-based state in the south as a bulwark against communism in the region, and when the time came supported South Vietnam's refusal to hold nationwide elections in consultation with Hồ's north.

This would be the beginning of America's long agony in Vietnam. On 1 June 1956, 39-year-old Senator John F. Kennedy, in a speech to the American Friends of Vietnam, described South Vietnam as 'the cornerstone of the free world in South East Asia'. 'This is our offspring – we cannot abandon it, we cannot ignore its needs,' he declared.[6]

If 1953's long shadow still stretches over the Korean peninsula today, the same could be said about Iran. In the immediate aftermath of the coup in 1953, the question of who owned and who controlled Iran's oil was settled by the Consortium Agreement of August 1954.

In legal terms, the agreement stated that Iran's nationalisation would remain in place for twenty-five-years; America, now the dominant player, recognised that to reverse it would fan the winds of nationalism. The new company set up to control the flow of oil was even given a nationalised name, the National Iranian Oil Company. It nominally owned the oil and facilities in the country.

But the reality of nationalisation was very different, with Western oil companies still firmly in control. Britain's objective of the full return of the Anglo-Iranian Oil Company (by this time renamed British Petroleum – BP) to its pre-eminent pre-nationalisation condition was never likely to be fulfilled. Anti-British sentiment, and the growing American influence, necessitated the setting up of an international consortium to operate the Iranian oil industry. So it was agreed that BP would hold the largest stake – 40 per cent – in the new holding company called Iranian Oil Participants Ltd, but four American companies took 32 per cent in total, while Gulf (8 per cent), Shell (14 per cent) and the French CFP (6 per cent) took the rest.[7]

The consortium agreed to share profits on a 50/50 basis with Iran – but not to open its books to Iranian auditors, nor to allow Iranians onto the board of directors. BP, despite its now diminished control, did have the satisfaction of receiving $90 million upfront as compensation for the nationalisation, plus ten cents a barrel royalty on the total production of the consortium until another $500 million had been paid.

The UK/US coup of 1953, coupled with this continuing 'exploitation' of the country's oil by the West, surely sowed the seeds of the 1979 Iranian Revolution. The Shah's corrupt regime, backed by America, only accelerated matters. The United States would become the 'Great Satan', but top of the slights Iran had endured at British hands over the years was 'The English Job' – the 1953 coup, with its overthrow of a democratically elected President.

In Europe, the proposed new supranational institutions fell by the wayside in 1954. First the ill-fated European Defence Community was finally put out of its misery when the French National Assembly rejected it in August. That then put paid to Paul-Henri Spaak's visionary European Political Community, its institutional corollary.

But the industrial arm of the new Europe, the European Coal and Steel Community, continued to develop. By 1954 virtually all barriers in coal, coke, steel, pig iron and scrap iron between its six members had been removed, and trade in these goods flourished in the 1950s. Spaak had not given up his ambitions for Europe, and would be a key player in setting up the Treaty of Rome in 1957, which established the European Economic Community (EEC) and the European Atomic Energy Community.

Britain, 'of, but not in' Europe, merely looked on as the European project gathered pace. She would eventually ask to sign up in 1961, but would not be admitted to the EEC until 1973. Forty-seven years later,

Britain's long, tortured relationship with these institutions of Europe would come to an end following a 'No' vote in a nationwide referendum.

America's witch-hunter-in-chief fell from grace in 1954. In the spring and early summer Joe McCarthy had turned his attention to the US Army, probing for security weaknesses in its ranks. The congressional hearings were fully televised and up to 20 million Americans tuned in.

What they witnessed made many of them change their minds about the senator from Wisconsin. His bullying tactics unleashed on a much-beloved institution did not sit well, and by June his Gallup approval rating of 50 per cent in January had fallen to 34 per cent.[8]

A seminal moment arrived on 9 June, the thirtieth day of the hearings, when an exasperated Joseph Welch, the army's chief counsel, responded to an accusation about the supposed communist leanings of one of his young associates with the words: 'Let us not assassinate this lad further, senator. You've done enough. Have you no sense of decency, sir? At long last, have you no sense of decency?'[9]

At this, all those in the room burst into applause. The McCarthy spell was broken. The senator was not helped in his investigation by accusations that he had used his own influence to win preferential treatment in the army for his own colleague, counsel David Schine.

By the end of the year even McCarthy's own party had turned against him. On 2 December, he was condemned by the US Senate for 'conduct unbecoming' of a senator. The vote was 67:22, with all the Democrats and half of the Republicans voting against him. McCarthy's influence dwindled away, and, turning increasingly to alcohol, he would die of hepatitis on 2 May 1957. But McCarthyism, the 'ideology', the fear extending to paranoia of communism, with its accompanying political repression, did not depart the scene so easily.

It took until 1 April 1954, a full seventeen months after the event, for the Eisenhower administration to finally release the full details of the H-bomb test at Eniwetok. Reporters at the White House were able to watch previously withheld footage of the stupendous blast, and were chilled by the announcement of Lewis Strauss that it was now possible to destroy New York or any other city with a single bomb. 'Indeed,' he said, 'there is no limit to the destructive power of the hydrogen bomb.'[10]

By then events had already moved on in America's expanding nuclear programme. A month earlier, at Bikini Atoll in the Marshall Islands, the first in a new series of thermonuclear tests had taken place code-named Operation Castle. The device that was detonated on 1 March – Castle Bravo – outstripped Ivy Mike with a yield of 15 megatons, two and a half times greater than expected and causing far higher levels of fallout and damage than expected.

Britain now felt she had no alternative but to join the H-bomb club. Sir William Penney, the leader of Britain's nuclear programme, told a secret Cabinet committee that although he believed Joe 4 had been a 'hybrid' bomb, the Soviets were likely to develop a 'true' hydrogen bomb before long. Churchill told Cabinet: 'We could not expect to maintain our influence as a world power unless we possessed the most up-to-date nuclear weapons.'[11]

There was a full-scale Cabinet debate on the matter with the moral, but principally the political, aspects tackled. Then, on 26 July 1954 – appearing as the third item on the agenda – after a short discussion, the Cabinet historically approved the production of the hydrogen bomb.

But it would be nearly three years, under Operation Grapple, before Britain successfully tested her first H-bomb, on 15 May 1957 at Christmas Island in the South Pacific. By then the Soviet Union had exploded her first 'true' thermonuclear device, RDS-37, on 22 November 1955, and the arms race was in full flow.

The concentration of resources on nuclear weapons meant that Britain's chemical and biological weapons programme was downgraded. The decision to abandon the development of the offensive use of these weapons was taken on economic, rather than moral, grounds. The last sea tests for biological weapons – Operation Negation, in the Bahamas – ended in March 1955. The nerve agent plant at Nancekuke in Cornwall would never move to full production.

After 1956, efforts were channelled into the development of protective clothing, agent detectors, medical counter-measures and decontamination. But over forty years later, those army volunteers who went to Porton Down in 1953 for tests began to ask questions about their unpleasant experiences.

The result was a major inquiry into allegations of malfeasance by the laboratory, run by the Wiltshire constabulary and codenamed Operation Antler. Detectives would eventually send eight cases of scientists to the Crown Prosecution Service for possible prosecution – none of which were acted upon.

The High Court did, however, quash the original verdict of misadventure that was reached for the death of Ronald Maddison and ordered a fresh inquest to take place. On 15 November 2004, after what was then the longest inquest ever held in England and Wales, lasting sixty-four days and featuring testimony from around 100 witnesses, the jury returned a verdict that Ronald Maddison was unlawfully killed at the hands of the state. The cause of his death was the 'application of a nerve agent in a non-therapeutic experiment'.[12]

Ronald's relatives received £100,000 in compensation from the Ministry of Defence. The ministry's acceptance of a charge of gross negligence was the basis for a further compensation claim by 360 Porton Down veterans who had undergone tests in 1953 and beyond. On 31 January 2008, the Defence Minister Derek Twigg announced a compensation package totalling £3 million for those who had been affected, along with an apology. He acknowledged 'that there were aspects of the trials where there may have been shortcomings and where, in particular, the life or health of participants may have been put at risk'.[13]

The experiments that were part of MKUltra, the CIA's mind control programme, continued into the 1960s before reducing in scope in 1964 and eventually petering out nine years later. Reports in the *New York Times* in late 1974 first laid bare the scandal of the project and prompted two government inquiries – the first, President Ford's 'Commission on CIA Activities within the United States' (the Rockefeller Commission), and the second, and more extensive, the Senate's Church Committee, which looked at abuses across all of America's intelligence agencies.

In 1953, as with Ronald Maddison, the US authorities succeeded in keeping a tight lid on the strange death of Frank Olson. But like Maddison, some of the details about Olson's death finally emerged decades later. In 1975, after the publication of the Rockefeller Commission report, the US government admitted that Olson had been dosed with LSD in the days before his death. The Olson family received an out-of-court settlement of $750,000, and personal apologies from President Ford and CIA director William Colby.

Frank's eldest son Eric continues to campaign for the full truth to come out about his father's death. In 1994, his body was exhumed and a second autopsy was carried out. A 'cold case' unit re-investigated the case, but advised that there was no new compelling evidence to send to a grand jury. In 2017, *Wormwood*, a docudrama miniseries, was released by Netflix, with Eric Olson a key participant, outlining his theory that his father may have been murdered because he was a potential security risk.

In the summer of 1953, a science-fiction movie based on a book by H. G. Wells about Martians attacking a small town in California was released to popular acclaim. Its opening words summed up the darkest fears of those living in that year:

In the First World War, and for the first time in the history of man, nations combined to fight against nations using the crude weapons of those days. The Second World War involved every continent on the globe, and men turned to science for new devices of warfare, which reached an unparalleled peak in their capacity for destruction. And now, fought with the terrible weapons of super-science, menacing all mankind and every creature on Earth, comes ... The War of the Worlds![14]

There was no one ultimate moment of heightened risk in 1953. But the hands of the Doomsday Clock had moved to two minutes to midnight by the end of the year because fear and suspicion abounded across the Iron Curtain, with little sign of it being lifted. The spectre of nuclear confrontation lurked menacingly in the background. It had certainly been a year of living dangerously.

NOTES

INTRODUCTION

1 'Clue to the Chain of Life', *New York Times*, 17 June 1953.
2 'Marion Keisker', Sun Record Company, http://www.sunrecordcompany.com/Marion_Keisker.html (accessed December 2020).
3 'Kinsey's Best Seller Book on Plant Life', *Herald-News*, 20 August 1953.
4 'Voters OK Kinsey Report by 3–1 Ratio, Says Gallup', *The Times* (Indiana), 20 August 1953.
5 Norman Giller, *Bill Wright: A Hero for All Seasons* (London: Robson Books, 2002).
6 Virginia A. Noble, *Inside the Welfare State: Foundations of Policy and Practice in Post-War Britain* (London: Routledge, 2009).
7 'Prejudice and Pride', *The Observer*, 1 February 1953.
8 'Trial For Murder', *The Times*, 24 September 1953.

PROLOGUE

1 Edward Teller, *Memoirs: A Twentieth-Century Journey in Science and Politics* (Oxford: Perseus Press, 2001), p. 352.
2 Alex Wellerstein, 'The Ivy Mike leak', The Nuclear Secrecy Blog, 13 June 2012, http://blog.nuclearsecrecy.com/2012/06/13/weekly-document-ivy-mike-leak-1952/ (accessed November 2020).
3 Mark Wolverton, 'Into the Mushroom Cloud', *Air & Space*, August 2009.
4 Richard Hewlett and Jack Holl, *Atoms for Peace and War, 1953–1961: Eisenhower and the Atomic Energy Commission* (Berkeley: University of California Press, 1989), p. 3.
5 Ibid.
6 Hansard, House of Commons, 23 October 1952.
7 Ibid.
8 John Colville, *The Fringes of Power: Downing Street Diaries, 1939–1955* (London: Phoenix, 2005), p. 311.

CHAPTER 1: 'TWO SCORPIONS IN A BOTTLE'

1 'State of the Union Address: Harry S. Truman (7 January 1953), Infoplease, 11 February 2017, https://www.infoplease.com/primary-sources/government/presidential-speeches/state-union-address-harry-s-truman-january-7-1953 (accessed December 2020).
2 *Ventura County Star-Free Press*, 8 January 1953.
3 Martin Gilbert, *Road to Victory: Winston S. Churchill, 1941–45* (London: Heinemann, 1989).
4 Winston Churchill, *The Second World War, Vol. 4: The Hinge of Fate* (S. l.: Cassell, 1951), p. 345.
5 National Archives, Kew, PREM 3/398/5 (409–411).
6 Hansard, House of Commons, 6 June 1944.
7 John Colville, *The Fringes of Power*.
8 *The Papers of Dwight David Eisenhower*, Johns Hopkins University Press, https://eisenhower.press.jhu.edu/index.html (accessed December 2020), 7 January 1953.
9 Ibid.
10 Ibid.

11 Evelyn Shuckburgh, *Descent to Suez: Diaries 1951–56* (London: Weidenfeld & Nicolson, 1986), 16 January 1953.

12 National Archives, PREM 11/422, 8 January 1953.

13 John Colville, *The Fringes of Power*, p. 320.

14 Richard Aldrich, *The Hidden Hand: Britain, America and Cold War Secret Intelligence* (London: John Murray, 2001), p. 12.

15 Interview with Fisher Howe, 3 February 1998, Association for Diplomatic Studies and Training, Oral History Project, https://www.adst.org/OH%20TOCs/Howe,%20Fisher.toc.pdf (accessed November 2020).

16 John Colville, *The Fringes of Power*, p. 321.

17 Churchill Papers, Churchill College, Cambridge, 4/379, 10 January 1953.

18 FBI, John Wheeler file.

19 National Nuclear Security Administration (NNSA), Wheeler statement, 3 March 1953, p. 13.

20 Ibid.

21 FBI, John Wheeler file.

22 Ibid.

23 Wheeler statement, 3 March 1953, p. 13.

24 Richard Gid Powers: *Broken: The Troubled Past and Uncertain Future of the FBI* (New York: Free Press, 2004), p. 206.

25 FBI, John Wheeler file.

26 Alex Wellerstein, 'The FBI file of John Wheeler', *Physics Today*, 3 December 2019.

27 FBI, John Wheeler file.

28 Ibid.

29 Ibid.

30 Ibid.

31 Ibid.

32 Richard Hewlett and Jack Holl, *Atoms for Peace and War*, p. 30.

33 *St Louis Post-Dispatch*, 29 December 1975.

34 Ibid.

35 Lisle A. Rose and Neal H. Peterson (eds), *Foreign Relations of the United States, 1952–1954: National Security Affairs, Vol. II, Part 2* (Washington: US Government Printing Office, 1984), p. 1109.

36 Ibid.

37 FBI, John Wheeler file.

38 Ibid.

39 Alex Wellerstein, 'The FBI file of John Wheeler'.

40 John Archibald Wheeler with Kenneth Ford, *Geons, Black Holes, and Quantum Foam: A Life in Physics* (New York: Norton, 1998), p. 286.

41 Lisle A. Rose and Neal H. Peterson (eds), *Foreign Relations of the United States, 1952–1954: National Security Affairs*, p. 1056.

42 Ibid.

43 Ibid.

44 Kai Bird and Martin J. Sherwin, *American Prometheus: The Triumph and Tragedy of J. Robert Oppenheimer* (London: Atlantic, 2008), p. 465.

45 Lisle A. Rose and Neal H. Peterson (eds), *Foreign Relations of the United States, 1952–1954: National Security Affairs*, p. 1056 onwards.

46 Ibid.

47 Ibid.

48 Kai Bird and Martin J. Sherwin, *American Prometheus*, p. 464.

CHAPTER 2: 'A GOOD TARGET'

1 *Salt Lake Tribune*, 25 October 1952.

2 'Executive Order 10450 – Security requirements for Government employment', Federal Register, US National Archives, 27 April 1953, https://www.archives.gov/federal-register/codification/executive-order/10450.html (accessed December 2020).

3 Nixon interview, John Foster Dulles Oral History Collection.

4 Robert Cutler, *No Time for Rest* (Boston: Little, Brown, 1966), p. 303.

5 Ibid.

6 'General James Gavin Argues A-Bomb Use Against Massed Troops', *Rapid City Journal*, 7 December 1950.

7   Lisle A. Rose and Neal H. Peterson (eds), *Foreign Relations of the United States, 1952–1954: National Security Affairs*, p. 770.

8   Ibid.

9   Ibid.

10 National Archives, DEFE 7/2209.

11 Ibid.

12 Ibid.

13 Wolfgang K. H. Panofsky, *Panofsky on Physics, Politics and Peace: Pief Remembers* (New York: Springer-Verlag, 2007), p. 61.

14 'Atom bomb checks', *Daily Telegraph*, 27 February 1952.

15 National Archives, DEFE 10/64.

16 Ibid.

17 National Archives, DEFE 7/2209.

18 National Archives, PREM 11/560.

19 Ibid.

20 Frederick Forsyth, *The Fourth Protocol* (London: Arrow, 2011).

21 Joseph and Alexander Poliakoff are the grandfather and father of the writer and director Stephen Poliakoff, who discussed how the pair were accused of spying in 'My father was accused of being a Soviet spy – and bugging Winston Churchill's hearing aid', *Daily Telegraph*, 11 May 2019.

22 National Archives, PREM 11/536.

23 Ibid.

24 Ibid.

25 National Archives, DEFE 5/48 (32).

26 Ibid.

27 National Archives, PREM 11/292, 15 November 1951.

28 National Archives, PREM 11/561.

29 Ibid.

30 Ibid.

31 Ibid.

32 'Tube Alloys', 18 September 1944, Atomic Heritage Foundation, https://www.atomicheritage.org/sites/default/files/19%20hyde%20park%20with%20markups.jpg (accessed December 2020).

33 Peter Hennessy, *Cabinets and the Bomb* (Oxford: Oxford University Press, 2007), p. 48.

34 Frederick Smith, *The Prof in Two Worlds: The Official Life of Professor F. A. Lindemann, Viscount Cherwell* (London: Collins, 1961), p. 307.

35 National Archives, CAB 129/58, 7 January 1953.

36 Ibid.

37 National Archives, CAB 195/11, 14 January 1953.

38 *St Louis Post-Dispatch*, 2 January 1953.

39 Ibid.

40 National Archives, PREM 11/561, 19 March 1953.

41 Ibid.

42 Warren F. Kimball, 'Churchill and the Presidents: Dwight Eisenhower, Sentiment and Politics', The Churchill Project, Hillsdale College, 23 July 2020, https://winstonchurchill.hillsdale.edu/president-eisenhower/ (accessed December 2020).

43 National Archives, CAB 195/11, 12 February 1953.

44 National Archives, PREM 11/330, 17 February 1953.

45 'Argentina Offered To Buy Falklands in 1953', *The Times*, 2 January 1984.

46 Ibid.

47 Ibid.

CHAPTER 3: 'NO CROCODILE TEARS'

1   Svetlana Alliluyeva, *Twenty Letters to a Friend* (London: Harper & Row, 1967).

2   Ibid.

3   Victor Zorza, 'How Moscow broke the news of Stalin's death', *Manchester Guardian*, 7 March 1953.

4   Ilya Zbarsky and Samuel Hutchinson, *Lenin's Embalmers* (London: Harvill, 1998), p. 165 and p. 167.

5   William Z. Slany (ed.), *Foreign Relations of the United States, 1952–1954: Eastern Europe; Soviet Union; Eastern Mediterranean, Vol. VIII* (Washington: US Government Printing Office, 1988), p. 1099.

6   Robert Cutler, *No Time for Rest*, p. 320.
7   Emmet John Hughes, *The Ordeal of Power: A Political Memoir of the Eisenhower Years* (London: Macmillan & Co, 1963), p. 101.
8   'Crocodile Tears', *Daily Mirror*, 6 March 1953.
9   *Daily Sketch*, 6 March 1953.
10 *Church of England Newspaper*, 6 March 1953.
11 Charles Wilson Moran, *Churchill: The Struggle for Survival: 1945–60* (London: Robinson, 2006), p. 112.
12 Ibid.
13 National Archives, PREM 11/422, 11 March 1953.
14 Ibid.
15 William Z. Slany (ed.), *Foreign Relations of the United States, 1952–1954: Eastern Europe; Soviet Union; Eastern Mediterranean, Vol. VIII*, p. 1117 onwards.
16 Ibid.
17 *The Papers of Dwight David Eisenhower*, Johns Hopkins University Press, 10 March 1953.
18 William Z. Slany (ed.), *Foreign Relations of the United States, 1952–1954: Eastern Europe; Soviet Union; Eastern Mediterranean, Vol. VIII*, p. 1117 onwards.
19 Ibid.
20 National Archives, CAB 131/12, 17 June 1952.
21 Ibid.
22 Ibid.
23 Ibid.
24 Author interview with Mike Parrish, January 2020.
25 Kelvedon Hatch Archives.
26 Ibid.
27 Ibid.
28 'RAF Portland ROTOR Radar Station', The Encyclopaedia of Portland History, https://www.portlandhistory.co.uk/raf-portland-rotor-radar-station.html (accessed December 2020).
29 National Archives, PREM 11/159, 21 December 1951.
30 Ibid.
31 Ibid.
32 Ibid.
33 Gregori Galofré Vilà et al., 'Economic consequences of the 1953 London Debt Agreement', VoxEU, 9 October 2016, https://voxeu.org/article/economic-consequences-1953-london-debt-agreement (accessed December 2020).
34 *Manchester Guardian*, 20 September 1946.
35 *Manchester Guardian*, 8 May 1948.
36 Earl of Kilmuir, *Political Adventure: The Memoirs of the Earl of Kilmuir* (S. I.: Wiedenfeld & Nicolson, 1964), p. 187.
37 National Archives, CAB 129/48.
38 *Time*, 5 August 1966.
39 Robert Coughlan, 'Design for the West', *Life*, 9 December, 1957.
40 Archive of European Integration, Pittsburgh University, http://aei.pitt.edu/.
41 Ibid.
42 'Draft Treaty embodying the Statute of the European Community', Archive of European Integration, http://aei.pitt.edu/991/1/political_union_draft_treaty_1.pdf (accessed December 2020).
43 'Britain and Europe', *The Observer*, 1 March 1953.
44 *Nevada State Journal*, 11 March 1953.
45 National Archives, AIR 55/291, 12 March 1953.
46 Ibid.
47 Ibid.
48 'Brutal Act of Aggression', *Kansas City Star*, 13 March 1953.
49 *The Times*, 14 March 1953.
50 Hansard, House of Commons, Vol. 512, 17 March 1953.
51 National Archives, PREM 11/896.
52 *San Francisco Examiner*, 13 March 1953.
53 Ibid.
54 *The Age* (Melbourne), 14 March 1953.
55 'Frontier Shots', *The Times*, 14 March 1953.

56 National Archives, CAB 195/11, 20 March 1953.

57 Ibid.

CHAPTER 4: MIND BLOWING

1 'Korea A-Bomb Use Urged by GI's at "Doom Town"', *San Francisco Examiner*, 18 March 1953.

2 'Times Man With GI's Sees Atomic Fury', *LA Times*, 18 March 1953.

3 'Korea A-Bomb Use Urged by GI's at "Doom Town"', *San Francisco Examiner*.

4 'Man and Doom in the Desert', *Deseret News*, 18 March 1953.

5 Quoted in *Seattle Times*, 9 October 2010.

6 Ibid.

7 John P. Glennon (ed.), *Foreign Relations of the United States, 1952–1954, Korea, Vol. XV, Part 1* (Washington: United States Government Printing Office, 1984), p. 817.

8 Ibid.

9 Ibid.

10 Ibid.

11 Ibid., p. 826.

12 Ibid.

13 *Time*, 5 February 1951.

14 Ibid., p. 827.

15 Ibid.

16 US Senate, 'Senate Select Committee to Study Governmental Operations with Respect to Intelligence Activities', 29 April 1976, p. 390.

17 Ibid.

18 Ibid.

19 Arthur Koestler, *Darkness at Noon* (London: Macmillan, 1940) and George Orwell, *1984* (London: Secker & Warburg, 1949).

20 Interview of Richard Helms by David Frost, CIA, 22 to 23 May 1978, https://www.cia.gov/library/center-for-the-study-of-intelligence/kent-csi/vol44no4/pdf/v44i4a07p.pdf (accessed November 2020).

21 Marcia Holmes, 'Edward Hunter and the origins of "brainwashing"', Hidden Persuaders, 26 May 2017, http://www.bbk.ac.uk/hiddenpersuaders/blog/hunter-origins-of-brainwashing/ (accessed December 2020).

22 Edward Hunter, *Brainwashing in Red China: The Calculated Destruction of Men's Minds* (US: Vanguard Press, 1951).

23 '"Malarkey," Says Mrs Schwable', *New York Times*, 23 February 1953.

24 Interview of Richard Helms by David Frost.

25 *New York Times*, 5 August 1976.

26 US Senate, 'Senate Select Committee to Study Governmental Operations with Respect to Intelligence Activities', pp. 392–3.

27 Allen Dulles, 'Brain Warfare', speech given at the National Alumni Conference of the Graduate Council of Princeton University, 10 April 1953, CIA, https://www.cia.gov/library/readingroom/docs/CIA-RDP80R01731R001700030015-9.pdf (accessed November 2020).

28 US Senate, 'Senate Select Committee to Study Governmental Operations with Respect to Intelligence Activities', p. 392.

29 Ibid., p. 394.

30 'Nuremberg Code', United States Holocaust Memorial Museum, https://www.ushmm.org/information/exhibitions/online-exhibitions/special-focus/doctors-trial/nuremberg-code (accessed December 2020).

31 US Senate, 'Project MKUltra, the CIA's Program of Research in Behavioral Modification: Joint Hearing Before the Select Committee on Intelligence', First Session, 3 August 1977, p. 199.

32 'Obituary: Sidney Gottlieb', *The Independent*, 16 March 1999.

33 *Courier-Journal* (Louisville, Kentucky), 9 July 1952.

34 Hansard, House of Commons, Vol. 515, 12 May 1953.

35 'Senator Joe McCarthy: Audio Excerpts, 1950–1954', Raynor Memorial Libraries, Marquette University, 21 October 1953, https://www.marquette.edu/library/archives/DC/JRM/JRM_1953_Leonardo_excpt.pdf (accessed November 2020).

36 Larry Tye, *Demagogue: The Life and Long Shadow of Senator Joe McCarthy* (Boston: Houghton Mifflin Harcourt, 2020), p. 235.

37 William Z. Slany (ed.), *Foreign Relations of the United States, 1952–1954, General: Economic and Political Matters, Vol. I, Part 2* (Washington: United States Government Printing Office, 1983), p. 1380.
38 David Oshinsky, *A Conspiracy So Immense: The World of Joe McCarthy* (Oxford: Oxford University Press, 2005), p. 266.
39 Ibid., p. 267.
40 Ibid.
41 'Uncover Plot in "Voice" to Sabotage US', *Chicago Tribune*, 13 February 1953.
42 Associated Press, 3 March 1953.
43 David Oshinsky, *A Conspiracy So Immense*, p. 272.
44 Associated Press, 7 March 1953.
45 US National Archives, Public Papers of the Presidents.
46 Thomas Reeves, *The Life and Times of Joe McCarthy: A Biography* (New York: Stein and Day, 1982), p. 479.
47 Ibid.
48 *Executive Sessions of the Senate Permanent Subcommittee on Investigations of the Committee on Government Operations, Vol. 2, 1953* (Washington: US Government Printing Office, 2003), p. 946.
49 Ibid., p. 947.
50 'Six Hours in London', *Manchester Guardian*, 21 April 1953.
51 Nicholas Von Hoffman, *Citizen Cohn* (New York: Doubleday, 1988), p. 167.
52 *News Chronicle*, 21 April 1953.
53 *Daily Express*, 21 April 1953.
54 Daniel Smith, *The Peer and the Gangster: A Very British Cover-up* (Cheltenham: The History Press, 2020), p. 68.
55 Quoted in 'Restive Britons', *The Nation*, 11 April 1953.
56 Ibid.
57 'Craig Backs Gal Who Tabbed Robin a Red', *The Times* (Munster, Indiana), 23 November 1953.
58 *Pravda*, 26 November 1953.
59 Arthur M. Schlesinger, *Robert Kennedy and His Times* (London: Deutsch, 1978), p. 101.
60 David Oshinsky, *A Conspiracy So Immense*, p. 297.
61 'Trade and Aid', *The Times*, 7 May 1953.
62 Hansard, House of Commons, Vol. 515, 12 May 1953.
63 *The Newark Advocate*, 14 May 1953.
64 Reuters, 15 May 1953.
65 Hansard, House of Commons debate, Vol. 516, CC 957–8, 17 June 1953.
66 David Oshinsky, *A Conspiracy So Immense*, p. 298.
67 Arthur M. Schlesinger, *Robert Kennedy and His Times*, p. 104.
68 *The Papers of Dwight David Eisenhower*, Johns Hopkins University Press, 18 May 1953.

CHAPTER 5: 'LEAST SAID, SOONEST MENDED'

1   'Peace Monger of Moscow', *Manchester Guardian*, 16 March 1953.
2   Emmet John Hughes, *The Ordeal of Power*, p. 104.
3   Ibid., p. 107.
4   Ibid., p. 109.
5   Peter G. Boyle, *The Churchill–Eisenhower Correspondence, 1953–1955* (Chapel Hill: University of North Carolina Press, 1990), p. 41.
6   Ibid., p. 42.
7   Emmet John Hughes, *The Ordeal of Power*, p. 113.
8   *New York Times*, 17 April 1953.
9   *The Times*, 17 April 1953.
10 *Daily Mirror*, 17 April 1953.
11 *Pravda*, 25 April 1953.
12 *Baltimore Sun*, 19 April 1953.
13 *Manchester Guardian*, 18 April 1953.
14 Charles Wilson Moran, *Churchill: The Struggle for Survival*, p. 113.
15 Interview with Barry Barnes, Imperial War Museum Sound Archive, April 2007, https://www.iwm.org.uk/collections/item/object/80028429 (accessed November 2020).

16 Ibid.
17 Ibid.
18 Ibid.
19 Ibid.
20 Ibid.
21 Ibid.
22 Ibid.
23 Ulf Schmidt, *Secret Science: A Century of Poison Warfare and Human Experiments* (Oxford: Oxford University Press, 2015), p. 250.
24 Antony Barnett, 'Final agony of RAF volunteer killed by sarin – in Britain', *The Observer*, 28 September 2003.
25 Ibid.
26 Ulf Schmidt, *Secret Science*, p. 233.
27 National Archives, CAB 131/12, 17 June 1952.
28 National Archives, CAB 131/13, 6 May 1953.
29 National Archives, CAB 131/13 Confidential Annex, 7 May 1953.
30 National Archives, CAB 131/13, 7 May 1953, p. 26.
31 National Archives, PREM 11/3099, 7 May 1953.
32 Ibid.
33 Ibid.
34 Ibid.
35 Ibid.
36 Ibid.
37 National Archives, WO 286/11, 13 July 1953.
38 Ibid.
39 Ibid.
40 Ibid.
41 Ibid.
42 'Poisoned by their own people', *The Independent*, 3 October 2000.
43 Ulf Schmidt, *Secret Science*, p. 236.
44 Ibid., p. 237.
45 Ibid., p. 240.
46 Ibid.
47 Ibid., p. 241.
48 Quoted in Ulf Schmidt, *Secret Science*.
49 *Daily Mail*, 25 May 1953.
50 *Sunday Dispatch*, 31 May 1953.
51 Hansard, House of Commons debate, 9 June 1953, Vol. 516, CC 7–8W.
52 Hansard, House of Commons debate, 22 June 1953, Vol. 516, C 104W.
53 Ulf Schmidt, *Secret Science*, p. 259.
54 'BW and BW Defence Field Trials Conducted by the UK: 1930–1979', Defence Evaluation and Research Agency, February 1999, https://whatcanidoaboutit.files.wordpress.com/2013/01/uk-bw-defence-field-trials-1940-1979-mod.pdf (accessed December 2020).
55 National Archives, CAB 131/12, 17 June 1952.
56 National Archives, PREM 3/89, 6 July 1944.
57 National Archives, CAB 131/12 (folio 51), 9 July 1952.
58 'Trawler Steamed Into Germ Warfare Site', *Daily Telegraph*, 20 September 2005.
59 National Archives, CAB 195/11, 10 August 1953.
60 Ibid.
61 Ibid.
62 National Archives, CAB 195/11, 18 August 1953.
63 Ibid.
64 Ibid.
65 National Archives, CAB 131/13, 1 October 1953.
66 National Archives, PREM 11/422.
67 Ibid.
68 Robert Rhodes James, *Anthony Eden* (London: Weidenfeld & Nicolson, 1986), p. 363.
69 Martin Gilbert, *'Never Despair': Winston S. Churchill, 1945–1965* (London: Minerva, 1990), p. 820.

70 National Archives, FO 371/106527, 9 May 1953.
71 Martin Gilbert, '*Never Despair*': *Winston S. Churchill, 1945–1965*, p. 817.
72 'Order of the Boot', International Churchill Society, https://winstonchurchill.org/resources/quotes/order-of-the-boot/#:~:text='How%20can%20I%20accept%20the,the%20Garter%2C%20which%20he%20declined (accessed December 2020).
73 Ibid., p. 824.
74 Anthony Nutting, *Europe Will Not Wait: A Warning and a Way Out* (London: Hollis & Carter, 1960), p. 50.
75 Peter G. Boyle, *The Churchill–Eisenhower Correspondence*, p. 48.
76 *The Papers of Dwight David Eisenhower*, Johns Hopkins University Press, 5 May 1953, p. 208.
77 Ibid.
78 Peter G. Boyle, *The Churchill–Eisenhower Correspondence*, p. 51.
79 Anthony Seldon, *Churchill's Indian Summer: The Conservative Government, 1951–55* (London: Hodder & Stoughton, 1981), p. 399.
80 Hansard, House of Commons debate, 11 May 1953, Vol. 515, CC 883–1004.
81 'The Supreme Event', *The Times*, 12 May 1953.
82 *Daily Herald*, 12 May 1953.
83 *Daily Worker*, 12 May 1953.
84 'Senator Likes Churchill's Idea', Associated Press, 12 May 1953.
85 Ibid.
86 Robert Rhodes James, *Anthony Eden*, p. 365.
87 Harold Macmillan, *The Macmillan Diaries: The Cabinet Years, 1950–1957* (London: Pan, 2004), 12 May 1953.
88 C. L. Sulzberger, *A Long Row of Candles: Memories and Diaries, 1934–1954* (London: Macdonald, 1969), p. 873.
89 'Mr H. Wilson meets Mr Molotov. Free and Frank Talks', *Manchester Guardian*, 22 May 1953.
90 Richard Crossman, *Backbench Diaries of Richard Crossman* (London: Hamish Hamilton & Jonathan Cape, 1981), p. 250.
91 'President Prods Russia To Back Up Peace Talk', *Charlotte Observer*, 15 May 1953.
92 John P. Glennon (ed.), *Foreign Relations of the United States, 1952–1954, Korea, Vol. XV, Part 1*, p. 1067.
93 Ibid., p. 1016.
94 Ibid., p. 977.
95 Ibid.
96 Ibid., p. 1015.
97 Ibid., p. 1016.
98 Ibid.
99 Ibid., p. 1066.
100 Ibid.
101 Ibid., p. 1067.
102 Ibid.
103 'Hints Eisenhower Doubts Red Peace', *Star-Gazette* (New York), 20 May 1953.

CHAPTER 6: 'WE GOVERN BY POPULAR WILL'

1   'The Coronation of Queen Elizabeth II', BBC News, https://www.bbc.com/historyofthebbc/anniversaries/june/coronation-of-queen-elizabeth-ii (accessed December 2020).
2   'Queen's Day – TV's Day', *Daily Express*, 3 June 1953.
3   'Few Shots Of Patient Crowds On TV', *Manchester Guardian*, 3 June 1953.
4   National Archives, CAB 195/10, 21 October 1952.
5   'New Pattern Occasion', *Manchester Guardian*, 3 June 1953.
6   'A Call to Social Responsibility', *The Times*, 4 June 1953.
7   Asa Briggs, *The History of Broadcasting in the United Kingdom* (London: Oxford University Press, 1995), p. 434.
8   Reported in *Baltimore Sun*, 14 June 1953.
9   *New York Daily News*, 12 June 1953.
10 Ibid.
11 Richard Nixon, '"Checkers" speech', 23 September 1952, University of Virginia, Miller Center, https://millercenter.org/the-presidency/presidential-speeches/september-23-1952-checkers-speech (accessed November 2020).
12 Kevin McDermott, 'Popular Resistance in Communist Czechoslovakia: The Plzeň Uprising, June 1953', *Contemporary European History*, Vol. 19, Issue 4, September 2010.

13 *Free Europe Press*, 1953, p. 22.

14 National Archives, PREM 11/673, 18 June 1953.

15 *Neues Deutschland*, 17 June 1953.

16 'When The Red Flag Came Down', *The Freeman*, 5 October 1953.

17 'Riots Caused By Oppression', *Chicago Tribune*, 18 June 1953.

18 Details about Willi Karl Göttling taken from 'Rebellion in the Rain', *Time*, 29 June 1953, RIAS radio report, featured in 'Berlin Documentary', 18 June 1953, New York Public Radio, https://www.wnyc.org/story/berlin-documentary/ (accessed December 2020) and *Life*, 29 June 1953.

19 'Rebellion in the Rain', *Time*, 29 June 1953.

20 Christian Ostermann (ed.), *Uprising in East Germany: The Cold War, the German Question, and the First Major Upheaval Behind the Iron Curtain* (Budapest: Central European University Press, 2001), p. 220.

21 RIAS radio report, featured in 'Berlin Documentary', 18 June 1953, New York Public Radio.

22 Christian Ostermann, '"This Is Not A Politburo, But A Madhouse": The Post-Stalin Succession Struggle, Soviet *Deutschlandpolitik* and the SED: New Evidence from Russian, German, and Hungarian Archives', *Cold War International History Project*, Bulletin 10 (March 1998), p. 95.

23 National Archives, FO 371/103839, 18 June 1953.

24 'Dr Adenauer at Berliners' Funeral', *Manchester Guardian*, 24 June 1953.

25 William Z. Slany (ed.), *Foreign Relations of the United States, 1952–1954, Germany and Austria, Vol. VIII, Part 2*, p. 1586 onwards.

26 Ibid.

27 Ibid.

28 Frank Roberts, *Dealing with Dictators: The Destruction and Revival of Europe, 1930–70* (London: Weidenfeld & Nicolson, 1991), p. 166.

29 National Archives, FO 371/103841, 18 June 1953.

30 Ibid.

31 Ibid.

32 M. Steven Fish, 'After Stalin's Death: The Anglo-American Debate Over a New Cold War', *Diplomatic History*, Vol. 10, Issue 4 (October 1986), pp. 333–55, p. 343.

33 National Archives, PREM 11/673, 22 June 1953.

34 Wilson Center Digital Archive, 'National Security Council Report, NSC 158, "United States Objectives and Actions to Exploit the Unrest in the Satellite States"', 19 June 1953, https://digitalarchive.wilsoncenter.org/document/116203.pdf?v=5805c643c092e3f2646bf4da6e857281 (accessed November 2020).

35 Ibid.

36 National Security Council meeting 132, 18 February 1953.

37 'Unrest in All Red Satellites', *Nashville Banner*, 30 June 1953.

38 William Z. Slany (ed.), *Foreign Relations of the United States, 1952–1954, Germany and Austria, Vol. VIII, Part 2*, p. 1617.

39 Ibid., p. 1618.

40 National Archives, PREM 11/673, 6 August 1953.

41 William Z. Slany (ed.), *Foreign Relations of the United States, 1952–1954, Germany and Austria, Vol. VIII, Part 2*, p. 1634.

42 *Rosenberg v United States*, 18 June 1953, FindLaw, https://caselaw.findlaw.com/us-supreme-court/346/273.html (accessed November 2020).

43 Lori Clube, 'Great Importance World-Wide: Presidential Decision-Making and the Executions of Julius and Ethel Rosenberg', *American Communist History*, Vol. 10, No. 3, 2011, pp. 271–3.

44 'Julius and Ethel Rosenberg', Eisenhower Library, www.eisenhowerlibrary.gov (accessed November 2020).

45 Letter from President Eisenhower to Clyde Miller, *The Papers of Dwight David Eisenhower*, Johns Hopkins University Press, 10 June 1953.

46 Letter from Clyde Miller to President Eisenhower, ibid., 8 June 1953.

47 Letter to John Eisenhower from President Eisenhower, ibid., 16 June 1953.

48 Letter from Ethel Rosenberg to President Eisenhower, ibid., 16 June 1953.

49 Emmet John Hughes, *The Ordeal of Power*, p. 80.

50 Ibid.

51 Ibid.

52 'Reject Final Appeal To Save Two Atomic Spies', *Brownwood Bulletin*, 19 June 1953.

53 Ibid.
54 Ibid.
55 'Enemies of Democracy', *Manchester Guardian*, 19 June 1953.
56 Associated Press, 19 June 1953.
57 'President's Statement', *Manchester Guardian*, 20 June.
58 'Atom Spies Walk Calmly to Death', *News-Palladium* (Michigan), 20 June 1953.

CHAPTER 7: THE EMERGENCY GOVERNMENT

1 National Archives, CP 1/28, 6 February 1953.
2 Churchill Papers, Chur 6/3A/92-93, 1 July 1953.
3 John Colville, *The Fringes of Power*, p. 311.
4 Charles Wilson Moran, *Churchill: The Struggle for Survival*, p. 116.
5 Kenneth Clark, *The Other Half: A Self-Portrait* (London: Hamish Hamilton, 1986), p. 128.
6 Mary Soames, *Clementine Churchill* (London: Doubleday, 2003), p. 434.
7 John W. Wheeler Bennett, *Action This Day: Working with Churchill* (London: Macmillan, 1968), p. 123.
8 Ibid.
9 Harold Macmillan, *Tides of Fortune, 1945–1955* (London: Macmillan, 1969), p. 516.
10 George Mallaby, *From My Level: Unwritten Minutes* (London: Hutchinson, 1965), p. 47.
11 Charles Wilson Moran, *Churchill: The Struggle for Survival*, p. 119.
12 Mary Soames, *Clementine Churchill*, p. 435.
13 Author interview with Lady Williams (Jane Portal), October 2019.
14 John Colville, *The Fringes of Power*, p. 329.
15 Letter from Jock Colville to Lord Beaverbrook, 25 June 1953, Beaverbrook Papers, Parliamentary Archive.
16 Quoted in Charles Wilson Moran, *Churchill: The Struggle for Survival*, p. 121.
17 Ibid., p. 120.
18 John Colville, *The Fringes of Power*, p. 328.
19 Quoted in 'Butler's Gag on Churchill's Stroke', *The Guardian*, 2 January 1984.
20 Anthony Howard, *Rab: The Life of R. A. Butler* (London: Cape, 1987), p. 196.
21 Bigmore Papers, courtesy of Peter Harrington Rare Books, Fulham Road, London.
22 Author interview with Lady Williams (Jane Portal), October 2019.
23 Charles Wilson Moran, *Churchill: The Struggle for Survival*, p. 124.
24 Bonham Carter Papers, Bodleian Library.
25 Ibid.
26 Harold Macmillan, *The Macmillan Diaries*, p. 239.
27 Hansard, House of Commons debate, 29 June 1953, Vol. 517, CC 27–32.
28 Ibid.
29 National Archives, PREM 11/517, 29 June 1953.
30 Ibid.
31 *Western Mail*, 1 July 1953, *Western Morning Herald*, 1 July 1953 and *Glasgow Herald*, 1 July 1953.
32 Charles Wilson Moran, *Churchill: The Struggle for Survival*, p. 128.
33 Churchill Papers, Chur 6/3A/92-93, 1 July 1953.
34 Author interview with Lady Williams (Jane Portal), October 2019.
35 Harold Macmillan, *The Macmillan Diaries*, p. 240.
36 Anthony Seldon, *Churchill's Indian Summer*, p. 65.
37 'Churchill Planning to Retire', *Liverpool Daily Post*, 9 July 1953.
38 'Beginning to Benefit from Rest?', *Manchester Guardian*, 1 July 1953.
39 John Colville, *The Fringes of Power*, p. 155.
40 Author interview with Lady Williams (Jane Portal), October 2019.
41 National Archives, PREM 11/517, 20 July 1953.
42 Ibid.
43 Charles Wilson Moran, *Churchill: The Struggle for Survival*, p. 152.
44 National Archives, PREM 11/517, 23 July 1953.
45 John Colville, *The Fringes of Power*, p. 333.
46 Harold Macmillan, *The Macmillan Diaries*, p. 246.
47 'Great Benefit from Month's Rest', *The Times*, 25 July 1953.
48 United Press International, 25 July 1953.

49 Clarissa Eden, *Clarissa Eden: A Memoir, From Churchill to Eden* (London: Weidenfeld & Nicolson, 2007), diary entry for 27 July 1953.

50 John Colville, *The Fringes of Power*, p. 333.

51 Ibid.

52 Evelyn Shuckburgh, *Descent to Suez: Diaries 1951–56*, 26 August 1953, p. 99.

53 Churchill Papers, 2/211, 12 August 1953.

54 Charles Wilson Moran, *Churchill: The Struggle for Survival*, p. 165.

55 Brendan Bracken, *My Dear Max: The Letters of Brendan Bracken to Lord Beaverbrook, 1925–1958* (London: Historians' Press, 1990), p. 148.

56 John Colville, *The Fringes of Power*, p. 337.

57 'Sir Winston's Illness', *New York Herald Tribune*, 7 August 1953.

58 'What is the Truth About Churchill's Illness?', *Daily Mirror*, 17 August 1953.

59 Charles Wilson Moran, *Churchill: The Struggle for Survival*, p. 170.

60 Harold Macmillan, *The Macmillan Diaries*, p. 255.

61 National Archives, CAB 195/11, 18 August 1953.

62 Charles Wilson Moran, *Churchill: The Struggle for Survival*, p. 158.

63 John P. Glennon (ed.), *Foreign Relations of the United States, 1952–1954, Korea, Vol. XV, Part 1*, p. 1068.

64 Quoted in Robert A. Pape, *Bombing to Win: Air Power and Coercion in War* (London: Cornell University Press, 1996), p. 166.

65 Ibid.

66 Mao Tse-Tung, *Selected Works of Mao Tse-Tung, Vol. 4* (Peking: Foreign Language Press, 1961), p. 100.

67 'Syngman Rhee – Deep Are The Roots of Freedom', *Time*, 9 March 1953.

68 *The Papers of Dwight David Eisenhower*, Johns Hopkins University Press, 24 July 1953, p. 420.

69 Quoted in 'US Had '53 Plan to Overthrow "Unreliable" Korean Ally', *Washington Post*, 17 December 1977.

70 Peter G. Boyle, *The Churchill–Eisenhower Correspondence*, p. 76.

71 Ibid.

72 National Archives, FO 800/784, 21 June 1953.

73 Ibid.

74 Martin Gilbert, *'Never Despair': Winston S. Churchill, 1945–1965*, p. 861.

75 Sherman Adams, *Firsthand Report: The Story of the Eisenhower Administration* (New York: Harper & Brothers, 1961), p. 101.

76 *Washington Post*, 17 December 1977.

77 Associated Press, 27 July 1953.

78 'Fought to a Draw', *The Times*, 27 July 1953.

79 Hansard, House of Lords, 27 July 1953, Vol. 183.

80 'President Eisenhower Announces Korean War Armistice', *Chicago Tribune*, 27 July 1953.

81 Andrew M. Condron, Richard G. Corden and Larance V. Sullivan, *Thinking Soldiers, by Men Who Fought in Korea* (Peking: New World Press, 1955), p. 123.

82 National Archives, CAB 134/98 HDC (53) 7, 24 July 1953.

83 Ibid.

84 Ibid.

85 Ibid.

86 Ibid.

87 'Corsham Ammunition Depot and Standby Government Headquarters', Subterranea Britannica, 1 June 1997, https://www.subbrit.org.uk/sites/corsham/ (accessed December 2020).

88 Robert Cutler, *No Time for Rest*, pp. 303–4.

CHAPTER 8: JOE 4

1 'Georgi Malenkov Dies at 86', *New York Times*, 2 February 1988.

2 Jonathan Haslam, *Russia's Cold War: From the October Revolution to the Fall of the Wall* (London: Yale University Press, 2011), p. 137 and 'Stalin's Successor', *Baltimore Sun*, 18 July 1953.

3 'Photo Trick Puts Malenkov Nearer Stalin and Mao', *New York Times*, 14 March 1953.

4 'Speech by G. M. Malenkov, Chairman of the Council of Ministers of the USSR', 8 August 1953, *Soviet News*, http://www.directdemocracy4u.uk/note/Malenkov_Speech8August1953.pdf (accessed November 2020).

5 Ibid.

6 'Mr Malenkov Surveys Russian Policy', *The Times*, 10 August 1953.

7   Ibid.
8   'H-Bomb Boast Discounted', *Fort Worth Star-Telegram*, 9 August 1953.
9   Ibid.
10 Ibid.
11 'Mr Malenkov Sets the Line', *The Times*, 10 August 1953.
12 'Thermo-Nuclear Experiment', *Manchester Guardian*, 21 August 1953.
13 Edward Teller, *Memoirs*, p. 365.
14 'The Doomsday Clock: A Timeline of Conflict, Culture, and Change', *Bulletin of the Atomic Scientists*, https://thebulletin.org/doomsday-clock/past-statements/ (accessed November 2020).
15 Eugene Rabinowitch, 'The Narrowing Way', *Bulletin of the Atomic Scientists*, October 1953.
16 Charles Wilson Moran, *Churchill: The Struggle for Survival*, p. 166.
17 Harold Macmillan, *Tides of Fortune, 1945–1955*, p. 522.
18 William Z. Slany (ed.), *Foreign Relations of the United States, 1952–1954, National Security Affairs, Vol. II, Part 1* (Washington: United States Government Printing Office, 1984), p. 457.
19 Ibid., p. 461.
20 Eisenhower Papers, Eisenhower Library, NSC 163, 24 September 1953.
21 Michael Amrine, 'US Could Suffer a New Pearl Harbor', *Daily Times*, Maryland, 2 September 1953.
22 'Preview of the War We Do Not Want – an Imaginary Account of Russia's Defeat and Occupation, 1952–60', *Collier's Weekly*, October 1951.
23 Val Peterson, 'Panic: The Ultimate Weapon', *Collier's Weekly*, 21 August 1953.
24 'C-Bomb Latest Way for World to End Itself', *Daily News*, 23 August 1953.
25 United Press International, 23 August 1953.
26 'The Nature of Modern War', *Hanford Sentinel*, 25 August 1953.
27 National Archives, CAB 195/11, 25 August 1953.
28 Unsourced, but widely attributed.
29 National Archives, FO 371/52735, 20 July 1946.
30 Josh Turner, 'A Splutter of Musketry – Britain and America's Destruction of Iranian Democracy', Repeater Books, 31 January 2018, https://repeaterbooks.com/a-splutter-of-musketry-britain-and-americas-destruction-of-iranian-democracy-part-one/ (accessed December 2020).
31 'Mohammed Mossadeq – Feet First Into Chaos', *Time*, 4 June 1951.
32 'Profile: Mohammed Moussadek', *The Observer*, 20 May 1951.
33 'Man of The Year – He Oiled The Wheels of Chaos', *Time*, 7 January 1952.
34 Josh Turner, 'A Splutter of Musketry – Britain and America's Destruction of Iranian Democracy'.
35 'Iran 1950–53', LHMA Woodhouse Papers, p. 3.
36 Ibid., p. 7.
37 State Department, memorandum of conversation, Byroade to Matthews, 'Proposal to Organize Coup d'état in Iran and Oil Problem', 26 November 1952, National Security Archive, https://nsarchive.gwu.edu/dc.html?doc=3914379-01-State-Department-Memorandum-of-Conversation (accessed November 2020).
38 State Department, memorandum of conversation, 'British Proposal to Organize Coup d'état in Iran', 3 December, 1952, https://nsarchive.gwu.edu/dc.html?doc=3914380-02-State-Department-Memorandum-of-Conversation (accessed November 2020).
39 Anthony Eden, *Full Circle: The Memoirs of Anthony Eden* (London: Cassell, 1960), p. 198.
40 Ibid., p. 205.
41 'Iran 1950–53', LHMA Woodhouse Papers, p. 11.
42 John P. Glennon (ed.), *Foreign Relations of the United States, 1952–1954, Iran, 1951–1954, Vol. X* (Washington: United States Government Printing Office, 1989), p. 689.
43 Ibid., p. 693.
44 Ibid.
45 Kermit Roosevelt, *Countercoup: The Struggle for Control of Iran* (New York: McGraw-Hill, 1979), p. 115.
46 John Prados, *Safe From Democracy: The Secret Wars of the CIA* (Chicago: Ivan R. Dee, 2006), p. 102.
47 Adam M. Howard (ed.), *Foreign Relations of the United States, 1952–1954, Iran, 1951–1954* (Washington: United States Government Printing Office, 2017), p. 523.
48 Donald N. Wilber, *Regime Change in Iran: Overthrow of Premier Mossadeq of Iran, November 1952–August 1953* (Nottingham: Spokesman, 2006), p. 74 onwards.
49 Kermit Roosevelt, *Countercoup: The Struggle for Control of Iran*, p. 12.
50 Ibid., p. 18.

51 Ibid.

52 John P. Glennon (ed.), *Foreign Relations of the United States, 1952–1954, Iran, 1951–1954, Vol. X*, p. 747.

53 'Shah Flees in Iran Coup', Associated Press, 17 August 1953.

54 John P. Glennon (ed.), *Foreign Relations of the United States, 1952–1954, Iran, 1951–1954, Vol. X*, p. 748.

55 Kermit Roosevelt, *Countercoup: The Struggle for Control of Iran*, p. 109.

56 'Mossadegh Flees; Top Aides Slain', *Indianapolis Star*, 20 August 1953.

57 Kermit Roosevelt, *Countercoup: The Struggle for Control of Iran*, p. 199.

58 Ibid., p. 206.

59 Ibid.

60 Diary, 8 October 1953, Whitman File, Box 1, Eisenhower Papers, Eisenhower Library.

61 National Archives, CAB 195/11, 25 August 1953.

CHAPTER 9: OVERTHROW

1   File on Anthony Blunt, FBI Records: The Vault, https://vault.fbi.gov/Anthony%20Blunt%20/Anthony%20Blunt%20Part%201%20of%201/view (accessed December 2020).

2   Hansard, House of Commons, 17 February 1953, Vol. 511.

3   'Missing Diplomat in Peace Moves', *Daily Express*, 14 May 1953.

4   Roland Philipps, *A Spy Named Orphan: The Enigma of Donald Maclean* (London: Vintage Digital, 2018), pp. 360–61.

5   *The Observer*, 27 July 1953.

6   Yuri Modin, *My Five Cambridge Friends* (London: Headline, 1994), pp. 225–7.

7   Roland Philipps, *A Spy Named Orphan*, p. 350.

8   Ibid.

9   'Missing Woman Left Car in Garage For a Week', *Odessa American* (Texas), 17 September 1953.

10 Ibid.

11 Yuri Modin, *My Five Cambridge Friends*, p. 246.

12 Roland Philipps, *A Spy Named Orphan*, p. 116.

13 'Winston Churchill made boozy £12,000 bet with British Empire would not fall … and won', *Daily Telegraph*, 10 March 2016.

14 National Archives, CAB 129/48, 29 November 1951.

15 Mark Curtis, 'The intervention in British Guiana, 1953', British Foreign Policy Declassified, 12 February 2007, http://markcurtis.info/2007/02/12/the-intervention-in-british-guiana-1953/ (accessed November 2020).

16 'Report on British Guiana by the Governor, Sir Alfred Savage', September 1953, declassified British documents, Guyana.org, http://www.guyana.org/govt/declassified_british_documents_1953.html (accessed November 2020).

17 'A Woman In White Plans Red Trip', *Daily Express*, 10 July 1951.

18 National Archives, KV 2/3604, 24 February 1953 and 'Janet Jagan Speaks Out for Colony', *Daily Worker*, 15 June 1953.

19 National Archives, KV 2/3600, 28 March 1953.

20 National Archives, KV 2/3604, 24 February 1953.

21 *The Gazette* (Quebec), 1 May 1953 and *Daily Oklahoman*, 1 May 1953.

22 'Communist Victory in British Guiana', *Manchester Guardian*, 30 April 1953.

23 'Extract of message from Queen Elizabeth II to the new Legislature of British Guiana', 30 May 1953, declassified British documents, Guyana.org, http://www.guyana.org/govt/declassified_british_documents_1953.html (accessed November 2020).

24 'Extract of the message from Colonial Secretary Oliver Lyttelton to the new Legislature of British Guiana', 30 May 1953, ibid.

25 National Archives, KV 2/3604, 30 May 1953.

26 Stephen Rabe, *US Intervention in British Guiana: A Cold War Story* (Chapel Hill: University of North Carolina Press, 2005), p. 39.

27 Ibid., p. 40.

28 National Archives, KV 2/3604, 9 July 1953.

29 'Extracts of the speech by Sir Alfred Savage, Governor of British Guiana to the new Legislature of British Guiana', 30 May 1953, Guyana.org, http://www.guyana.org/govt/declassified_british_documents_1953.html (accessed November 2020).

30 National Archives, KV 2/3605, 2 September 1953.

31 Ibid.

32 Quoted in Winston McGowan, 'Guyana Politics: The suspension of the British Guiana constitution in 1953', *Stabroek News*, 31 October 2002, Guyana.org, https://guyaneseonline.files.wordpress.com/2019/03/guyana-politics-the-suspension-of-the-british-guiana-constitution-in-1953-1.pdf (accessed November 2020).

33 'Letter from Timothy Luke to Philip Rogers of the Colonial Office, 12 September 1953, Guyana.org, http://www.guyana.org/govt/declassified_british_documents_1953.html (accessed November 2020).

34 'Telegram (No. 21) from Colonial Secretary to Governor of British Guiana', 24 September 1953, ibid.

35 'Telegram (No. 66) from Governor of British Guiana to Colonial Secretary', 29 September 1953, ibid.

36 National Archives, CAB 195/11, 2 October 1953.

37 'Suspension of British Guiana Constitution', *The Times*, 10 October 1953.

38 Mark Curtis, 'The intervention in British Guiana, 1953'.

39 'Broadcast by Sir Alfred Savage, Governor of British Guiana on Radio Demerara', 9 October 1953, Guyana.org, http://www.guyana.org/govt/declassified_british_documents_1953.html (accessed November 2020).

40 National Archives, KV 2/3606, 12 October 1953.

41 National Archives, CAB 195/11, 7 October 1953.

42 'MP Attacks "Gunboat Diplomacy" in British Guiana', *Manchester Guardian*, 19 October 1953.

43 Hansard, House of Commons, 22 October 1953, Vol. 518.

44 US National Archives, Department of State records, 16 October 1953.

45 'Sharp Dig At Guatemala', *Kansas City Star*, 14 October 1953.

46 Mary Soames, *Clementine Churchill*, p. 438.

47 Richard Austen Butler, *The Art of the Possible: The Memoirs of Lord Butler* (London: Hamilton, 1971), p. 171.

48 Letter from Albert Nockels to Lord Beaverbrook, September 1953, Beaverbrook Papers.

49 Martin Gilbert, 'Never Despair': Winston S. Churchill, 1945–1965, p. 887.

50 Ibid.

51 Harold Macmillan, *The Macmillan Diaries*, p. 263.

52 Anthony Seldon, *Churchill's Indian Summer*, p. 520.

53 Woolton diaries, 1 October 1953, held at the Bodleian Library, Oxford.

54 Charles Wilson Moran, *Churchill: The Struggle for Survival*, p. 194.

55 Robert Rhodes James, *Anthony Eden*, p. 371.

56 Ibid.

57 National Archives, CA 2/216 2 October 1953.

58 Harold Macmillan, *The Macmillan Diaries*, p. 268.

59 Charles Wilson Moran, *Churchill: The Struggle for Survival*, p. 196.

60 'In Search of Peace', *The Times*, 12 October 1953.

61 Ibid.

62 'Prime Minister on Defence of Europe', *The Times*, 12 October 1953.

63 Author interview with Lady Williams (Jane Portal), October 2019.

64 Harold Macmillan, *The Macmillan Diaries*, p. 269.

65 Charles Wilson Moran, *Churchill: The Struggle for Survival*, p. 199.

66 Ibid., p. 198.

67 'Churchill Passes an Ordeal', *The Observer*, 11 October 1953.

68 *Sunday Pictorial*, 11 October 1953, quoted by Lord Moran in *Struggle for Survival*, p. 198.

69 Churchill Archives Centre, Cambridge, Papers of Patrick Buchan-Hepburn.

70 'Winston Churchill – Facts', NobelPrize.org, 20 November 2020, https://www.nobelprize.org/prizes/literature/1953/churchill/facts/ (accessed November 2020).

71 Churchill Archives Centre, Cambridge, Papers of Patrick Buchan-Hepburn.

CHAPTER 10: 'AN EXTREME MEASURE'

1 'Eisenhowers Scurry to White House Shelter in Mock Enemy Air Raid', *Tampa Tribune*, 6 November 1953 and 'Washington Atomic Bomb Test Sends Eisenhowers To Shelter', *St Louis Post-Dispatch*, 5 November 1953.

2 *The Papers of Dwight David Eisenhower*, Johns Hopkins University Press, 23 October 1953, p. 597.

3 National Archives, CAB 131/13, 1 October 1953.

4 William Z. Slany (ed.), *Foreign Relations of the United States, 1952–1954, National Security Affairs*, Vol. II, Part 1, p. 546.

5 Quoted in Michael G. Jackson, 'Beyond Brinkmanship: Eisenhower, Nuclear War Fighting, and Korea, 1953–1968', *Presidential Studies Quarterly* (2005), Vol. 35, Part 1, pp. 52–75, p. 57.

6 US National Archives, State Department (declassified document), 'Use of United Kingdom Bases and Consultation with the United Kingdom on the Use of Atomic Weapons', 6 March 1953.

7 Ibid.

8 William Z. Slany (ed.), *Foreign Relations of the United States, 1952–1954, National Security Affairs, Vol. II, Part 1*, p. 739.

9 Edward C. Keefer (ed.), *Foreign Relations of the United States, 1952–1954, Korea, Vol. XV, Part 2* (Washington: United States Government Printing Office, 1984), pp. 1626–29.

10 Hansard, House of Commons, 10 November, Vol. 520.

11 National Archives, CAB 128/26, 29 November 1953.

12 National Archives, CAB 195/11, 29 November 1953.

13 'Savage and Shockingly Prophetic: On Ray Bradbury's *Fahrenehit 451*', Literary Hub, 2 January 2018, https://bookmarks.reviews/savage-and-shockingly-prophetic-on-ray-bradburys-fahrenheit-451/ (accessed November 2020).

14 'Eisenhower Raps Book Burners', *Fort Worth Star-Telegram* (Texas), 15 June 1953.

15 Ibid.

16 'A Visit To An Eisenhower Press Conference', *Tampa Bay Times*, 21 June 1953.

17 'Ike Has No Objection to Burning of Propaganda Books', *Albuquerque Journal*, 22 June 1953 and 'Ike Okeh's "Propaganda" Book Burning', *Knoxville Journal*, 22 June 1953.

18 Associated Press, 17 June 1953.

19 Richard M. Fried, *Men Against McCarthy* (New York: Columbia University Press, 1976), pp. 277–8.

20 'Brownell Accuses Truman', *Morning Call* (Pennsylvania), 6 November 1953.

21 Stephen Ambrose, *Eisenhower: The President, 1952–1969, Vol. 2* (London: Allen & Unwin, 1984), p. 137.

22 'Eisenhower Has More At Stake Than Truman', *New York Times*, 11 November 1953.

23 United Press International, 11 November 1953.

24 Associated Press, 17 November 1953.

25 'Text of Truman Defense of Action in White Case', *The News* (New Jersey), 17 November 1953.

26 Associated Press as reported in 'McCarthy Hurls Red Charges, Hits Trumanism', *Sacramento Bee*, 25 November 1953.

27 Letter from C. D. Jackson to Sherman Adams, 25 November 1953, Eisenhower Papers, Eisenhower Library.

28 'Dulles Lashes Out At McCarthy's Talk Against US Policy', United Press International, 1 December 1953.

29 Associated Press, 3 December 1953.

30 'No Change of Heart – Adroit Reply By McCarthy', *Manchester Guardian*, 4 December 1953.

31 McCarthy hearings transcripts, United States Senate, https://www.senate.gov/about/powers-procedures/investigations/mccarthy-transcripts.htm (accessed December 2020).

32 Quoted in David Oshinsky, *A Conspiracy So Immense*, p. 356.

33 *Washington Post*, 16 July 1953.

34 Mike Mansfield Papers, Series 21, Box 37, Folder 46, Mansfield Library, University of Montana, exhibits.lib.umt.edu.

35 Stephen Ambrose, *Eisenhower: The President*, p. 135.

36 Associated Press, 29 November 1953.

37 'Dr Frank R Olson Dies in New York City', *Iron County Miner*, 4 December 1953.

38 H. P. Albarelli, *A Terrible Mistake: The Murder of Frank Olson and the CIA's Secret Cold War Experiments* (Walterville, Or.: Trine Day, 2009), p. 80.

39 'A Study of Assassination', The National Security Archive, George Washington University, https://nsarchive2.gwu.edu/NSAEBB/NSAEBB4/ciaguat2.html (accessed November 2020).

40 National Archives, KV 2/3875, 7 October 1953.

41 Ibid.

42 Ibid.

43 Robert Oppenheimer, 'The Sciences and Man's Community', BBC Reith Lectures, November 1953, https://www.bbc.co.uk/programmes/p00h9lm8 (accessed November 2020).

44 'Oppenheimer Tells Of New Sub-Atomic World', United Press International, 22 November 1953.

45 National Archives, PREM 11/785, 13 April 1954.

46 *The Papers of Dwight David Eisenhower*, Johns Hopkins University Press, December 1953, p. 578.

47 US Atomic Energy Commission, *In the Matter of J. Robert Oppenheimer* (Washington: US Department of Energy, 2014), pp. 837–8.
48 *The Papers of Dwight David Eisenhower*, Johns Hopkins University Press, 3 December 1953, p. 584.
49 Ibid.
50 Richard Hewlett and Jack Holl, *Atoms for Peace and War*, p. 69.

CHAPTER 11: 'WINSTON'S BABY'

1 'Recalling Mark Twain's Time In Bermuda', Bernews, 30 November 2013, https://bernews.com/2013/11/recalling-mark-twains-time-in-bermuda/#:~:text=Mark%20Twain%20%E2%80%94%20who%20famously%20remarked,ago%20today%20%5BNov%2030%5D.&text=%E2%80%9CThe%20island%20is%20not%20large%2C%E2%80%9D%20said%20Twain (accessed November 2020).
2 National Archives, PREM 11/418, 8 November 1953.
3 Peter G. Boyle, *The Churchill–Eisenhower Correspondence*, p. 96.
4 *Ottawa Citizen*, 18 January 1942.
5 'Will Our Officials Never Learn?', *Daily Mirror*, 25 November 1953.
6 *Daily Herald*, 25 November 1953.
7 'Big 3 Dinner Makes up for "Color" Controversy', *Vancouver-News Herald*, 5 December 1953.
8 *Vancouver Sun*, 4 December 1953.
9 Evelyn Shuckburgh, *Descent to Suez: Diaries 1951–56*, p. 112.
10 Charles Wilson Moran, *Churchill: The Struggle for Survival*, p. 223.
11 William Z. Slany (ed.), *Foreign Relations of the United States, 1952–1954, Western European Security, Vol. V, Part 2* (Washington: United States Printing Office, 1983), p. 1721.
12 Ibid., p. 1758.
13 Ibid., p. 1760.
14 Ibid., p. 1761.
15 John Colville, *The Fringes of Power*, p. 348.
16 *The Papers of Dwight David Eisenhower*, Johns Hopkins University Press, 10 December 1953, p. 744.
17 Ibid.
18 Charles Wilson Moran, *Churchill: The Struggle for Survival*, p. 226.
19 Ibid., p. 228.
20 C. L. Sulzberger, *A Long Row of Candles*, p. 931.
21 William Z. Slany (ed.), *Foreign Relations of the United States, 1952–1954, Western European Security, Vol. V, Part 2*, p. 1775.
22 Ibid., p. 1781.
23 Ibid., p. 1783.
24 Ibid.
25 C. L. Sulzberger, *A Long Row of Candles*, p. 932.
26 *The Papers of Dwight David Eisenhower*, Johns Hopkins University Press, 6 December 1953, p. 733.
27 Ibid.
28 Evelyn Shuckburgh, *Descent to Suez: Diaries 1951–56*, p. 114.
29 Quoted in Robert Rhodes James, *Anthony Eden*, p. 351.
30 'Address by Mr Dwight D. Eisenhower, President of the United States of America, to the 470th Plenary Meeting of the United Nations General Assembly', International Atomic Energy Agency, 8 December 1953, https://www.iaea.org/about/history/atoms-for-peace-speech (accessed November 2020).
31 Quoted in Peter G. Boyle, *The Churchill–Eisenhower Correspondence*, p. 110.
32 Ibid.
33 William Z. Slany (ed.), *Foreign Relations of the United States, 1952–1954, Western European Security, Vol. V, Part 2*, p. 1830.
34 Ibid., p. 1833.
35 Ibid.
36 William Z. Slany (ed.), *Foreign Relations of the United States, 1952–1954, Western European Security, Vol. V, Part 2*, p. 1839.
37 Evelyn Shuckburgh, *Descent to Suez: Diaries 1951–56*, p. 116.
38 Charles Wilson Moran, *Churchill: The Struggle for Survival*, p. 230.
39 William Z. Slany (ed.), *Foreign Relations of the United States, 1952–1954, Western European Security, Vol. V, Part 2*, p. 1843.
40 Ibid., p. 1844.

41 'Platitudinous Communique On The Bermuda Talks', *Manchester Guardian*, 9 December 1953.

42 C. L. Sulzberger, *A Long Row of Candles*, p. 934.

43 Evelyn Shuckburgh, *Descent to Suez: Diaries 1951–56*, p. 11.

44 Quoted in Helen McCarthy, *Women of the World: The Rise of the Female Diplomat* (London: Bloomsbury, 2014), p. 281.

45 'Soviet Policy on Agriculture – Wide Powers For Mr Khrushchev', *The Times*, 14 September 1953.

46 *Manchester Guardian*, 17 December 1953.

47 Reported in *Nedyela (Izvestia)*, 28 February 1988.

48 William Z. Slany (ed.), *Foreign Relations of the United States, 1952–1954, Western European Security, Vol. V, Part 2*, p. 1827.

49 'Soviet Aggression in Indo-China Test For US', *Lexington Leader*, 30 December 1953.

50 Ronald H. Spector, *Advice and Support: The Early Years 1941–1960, The US Army in Vietnam* (Washington: Center of Military History, 1983), p. 167.

51 *The Pentagon Papers, Vol. 1* (Boston: Beacon Press, 1971), pp. 75–107.

52 William Z. Slany (ed.), *Foreign Relations of the United States, 1952–1954, Western European Security, Vol. V, Part 2*, p. 1829.

53 Ibid., p. 1828.

54 Associated Press in 'Determined Red Drive Foreseen in Indochina', *San Bernadino County Sun*, 31 December 1953.

55 United Press International in 'Dulles Rattles Sabre At China', *Beckley Post-Herald*, 30 December 1953.

POSTSCRIPT

1 Richard Crossman, *Backbench Diaries of Richard Crossman*, p. 343.

2 National Archives, CAB 129/70, 18 August 1954.

3 Martin Gilbert and Larry P. Arnn (eds), *The Churchill Documents, Vol. 23: Never Flinch, Never Weary, November 1951 to February 1965* (London: C & T Publications Limited, 2018), p. 1795.

4 John Colville, *The Fringes of Power*, p. 316.

5 Ibid., p. 379.

6 'Remarks of Senator John F. Kennedy at the Conference on Vietnam', Washington, 1 June 1956, John F. Kennedy Presidential Library and Museum, https://www.jfklibrary.org/archives/other-resources/john-f-kennedy-speeches/vietnam-conference-washington-dc-19560601 (accessed December 2020).

7 'The Consortium Agreement of 1954', Iran Review, 12 September 2016, http://www.iranreview.org/content/Documents/The-Consortium-Agreement-of-1954.htm (accessed December 2020).

8 David Oshinsky, *A Conspiracy So Immense*, p. 464.

9 Associated Press reporting in 'Welch Tags McCarthy Cruel, Reckless in Dramatic Clash', *Wisconsin State Journal*, 10 June 1954.

10 'Unlimited Power of H-Bombs', *Manchester Guardian*, 1 April 1954.

11 National Archives, CAB 1238/27, 7 July 1954.

12 Rob Evans and Sandra Laville, 'Porton Down unlawfully killed airman in sarin tests', *The Guardian*, 16 November 2004.

13 Hansard, House of Commons debate, 31 January 2008, C26WS.

14 *The War of the Worlds* (Paramount Pictures, August 1953).

BIBLIOGRAPHY

Adams, Sherman, *Firsthand Report: The Story of the Eisenhower Administration* (New York: Harper & Brothers, 1961).

Aldrich, Richard, *The Hidden Hand: Britain, America and Cold War Secret Intelligence* (London: John Murray, 2001).

Aldrich, Richard, and Rory Cormac, *The Black Door: Spire, Secret Intelligence and British Prime Ministers* (London: William Collins, 2016).

Ambrose, Stephen, *Eisenhower: The President, 1952–1969, Vol. 2* (London: Allen & Unwin, 1984).

Ambrose, Stephen, *Eisenhower: Soldier and President* (London: Simon & Schuster, 1990).

Bird, Kai, and Martin J. Sherwin, *American Prometheus: The Triumph and Tragedy of J. Robert Oppenheimer* (London: Atlantic, 2008).

Blake, George, *No Other Choice: An Autobiography* (London: Jonathan Cape, 1990).

Booker, Christopher, *The Great Deception: Can the European Union Survive?* (London: Bloomsbury, 2016).

Bradbury, Ray, *Fahrenheit 451* (New York: Spark Pub., 2002).

Brendon, Piers, *Ike: The Life and Times of Dwight D. Eisenhower* (London: Secker & Warburg, 1987).

Browne, Anthony Montague, *Long Sunset: Memoirs of Winston Churchill's Last Private Secretary* (London: Cassell, 1995).

Butler, Richard Austen, *The Art of the Possible: The Memoirs of Lord Butler* (London: Hamilton, 1971).

Campbell, Duncan, *War Plan UK: The Truth About Civil Defence in Britain* (London: Burnett, 1982).

Carter, Miranda, *Anthony Blunt: His Lives* (London: Macmillan, 2001).

Chandos, Viscount, Oliver Lyttelton, *The Memoirs of Lord Chandos* (S.I.: The Bodley Head, 1962).

Cocroft, Wayne, and Roger Thomas, *Cold War: Building for Nuclear Confrontation 1946–1989* (Swindon: English Heritage, 2003).

Colville, John, *The Churchillians* (London: Weidenfeld & Nicolson, 1981).

Cook, Blanche Wiesen, *The Declassified Eisenhower: A Divided Legacy* (Garden City, New York: Doubleday, 1981).

Cutler, Robert, *No Time for Rest* (Boston: Little, Brown, 1966).

Davies, Philip, *MI6 and the Machinery of Spying* (London: Frank Cass, 2004).

Dorril, Stephen, *MI6: Fifty Years of Special Operations* (London: Fourth Estate, 2000).

Eden, Sir Anthony, *Full Circle: The Memoirs of Anthony Eden* (London: Cassell, 1960).

Eisenhower, Dwight, *Mandate for Change 1953–56* (Garden City, New York: Doubleday, 1963).

Evans, Robert, *Gassed: Behind the Scenes at Porton Down* (Thirsk: House of Stratus, 2000).

Forsyth, Frederick, *The Fourth Protocol* (London: Arrow, 2011).

Fort, Adrian, *Prof: The Life of Frederick Lindemann* (London: Jonathan Cape, 2003).

Gilbert, Martin, *'Never Despair': Winston S. Churchill, 1945–1965* (London: Minerva, 1990).

Gilbert, Martin, and Larry P. Arnn (eds), *The Churchill Documents, Vol. 23: Never Flinch, Never Weary, November 1951 to February 1965* (London: C & T Publications Limited, 2018).

Graff, Garrett M., *Raven Rock: The Story of the US Government's Secret Plan to Save Itself – While the Rest of Us Die* (London: Simon & Schuster, 2017).

Grose, Peter, *Gentleman Spy: The Life of Allen Dulles* (London: Andre Deutsch, 1995).

Halberstam, David, *The Fifties* (New York: Villard Books, 1993).

Hastings, Max, *The Korean War* (London: Pan, 2012).

Hennessy, Peter, *Cabinets and the Bomb* (Oxford: Oxford University Press, 2007).

Hennessy, Peter, *Having it So Good: Britain in the Fifties* (London: Penguin, 2007).

Hennessy, Peter, *Never Again: Britain 1945–1951* (London: Penguin, 2006).

Hennessy, Peter, *The Secret State: Whitehall and the Cold War* (London: Penguin, 2002).

Hennessy, Peter, *Whitehall* (London: Pimlico, 2001).

Hewlett, Richard, and Jack Holl, *Atoms for Peace and War, 1953–1961: Eisenhower and the Atomic Energy Commission* (Berkeley: University of California Press, 1989).

Hoopes, Townsend, *The Devil and John Foster Dulles* (London: Deutsch, 1974).

Howard, Anthony, *Rab: The Life of R. A. Butler* (London: Cape, 1987).

Hughes, Emmet John, *The Ordeal of Power: A Political Memoir of the Eisenhower Years* (London: Macmillan & Co., 1963).

Humes, James C., *Eisenhower and Churchill* (New York: Three Rivers Press, 2001).

James, Robert Rhodes, *Anthony Eden* (London: Weidenfeld & Nicolson, 1986).

Jefferson, Louis, *The John Foster Dulles Book of Humor* (New York: St Martin's Press, 1986).

Kaku, Michio, and David Axelrod, *To Win a Nuclear War: The Pentagon's Secret War Plans* (London: Zed, 1987).

Kinzer, Stephen, *All the Shah's Men: The Hidden Story of the CIA's Coup in Iran* (New York: Wiley, 2003).

Kinzer, Stephen, *The Brothers: John Foster Dulles, Allen Dulles and Their Secret World War* (New York: St Martin's Press, 2013).

Kynaston, David, *Family Britain 1951–57* (London: Bloomsbury, 2009).

Lashmar, Paul, *Spy Flights of the Cold War* (Stroud: Sutton, 1996).

Lownie, Andrew, *Stalin's Englishman: The Lives of Guy Burgess* (London: Hodder & Stoughton, 2015).

McCamley, Nick, *Cold War Secret Nuclear Bunkers: The Passive Defence of the Western World During the Cold War* (London: Leo Cooper, 2002).

McCamley, N. J., *Secret History of Chemical Warfare* (Barnsley: Pen & Sword Military, 2006).

Macmillan, Harold, *Tides of Fortune, 1945–1955* (London: Macmillan, 1969).

Malkasian, Carter, *The Korean War 1950–53* (Oxford: Osprey Publishing, 2001).

Mallaby, George, *From My Level: Unwritten Minutes* (London: Hutchinson, 1965).

Marks, John, *The Search for the 'Manchurian Candidate': The CIA and Mind Control* (London: Norton, 1979).

Modin, Yuri, *My Five Cambridge Friends* (London: Headline, 1994).

Nichols, David A., *Ike and McCarthy: Dwight Eisenhower's Secret Campaign Against Joseph McCarthy* (London: Simon & Schuster, 2017).

Nutting, Anthony, *Europe Will Not Wait: A Warning and a Way Out* (London: Hollis & Carter, 1960).

Oshinsky, David, *A Conspiracy So Immense: The World of Joe McCarthy* (Oxford: Oxford University Press, 2005).

Pelling, Henry, *Churchill's Peacetime Ministry, 1951–55* (Basingstoke: Macmillan, 1997).

Philipps, Roland, *A Spy Named Orphan: The Enigma of Donald Maclean* (London: Vintage Digital, 2018).

Reeves, Thomas, *The Life and Times of Joe McCarthy: A Biography* (New York: Stein and Day, 1982).

Rhodes, Richard, *Dark Sun: The Making of the Hydrogen Bomb* (New York: Simon & Schuster, 2005).

Roberts, Andrew, *Churchill: Walking With Destiny* (London: Penguin, 2018).

Roberts, Frank, *Dealing with Dictators: The Destruction and Revival of Europe, 1930–70* (London: Weidenfeld & Nicolson, 1991).

Ruane, Kevin, *Churchill and the Bomb* (London: Bloomsbury Academic, 2016).

Schlesinger, Arthur, *Robert Kennedy and His Times* (London: Deutsch, 1978).

Schmidt, Ulf, *Secret Science: A Century of Poison Warfare and Human Experiments* (Oxford: Oxford University Press, 2015).

Seldon, Anthony, *Churchill's Indian Summer: The Conservative Government, 1951–55* (London: Hodder & Stoughton, 1981).

Shinkle, Peter, *Ike's Mystery Man: The Secret Lives of Robert Cutler* (Hanover, US: Steerforth Press, 2018).

Straw, Jack, *The English Job* (London: Biteback Publishing, 2019).

Sulzberger, C. L., *A Long Row of Candles: Memoirs and Diaries, 1934–1954* (London: Macdonald, 1969).

Talbot, David, *The Devil's Chessboard: Allen Dulles, the CIA, and the Rise of America's Secret Government* (London: William Collins, 2016).

Thomas, Evan, *Eisenhower's Bluff: The World's Secret Battle Against Nuclear Annihilation* (London: Gibson Square, 2013).

Thorpe, D. R., *Eden: The Life and Times of Anthony Eden, First Earl of Avon, 1897–1977* (London: Vintage Digital, 2011).

Weiner, Tim, *Legacy of Ashes: The History of the CIA* (New York: Anchor Books, 2008).

Wolf, Markus, *Memoirs of a Spymaster* (London: Pimlico, 1997).

Wright, Peter, *Spycatcher* (New York: Viking, 1987).

Wynn, Humphrey, *The RAF Strategic Nuclear Deterrent Forces: Their Origins, Roles and Deployment, 1956–1969* (London: The Stationery Office, 1994).

Young, Hugo, *This Blessed Plot: Britain and Europe from Churchill to Blair* (London: Papermac, 1998).

Young, John, *Winston Churchill's Last Campaign: Britain and the Cold War, 1951–55* (Oxford: Clarendon Press, 1996).

Zbarsky, Ilya, and Samuel Hutchinson, *Lenin's Embalmers* (London: Harvill, 1998).

ACKNOWLEDGEMENTS

Sixty-eight years on and government papers, archives, diaries and memoirs have principally shaped this book. But one key participant at the time who I was able to interview was Baroness Williams of Elvel – Jane Portal as she was back then. In 1953 she was Churchill's 23-year-old personal secretary, and I'm very grateful for her illuminating recollections on the Prime Minister's stroke in the summer of 1953, chronicled in Chapter 7: The Emergency Government.

I owe a huge debt of thanks to two other people – nuclear historians Alex Wellerstein and Brian Burnell. Alex is assistant professor of science and technology at the Stevens Insititute of Technology in Hoboken, New Jersey, who also runs a brilliant website called The Nuclear Secrecy Blog: Restricted Data.

Alex has assiduously ferreted out many fascinating files and generously made them available to Cold War historians like myself. I have drawn heavily on one set of those files in particular – the case of John Archibald Wheeler (Chapter 1: Two Scorpions in a Bottle). Alex wrote a superb essay about the Wheeler story in *Physics Today*, and I have used the FBI documents he unearthed to expand the story further.

Brian, a former nuclear engineer, is an equally proficient hunter of archival gems. It is thanks to him – among other things – that I became aware of the work of the secret Imports Research Committee in the early 1950s, and the No Name Committee on nuclear policy. He has been most generous with his insights.

I must also thank Mike Parrish, the owner of Kelvedon Hatch (now a superb museum), whose father Jim complied with the government's desire to transform part of his land into a secret underground nuclear bunker back in 1952. Mike generously gave me access to his archives, and to the memories of those who were there when the site first opened in 1953.

For the section in Chapter 5: Least Said, Soonest Mended on Porton Down, I drew on the excellent book by Ulf Schmidt, *Secret Science: A Century of Poison Warfare and Human Experiments*, while *Gassed: Behind the Scenes at Porton Down* by investigative *Guardian* journalist Rob Evans (and his newspaper reports) also helped greatly to shape it.

Once more, the splendid Churchill Archives Centre at Cambridge has aided and abetted my studies considerably. I received a grant from the newly created Jennie Churchill Fund – named after Sir Winston Churchill's great-granddaughter – and archive director Allen Packwood and his staff have provided constant help and encouragement.

Many more government papers and files from the early 1950s have been opened up in the last decade or so. One valuable source for this book has been the transcripts of British Cabinets (made available in 2006) which – with the individual comments from those around the table all chronicled – have brought those meetings to life.

Likewise, the minutes of the crucial National Security Council gatherings in the first half of 1953 are all available in the online *Foreign Relations of the United States* papers. Once again, although couched in more formal language, they help paint a vivid picture of those meetings.

Some fascinating documents have emerged in America in recent years about the US/UK-inspired coup in Iran, and the National Security Archive has been a most valuable source for this fresh information. But while the American authorities seem willing to disclose more, there is no such move in Britain, where of course the MI6 archives remain closed on this subject.

Another valuable source for this book has been the complete electronic edition of *The Papers of Dwight David Eisenhower*, hosted online by Johns Hopkins University Press. Like so many public figures at the time, President Eisenhower kept a diary, and his carefully considered thoughts about colleagues and world leaders, and analysis of the key problems he encountered, are all there in these 14,000 pages. I am grateful to the Eisenhower Presidential Library for allowing me to quote from them.

I have also drawn on much material from the National Archives, and some from the Bodleian Library, Liddell Hart Centre for Military Archives and the Imperial War Museum. My thanks to the staff at these establishments for their patience and support.

My agent, Andrew Gordon, has, as always, offered great support and wise counsel throughout this project. I must also thank everyone at new publisher Biteback for their generous backing and encouragement – James Stephens, Olivia Beattie and my excellent, assiduous editor James Lilford.

ABOUT THE AUTHOR

Roger Hermiston is a writer and journalist who worked as assistant editor of BBC Radio 4's *Today* programme from 1998 to 2010. He began his career on weekly newspapers in Kent and Yorkshire before becoming crime reporter on the daily *Sunderland Echo*. He then moved to the *Yorkshire Post* before joining the BBC in the early 1990s.

Roger is the author of *The Greatest Traitor: The Secret Lives of Agent George Blake*; *All Behind You, Winston*; and *Clough and Revie*. He lives in Suffolk with his partner and their pony, two donkeys, three cats, three guinea fowl and two peacocks. He is a season ticket holder at Ipswich Town, plays golf and enjoys cinema and theatre.

INDEX